To Kevin, Luke and Meadbh (ST)
To Noreen, Oisín, Alannah, Óran and Fionnán (MM)

Preface

M uch has changed since the last edition of *Modern Management* was published in 2006. Ireland has gone from the much-lauded Celtic Tiger to a country in the front line of the financial crisis. Sovereign debt, coupled with the growing bank debt, gave rise to a very severe financial crisis, which ultimately led to an EU/IMF bailout in November 2009. Changes over the last decade in Irish business mirror developments internationally, but the onset of recession has been particularly evident in Ireland. As the country transitions and adapts to the new economic realities, managers in Ireland face a rapidly changing global business world.

The search for a sustained competitive advantage in a changing environment, with added competition from the BRIC and other emerging economies, has become critically important for organisations. New approaches to management with a focus on recovery and renewal in a post-global financial crisis era reflect the requirement for ethical, sustainable and socially responsible behaviours. All of these challenge our traditional assumptions in relation to management education and development, but most particularly in relation to the requirement for socially engaged, dynamic and ethically aware professionals.

Any summative account of management in Ireland – as this book is – cannot claim to be all-inclusive. Managerial backgrounds and styles, organisational practices and business environments vary widely. This book is intended as an introductory text for students studying management in Ireland. A mixture of theory and practice has been employed in the completion of the manuscript, and theoretical principles are supported by Irish case examples, case studies at the end of each chapter and Irish data where available.

The ten chapters trace the history of management thought, examine the development of Irish industrial policy and business development, the current global business environment, and the key managerial roles of planning, decision making, organising, motivating, leading and controlling. The text is enhanced by the inclusion of chapter learning objectives at the start of each chapter and a summary of key propositions at the end of each chapter. Student revision is facilitated by the provision of end-of-chapter discussion questions. Each chapter contains an Irish case study relevant to the material covered in the chapter, and website addresses are given for the companies around which the case is written so that students can keep up to date with current developments.

A number of people have provided valuable assistance in the preparation of this book and we take this opportunity to place on record our thanks to them.

To all our colleagues in the Kemmy Business School of the University of Limerick, in particular our Dean, Dr Philip O'Regan, along with Marese Kelly, Stephen Kinsella and Donal Palcic, who were kind enough to give their time in reviewing earlier drafts of the manuscripts.

To our co-author on the last three editions of *Modern Management*, Edel Foley of Dublin Institute of Technology. Edel's 1989 text, *Irish Business Management*, provided the impetus for our collaboration in the development and evolution of this text over the past 20 years.

Siobhán Tiernan
Michael J. Morley

Limerick, Spring 2013

Contents

Preface   v

Chapter 1 Management: Concepts and Evolution   1

Chapter Learning Objectives   1

1.1   Introduction   2
1.2   The functions of management   4
       1.2.1   Planning   4
       1.2.2   Organising   4
       1.2.3   Staffing   4
       1.2.4   Leading   4
       1.2.5   Controlling   4
1.3   Management levels and skills   5
1.4   Managerial roles   7
1.5   The manager's job: folklore versus fact   9
1.6   Early management theories   10
1.7   The Industrial Revolution   12
1.8   The classical approaches   13
       1.8.1   Scientific management   14
       1.8.2   Bureaucracy   16
       1.8.3   Administrative management   18
       1.8.4   Human relations   20
       1.8.5   The classical approaches: a summary   24
1.9   Contemporary approaches   25
       1.9.1   Organisational behaviour   25
       1.9.2   Systems theory   26
       1.9.3   Contingency theory   28
       1.9.4   The contemporary approaches: a summary   31
1.10   Summary of key propositions   32
       Discussion questions   33
       Concluding Case: McDonald's and management theory   34
       Case questions   35
       Notes and References   35

Chapter 2 The Development of Business in Ireland 37

Chapter Learning Objectives 37

2.1   Introduction 38
2.2   The early years 38
2.3   The Irish Free State (1922) 38
2.4   Self-sufficiency and protectionism (1932–58) 40
2.5   The move to free trade and foreign direct investment (1958) 43
2.6   Membership of the European Economic Community (1973) 47
2.7   Recession and recovery (1980–93) 49
2.8   The Celtic Tiger (1993–2007) 51
2.9   Financial crisis and the end of the Celtic Tiger (2008–) 54
2.10 Future prospects 59
2.11 Summary of key propositions 64
       Discussion Questions 65
       Concluding Case: The International Financial Services Centre (IFSC) –
            looking for direction? 66
       Case Questions 68
       Notes and References 68
       Appendix 1 The structure of Irish business following the Celtic Tiger era 72

Chapter 3 The Global Business Environment 80

Chapter Learning Objectives 80

3.1   Introduction 81
3.2   Understanding the global business environment 81
3.2.1 Globalisation 81
      3.2.2   Regional trading alliances 83
      3.2.3   The BRICs and other emerging economies 89
3.3   Managing the global business environment 91
      3.3.1   The political–legal context 92
      3.3.2   The economic context 94
      3.3.3   The technological context 95
      3.3.5   The socio-cultural context 99
3.4   The competitive environment 102
      3.4.1   Rivalry among existing firms 104
      3.4.2   The threat of substitutes 105
      3.4.3   The threat of new entrants 105
      3.4.4   The bargaining power of suppliers 106
      3.4.5   The bargaining power of buyers 107

3.4.6   Identifying favourable and unfavourable business environments   107
3.5   Entering international markets   108
3.6   Summary of key propositions   110
Discussion Questions   111
Concluding Case: The Irish airline industry – the Dublin–London route   111
Case Questions   116
Notes and References   116

Chapter 4 Planning   118
Chapter Learning Objectives   118
4.1   Introduction   119
4.2   The nature and importance of planning   119
4.3   Types of planning   120
4.4   Types of plan   122
4.4.1   Purpose or mission   124
4.4.2   Objectives/goals   125
4.4.3   Strategies   125
4.4.4   Policies   126
4.4.5   Procedures   126
4.4.6   Rules   127
4.4.7   Programmes   127
4.4.8   Budgets   127
4.5   Management by objectives (MBO)   128
4.6   The planning process   129
4.6.1   Define corporate objectives   129
4.6.2   External and internal analysis   131
4.6.3   Revise objectives   133
4.6.4   Formulate strategic plans   133
4.6.5   Formulate tactical plans   133
4.6.6   Implement action/operational plans   133
4.7   Business-level planning and strategies   134
4.7.1   The Miles and Snow typology   134
4.7.2   Porter's generic strategies   134
4.8   Corporate-level planning strategies   135
4.8.1   Related diversification   135
4.8.2   Unrelated diversification   135
4.8.3   Managing diversification strategies   136
4.9   Summary of key propositions   137

Discussion Questions   138
Concluding Case: Ryanair's competitive strategy   138
Case Questions   141
Notes and References   142

Chapter 5 Decision Making   **144**
Chapter Learning Objectives   144
5.1   Introduction   145
5.2   Characteristics of decisions   145
      Decision-making conditions   146
5.4   The decision-making process   148
      5.4.1   Step 1: Problem identification and diagnosis   149
      5.4.2   Step 2: Identification of alternatives   149
      5.4.3   Step 3: Evaluation of alternatives   149
      5.4.4   Step 4: Choice of alternative   150
      5.4.5   Step 5: Implementation   150
      5.4.6   Step 6: Evaluation   150
5.5   Barriers to making good decisions   151
5.6   Approaches to decision making   152
      5.6.1   The concept of rationality   152
      5.6.2   Bounded rationality   153
      5.6.3   The political model   154
      5.6.4   Escalation of commitment   155
5.7   Group versus individual decision making   155
5.8   Improving group decision making   157
5.9   Summary of key propositions   158
      Discussion Questions   159
      Concluding Case: Glanbia – big plans; key decisions   159
      Case Questions   161
      Notes and References   162

Chapter 6 Organisational Structure and Design   **163**
Chapter Learning Objectives   163
6.1   Introduction   164
6.2   The nature and importance of organising   164
6.3   Components of organisational structure   164
      6.3.1   Structural configuration   164
      6.3.2   Structural operation   170

6.4	Universal approaches to organisational design	171
6.5	The Mintzberg framework	174
	6.5.1 Simple structure	174
	6.5.2 Machine bureaucracy	174
	6.5.3 Professional bureaucracy	174
	6.5.4 Divisionalised structure	175
	6.5.5 Adhocracy	175
6.6	Contemporary organisation design	175
	6.6.1 Matrix and project structures	177
	6.6.2 Team-based work and new organisational forms	178
6.7	Summary of key propositions	180
	Discussion Questions	180
	Concluding Case: Tronics plc	181
	Case Questions	181
	Notes and References	181

Chapter 7 Managing Human Resources 183

	Chapter Learning Objectives	183
7.1	Introduction	183
7.2	The historical development of the HR function	184
	7.2.1 The early 1900s	185
	7.2.2 The mid-1900s	186
	7.2.3 The 1970s: centralised pay bargaining	186
	7.2.4 The 1980s: the emergence of HRM?	187
7.3	Activity areas in HRM	188
	7.3.1 HR planning	188
	7.3.2 Recruitment	191
	7.3.3 Selection	194
	7.3.4 Pay and benefits	196
	7.3.5 Performance appraisal	199
	7.3.6 Training and development	201
7.4	The employee relations context	204
	7.4.1 Trade unions	206
	7.4.2 Employer organisations	209
	7.4.3 State institutions	210
7.5	Summary of key propositions	213
	Discussion Questions	214

Concluding Case: Change at Leeway and the implications for human resource
    management and development   214
  Case Questions   215
  Notes and References   215

Chapter 8 Leadership   216
Chapter Learning Objectives   216
8.1   Introduction   216
8.2   Leadership defined   218
8.3   Distinguishing leadership and management   219
8.4   Different schools of thought on leadership   221
    8.4.1   Trait theories of leadership   221
    8.4.2   Behavioural theories of leadership   222
    8.4.3   Contingency leadership theory   225
    8.4.4   Charismatic leadership theories   228
8.5   Leadership and leadership development in Ireland   230
8.7   Summary of key propositions   233
  Discussion Questions   233
  Concluding Case: Leadership at Leadmore Ice Cream   234
  Case Questions   235
  Notes and References   235

Chapter 9 Motivation   237
Chapter Learning Objectives   237
9.1   Introduction   237
9.2   The ongoing centrality of motivation in organisational life   238
9.3   Motivation defined   238
9.4   Content theories of motivation   239
    9.4.1   Maslow's hierarchy of needs   239
    9.4.2   Existence–relatedness–growth theory   241
    9.4.3   McClelland's achievement theory   242
    9.4.4   The two-factor theory   242
9.5   Process theories of motivation   244
    9.5.1   Theory X, theory Y   244
    9.5.2   Expectancy theory   245
    9.5.3   Equity theory   247
9.6   Motivation and pay   248
9.7   Motivation and the design of work   250

	9.7.1	Task specialisation	251
	9.7.2	Job enlargement and job enrichment	252
	9.7.3	The quality of working life movement	254
	9.7.4	High-performance work design	255
9.8	Summary of key propositions		256
	Discussion Questions		257
	Concluding Case: Motivation case study		257
	Case Questions		259
	Notes and References		259

Chapter 10 Control

260

Chapter Learning Objectives

260

10.1	Introduction		260
10.2	The nature and importance of control		261
10.3	Stages in the control process		262
	10.3.1	Setting performance standards	263
	10.3.2	Measuring and comparing performance	264
	10.3.3	Taking action	265
10.4	Types of control		265
	10.4.1	Feedforward control	266
	10.4.2	Concurrent control	266
	10.4.3	Feedback control	266
10.5	Characteristics of effective control		267
	10.5.1	Appropriatenes	267
	10.5.2	Cost-effectiveness	267
	10.5.3	Acceptability	268
	10.5.4	The relative emphasis on exceptions at control points	268
	10.5.5	Flexibility	268
	10.5.6	Reliability and validity	268
	10.5.7	Controls based on valid performance standards	269
	10.5.8	Controls based on accurate information	269
10.6.	Methods of control		269
10.7	Financial controls		269
	10.7.1	Budgetary control	269
	10.7.2	Break-even analysis	272
	10.7.3	Ratio analysis	273
10.8	Non-financial controls		277
	10.8.1	Project controls	277

	10.8.2	Management audits	280
	10.8.3	Inventory control	280
	10.8.4	Production control	282
	10.8.5	Quality control	283
10.9	Summary of key propositions		286
	Discussion Questions		286
	Concluding Case: Roads authority pay £2.8 million after mistake		288
	Case Questions		288
	Notes and References		289

Index   **290**

CHAPTER 1

Management: Concepts and Evolution

CHAPTER LEARNING OBJECTIVES

- To define the terms *management*, *managing* and *managers* and to understand the role management has played in the pattern of industry as we know it today.
- To understand the five main functions of management.
- To understand the ten key managerial roles performed by managers.
- To appreciate the earliest contributions to management thought, including those of the ancient Egyptians, the ancient Romans and the Catholic Church.
- To appreciate the pivotal role played by the Industrial Revolution, which led to the development of new management techniques to cope with the issues presented by industrialisation: production, efficiency and cost savings.
- To understand the term *scientific management* and its emphasis on the development of one best way of performing a task through the application of scientific methods.
- To understand the term *bureaucracy* and the role of bureaucracy in the development of management theory.
- To understand the role played by *administrative management* and the principles of Henri Fayol, who identified management as a separate business activity with five functions.
- To understand the human relations movement in order to see how social and psychological factors influence performance.
- To understand organisational behaviour and management activities that encourage employee effectiveness by analysing and exploring individual, group and organisational processes.
- To understand *systems theory*, which argues that organisations should be viewed as systems that transform inputs into outputs to the environment.
- To understand *contingency theory*, which argues that because organisations face different situations or contingencies there is no one best way of managing.

1.1 Introduction

This chapter provides an introduction to the topic of management and its evolution. First, a definition of management is provided and its nature and importance in modern society explained. The main functions of all managers are outlined, along with the various skills they typically use. The different roles played by managers at the top, middle and bottom of the organisation are explained, and the characteristics of effective managers are then considered. The historical evolution of management, from traditional classical ideas to contemporary approaches, is also discussed.

Peter Drucker, one of the most influential management theorists, states that over the last 150 years management has revolutionised the social and economic fabric of the developed regions of the world.[1] Management has also made the structure of modern industry possible. Before the advent of management, society could only support small groups of workers. Management has permitted the use of large numbers of knowledgeable and skilled employees to achieve organisational goals. As a result, effective management has become one of the most important resources of the developed world and one that is eagerly sought by developing regions.

Finding an adequate definition of management is not always easy because the word has been used in so many different ways. 'Management' can refer to:

- the process that managers go through to achieve organisational goals
- a body of knowledge that provides information about how to manage individuals who guide and control organisational activities
- a career involving the task of guiding and controlling organisations.

In this book we take management to mean the process by which managers achieve organisational goals. Most definitions – of which there are many in the literature – have three characteristics in common:

1. Management is viewed as a process or series of continuing and related activities.
2. It is seen as involving the achievement of organisational goals.
3. It reaches these organisational goals by working with and through people.

Management therefore concentrates on achieving specific organisational goals by employing human and financial resources. Managers can thus be viewed as individuals in organisations whose principal aim is to achieve organisational goals by holding positions of authority and making decisions about the allocation of resources. Managers are therefore professionals who pursue a particular career in an organisation. They are either promoted up through the ranks of the organisation or recruited externally. Management Focus 1.1 illustrates the varied backgrounds of some of Ireland's senior managers. The advantages of having managers with a diverse background include: a broader intellectual base; strong human skills; and experience of a variety of industry sectors – which probably means that the person has experienced a range of management styles and ways of doing things.

Management Focus 1.1 Routes to the top

Brendan Murphy, Chief Executive Officer (CEO), Allianz Ireland. Murphy graduated from UCD with a BComm, was articled and became a member of the Institute of Chartered Accountants while working for Deloitte. He worked in general audit, consulting and solvency, specialising in insurance. In 1984 he became Head of Internal Audit with the Insurance Corporation of Ireland (ICI), and later became its General Manager and Chief Executive. He joined Allianz Ireland in 1999 as Director of Operations; by 2000 he was Chief Operations Officer (COO) and was appointed CEO in 2002.

Danuta Gray, Non-Executive Chairman, Telefonica 02 Ireland. Gray joined Telefonica 02 from BT Europe in Germany, where she had been Director. Before that she was General Manager at BT Mobile in the UK. She holds a BSc in Biophysics and an MBA.

Stan McCarthy, CEO, Kerry Group. Almost all of McCarthy's career has been with Kerry Group. A native of Kerry, he joined the company in 1976 through the graduate recruitment programme, working in finance in Ireland until his appointment in 1984 as Financial Controller in the USA. In 1988 he was appointed Vice-President (VP) Materials Management and Purchasing, in 1991 VP Sales and Marketing, and in 1996 President of Kerry Ingredients Americas. In 1999 he was appointed Director of the Group and in 2008 its CEO.

Patrick Kennedy, CEO, Paddy Power. Patrick Kennedy is one of the youngest CEOs of a public company in Ireland. He was appointed to that position in 2006, having served on the board of Paddy Power since 2005. He had previously been employed by Greencore, taking responsibility for group development since 1998, and assuming the role of Chief Financial Officer (CFO) in 2002.

Niall Gibbons, CEO, Tourism Ireland. Niall Gibbons graduated from Trinity College Dublin with a BBS degree in 1988. He then worked with Coopers and Lybrand and qualified as a Chartered Accountant in 1992. He moved into the public service in 1994, joining the Marine Institute (established to expand Ireland's capacity in marine research and development) in the role of Director of Corporate Services. He has been with Tourism Ireland, which was set up under the framework of the Good Friday Agreement to market the island of Ireland internationally, since 2001 and took up the role of CEO in 2009.

Source: Business and Finance (2011) 'Top 500 Companies 2012'.

All managers operate within an organisation of some sort. An organisation can be viewed as a system that is designed and operated to achieve specific organisational objectives. Organisations are consciously and formally established to achieve goals that their members would be unable to achieve by working on their own. Management is universal in that it occurs in all types of organisation, whether public or private, large or small, profit- or non-profit-making. While the techniques and emphasis may vary depending on the organisation, the general principles of management apply to all organisations.

As all organisations exist for a purpose, managers have the responsibility of combining and using organisational resources to ensure that the organisation achieves its purpose. If these activities are designed effectively, the production of each individual worker represents a contribution to the achievement of organisational goals. Management tries to encourage individual activity that will lead to the achievement of organisational objectives, and to discourage individual activity that hinders organisational goal attainment.

1.2 The functions of management

In order to achieve organisational goals all managers perform several major functions or activities. The key management functions are planning, organising, staffing, leading, and controlling.

1.2.1 Planning

Planning is the process of establishing goals and objectives and selecting a future course of action in order to achieve them. Plans are developed by all parts of the organisation, including business units, work groups and individuals. Such plans can be long term (five to fifteen years), medium term (one to five years) or short term (less than one year). Managers are responsible for gathering and evaluating the information on which the plans are based, setting the goals that need to be achieved and deciding how the plans will be implemented in order to reach the goals.

1.2.2 Organising

Once the plans have been established, adequate resources will have to be allocated to ensure that they can be achieved. Organising is therefore the next logical step in the management process. It involves dividing tasks into sub-tasks, allocating resources to get the tasks done, and co-ordinating employees. It also involves establishing managerial authority.

1.2.3 Staffing

The staffing and personnel function ensures that effective employees are selected, trained, developed and rewarded for accomplishing organisational goals.

1.2.4 Leading

The fourth main function of management is leading, which involves getting individuals or groups to assist willingly and harmoniously in attaining organisational goals. Leading usually involves directing, motivating and communicating with employees. The leading function is almost entirely concerned with managing people within the organisation.

1.2.5 Controlling

The final function of management is controlling, which is the process of monitoring progress made by the organisation, business unit or individual and, where necessary, taking action to ensure that goals match targets. The other management functions focus on developing plans, organising the resources needed to put the plans into practice and directing and motivating employees toward their realisation. However, good plans, solid organisation and effective leaders are no guarantee of success unless the organisation's activities are measured, evaluated and corrected. Successful organisations pay close attention to the control function to make sure that they are on target to achieve their goals.

The five management functions are carried out by all managers and are interrelated. They make up a set of interdependent activities that shape the *management process*, as shown in Figure 1.1.

FIGURE 1.1 THE MANAGEMENT PROCESS

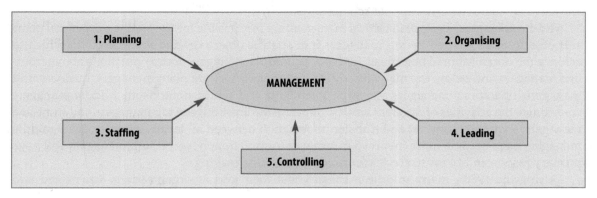

Although the various functions take place concurrently throughout most organisations, they follow a logical sequence.

* **Planning** establishes the direction of the organisation.
* **Organising** divides activities among work groups and co-ordinates results.
* **Staffing** allocates the required people to achieve tasks.
* **Leading** motivates employees to achieve organisational goals.
* **Control** measures and evaluates organisational performance.

1.3 Management levels and skills

Managers are located at different levels in the organisations. Typically managers at different levels perform a range of different activities. Three distinct but sometimes overlapping levels of management can be identified in most organisations, as shown in Figure 1.2.

FIGURE 1.2 LEVELS OF MANAGEMENT

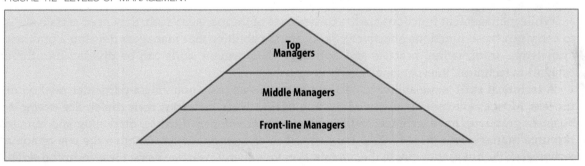

Top managers, sometimes referred to as strategic managers, are the top executives of an organisation. Top managers include the CEO, president, chairman, chief operating officer (COO), directors and members of the board. These managers are responsible for the overall mission and direction of the organisation. Top managers shape organisational goals, provide resources, monitor progress and make strategic decisions. In this sense they act as the interface between the organisation and its external environment. They represent the organisation at external meetings and develop customer and supplier relationships.

Middle managers, also called tactical managers, are responsible for translating the general plans and objectives developed by top managers into specific objectives and activities with which to achieve the organisational objectives. In this way, middle managers occupy positions above front-line managers and below top managers. Middle managers include plant managers, business unit managers, operations managers and superintendents and senior supervisors. Middle managers co-ordinate the activities of different work groups. As the link between top managers and front-line managers, they communicate and transfer information between all levels. In recent years middle managers have become more involved in strategy formulation; however, top managers still have primary responsibility for strategic planning and decision making.

During the 1980s, many middle managers lost their jobs as organisations downsized and delayered in order to reduce costs and become more competitive. Developments in information technology have meant that middle managers are no longer required to serve as information and communication channels between top managers and front-line managers. Many organisations have not replaced the middle managers they eliminated in the past, and it is unlikely that they will do so in the future.

Front-line managers, sometimes referred to as operational managers or supervisors, form the largest group of managers in most organisations. They are responsible for directly supervising and managing employees and resources. They make sure that the plans developed by top managers are fulfilled by the employees who actually produce the organisation's goods and/or provide its services. They are a critically important managerial group as they are the link between management and non-management personnel. How they interpret information and pass it on to employees has an important impact on employees' reactions.

While the number of middle managers has been reduced, the role of front-line managers has also changed. Many of the responsibilities of the traditional middle manager have been passed down to the front-line manager, who has become increasingly responsible for shop-floor operations and has been given more authority and responsibility. Some observers have predicted that no job is going to change more in the future than that of the front-line manager.

While management functions are the cornerstone of the manager's job, they need certain skills to carry out these functions effectively. Skills are the abilities that managers develop from their knowledge, information, practice and aptitude. Management skills can be divided into three categories: technical; interpersonal; and conceptual.

A **technical skill** is the ability to perform a specialised task involving a particular method or process. Most employees develop a set of technical skills as they start their career. For example, business graduates have technical skills in relation to accounting, finance, marketing and human resource management (HRM). The daily activities of most managers involve the use of some technical skills, but as they rise in the organisation they spend less time using these technical skills. For example, when an engineer is recruited s/he will rely heavily on technical skills, but as s/he is promoted and manages other employees, other skills will become more important.

In order to work well with other people a manager needs good **interpersonal skills**, sometimes called human skills. Most top managers spend about half of their time dealing with other people.[2] If managers are to deal with employees effectively they must develop their ability to motivate and communicate effectively with those around them. Interpersonal skills are required by all managers because they all have to deal with other people.

Conceptual skills involve the ability to see the organisation as a whole, recognising complex and dynamic issues, examining factors that create problems and resolving difficult situations. As managers are promoted up the organisation they depend more and more on conceptual skills. In fact, most managers are promoted on the basis of their ability to make sound decisions and their vision and ability to chart the organisation's future. While conceptual skills are used by most managers, top managers require them most of all, particularly when making strategic decisions.

Figure 1.3 shows the various skills necessary at different management levels. As the diagram shows, for front-line managers the most important skills are technical and interpersonal. For middle managers, interpersonal skills are the most important, and they need medium amounts of technical and conceptual input. For top managers the most important skills are conceptual and interpersonal, with little need for technical input.

FIGURE 1.3 MANAGEMENT SKILLS AT DIFFERENT LEVELS

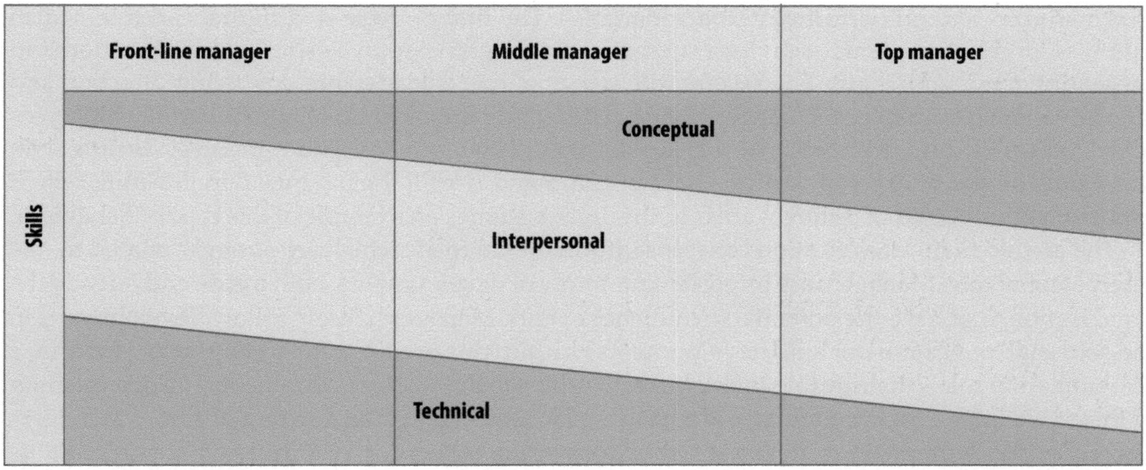

Source: Adapted from Mintzberg, H. (1990) 'The Manager's Job: Folklore and Fact', *Harvard Business Review*, March–April, 163–176.

1.4 Managerial roles

Further insights into the world of the manager can be found by examining the key roles that s/he plays during the course of daily working life. Managerial roles essentially tell us what activities the manager undertakes. The most useful work in this area has been written and researched by Henry Mintzberg,[3] who believed that the classical view that managers purely undertake planning, organising, leading, staffing and controlling was a little misleading and not representative of an average manager's activities.

Mintzberg studied CEOs' managerial behaviour and day-to-day activities, and concluded that his sample displayed ten main managerial roles, which could be further classified into three distinct areas, as shown in Figure 1.4. While each of the roles is distinct, Mintzberg believes that they are all closely related.

FIGURE 1.4 MANAGERIAL BASIC ROLES

Classification	Role	Typical Activities
Interpersonal	Figurehead Leader Liaison	Attending employee's wedding Co-ordinating teams Interacting with peers from other areas of the organisation
Informational	Monitor Disseminator Spokesperson	Tracking developments in the business environment E-mailing staff to keep them abreast of developments Making an address at a breakfast meeting
Decisional	Entrepreneur Disturbance Handler Resource Allocator Negotiator	Creating a new business project Resolving disputes over work allocation Making decisions about staff deployment Dealing with trade unions

The first group of managerial roles concerns the interpersonal aspect of the manager's job. Given that interpersonal skills are so important at all levels of management, it is not altogether surprising that managers should perform interpersonal roles. The first of these is a figurehead role, which involves largely ceremonial activities such as attending an employee's retirement function and presenting them with a gift. The second interpersonal role is leadership, involving direction and co-ordination of employees. Managers play a particularly important role in motivating employees to perform. The third interpersonal role is a liaison or connector role and it involves dealing with those outside the traditional vertical chain of command within the organisation. Meeting with a group of peers located in different areas in the organisation is an example of this type of behaviour.

The second main classification concerns informational roles, which are strongly related to the interpersonal role. Managers are important monitors of developments, both inside and outside the organisation, that have the potential to influence events. Managers closely follow developments in the external environment and developments within the organisation. They also perform a dissemination role – distributing information to others in the work environment. The combination of these two roles – monitor and disseminator – place the manager in a strong position. Managers also act as spokespeople for the organisation, providing others with information about it and its position on key issues. This role assumes even greater importance during a crisis, when the manager becomes the human face of the organisation. The spokesperson role is similar to that of the figurehead role described earlier. However, the latter is primarily a symbolic role, whereas the former is involved in sharing and disseminating organisational information.

The final classification concerns decisional roles, which again reflect the importance of conceptual skills. The entrepreneurial role is concerned with change and innovation, either through new project/business developments or through changes in work practices. The disturbance handler role consists of dealing with problems that are outside the manager's control, such as threatened strikes or go-slows. The resource allocator role involves making decisions about the allocation of key resources within the organisation. In this regard, managers typically have to make decisions about competing demands for scarce resources. The final role is negotiator: the manager discusses issues and tries to reach agreement with all the parties involved.

The role of the manager is therefore more varied than the traditional view would suggest. Mintzberg also found that different managers spend different amounts of time involved in each of the ten roles. For example, he found that sales managers spent relatively more of their time involved with interpersonal roles, a fact he attributes to their more extrovert nature. Production managers, Mintzberg found, spend more time on decisional roles, reflecting their concern for efficiency in the work process. Staff managers spent most time on informational roles.

1.5 The manager's job: folklore versus fact

As we have seen, managers pursue a variety of roles in their daily working lives. These roles extend far beyond the traditional view that managers only plan, organise, staff, lead and control. Mintzberg summarises a number of studies on the nature of the manager's job and concludes that many myths still exist in this regard.[4] He argues that it is impossible to improve management practice if we do not know what managers really do. He presents four commonly held myths about the nature of managerial work.

- **Myth 1: The manager is a reflective, systematic planner.** Managers work at an unrelenting pace, and their work is often characterised by discontinuity and variety. They are strongly oriented to action and do not in fact like reflective activities. Mintzberg found that half the activities engaged in by five of the CEOs he studied lasted less than nine minutes and only 10 per cent were longer than an hour. These CEOs were constantly interacting with callers and subordinates, and dealing with mail. When managers plan, they do so on a daily basis and in a flexible way. Mintzberg concluded that management does not produce reflective thinkers, but people who are conditioned by their jobs and prefer action to delay.
- **Myth 2: The effective manager has no regular duties to perform.** We already know that managers perform a wide variety of regular duties, ranging from ceremonial to informational. They spend time meeting and greeting outside guests, presiding over ceremonies, and securing 'soft' external information and disseminating it throughout the organisation. All of these tasks are regularly performed by managers.
- **Myth 3: Senior managers need aggregated information and data, which is best generated by a formal management information system.** The formal management information system (MIS) generates formal documents for managers to read on a range of internal organisational topics. However, Mintzberg's evidence is that managers prefer oral means of communication (such as phone conversations and casual meetings) to a formal MIS. The role played by gossip, hearsay and 'soft' information is also interesting. Managers find this source invaluable for information generation and this produces two important outcomes. First, because informally conveyed information remains in the manager's mind it is not contained in any formal organisational databank. Second, managers are reluctant to delegate because instead of simply handing over a file they would need to spend time recalling their knowledge of the relevant topic.
- **Myth 4: Management is a science and a profession.** Mintzberg argues that a science involves 'the enaction of systematic, analytically determined procedures or programmes'.[5] As we have seen, management does not involve such clearly identifiable procedures and programmes and is in fact largely based on judgement and intuition.

To be effective, a manager should be an active leader. As we have seen, leading is one of the key functions of management. The main difference between managers and leaders is that managers do things right whereas leaders do the right things. Leaders have a vision, which they successfully communicate to employees. Active leaders concentrate on achieving the task at hand in an active rather than a passive manner. They participate in the activities of the organisation at work group and business unit level. In this way they are highly visible to employees and demonstrate that they have a thorough knowledge of the business.

In order to provide the opportunity for high performance, both managers and employees must understand their jobs and what they do, as opposed to what they should do. They must also have a sense of the future for their particular task. Involving employees in the design and execution stages is one method of providing the opportunity to achieve high performance. The Japanese have used this philosophy very effectively, especially in relation to quality circles. Japanese managers work closely with employees to plan and implement changes for the benefit of everyone. Managers can also provide the opportunity to achieve high performance by making sure that all employees have the necessary resources. Effective managers are constantly searching for ways to help employees do their jobs well and to focus their activities and efforts on production matters.

In order to provide incentives for employees to achieve high performance, the manager needs to identify the factors that motivate employees and build those factors into the work environment. Incentives can include rewards such as money and promotion, a challenging job or relationships with co-workers. The manager then needs to link these factors to clear objectives. In other words, effective managers identify the important objectives they need to achieve and they focus everyone's efforts towards achieving those objectives.

Before focusing on the manager's role in a modern business organisation we shall first look at historical approaches to the study of management. By studying earlier ideas we can learn from them and build on them to reach an integrated view of the concept of management.

1.6 Early management theories

Attempts to understand and develop a theory of management can be traced back to the earliest efforts of humankind to achieve goals by working in groups. However, the Industrial Revolution heightened awareness of and interest in management theory and practice as managers sought to achieve internal efficiency. The opportunities created by the Industrial Revolution led to a period of considerable debate on the most effective management theory and practice, which resulted in what we now call *classical management*.

A thorough knowledge and understanding of the classical approaches to management is necessary because they laid the foundations for many of the contemporary theories of management. In fact, the most modern approaches to management have integrated and expanded the key concepts developed by the classical approaches. The following sections will examine the earliest contributions to management thought, the classical approaches to management and, finally, the contemporary approaches available to managers today.

For thousands of years people have been faced with the same issues and problems that continue to confront managers today. The earliest thoughts and ideas in relation to management can be traced back to the written records of the Sumerians (around 5000 BC), who documented the formation of their government, their tax-collecting systems and their conduct of commerce.

Management Focus 1.2 Early management practice

The ancient Egyptians used managerial skills to build their vast pyramids. The construction of the Great Pyramids, which were built using levers and rollers, took nearly thirty years to complete and involved over 100,000 workers of various trades. To achieve such a vast undertaking, managers had to plan in advance the type and size of stone required, organise available staff and resources, provide leadership and, finally, control the process to ensure that the end result matched the original plans. The Egyptians developed managerial skills to organise human labour and found that the best way to delegate the multitude of tasks required to complete the undertaking was through a hierarchy.

Greek civilisation (c. 800–150 BC) also contributed to early management thought with the development of separate courts, an administration system and an army, highlighting the need for different management functions. The Greek philosopher Socrates differentiated between management and other technical functions, providing the first written example of the concept that management is a separate and specialist skill.

The Roman Empire (c. 300 BC–AD 300) provides further evidence of the development of management thought. Because the Roman Empire extended over such a vast area, the Romans were faced with the problem of the management and control of their conquests. In order to effectively manage the empire, delegation of power and the scalar principle of authority were used, coupled with a system of communication between the outposts and the central command. This tight organisation ensured that the Roman Empire could maintain control over regions.

One of the most enduring examples of early management thought, and certainly the most prevalent in Ireland, can be found in the Roman Catholic Church, which combined managerial skills with a spiritual message to successfully achieve its objectives. Managerial techniques employed by the Church included a strict hierarchy of authority and the specialisation of members on a functional basis. The hierarchical structure still employed by the Catholic Church includes five main levels: parish priest, bishop, archbishop, cardinal and pope. The concept of centralisation of authority in Rome remains the same today as when it was first introduced. The Catholic Church became a model for the management of other religious organisations and also for the army, which further developed the concepts of leadership, unity of command, line authority and staff authority.

In the 1300s, Venetian merchants made their contribution to management thought by establishing legal foundations for their trade. Financial records were formalised into double-entry bookkeeping, first described by Pacioli in 1494. Machiavelli, whose *The Prince* was published in 1532, further developed management thought in relation to the political organisation.[6] He suggested that the prince or leader should build a cohesive organisation, binding his allies with rewards and making sure they knew what was expected of them. Machiavelli's ideas on leadership and consent of the masses for effective rule still have relevance in today's environment.

Collectively, the contributors to the development of early management thought have produced many ideas that are relevant to modern theory and practice. However, early managers tended to operate on a trial and error basis. Communication and transport problems prevented the widespread growth of business ventures, which meant that advances in management techniques and skills could not significantly improve performance. The advent of the Industrial Revolution changed the situation and led to the development of management as a formal discipline.

1.7 The Industrial Revolution

The Industrial Revolution marked a major watershed in the development of management thought. Until the 1700s large organisations were mainly military, political or religious, rather than industrial. Most skilled work was performed by craft workers, who operated alone, using fairly simple tools to produce clearly identifiable goods such as clocks or clothing. These goods were then sold directly to individual customers in the worker's locality.

The Industrial Revolution significantly changed this pattern of industrial activity. The invention of machines such as Watt's steam engine (1765), Arkwright's water frame (1769) and Cartwright's power loom (1785) effectively transferred skills from the craft worker to the machine. These new machines could be operated by unskilled workers, who simply had to insert raw materials and extract the finished goods. Eventually fully automated machines were developed which no longer required worker input. Such developments also made possible the establishment of large-scale factories, which stood in marked contrast to the local nature of craft work.

As a result of these advances the productive capability of humans and indeed animals was greatly increased. Productivity began to increase steadily and industry started to feel the benefits of *economies of scale*, whereby the average unit cost of producing an item decreases as the volume of production increases. Consequently prices fell and consumption rose. Developments in transportation and communications further opened up new markets and promoted economic growth. Industry and commerce boomed and entrepreneurs formed a new social class – the bourgeoisie. The growth of industry gave people the opportunity to leave the land and move into the cities to avail of industrial work. The social implications of the Industrial Revolution were enormous as people had to leave their homes to work long hours for poor pay and conditions. As industry and commerce expanded to capitalise on new markets and production processes, organisations became increasingly large and complex. This meant that new management techniques had to be developed to cope with the problems and opportunities presented by industrialisation. As early as 1776, Adam Smith advocated in *The Wealth of Nations* that the key to profitability lay in the specialisation of labour, whereby workers are assigned a specific task to complete, ensuring a sharp division of labour. [7]

The Industrial Revolution created huge opportunities for mass production. This, coupled with the increasing size and complexity of organisations, resulted in an upsurge of systematic thought on the key managerial problems presented by industrialisation, namely production, efficiency and cost savings. An era of renewed interest and debate on management ensued, which led to the emergence of management as a formal discipline distinct from other technical areas.

Management Focus 1.3 The Industrial Revolution in Ireland

In Ireland before the Industrial Revolution, agriculture was the main occupation. While some of the larger towns had small water-powered factories producing beer, whiskey and flour, only about one in ten people lived in towns, and most of these were craft workers. The impact of the Industrial Revolution in Ireland was less evident than in the UK or the USA; in fact Irish industry suffered from competition from the UK, particularly in the woollen and cotton industries, which virtually collapsed in the mid-1800s. However, in the linen industry, production moved from the home to large-scale factories. Nonetheless, Ireland remained an agricultural economy and only experienced the shift to industrial employment in the 1950s (for further discussion, see Chapter 2).

The evolution of management thought since the Industrial Revolution can be divided into classical and modern approaches. Figure 1.5 provides a historical picture of the evolution of management thought. Many of the approaches were developed simultaneously and have therefore affected one another, but some of the approaches were developed as a direct response to some of the weaknesses of earlier approaches. The remainder of the chapter will concentrate on the contribution of both the classical and the contemporary approaches to the study of management.

FIGURE 1.5 THE EVOLUTION OF MANAGEMENT THOUGHT

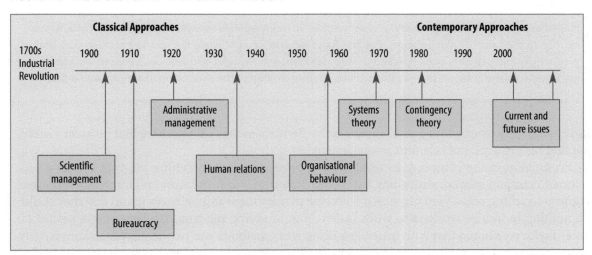

Note: The year associated with each school of thought is the year when the approach began. The beginning of the next school of thought does not denote the end of the previous one.

1.8 The classical approaches

The classical approach to the study of management was born at the end of the nineteenth century as a response to the managerial challenges posed by over a century of intense industrialisation. The major approaches associated with this era are scientific management, bureaucracy, administrative management and human relations, and they were generally developed from the personal experiences of key contributors.

In order to avoid confusion about the period that each approach dates from, it is important to distinguish between: the date a particular work was written; the date it was translated into English; and the date the work became popular in management thought. For many of the approaches each of these categories will have a different date.

1.8.1 Scientific management

Scientific management is concerned with the development of one best way of performing a task through the application of *scientific methods*. The birth of scientific management is attributed to Frederick Taylor. According to Taylor, the principle objective of management should be to secure the maximum prosperity for the employer coupled with the maximum prosperity of each employee.[8] This prosperity meant not only monetary profit, but also the development of each employee to perform to the highest level that s/he was capable of. In order to achieve this, Taylor advocated that scientific methods should be used to analyse the one best way to do tasks.

Management Focus 1.4 Frederick Taylor: background

Frederick Taylor (1856–1917), whose ideas were developed in two books, *Shop Management* (1903) and *Principles of Scientific Management* (1911) (published together in one volume, entitled *Scientific Management,* in 1947), trained as an engineer. After completing his apprenticeship he joined Midvale Steel Works in Pennsylvania, where he rose to the rank of chief engineer. His first-hand experience at Midvale led him to conclude that both productivity and pay were poor, operations were inefficient and wasteful, and relations between workers and management were antagonistic – a picture that he believed reflected the wider state of industry at the time.

In 1898 Taylor was employed as a consultant by Bethlehem Steel. It was here that he most visibly applied his principles of scientific management.

Production in the company focused on two processes: first, handling pig-iron blocks on to railroad cars; and second, shovelling fuel (sand, limestone, coal and iron ore) into blast furnaces. Pig-iron handling was a very physical job and the management at Bethlehem found that they could do nothing to induce workers to work faster. After studying pig-iron handlers over a period of time, Taylor concluded that with better, less tiring work methods and frequent breaks, daily output per worker could be quadrupled. In order to do this a piece-rate pay system was developed under which workers would be paid extra when they produced more than a standard level of output. The results were staggering; not only did output per worker increase from 12.5 to 47.5 tons, but wages per day increased from $1.15 to $1.85.

Taylor then tackled the problem of shovelling, which was completed by work groups of fifty to sixty men under a single foreman. Taylor used time and motion studies to establish the one best way of shovelling, including the type of shovel to be used, which Taylor believed depended on the raw material. As a result of his findings a tool room was set up and each morning workers were given written instructions stating what tools were needed for the day. A piece-rate system was also introduced. Once again the results were outstanding. The amount shovelled per day increased from 16 to 59 tons and wages went up from \$1.15 to \$1.88. Taylor's experience at Bethlehem led him to develop four main principles of management, which became the cornerstones of scientific management.

1   **The development of a true science of work.** Taylor believed that both management and workers were essentially unaware of what a fair day's work was and this gave employers room for complaint about employee inadequacies. Taylor therefore argued that rules of thumb should be replaced by a scientific approach to work: each task would be broken down into basic movements that could be timed to determine the one best way of doing the task. A worker would thus know what constituted a fair day's work, for which he would receive a fair day's pay. The level of pay would be higher than the average worker would get in unscientific factories, but if workers failed to perform they would lose income.

2   **The scientific selection and development of workers.** Taylor was aware of the importance of hiring and training the appropriate worker for the job with regard to physical and mental aptitudes. Once properly matched to the job the worker could then be developed to the highest capacity by a piece-rate system of pay. Taylor believed that as workers were motivated by money, both workers and managers would benefit from increased productivity.

3. **The co-operation of workers and management in studying the science of work.** Taylor believed that management and workers should co-operate to ensure that the job, plans and principles all match. To achieve this end he advocated standardised tools, instruction cards to assist workers, and breaks to reduce tiredness.

4. **The division of work between management and the workforce.** Taylor believed that workers and those in management should do the tasks for which they were best equipped: managers would therefore direct and allocate work, and workers would complete the tasks.

The principles of scientific management were widely accepted and one of the most famous applications of the approach was in Henry Ford's Model T factory. Other proponents of scientific management included Henry Gantt, and Frank and Lillian Gilbreth[9] (see Management Focus 1.5). Gantt (1861–1919) was a contemporary and acquaintance of Taylor who modified some of his ideas. Gantt proposed that every worker should be entitled to a set wage rate, with a bonus if output was exceeded (the application of the principle of management by exception). This would allow supervisors to spend more time coaching the less able worker and left room for initiative and discretion.

Management Focus 1.5 The Gilbreths

Frank Gilbreth (1868–1924) and his wife Lillian (1878–1972) were also contemporaries of Taylor. They were primarily concerned with the elimination of waste and, like Taylor, discovering the one best way of doing a job. They believed that by doing this an individual could achieve his or her personal potential. Frank Gilbreth, who owned a construction company in Boston, began to analyse each task he did, constantly trying to eliminate unnecessary work movements. He identified seventeen hand motions, which he called therbligs (a slightly altered backward spelling of the family name). Frank believed that by isolating the therbligs in a task one could eliminate or shorten them. In applying this system to bricklaying he reduced the motions or therbligs from eighteen to 4.5.

⟶

After her husband's death, Lillian continued his pioneering work. As an industrial psychologist, she emphasised the need for understanding workers' personalities and needs and pioneered the development of human resource management. Her interests lay in the human factor and the scientific selection, training and development of workers. The Gilbreths proved to be a formidable team in terms of their contribution to management theory, the handling of materials, monotony, and modern human resource management.

Scientific management and its advocates had a phenomenal effect on managerial practices at the turn of the last century. Taylor's *Principles of Scientific Management* was first published in 1911 and within a few years had been translated into eight different languages. Scientific management spread as far as the Soviet Union, where the principles were incorporated into various five-year development plans. Scientific management dramatically improved productivity and efficiency in manufacturing organisations and introduced scientific analysis into the world of work. The piece-rate pay system gained wide acceptance as a result of its link between effort and reward. Scientific management instilled a sense of co-operation between workers and management and, finally, the concept of a management specialist gained widespread acceptance.

However, scientific management was not without its critics. In emphasising the link between worker effort and monetary reward, Taylor assumed that people are motivated solely by money. Worker motivation is, however, far more complex, and involves job-related social and psychological factors that Taylor ignored. Advocating one best way of completing tasks meant that work activities frequently became routine and mechanistic, which led to boredom and apathy among the workforce.

Trade unions strongly opposed scientific management techniques. They viewed the piece-rate system as a return to 'sweat shop' exploitation of labour by management. Scientific management techniques frequently resulted in lay-offs and, as a result, unions feared that its application would lead to widespread job losses. Scientific management also ignored the role of senior management within the organisation; and it failed to deal with the relationship between the organisation and the environment, such as competitors and regulators, especially at the senior level of the organisation.

Despite these criticisms the legacy of scientific management is pervasive. It formally established management as a specialist area, introduced scientific analysis to the workplace and provided a framework for solving the managerial problems of efficiency and productivity. While Taylor's theories were accused of causing unemployment, his real aim was to bring about a mental revolution so that both sides would stop viewing the division of the surplus as all-important and, together, turn their attention to increasing the size of the surplus.[10]

1.8.2 Bureaucracy

Max Weber (1864–1920), a German sociologist, wrote most of his work at the turn of the last century, though it was not translated into English until the 1920s.[11] While Taylor focused on the problems of effectively managing an organisation, Weber concentrated on how to structure organisations for success. Weber outlined key elements of an ideal form of structure that he believed would promote efficiency and he called it *bureaucracy*. It is important to note that while the term 'bureaucracy' may have negative connotations in today's society, at the beginning of the twentieth century it was viewed as the ultimate structure.

The ideal bureaucracy that Weber advocated had six main elements.

1. **Division of labour.** Tasks were divided and delegated to specialists so that responsibility and authority were clearly defined.
2. **Hierarchy.** Positions were organised in a hierarchy of authority from the top of the organisation to the bottom, with authority centralised at the top of the organisation.
3. **Selection.** Employees were recruited on the basis of technical qualifications rather than favouritism.
4. **Career orientation.** Managers were viewed as professionals who were pursuing a career rather than having ownership in the organisation.
5. **Formalisation.** The organisation was subject to formal rules and procedures in relation to performance.
6. **Impersonality.** Rules and procedures were applied uniformly to all employees.

Weber's ideal bureaucracy gained widespread acceptance as soon as his work was translated in the 1920s and 1930s. Because it allowed large organisations to perform the many routine activities necessary for survival the structure became extensively used in large-scale organisations worldwide. Bureaucracy was particularly popular in public organisations and civil service-type organisations. Many of the early Irish semi-state bodies, including Aer Lingus and Iarnród Éireann (part of CIÉ), and the Irish civil service were structured along bureaucratic lines.

The bureaucratic structure had a number of important advantages for large organisations. The division of labour increased efficiency and expertise because similar tasks were undertaken by the same people. Setting out a hierarchy allowed a chain of command to develop in line with Fayol's scalar chain idea (see section 1.7.3). Formal selection meant that employees were hired on merit and expertise and no other criteria would be used. Career orientation ensured that career professionals would give the organisation a degree of continuity in operations. Rules and procedures controlled employee performance and increased efficiency. The impersonality of the organisation ensured that rules were applied equally to all.

While bureaucracy might be an extremely rational and efficient form of organisation, it has a number of disadvantages. Rules and procedures can sometimes become ends in themselves; in other words, obeying rules at all costs becomes important, irrespective of whether this helps to achieve organisational goals. Bureaucracy promotes stability but over time it can become very rigid. Rules and procedures are blindly applied to all situations even though they may not be the most appropriate. Consequently the organisation comes to believe that what has worked well in the past will continue to do so in the future, despite changed conditions. Delegation of authority in the bureaucratic organisation can lead to a situation where the goals of the work groups become more important than organisational goals, which can adversely affect the organisation in the long run. A strict division of labour can lead to jobs becoming routine and boring and to workers feeling apathetic and demotivated. Extensive rules can lead to the establishment among workers of a minimum acceptable standard as laid down by the rules, above which workers will not go. So, instead of acting as a controlling device, the rules actually reduce performance.

The fact that elements of Weber's bureaucratic structure can be found in so many organisations today is testimony to the importance of his work. Bureaucracy is both rational and efficient. However, organisations need to understand bureaucracy in order to avoid being controlled by it. Like that of Taylor, Weber's work had enormous influence on management thought and is still relevant in today's business environment, particularly for organisations operating in a stable environment.

1.8.3 Administrative management

Administrative management was based on the personal experiences of its key advocates. It focused on senior managers and the policy issues they faced. In doing so, administrative management offered universal principles of management. The most important contributor to administrative management was Henri Fayol.[12]

Management Focus 1.6 Henri Fayol: background

Henri Fayol (1841–1925) is commonly known as the father of modern management. Unlike earlier management theorists, who were predominantly American, Fayol was French, and he worked independently during the same period in which scientific management was gaining momentum. Fayol was a mining engineer and came to realise that managing an enterprise required a host of skills apart from technical ones. In 1916 he wrote *Administration Industrielle et Générale* (later published in an English translation as *General and Industrial Management*), which established him as the pioneer of European management in the early 1900s.

Unlike Taylor, who concentrated on work group management, the focus of Fayol's work, reflecting his managerial experiences, was the senior executive of the organisation. Concentrating on the problems faced by the senior executive in managing an organisation, Fayol concluded that all business activities could be divided into six essential areas:

1. **Technical** – production and manufacturing.
2. **Commercial** – buying, selling and exchange.
3. **Financial** – funding and using capital.
4. **Security** – guarding property.
5. **Accounting** – costing and stock-taking.
6. **Managerial** – planning, organising, controlling, commanding and co-ordinating.

The inclusion of management as a separate business activity with five main functions gained Fayol widespread recognition. Fayol believed that the six groups of activities were interdependent and that all of them need to be running effectively for the organisation to prosper. Figure 1.6 outlines the manager's main activities according to Fayol. It is interesting to note the similarity between Fayol's five main managerial activities and the modern five functions of management (planning, organising, staffing, leading and controlling) discussed in Section 1.2.

In addition to the five management functions, Fayol identified fourteen basic principles of management which he had found most useful during his career (see Figure 1.7). Fayol emphasised that such principles of management should be applied in a flexible manner. Fayol's principles remain important not only because of his influence on succeeding generations of managers, but also because of the continuing validity of his work.

FIGURE 1.6 FAYOL'S BUSINESS ACTIVIES

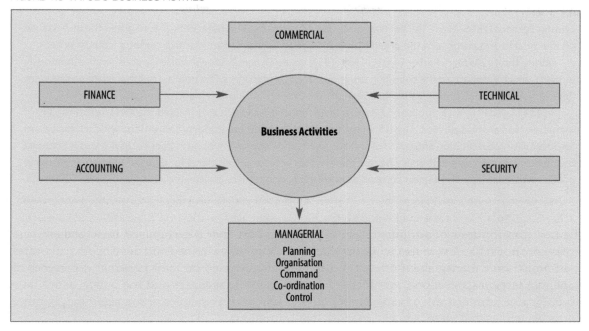

FIGURE 1.7 FAYOL'S FOURTEEN MANAGEMENT PRINCIPLES

1. Division of labour: Divide work into specialised tasks and assign responsibility to individuals.
2. Authority: Equal delegation of responsibility and authority.
3. Discipline: Establish clear expectations and penalties.
4. Unity of command: Each employee should report to one supervisor.
5. Unity of direction: Employee efforts should be guided to achieve organisational goals.
6. Subordination of individual interest to general: Individual interests should not precede the general interests of the group.
7. Remuneration: Equitable rewards for work.
8. Scalar chain: Lines of authority and communications from the highest to the lowest level.
9. Order: Order tasks and materials to support organisational direction.
10. Equity: Treat employees fairly.
11. Stability of tenure: Minimise turnover to ensure loyalty of personnel.
12. Initiative: Employees should have freedom and discretion.
13. Esprit de corps: Unity of interest between management and workers.
14. Centralisation: Decide the importance of superior and subordinate roles.

Other executives who used their personal experiences to contribute to administrative management include Chester Barnard,[13] Mary Parker Follett[14] and Lyndall Urwick.[15]

Management Focus 1.7 Barnard, Follett and Urwick

Chester Barnard (1886–1961), in *The Functions of the Executive* (published in 1938), highlighted the importance of: the mission and purpose of the organisation; hiring specialists; and an effective communications system.

During the 1920s Mary Parker Follett (1868–1933) wrote *Dynamic Administration* (published posthumously in 1941), which emphasised the changing situations faced by managers. She pointed out that all managers want flexibility, and she also distinguished between the motivation of individuals and of groups.

In 1947 Lyndall Urwick published *Elements of Administration,* which emphasised the social responsibility of managers toward employees. Urwick drew up ten principles for good organisation, which focused on responsibility, job definition and spans of control. As an employee of Rowntree in the UK, Urwick was influenced by the humane management policy he saw there, which acted as a trail blazer for many of the human resource policies we have today. The earliest companies in Ireland to adopt these policies included Cadbury and Guinness.

The key contributions of administrative management are that it recognised management as a profession, much like law or medicine, in which people could be trained and developed. Advocates of administrative management offered recommendations based on their personal experience of managing large organisations, and focused on senior-level managers and the policy issues they faced. Finally, administrative management offered universal principles of management, in other words principles that were believed to work in all situations.

The main criticism levelled at the approach is that universal principles do not take account of variations in the environment, technology or personnel, which may require alternative management action.

Administrative management is remembered for its enormous influence on successive generations of managers and because of the continued relevance and validity of its principles, particularly those of Fayol.

1.8.4 Human relations

The human relations (or behavioural) approach to management emerged in the 1920s and 1930s. In contrast to previous approaches, the human relations movement concentrated on the human side of management and sought to understand how psychological and social factors interact with the work environment in influencing performance. The approach built on the ideas and concepts developed by its predecessors, most notably Gantt and the Gilbreths' scientific management.

The human relations approach emerged from a research study that began as a scientific management approach to determining the impact of working conditions on performance and ended up discovering the effect of the human factor on productivity. Elton Mayo (1880–1949)[16] and Fritz Roethlisberger, both Harvard researchers, were employed in 1927 by the Western Electric Company to study the effect of physical working conditions on worker productivity and efficiency. Commonly known as the Hawthorne Studies, and chronicled by Roethlisberger and Dickson (1939)[17] in *Management and the Worker,* this research was one of the most important watersheds in the evolution of management thought.

Western Electric (now AT&T Technologies) manufactured equipment for the telephone industry. Between 1924 and 1932 a series of studies were carried out within the company. The Hawthorne

Studies can be divided into three main phases, each phase adding to the knowledge acquired in the last:
1. The Illumination Experiments 1924–27.
2. The Relay Assembly Test Room Experiments 1927–32.
3. The Bank Wiring Observation Room Experiments 1931–32.

The Illumination Experiments 1924–27

Before the arrival of Mayo and his research team, the US National Research Council had made an initial investigation, marking the first stage of the Hawthorne Studies. Between 1924 and 1927 the Illumination Experiments were conducted in several departments employing female coil-winders, relay assemblers and small parts inspectors. The investigation was designed to determine how the level of lighting affected worker output and the researchers expected that better lighting would increase output. Two groups were isolated and the conditions in one were held constant, while the level of light was systematically changed in the second group. The results, surprisingly, showed that output increased in both groups. When Mayo and his research team were employed in 1927 they concluded that there was no simple cause and effect relationship between illumination and productivity and that the increase in output was caused by the fact that the workers were aware of being observed. This phenomenon – the Hawthorne Effect – is that workers are influenced more by psychological and social factors (observation) than by physical and logical factors (illumination).

The Relay Assembly Test Room Experiments 1927–32

The Relay Assembly Test Room (RATR) Experiments were designed to study the effects on productivity of rest breaks, work day length, refreshments and incentive payments.

Six skilled women involved in the assembly of phone relays were selected and placed in a test room without their normal supervisor. An observer was placed in the test room to record observations and to create a friendly and relaxed atmosphere. The various changes were introduced with the women's knowledge and consent. The result was that output increased.

The next stage was to return the women to their original conditions (a 48-hour, six-day week, with no refreshments, no incentives and no pauses) by withdrawing the concessions, and once again output increased.

In trying to explain these results Mayo concluded that the research team had unintentionally changed the human relations of the work group under observation. They found that the test room was significantly different from regular departments in four main ways. First, the supervisory style in the test room, with the absence of a formal supervisor, was more open and friendly and workers enjoyed being the centre of attention. Second, the test room was less controlled than regular work groups and the women actually participated in decisions affecting the job and could set their own work pace. Third, group formation resulted in a cohesive group that was loyal and co-operative. Finally, the attitudes of the women were different as they no longer felt part of a large department subject to managerial control, but felt involved. This consequently affected their job satisfaction.

Mayo was rather puzzled and surprised by the results of his observations and decided to interview the factory workers about their conditions. From these interviews he found that many of the management problems were related to human factors. In other words, people were underproductive because of things they felt were wrong, rather than because of ignorance about the company's objectives. This contradicted Taylorism, which claimed that once a worker was convinced of the one best way, s/he would adopt it.

The Bank Wiring Observation Room Experiments 1931–32

The Bank Wiring Observation Room (BWOR) Experiments involved fourteen men who were kept in their natural work setting (i.e. non-experimental) with an observer but with no changes in their working conditions. The aim of the study was to analyse the behaviour of the work group and how it functioned. Observation and interviews showed that the group had well-established norms or rules of behaviour. The results showed that the men restricted their output; the group had standards for output and these were not exceeded by any worker. They had their own idea of what constituted a fair day's work: employees who exceeded the agreed daily output were called 'rate busters'; and those producing below it were called 'rate chisellers'. These norms were enforced by the group through sarcasm and 'binging' – a group member hitting another on the arm to show displeasure. Group members were united in their opposition to management and were indifferent to the financial incentives offered for higher output.

All these observations led Mayo to conclude that informal work group relations had enormous influence on motivation and performance. When Mayo reviewed the overall findings, he concluded that an 'informal' organisation existed among the workers, in addition to the 'formal' organisation recognised by management.

The important contribution made by the Hawthorne Studies was the finding that social needs take precedence over economic needs and that the informal work group can exert control over employee behaviour and performance. Consequently Mayo argued that managers should focus on motivation, communications and employee welfare to gain the co-operation of the group and promote job satisfaction and norms consistent with the goals of the organisation.

However, in recent years doubt has been cast on the authenticity of a 'Hawthorne Effect' with researchers arguing that we have naively taken on board the assumption, when in reality the evidence does not support its existence.[18] Whatever our feelings on this debate, there can be no doubt that the Hawthorne Studies played a monumental role in the development of managerial thought by voicing concerns about the role human beings play in the organisation.

Another key contributor to the human relations approach to management was Abraham Maslow.[19] He was concerned with the issue of worker motivation and sought to explain how workers could be motivated to achieve better performance. Maslow's studies led him to propose a theory of human motivation that is still referred to in current discussions of management. Maslow believed that people try to satisfy a hierarchy of needs, as shown in Figure 1.8.

The most basic needs Maslow identified are physiological needs, which include food and shelter. Safety needs refer to the need to feel secure and physically protected; acceptance needs are concerned with the need to relate to and be accepted by other people; esteem needs include the need for self-respect and for the esteem of others; and self-actualisation refers to the need for achievement and fulfilment. The first three have been termed 'deficiency needs' because they need to be satisfied for basic comfort, while the top two are growth needs, as they focus on growth and development.

FIGURE 1.8 MASLOW'S HIERARCHY OF NEEDS

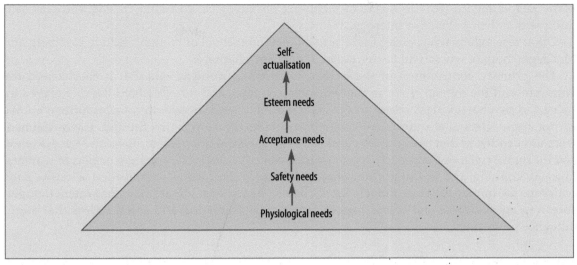

Maslow argued that people try to satisfy their needs systematically, starting from the bottom and working up so that once a given level of needs has been satisfied it no longer acts as a motivator and people move on to try to satisfy higher-order needs: so, for example, people try to satisfy food and shelter needs before considering love and esteem. It is possible to apply these basic needs to the organisational setting, which offers more insight into how people can be motivated. Figure 1.9 is an example of how Maslow's hierarchy of needs can be applied to the organisation.

FIGURE 1.9 MASLOW'S HIERARCHY OF ORGANISATIONAL NEEDS

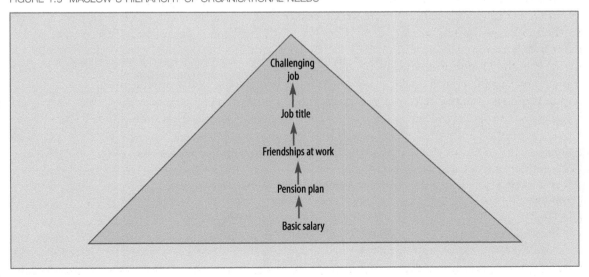

It has been concluded that in many instances managers help workers to satisfy the first three needs but neglect the top two and that consequently many employees remain undermotivated. Maslow's research gave important managerial insights into how people seek self-actualisation in their work. Many people regard work as a way of satisfying physiological and safety needs, and seek self-fulfilment in their hobbies or interests.

Other researchers who belong to the human relations school of thought include Herzberg and McGregor, both of whom will be discussed in detail in Chapter 9.

The primary contribution of the human relations movement was that it emphasised the importance of the human factor in the work environment, and it highlighted the role played by social and psychological processes and the satisfaction of needs in determining performance. Like earlier approaches, it also drew criticism: for example, the Hawthorne Studies, it was claimed, were unscientific in that many of the conclusions reached did not necessarily follow the evidence; and the human relations approach in general has been criticised for its apparent neglect of workers' rational thinking and the important characteristics of the formal organisation. Despite such criticisms the human relations movement has had a phenomenal impact on management thought, encouraging managers and researchers to consider psychological and social factors that might influence performance.

1.8.5 The classical approaches: a summary

The various classical approaches to the study of management laid the foundations for the principles behind the management of organisations that still exist today. Figure 1.10 summarises the main contributions and limitations of the various approaches. The classical approaches sought to provide managers with skills and techniques to confront the important issues of the time, namely productivity and efficiency. Primarily based on the personal experience of key contributors, they focused on the basic managerial functions, co-ordination of work and supervision. Apart from the

FIGURE 1.10 THE CLASSICAL APPROACHES: A SUMMARY

School of thought:	Scientific management: 1898–present day
Proponents:	Taylor, Gantt and the Gilbreths
Contribution:	Application of scientific principles to the study of work through work studies and incentives
Limitations:	Simplistic view of motivation; ignored the role of the external environment
School of thought:	Bureaucracy: 1920s–present day
Proponents:	Weber
Contributions:	Bureaucratic structure emphasising efficiency and stability
Limitations:	Ignored the human element and the role of the external environment
School of thought:	Administrative management: 1916–present day
Proponents:	Fayol, Follet, Barnard and Urwick
Contribution:	Universal principles of management for senior executives
Limitations:	Ignored environmental differences
School of thought:	Human relations: 1927–present day
Proponents:	Mayo, Roethlisberger and Maslow
Contributions:	Importance of social and psychological factors in influencing work performance
Limitations:	Ignored the role of the formal work group and worker rationality

human relations school and elements of administrative management, they concentrated on the formal aspects of the organisation. With the benefit of hindsight, some of the approaches take a simplistic view of the needs and interests of workers and fail to address the important issue of the role of the external environment in determining success. More modern approaches to the study of management attempt to further these basic concepts and overcome key criticisms.

1.9 Contemporary approaches

Since the 1950s, contemporary approaches to the study of management have sought to build on and integrate many of the elements of the classical approaches and, in so doing, to provide a framework for managing the modern organisation. As industries have matured and evolved and competition has steadily increased, researchers and practitioners have become more concerned about how to manage for competitive success. As a result there has been an ever-increasing amount of literature on management, to such an extent that Koontz referred to the 'management theory jungle'.[20] Rather than giving an exhaustive list of all the modern contributions to management theory, this section concentrates on three critically important approaches – organisational behaviour, systems theory and contingency theory – that are the most dominant and influential modern management theories.

1.9.1 Organisational behaviour

The organisational behaviour (OB) approach to management has its roots in the human relations approach that was so popular in the 1930s and 1940s. Theorists began to recognise that the assumptions of the human relations approach were simplistic, and that they failed to adequately explain human behaviour. Assumptions about job satisfaction and subsequent performance illustrate this point. According to the human relations view, happier employees are more productive. However, repeated research studies failed to find a definitive causal relationship between job satisfaction and employee performance.[21]

As a result, a group of theorists recognised that human behaviour and its outcomes are far more complex than the early human relations approach had envisaged and they started to focus more on management activities that encourage employee effectiveness by understanding and exploring individual, group and organisational processes – all of which play critically important roles in contemporary management theory. OB, which borrows heavily from sociology, psychology and anthropology, came to dominate the behavioural approach to management from the 1950s.

The OB school of management recognised the importance of developing human resources in the organisational context. Key areas studied under the OB framework include worker stress, job satisfaction, learning and reinforcement, group dynamics, job and organisational design, and organisational change.[22] In fact, many of the theorists discussed in subsequent chapters on organising (Chapter 6) and motivation (Chapter 9) have made significant contributions to the field of OB. The most famous researchers in this school of thought are Douglas McGregor (theory X theory Y), and Frederick Herzberg (the two factor theory), who will be discussed in Chapter 9.

The main contribution of the OB approach to management is that it focuses attention on how individual, group and organisational processes can influence employee participation and performance. Its focus on enriching jobs and changes in job design are still very important components of current approaches to organisational design and employee motivation. It has been criticised for failing to take account of situational factors such as the role of technology and the external environment. However, its contribution to management theory is undeniable and evidenced by the fact that so many OB theorists still play prominent roles in management theory and practice.

1.9.2 Systems theory

The systems approach to the study of management, which originated in the work of Chester Barnard,[23] came to the forefront of management literature in the 1950s. Many of the classical approaches had ignored the role of the external environment and tended to concentrate on particular aspects of the organisation rather than viewing it as a whole. In the 1950s, management theorists began to consider the organisation as a whole system and developed systems theory as a means of interpreting organisations.

A *system* is a set of interdependent parts or elements that function as a whole to achieve certain goals or objectives. Systems theory argues that organisations should be seen as systems that transform inputs *from* the external environment into outputs *to* the external environment. Figure 1.11 outlines the basic model of systems theory. The inputs an organisation uses are commonly termed 'factors of production' and include materials, money, information and people. The organisation transforms such inputs into outputs in the form of goods or services, which are then exchanged in the external environment. Such outputs to the environment provide feedback for the organisation, enabling it to begin the whole process again. Figure 1.12 provides an example of the application of systems theory to an Irish university or third-level institution and shows how an organisation can be viewed as a system using various inputs and producing outputs to the external environment through its transformation process.

The cycle of inputs, transformation and outputs must be maintained if the organisation is to stay in existence; so the organisation has to be able to produce outputs that will result in energy or feedback from the environment to enable it to begin the process again. An organisation will be profitable when the value created, or what customers are willing to pay, is greater than the cost of inputs and transformation.

FIGURE 1.11 THE ORGANISATION AS A SYSTEM

Inputs	Transformation process	Outputs
People	Purchasing	Products
Materials	R & D	Services
Money	Manufacturing	Waste
Information		

THE ENVIRONMENT

FEEDBACK FROM ENVIRONMENT

FIGURE 1.12 AN IRISH EXAMPLE OF THE SYSTEMS MODEL

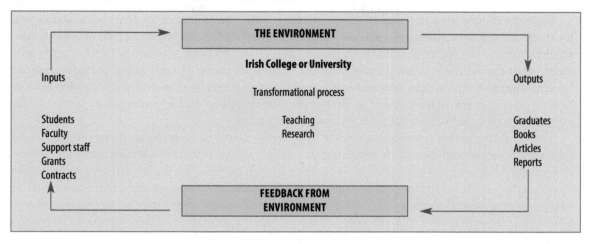

One of the key elements of systems theory was that organisations should be viewed as *open systems* rather than *closed systems.* Many of the classical approaches treated organisations as closed systems, which means that the organisation does not depend on interactions with the external environment for survival and thus acts as a 'closed' entity. The classical approaches, in concentrating on closed systems and internal efficiency, ignored the fact that an organisation depends on the environment for inputs and on a market for outputs.

Systems theory advances the idea of the organisation as an open system and views the organisation as a system that depends on the external environment for inputs and outputs. In other words, the organisation depends on other systems. For example, universities or third-level institutions depend on inputs in the form of students and faculty. In addition, they are dependent on the environment to sell or market their outputs in the form of graduates and research. So if the organisation is to survive it must not only be aware of, but also respond to, systems that supply it and, in turn, those it supplies.

In viewing organisations as closed systems many of the classical approaches were solely concerned with internal efficiency. By taking an open systems view another important dimension for managers becomes apparent – *effectiveness*. Effectiveness is the extent to which the organisation's outputs match the needs and wants of the external environment. The effectiveness of, for example, a university or third-level institution can be determined by the extent to which the external environment needs and wants students and research. If the environment does not need or want the outputs, the organisation cannot be effective, no matter how efficient it is.

As all systems tend to have *sub-systems*, the organisation can be viewed as a series of sub-systems that comprise a whole system – the organisation. Each sub-system can itself be viewed as a system with its own sub-systems. The organisation can also be viewed as a sub-system of a wider system. For example, the world economy can be viewed as a system, with each of the national economies as sub-systems. In turn, the Irish national economy is made up of various sub-systems, which include industries; and Glanbia , for instance, is a sub-system of the wider food industry. The realisation that an organisation is both a system and a sub-system encourages those who run the organisation to think in a holistic way; and, as a result, it should be easier for the organisation to see the effect that any action it takes will have on its ability to achieve wider organisational goals.

Systems theory also highlights the point that if the performance of the organisation is the product of the interactions of its various parts it is possible for the action of two or more parts to achieve more than either is capable of individually. This concept is referred to as *synergy* and it means that the whole is often greater than the sum of its parts. Therefore the performance of an organisation as a whole depends more on how well its parts relate than on how well each operates. The implication for management is that organisations need to be managed in terms of their interactions, not on the basis of their independent actions.

The most important contribution made by systems theory is its recognition of the relationship between an organisation and its environment, especially in relation to achieving organisational effectiveness. Viewing an organisation as an open system emphasises the importance of the external environment, both for inputs and for markets for outputs. As a system the organisation also has various sub-systems which must interact well with each other, sometimes achieving a synergy in which the whole is greater than the sum of the parts. One limitation of this approach, however, is that it does not provide details on the functions and duties of managers working in open systems. Nonetheless, systems theory marked a step away from a sole focus on internal operations to one that incorporated the external environment.

1.9.3 Contingency theory

The second contemporary approach to the study of management attempts to integrate the concepts of earlier approaches, especially systems theory. Contingency theory advocates that managerial practice depends on the situation facing an organisation. Advocates of contingency theory, and therefore contingency management, argue that it is impossible to specify a single way of managing that works best in all situations because circumstances facing organisations are varied and continually changing. Consequently, contingency theory rejects the idea that there are universal principles of management that can be applied in every case.

Contingency theory accepts that every organisation is distinct, operating in a unique environment with different employees and organisational objectives. Such differences mean that managers have to consider the circumstances of each situation before taking any action. The different circumstances or situations facing organisations are called contingencies. Managerial response depends on identifying key contingencies in an organisational setting. The main contingencies are:

* the rate of change and complexity of the external environment
* the types of technology, tasks and resources used by the organisation
* the internal strengths and weaknesses of the organisation
* the values, skills and attitudes of the workforce.

These various contingencies affect the type of managerial action required by the organisation and its degree of success. For example, a universal strategy of low-cost products will only be effective if the market is cost-conscious. If the market emphasises quality, this strategy will not be effective. In this example the success of the strategy is contingent on the demands of the external environment. (It should be noted, however, that low costs do not necessarily lead to poor quality, but high quality is usually associated with higher cost.) Only when a manager understands the contingencies facing the organisation is it possible to identify which situations demand particular managerial action. Depending on the situation at hand or the contingency, the organisation can categorise the situation and use an appropriate form of structure, managerial process or competitive strategy.

Much of the research conducted in the contingency framework concentrated on how different environments and technologies affect the structure and processes of the organisation.

Lawrence and Lorsch, both from Harvard Business School, argued that the structure of an organisation is contingent on the environment within which it operates.[24] Their approach to structure was based on research undertaken in ten organisations in three different industrial sectors: plastics (six organisations); food (two); and containers (two). In order to deal effectively with the external environment, organisations develop segmented units to deal with specific aspects of the environment. For example, organisational functions are typically divided into production, sales, research and development (R&D), and finance, each of which has to cope with different subsections of the environment. Lawrence and Lorsch used the term *differentiation* to describe this segmentation or breaking down of functions. They defined differentiation as 'the differences in cognitive and emotional orientation of managers in various functional areas'.[25]

However, organisations also need to be co-ordinated to achieve effective transaction with the environment. This co-ordination and collaboration is achieved through integration, which Lawrence and Lorsch define as 'the quality of the state of collaboration existing among departments that are needed to achieve unity of effort demanded by the environment'.[26] Integration can be achieved through mechanisms such as direct managerial contact, hierarchy, formal and informal communication, and through more sophisticated devices such as permanent integrating teams and integrative departments.

During the course of their research Lawrence and Lorsch found that the greater the level of uncertainty in the environment the greater the diversity or differentiation among organisational sub-units. For example, organisations in the plastics industry, faced with a high degree of uncertainty, significantly differentiated between sales, R&D, finance and production. In contrast, organisations in the container industry, which faced a more certain environment, employed less differentiation.

Greater differentiation, however, creates the potential for conflict between sub-units as the specialist groups develop their own ways of dealing with uncertainty in the environment. Highly differentiated organisations consequently require appropriate methods of integration and conflict resolution. Lawrence and Lorsch found that the greater the degree of differentiation the greater the need for integration. For example, high-performing organisations in the plastics sector, which had the highest level of differentiation, used a variety of integrative mechanisms including direct managerial contact, hierarchy, communications, permanent cross-functional teams and integrative departments. In contrast, the container industry's lower levels of differentiation required less integration in the form of direct managerial contact, hierarchy and communications.

Lawrence and Lorsch concluded that effective organisational functioning depends on an appropriate three-way relationship between uncertainty and diversity within the environment, the degree of differentiation and the state of integration achieved. In this way the structure of a successful organisation is contingent upon its environment, as shown in Figure 1.13.

FIGURE 1.13 THE LAWRENCE AND LORSCH FRAMEWORK

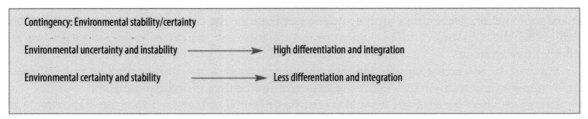

In relation to technology, Burns and Stalker[27] argued that the structure of the organisation is contingent on the rate of technological change, as shown in Figure 1.14. Based on research in the UK, they found that if the rate of technological change is slow the most effective structure is mechanistic, but if the rate of change is rapid a more flexible – organic – type of structure is required, which allows flexibility as demanded by the pace of change.

FIGURE 1.14 THE BURNS AND STALKER FRAMEWORK

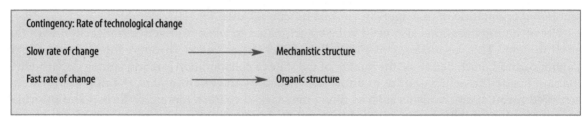

A mechanistic-type structure is mainly hierarchical in nature, with communications and interaction occurring vertically. In this form of structure knowledge is concentrated at the top and continued membership of the organisation is based on obedience and loyalty. Therefore the mechanistic form of structure is similar to a bureaucracy. In contrast, an organic structure is like a network with interactions and communications occurring both horizontally and vertically. Knowledge is based wherever it is most suitable for the organisation and membership requires commitment to the organisation.

The main contribution of contingency theory is that it recognised the limitations of universal principles of management and identified contingencies under which different actions are required. These ideas gained widespread acceptance, especially in relation to the role of technology and the external environment.

The main problem associated with the approach is that it may not be applicable to all managerial issues and it is almost impossible to identify all contingencies facing organisations. Despite these problems, contingency theory is still popular today because it emphasises the need for managers to be flexible and to adapt to changing conditions. In recognising that the world is too complex for one best way of managing to exist, contingency theory has provided much food for thought in contemporary management.

1.9.4 The contemporary approaches: a summary

Contemporary management approaches have dominated the field of management thought since the 1950s and are still influential, both in theory and practice. The key contributions and limitations of the various approaches are outlined in Figure 1.15.

FIGURE 1.15 CONTEMPORARY APPROACHES: A SUMMARY

School of thought:	Organisational behaviour: 1950s–present day
Proponents:	McGregor, Likert
Contribution:	Focused on management activities that encouraged employee effectiveness by understanding and exploring individual, group and organisational processes
Limitations:	Ignored situational factors
School of thought:	Systems theory: 1950s–present day
Proponents:	Barnard; Katz and Khan
Contribution:	Organisation seen as open system interacting with the environment; organisation is both a system and a sub system; synergies exist and multiple ways to achieve the same outcome
Limitations:	No specific guidelines on the functions and duties of managers
School of thought:	Contingency theory: 1960s–present day
Proponents:	Burns and Stalker; Lawrence and Lorsch
Contribution:	Appropriate managerial action depends on situational contingencies; no one best way of managing
Limitations:	Not possible to identify all contingencies; may not apply to all managerial issues

OB focused on employee effectiveness through individual, group and organisational processes. Systems theory recognised the organisation as an open system that depends on the external environment for survival, and emphasised that efficiency alone is not sufficient for survival. In order to be successful, organisations have to be effective in ensuring a match between what they produce and what the external environment wants and needs.

Contingency theory argues that best management practice depends on or is contingent upon the situation at hand. The technology employed by the organisation and the environment within which it operates often influence the managerial action required for success.

These approaches are still popular today in the field of management thought and they represent some of the most critical issues facing managers as they try to achieve competitive advantage in an increasingly competitive external environment. Systems theory highlights the importance of the environment for organisational survival; contingency theory emphasises that best management practice depends on the situation and that this must be evaluated by the manager. All of these factors need to be adequately addressed by managers in today's environment if the organisation is to be successful. These points will be further developed throughout this book.

1.10 Summary of key propositions

- Management has been largely responsible for the development of the pattern of industry as we know it today. Management has facilitated the co-ordination of people with different skills and knowledge to achieve organisational goals.

- Management is the process of achieving desired results through an efficient utilisation of human and material resources. Managers are individuals within organisations who are responsible for the process of management.

- Management typically has five main functions which logically follow on from one another: planning involves establishing what needs to be done; organising establishes how tasks should be completed; staffing and personnel ensures the availability of human resources to achieve such tasks; leading involves directing and motivating employees toward the attainment of organisational goals; and control involves measuring actual performance against desired performance and taking corrective action.

- Managers perform ten key managerial roles: interpersonal (figurehead, leader, liaison); informational (monitor, disseminator, spokesperson); and decisional (entrepreneur, disturbance handler, resource allocator, negotiator).

- The earliest contributions to management thought can be traced back to the Sumerians, the ancient Egyptians and the ancient Romans. One of the most enduring examples of early management practice is the Roman Catholic Church.

- The Industrial Revolution marked a watershed in the development of management thought. As industries expanded to take advantage of new markets and technological innovations, organisations became larger and more complex. This led to the development of new management techniques to cope with the issues presented by industrialisation, namely production, efficiency and cost savings.

- In response to the managerial challenges posed by industrialisation, the 'classical' approach to management emerged in the early twentieth century. The major schools of thought associated with the classical approach are scientific management, bureaucracy, administrative management and human relations.

- Scientific management emphasised the development of one best way of performing a task through the application of scientific methods. The birth of scientific management is attributed to Taylor and his pioneering work in the Bethlehem Steel Works.

- Max Weber concentrated on how organisations should be structured to ensure efficiency. He developed what he perceived to be the ideal form of structure and called it bureaucracy. The bureaucratic structure emphasised detailed rules and procedures, hierarchy and impersonal relationships between organisational members.

- Administrative management was based on the personal experiences of its key proponents and focused on senior managers and the policy issues they faced. The father of administrative management is Henri Fayol, who identified management as a separate business activity with five functions. Fayol also developed 14 principles of management.

- The human relations movement concentrated on the human side of management and tried to understand how social and psychological factors influence performance. Mayo and his associates conducted the Hawthorne Studies, which proved that social needs take precedence over economic needs and that the informal work group exerts control over employee performance.
- Contemporary approaches to management that have emerged since the 1950s include organisational behaviour (OB), systems theory and contingency theory.
- OB, developed in the 1950s, focused on management activities that encourage employee effectiveness by understanding and exploring individual, group and organisational processes. However, it ignored situational factors.
- Systems theory argues that organisations should be viewed as systems that transform inputs into outputs to the environment. Consequently, the organisation constantly interacts with its environment. Key advocates of this approach include Barnard, and Katz and Kahn.
- Contingency theory argues that there is no one best way of managing because organisations face different situations – or contingencies. The most common contingencies are the external environment, technology, the organisation's internal strengths and weaknesses, and the values and skills of its workforce. Burns and Stalker, and Lawrence and Lorsch examined the contingencies affecting structure.
- All of the issues raised by the various approaches need to be considered by managers when striving to compete in today's business environment.

Discussion Questions

1 What is scientific management? Why was it so popular?
2 What effect did the Industrial Revolution have on management?
3 Compare and contrast scientific and administrative management.
4 What were the Hawthorne Studies? Why were they so important in the development of management thought?
5 What are the main elements of bureaucracy? What are its advantages and disadvantages?
6 How did systems theory try to overcome the limitations of earlier approaches?
7 Explain why contingency theory has become so popular.
8 How do the contemporary approaches to management differ from the classical approaches?
9 Taylor and Fayol have both been accused of seeking a one best way of managing organisations. To what extent is this statement true?

Concluding Case: McDonald's and management theory

McDonald's is one of the world most famous and instantly recognisable brands. It is a global food service retailer with more than 33,500 local restaurants serving approximately 69 million people in 119 countries every day, and its world-famous French fries, Big Mac, Quarter Pounder and Chicken McNuggets have become synonymous with 'fast food'.

McDonald's largely operates on a franchise basis; over 80 per cent of its restaurants worldwide are owned and operated by independent local entrepreneurs. Of its total restaurants worldwide, nearly 59 per cent are conventional franchises, 21 per cent are licensed to foreign affiliates or developmental licensees, and nearly 20 per cent are company operated. The strength of the alignment between the company, its franchisees and suppliers (collectively referred to as the 'System') has been key to McDonald's success.

McDonald's Plan to Win strategy provides a common framework for the global business yet allows for local adaptation. Through the execution of initiatives surrounding the five elements of the Plan to Win – People, Products, Place, Price and Promotion – McDonalds has grown comparable sales and customer visits in each of the last eight years.

This business model allows McDonalds to be a global giant but also to remain locally responsive. The food industry is one in which there are still regional differences, and ensuring local franchise arrangements means that McDonald's is uniquely placed to respond to local market preferences. For example, in China, the menu had to be modified to take account of the local preference for more chicken-based products. In France, the company added a variety of breads, such as brioche, and espresso to meet customer requirements. McDonald's can therefore respond to local market contingencies. The business is managed in distinct geographical segments that include the USA; Europe; Asia/Pacific, Middle East and Africa (APMEA); and other countries/regions, including Canada and Latin America.

Despite the onset of the recession, McDonald's has continued to increase its operating income year on year. In 2011 the company reported an operating income of $8.5 billion, up from $6.8 billion in 2009; and in the USA the company expanded its core business, adding more than 350 million customer visits in 2011. Growth also continued in Europe, where 40 per cent of its overall income is now generated. The APMEA section doubled its income between 2005 and 2011. Growth for the years 2011 and 2010 is shown in Table 1.1.

TABLE 1.1 MCDONALD'S GROWTH, 2011 AND 2010

	USA	Europe	APMEA	Other Countries & Corporate	Total
2011	4.8%	5.9%	4.7%	10.1%	5.6%
2010	3.8%	4.4%	6.0%	11.3%	5.0%

McDonald's uses a very strict division of labour in all its branches. Most of the food is pre-cooked and then shipped to each outlet. The tasks are then divided and very clearly allocated to specific staff members. The main tasks are:

1 Customer service at the till.
2 Preparation of fries.
3 Preparation of burgers.
4 Assembly of buns and burgers.
5 Lobby clean-up.

In contrast to a smaller food outlet, where one person may be involved in all of those tasks, McDonald's employs a strict division of labour, with staff involved in narrowly defined tasks. Job specialisation results in speed and familiarity with the processes involved in fast food production; and the procedure is similar to the principles of assembly line manufacture. The layout of each branch is also designed to minimise time delays in moving from one location to another. As the whole 'fast food' concept is based on speed and ease of delivery, this is an important element.

Keep up to date
www.mcdonalds.com

Source: www.aboutmcdonalds.com/mcd/investors/annual_reports.html

Case Questions
1 What schools of management thought are evident in the McDonald's case above?
2 Why does scientific management work so well for McDonald's?
3 What disadvantages could there be in using a strict division of labour?

Notes and References

1 Drucker, P. (1980) *Managing in Turbulent Times*. London: Heinemann.
2 Mintzberg, H. (1990) 'The Manager's Job: Folklore and Fact', *Harvard Business Review*, March–April, 163–76.
3 Ibid.
4 Ibid.
5 Ibid.
6 Machiavelli, N. (1532) *Il Principe*. English translation (1985) *The Prince*. London: Penguin.
7 Smith, A. (1937, first published 1776) *An Inquiry Into the Nature and Causes of the Wealth of Nations*. New York: Random House.
8 Taylor, F. (1947) *Scientific Management*. New York: Harper Row.
9 Gilbreth, F. and Gilbreth, L. (1916) *Fatigue Study*. New York: Sturgis and Walton.
10 Taylor, F., *op. cit.*
11 Weber, M. (1947) *The Theory of Social and Economic Organisation* (trans. Henderson and Talcott). New York: Free Press.
12 Fayol, H. (1916) *Administration Industrielle et Générale*. English translation (1949) *General and Industrial Management*. London: Pitman.

13 Barnard, C. (1938) *The Functions of the Executive.* Cambridge, MA: Harvard University Press.

14 Metcalf, H. and Urwick, L. (eds) (1941) *Dynamic Administration: The Collected Papers of Mary Parker Follett.* New York: Harper and Brothers.

15 Urwick, L. (1973) *The Elements of Administration.* London: Pitman.

16 Mayo, E. (1949) *The Human Problems of an Industrial Civilisation.* New York: Macmillan.

17 Roethlisberger, F. and Dickson, W. (1939) *Management and the Worker.* Cambridge, MA: Harvard University Press.

18 Carey, A. (1967) 'The Hawthorne Studies: A Radical Criticism', *American Sociological Review* 32, 403–16; Jones, S. (1990) 'Worker Interdependence and Output: The Hawthorne Studies Reevaluated', *American Sociological Review* 55, April, 176–90; Jones, S. (1992) 'Was there a Hawthorne Effect?', *American Journal of Sociology* 98(3), 451–68; Yunker, G. (1993) 'An Explanation of Positive and Negative Hawthorne Effects: Evidence from the Relay Assembly Test Room and Bank Wiring Observation Room Studies', paper presented to the Academy of Management Annual Meeting, Atlanta, Georgia.

19 Maslow, A. (1943) 'A Theory of Human Motivation', *Psychological Review* 50(2), 370–96.

20 Koontz, H. (1980) 'The Management Theory Jungle Revisited', *Academy of Management Review*, April, 175–87.

21 Brayfield, A. and Crockett, W. (1955) 'Employee Attitudes and Employee Performance', *Psychological Bulletin* 51, 396–424; Vroom, V. (1969) *Work and Motivation,* New York: Wiley; Iaffaldano, M. and Muchinsky, P. (1985) 'Job Satisfaction and Job Performance: A Meta Analysis', *Psychological Bulletin* 97, 251–73.

22 For a fuller discussion of OB techniques see Morley, M., Moore, S., Heraty, N., Linehan, M. and MacCurtain, S. (2011), *Principles of Organisational Behaviour* (3rd edn). Dublin: Gill & Macmillan.

23 Barnard, C. (1938) *The Functions of the Executive.* Cambridge, MA: Harvard University Press.

24 Lawrence, P. and Lorsch, J. (1969) *Organisations and Environment: Managing Differentiation and Integration.* Illinois: Irwin.

25 Ibid.

26 Ibid.

27 Burns, T. and Stalker, G. (1961) *The Management of Innovation.* London: Tavistock.

CHAPTER 2

The Development of Business in Ireland

CHAPTER LEARNING OBJECTIVES

- To understand the pattern of industrial development in Ireland before 1922.
- To understand the conservative approach to industrial development taken by the Free State government and the priority given to the agricultural sector.
- To appreciate the rationale for the policy of self-sufficiency pursued between 1932 and 1958.
- To understand the significance of the move to free trade and a policy of foreign direct investment from 1958 onwards.
- To understand the significance of joining the EEC (EU) from an industrial development perspective.
- To understand why the 1980s forced the IDA to rethink their strategy and to concentrate on attracting companies with high output, using the best technology while spending significant amounts on Irish materials and related services.
- To understand the role played by fiscal rectitude and social partnership in the recovery from the late 1980s onwards.
- To understand the basis of the Celtic Tiger years and explain the extent of economic growth.
- To understand the nature and causes of the financial crisis of 2008 and its effect on businesses.
- To understand the structure of business in Ireland and future prospects for the sector.

2.1 Introduction

This chapter[1] charts the development of the Irish business sector from its earliest industrial activity to the present. Historical approaches to industrial development, from early protectionism to free trade and foreign direct investment, are considered. The role played by membership of the European Community in 1973 is also highlighted, and the economic recession and subsequent recovery of the 1990s is explained. The recent financial crisis and recession are analysed, and the chapter concludes with a discussion of the future prospects for business in Ireland.

2.2 The early years

Ireland was largely unaffected by the Industrial Revolution that swept through the UK and the USA and changed the pattern of industrial development. Despite this, according to the 1821 Census of Population, more than one-third of Irish counties (six of which were outside Ulster) had a significant number of people involved in manufacture, trade or handicraft. The census also indicated that 700,000 people were employed in the Irish textile industries, most notably cotton and linen.[2] From the 1840s to the early 1900s the country's per capita income rose steadily, averaging 40 per cent of the UK level in the 1840s and increasing to 60 per cent in 1913. In fact, Irish incomes were higher than those in Finland, Italy and Portugal.[3] The population, however, continued to decline in the post-famine era, falling from 6.6 million in 1851 to just over four million in the early 1900s.

The first census of production in Ireland (the thirty-two counties), undertaken in 1907, found that industrial activity came a poor second to agriculture in terms of employment and output. However, Irish industry still employed about 20 per cent of the entire workforce and 50 per cent of industrial output was exported. The country had also earned worldwide recognition in key industrial sectors such as linen, shipbuilding, distilling and brewing, with names like Guinness and Harland and Wolff well established in their industrial sectors. In addition, Ireland's volume of trade per capita was higher than the British figure. It is important to note, however, that the bulk of industrial activity was centred on the six northeastern counties.

An important challenge confronted by Irish businesses, and most European businesses, in the early years of the nineteenth century was the emergence of an organised labour movement. The development of a strong labour movement, particularly in Dublin and Cork, posed difficulties for Irish industry, and the tensions between management and unions culminated in the now famous Dublin Lockout of 1913. Dublin employers, led by William Martin Murphy, came into conflict with the Irish Transport and General Workers' Union (ITGWU), led by Jim Larkin. Workers refused to sign statements undertaking not to acquire or retain union membership, went on strike and were subsequently locked out by their employers. At its height, 20,000 workers from 300 different companies were involved. After six months the workers drifted back to work, but many of them had been radicalised by the experience.[4]

2.3 The Irish Free State (1922)

With the emergence of the Irish Free State in 1922, Ireland was not only politically but also, in theory, economically independent. The extent of such economic independence has to be qualified by the fact that the Irish economy remained closely dependent on the UK. The currency tie between the two countries remained and the UK market was the largest Irish export market. In addition, much industry in Ireland at the time took the form of UK subsidiary companies.

The most pressing task for the new government was building a nation. The country inherited a fully developed banking system, a reasonable communications system, schools, hospitals and valuable external assets.[5] But it also inherited the devastation that had been wrought by both the War of Independence and, later, the Civil War. The population had also fallen significantly to 3.1 million in 1922.

In relation to industry, the most devastating blow to Ireland was the loss of the industrialised northeast, especially the thriving region of Belfast. By the 1920s the industrial labour force amounted to just over 100,000 workers or about 7 per cent of the total labour force.[6] The prospects for the fledgling economy were further undermined by Ireland's lack of an entrepreneurial tradition, which had resulted from the colonial status of the economy – by definition, the native population had had limited access to business opportunities and managerial positions. In addition, the recent turbulent environment meant that in many cases the 'brightest and best' opted for the relatively safe employment of the civil service, rather than establishing businesses or seeking employment in the private sector.

The government adopted a conservative approach to both economic and industrial development. It received the backing of the banks, large farmers and the Anglo-Irish community, which provided a useful base from which to construct the new state, and it avoided the mistakes made by countries such as Poland and Germany, which printed their own money and consequently suffered severe inflation.

In relation to economic development the government very firmly prioritised the agricultural sector, which at the time employed 50 per cent of the workforce and was the country's largest exporter. Key members of the government believed that what was good for agriculture would automatically be good for industry. In this sense agriculture was viewed as a vehicle for economic and industrial growth. State intervention in industry was, therefore, kept to a minimum.

Despite its conservative stance on the economy and developing the industrial sector, the government was responsible for the establishment of an electricity supply service (see Management Focus 2.1); and the Agricultural Credit Corporation was also established in 1927 to finance the development and expansion of farming and agribusiness.

Management Focus 2.1 Ardnacrusha power plant

The decision to construct a hydroelectric plant at Ardnacrusha was taken in 1924 and was largely the brainchild of Dr Thomas McLoughlin, an Irish engineer who had been approached by the government in 1923 to survey Ireland's electricity capacity. The government established the Electricity Supply Board (ESB) in 1927 to supervise the distribution of electricity nationally. The Shannon Scheme, when it became operational in 1929, was an immediate success, and the introduction of electricity changed the face of rural Ireland. In the decades that followed, industry also benefited from this ambitious development, which added significantly to Ireland's industrial infrastructure.

While agriculture was prioritised during the early years of the state, important inroads were nonetheless made into providing a base from which industry could, many years later, develop. However, in this period the development of a vibrant export-driven industrial economy was still a distant hope.

2.4 Self-sufficiency and protectionism (1932–58)

In 1932 Fianna Fáil came to power and began to pursue an entirely different approach to industrial policy, one that was economically, but also politically, motivated. This was the first period during which a native Irish government had a coherent economic philosophy. Protectionism and self-sufficiency, which was particularly espoused by Arthur Griffith, was based on Friedrich List's infant industry argument, which advocated a protectionist policy. Like many other countries in Europe at the time, de Valera's government had a strong ideological belief in self-sufficiency. For Ireland self-sufficiency was viewed as a means of ensuring economic growth, but it was also a measure of the political independence that had been achieved by the state. Self-sufficiency effectively meant that the government protected domestic industries from competition by placing high tariffs on imported goods, thereby rendering them more costly than domestic produce (see Management Focus 2.2). Irish tariffs were as high as 45 per cent in the following years and only countries like Spain and Germany had higher barriers. A number of new industries, such as car assembly, successfully grew up behind tariff barriers during this period. The Control of Manufacturers Act 1932 required that more than 50 per cent of the equity in new companies should be Irish-owned.

Management Focus 2.2 Difficulties with tariffs

Imposing tariffs wasn't the simple thing that many thought. The 1934 budget, for instance, was forced to address the problem that brush handles were escaping duties by masquerading as duty-free handles for chimney scrapers. However, the most persistent problem was with the importation of rosary beads. Despite a 33.3 per cent duty, imports continued to be stubbornly strong. A minimum duty of 2d per rosary was imposed to stop the deluge. Soon, however, cunning types began to import beads with a full 15 decades on each (presumably to encompass Glorious, Sorrowful and Joyful Mysteries in one compendium). The government countered this threat to the national endeavour by slapping a 3s/4d tax on every decade of imported foreign rosaries. That put a stop to the gallop of the bead importers.

Source: Fitzpatrick, M. (2000) 'A Century of Irish Business', *Sunday Independent* 2 January, 18L–19L.

The 1930s were characterised by severe depression in the aftermath of the Wall Street Crash in 1929 and the government found the €3.81 million annual payment to the UK in land annuities a serious drain on public finances.* In 1932 the government withheld payment and the UK responded by imposing duties on the importation of Irish livestock, meat and dairy products. The Irish

Note: All sums in Irish punts have been converted to euro equivalents.

government in turn imposed additional tariffs on UK goods, at which the Economic War ensued between the two countries, which continued until 1937. The Irish economy fared badly during the Economic War, with cattle exports to the UK falling from 750,000 in 1930 to 500,000 in 1934, while total agricultural exports fell from €54 million in 1929 to €17.6 million in 1935. As a result the cattle industry was severely hit, farm incomes dropped and unemployment and emigration both increased.

However, the Economic War also affected industry. One of the most negative consequences saw Ireland's largest brewer, Guinness, establish manufacturing operations outside Ireland for the first time. The reasons behind the move by Guinness were clear: American Prohibition had increased the company's reliance on the UK market. However, with the introduction of tariffs, the UK market came under significant threat. Rather than put trade with the UK at risk, Guinness decided to establish its first brewery outside Ireland. Eventually, Guinness was no longer viewed as an Irish company.[7]

Throughout the period of protectionism, the government took pragmatic decisions to develop Ireland's economic infrastructure. Many semi-state bodies were established to provide essential services that the market might fail to do (Aer Lingus in 1936, CIÉ in 1944 and Irish Shipping in 1951), and to exploit natural resources (Bord na Móna in 1946 and Comhlucht Siúcra Éireann in 1933). In 1933 the Industrial Credit Corporation (ICC) was established to provide capital for the development of industry. The ICC essentially acted as an underwriter to issues of new companies.

Despite high rates of emigration and the effects of the Economic War, the 1930s brought growth in both industrial employment and output. With the onset of the Second World War self-sufficiency was no longer a choice but an economic necessity. In Ireland the period 1939–45 was termed 'the Emergency' and it was a particularly difficult time for the economy. One of the main problems was importing raw materials and supplies, the sources of which were limited to the UK and the USA, as the Germans occupied most of Europe. The war caused extreme hardship for some industries that depended on imported raw materials, for example car assembly (Ford), soap making (Creans) and candle manufacturing (Rathbornes).

The war further heightened economic divisions between the North and South. While the North had been particularly badly affected by the Great Depression of the 1930s, the situation changed completely with the start of the war, which meant rearmament and huge ship-building projects. The economy of the North benefited from such orders, but the South failed to experience the same economic boom. In the South incomes grew by only 14 per cent between 1939 and 1947, while in the North they grew by 84 per cent over the same period.[8]

The immediate post-war years continued to provide problems for the government, who had envisaged a fast economic recovery. However, Ireland continued to experience rising unemployment, high emigration (125,000 people emigrated between 1945 and 1948), higher prices, and rationing. The late 1940s were characterised by bad harvests and public sector strikes. The winter of 1946/47 was particularly harsh and a fuel crisis during the early part of 1947 crippled industry and transport. A national teachers' strike in 1948 further intensified problems.

In 1949 the government established the Industrial Development Authority (IDA), which had a dual function: to advise the Minister for Industry and Commerce on industrial development; and to promote greater investment in Irish industry.

The passing of the Underdeveloped Areas Act 1952 introduced financial grants for industries to set up in undeveloped areas, mostly in the western and midland regions. In the same year the government decided to separate the grant-giving function of the IDA from the promotion of new industry. As a result the IDA's function was limited to promoting new investment; and a new body, An Foras Tionscal, was created with the remit of awarding grants and incentives. In 1956, Export Profits Tax Relief, introduced in the Finance Act, gave 50 per cent tax remission on export sales; this was increased to 100 per cent two years later.

There were some success stories from the protectionist self-sufficiency years in Ireland's development, the most famous of which is Jefferson Smurfit (see Management Focus 2.3). The experience of the Smurfit Group, however, is at odds with the more familiar spectre associated with Irish industry in the 1950s.

Management Focus 2.3 Jefferson Smurfit: a success story

In the 1930s Jefferson Smurfit set up a box-making business in Dublin. During the war years, as Smurfit's supplies all but disappeared, he pioneered the development of a machine to use waste paper, and through this was able to keep his business growing. The company continued to expand through acquisitions, both domestic and international, and by 1964 the company was quoted on the Irish Stock Exchange.

Source: Fitzpatrick, M. (2000) 'A Century of Irish Business', *Sunday Independent* 2 January, 18L–19L.

Economic difficulties continued throughout the 1950s, a period often referred to as the Great Slump. Emigration continued at an alarming rate, with 400,000 people leaving the country between 1951 and 1961. Almost 90 per cent of exports were to the UK, which marked an extreme over-reliance on one market. Living standards failed to increase and the move to international free trade by other countries during the early 1950s passed Ireland by.

The situation in Ireland during the 1950s was unique in comparison to other European countries, all of which were rebuilding and experiencing growth. The late 1950s was a period of great prosperity in the UK, prompted in part by the need for post-war recovery and facilitated by a strong manufacturing base. In contrast, Ireland in the 1950s was characterised by a deep conservatism generated by the influence of the Roman Catholic Church and close links between political and church leaders. The political scene was still dominated by the War of Independence/Civil War generation, in contrast to the familiar left–right divide that was evident in many other countries at the time.

Domestic companies were small and uncompetitive, sheltering behind high tariff walls where there was no incentive to become efficient and effective. The industrial base simply was not large enough to employ surplus labour and to reduce unemployment through job creation. By 1950 manufactured goods accounted for only 6 per cent of exports, with food and food products making up 73 per cent. A sizeable proportion of the labour force, 44 per cent, was employed in agriculture compared to only 15 per cent in industry.[9] Ireland was faced with growing balance of payments crises fuelled in part by the devaluation of sterling, the Korean War and the Suez Crisis.

2.5 The move to free trade and foreign direct investment (1958)

By the late 1950s Ireland was facing an economic crisis that began to threaten the economic viability of the country as a separate entity. Given the huge number of people emigrating to seek work and success elsewhere (one million people had emigrated since the foundation of the state), questions were raised as to whether the country could survive independently on a long-term basis.

In the mid-1950s the government set up the Capital Investment Advisory Committee to examine ways of improving the economy. T. K. Whitaker, the new Secretary of the Department of Finance, was appointed chairman. In 1958 Whitaker produced a report called *Economic Development*, which advocated a reversal of the protectionist policy that had been pursued since 1932. The thrust of industrial policy should, according to the report, concentrate on free trade and reflect a move by the government towards productive rather than social investment. The document also recommended that a policy of foreign direct investment (FDI) should be pursued; in other words, foreign companies should be encouraged to invest in Ireland. Whitaker's plan was implemented by the government through a series of economic programmes, starting with the First Programme for Economic Expansion (1959–64). The main elements of the First Programme were:

- increased state expenditure on productive investment areas
- an export drive in both agriculture and industry
- the encouragement of FDI in Ireland
- the adaptation of Irish industry to modern markets and methods of production.

The implementation of the First Programme therefore marked a huge change in industrial policy, one that would open up Ireland's small closed economy and develop important links with other countries, thereby promoting industrial and economic growth. It was followed by a second programme, which had been designed to cover 1964 to 1970, but which was shelved in 1967. According to Kennedy this new outward-looking policy was composed of three main strategies, which the government pursued during the 1960s.[10]

1. Protectionism was gradually replaced by free trade and greater market access, which culminated in the Anglo-Irish Free Trade Area Agreement (AIFTAA) in 1965 and European Economic Community (EEC) membership in 1973.
2. The IDA was given the task of actively generating FDI in Ireland to aid job creation and further develop the export orientation recommended in Whitaker's report.
3. Financial grants and incentives were given to encourage the development of an export-focused manufacturing industry.

Each of these strategies was vigorously pursued by different means throughout the 1960s. In relation to the first strategy of promoting free trade, Ireland joined the World Bank and the International Monetary Fund (IMF). The transition to free trade was eased by two developments – the AIFTAA in 1965 and Ireland's 1961 application and subsequent membership of the EEC in 1973. (The French had vetoed Britain's entry in 1961 and it was considered too risky for Ireland to enter without its largest trading partner.) The AIFTAA was signed in December 1965 and resulted in a phased reduction of tariffs between Ireland and Britain. It comprised the following terms:

- Irish industrial goods were guaranteed tariff-free access to British markets.
- Irish store cattle were given a guaranteed market and butter import quotas to Britain were increased.
- Ireland would reduce tariff barriers on British imports by 10 per cent annually, reaching free trade after a period of ten years in 1975.

The time frame associated with the agreement was long enough to allow Irish industry time to adapt to the changed circumstances. AIFTAA can be viewed as a stepping stone to membership of the General Agreement on Tariffs and Trade (GATT), which Ireland secured in 1967.

The second strategy – increasing FDI – was handled by the IDA and was viewed as critical to the IDA's efforts to promote Ireland as a location for foreign investment. The IDA attempted to create a one-stop shop for potential investors: it provided packages to attract them in the first instance; and once they were located in Ireland, the IDA maintained the investment through communication with the foreign parent and the Irish facility. In 1958 the Control of Manufacturers Act 1932, which had placed restrictions on foreign ownership of industry in Ireland, was eased.

Traditionally the main source of foreign investment in Ireland had come from UK firms hoping to avoid high tariffs in the Irish market. Throughout the 1960s the UK remained the single largest source of foreign investment and resultant job creation, until the USA overtook it in the 1970s. In the late 1950s and the early 1960s West German companies were particularly interested in Ireland. Marshall Aid had helped West German companies to recover from the ravages of the Second World War and they were ready to consider new locations. These West German companies were the first foreign-owned businesses to build new factories whose output was produced solely for export purposes. These companies included Krups (Limerick), Faber-Castell (Cork) and Liebherr (Kilkenny).

In the 1960s the pattern of FDI began to change as a result of the IDA's promotional efforts in the USA. General Electric established two electronics industries, EI in Shannon (1963) and ECCO in Dundalk (1966).[11] Another US giant, the Pfizer Corporation, set up a chemical plant in Ringaskiddy, Cork in 1969. The promotional campaigns undertaken by the IDA produced results. During the 1960s 450 foreign companies established facilities in Ireland and by 1972 they were employing 34,000 people.[12]

Despite IDA success in promoting FDI through its home base and network of six foreign offices, there was a feeling that the twin agencies (IDA and An Foras Tionscal) were suffering from the civil service employment structure within which they operated. It was argued that such a structure prevented the agencies developing. A report published in 1967 reflected these fears and recommended that IDA staff should no longer be regarded as civil servants. The report was accepted by the Minster for Industry and Commerce and implemented through the Industrial Development Act 1969, which gave the IDA a mandate to act under the minister as a body with responsibility for industrial development. The IDA now had sole responsibility for allocating grants and incentives and providing factories and industrial estates, and could for the first time take an equity stake in selected companies. Coupled with this role, the IDA now held responsibility for the promotion in Ireland of indigenous companies, especially small start-ups. The change in the IDA from civil service department to state-sponsored body marked a major transition in its development. Almost all civil servants previously employed in the IDA returned to the Department of Industry and Commerce when the new agency was established.

In pursuing the third and final strategy – developing an export-focused manufacturing industry – the government set up the Committee on Industrial Organisation (CIO) in 1961 in order to generate adjustment measures for Irish industry. The CIO carried out detailed analyses of the levels of efficiency across many different industrial sectors and recommended various aids and incentives for Irish companies.[13] Irish companies were left in no doubt that they had to adapt to the concept of export-led growth or face decline and extinction. Some Irish companies responded to the challenge: companies such as Youghal Carpets and Waterford Glass saw a significant growth in earnings, boosted by generous tax relief from the government.[14] Others, however, were less successful, and the sugar confectionery business (see Management Focus 2.4) is a good example of the failure of Irish companies to develop with free trade.

Management Focus 2.4 Irish confectionery

Throughout the 1940s and 1950s Lemon's had become a highly successful sweet manufacturer, with the company's image successfully displayed through a very effective advertising campaign. The campaign consisted of a series of line drawings accompanied by the slogan, 'This is Saturday – time for your Lemon's pure sweets'. Lemon's competed against foreign companies such as Cadbury and Rowntree Mackintosh, and also against other domestic companies such as Urney of Tallaght and J. Milroy & Sons (manufacturer of the famous toffee bars). These domestic sweet manufacturers produced confectionery for the Irish public behind tariff walls. However, they had no economies of scale when compared to their UK rivals. Instead they produced a large variety of products for a small-scale unexpanding market. When the tariffs ended after the change in industrial policy, so too did the small Irish independents. Lemon's was eventually bought out by a UK manufacturer and subsequently closed in 1983. Urney was taken over by a US company in 1963 and latterly by Unilever. However, this company was also closed eventually when, like Lemon's, it failed to develop a strong export business.

Source: Fitzpatrick, M. (2000) 'A Century of Irish Business', *Sunday Independent* 2 January, 18L–19L.

Further developments throughout the 1960s greatly enhanced Ireland's current and potential competitive infrastructure. The Irish banking industry went through a period of amalgamation to produce two major banking groups, Allied Irish Banks and the Bank of Ireland. The banks were willing to lend money to industry and the growing range of financial services offered by the banks provided corporate customers with a complete range of business financial services.[15]

Ireland became more aware of deficiencies in Irish management and of the importance of management training. The types of management skill required to operate in a free trade export-led industry are obviously very different from those needed in a small, sheltered domestic sector. Recognition of this resulted in the establishment of the Irish Management Institute (IMI) to provide management training for organisations in Ireland.

Developments in the educational sector during the 1960s, however, were to have an enormous impact in later years. By the 1960s Ireland lagged behind most of Europe in relation to the development of the educational system. Apart from the Vocational Education Act 1930, the system had remained largely unchanged since the foundation of the state. Educational opportunities at second and third level were limited to those who could afford to pay the fees, rather than being open to the most intellectually gifted. In the early 1960s a highly critical report by the Organisation for Economic Co-operation and Development (OECD) entitled *Investment in Education* highlighted the lack of opportunity available to poorer students to enter secondary and third-level education. It also argued that the system did not foster talent due to the low intellectual yet high cost requirements for education.

As an immediate response to the report the decision was made to establish comprehensive schools in areas where adequate secondary schooling was unavailable. However, the most significant change to education was introduced between 1965 and 1967 by Donagh O'Malley, Minister for Education. In 1966 O'Malley announced the free secondary school education scheme for all children. The scheme also provided free transport for all children living over five kilometres from the nearest school. In addition, the government provided support for capital expenditure in schools. These developments marked a decisive step forward for Irish education. As a direct result of the scheme the numbers availing of secondary education increased from 104,000 in 1966 to 144,000 in 1969.[16]

The third-level sector also witnessed change. The government established the Higher Education Authority (HEA) in 1969 to help guide expenditure in third-level education. Polytechnic-style initiatives were promoted to cater for aspects of education neglected by the universities at the time. The full impact of these developments in education was to be felt in subsequent decades when they significantly affected the promotional policies of the IDA. This point will be elaborated on later in the chapter.

As part of its regional development drive, the IDA established the first industrial estates in the early 1970s in Galway and Waterford.[17] It is interesting to note that Dublin was not specifically promoted as a location for FDI until the late 1970s, when the clothing industry that had thrived in inner Dublin collapsed due to stiff competition and recession. It was only in 1976 that the IDA began actively to promote Dublin by developing industrial estates in areas on the periphery of the city such as Coolock, Santry and Clondalkin.

The 1960s can be viewed as a decade of prosperity and economic boom for the country. The economy grew at a rate of 4 per cent between 1959 and 1964, compared to 1 per cent in the preceding years. Between 1958 and 1970 the economy grew by 61 per cent. During the 1960s Ireland began to discover industry and business and gradually the country became less agricultural and more industrial. Industry rather than agriculture came to be viewed as the vehicle for economic growth.

The marked increase in the relative importance of industry in the Irish economy is clear, amounting to 35.7 per cent of gross national product (GNP) in 1969. The expanding export market, particularly in manufacturing, accounted for much of the growth during this period. There were also important changes in the value and composition of exports. The value of manufacturing exports had trebled between 1953 and 1960 and according to Lee this was no mere recovery but a shift in trajectory.[18] The relative importance of manufacturing exports increased from 49.7 per cent in 1958 to 70 per cent in 1969. There was also a change in the pattern of manufacturing exports, with growth occurring in the newer, modern industry sectors, such as chemicals and machinery, marking a shift in the balance of power in manufacturing. Such new, modern industries do not use large quantities of raw materials, and have a high import content; that is, they import a large proportion of their raw materials.

Also during the 1960s the population of the country increased, reaching 2.98 million in 1971, with emigration continuing to fall. Employment was the only area not recording a significant improvement, mainly due to the continuing reduction in the numbers employed in agriculture. There can be no doubt that in relation to economic performance and industrial development the 1960s were heady years. However, there is less consensus among commentators about the causal relationship between the new policies introduced after 1958 and the phenomenal growth rate. Some have argued that even in the absence of free trade and FDI, the Irish economy would still have grown. It seems unlikely, however, that such a scale of economic growth could have been achieved without the changes in industrial policy. Lee concludes that, while difficult to quantify, policy played a preponderant role in turning recovery into growth, and that the policy makers were lucky in that the new policy coincided with favourable international circumstances.[19]

The industrial policy pursued by the IDA during this period was not without its critics. The 1973 Cooper and Whelan Report[20] (co-authored by Noel Whelan, who became Secretary to the Department of An Taoiseach in 1979), expressed concern about the long-term impact of Ireland's heavy reliance on foreign investment. The report concluded that:

- Dependence on foreign enterprise should be more selective and there should be a more complete cost–benefit comparison of the advantages of foreign as opposed to Irish enterprise.
- Foreign enterprise should be conceived of as providing a complementary source of technology rather than substituting for the development of Irish skills.
- Support for Irish enterprise should shift from the current policy of attempting marginal improvements within the existing structure of inefficient, protected, small firms to the creation of a new structure of production.

While some of the suggestions were taken on board by the IDA, the issue of the lack of Irish enterprise development was to re-emerge in the early 1980s. The next most immediate challenge to face Ireland was accession to the European Economic Community (EEC).

2.6 Membership of the EEC (1973)

In January 1973, Ireland, along with the UK and Denmark, joined the EEC. In 1951 the European Coal and Steel Community (ECSC) had been established by the main European countries with the aim of fostering co-operation. This was followed in 1957 by the formation, under the Treaty of Rome, of the EEC and the European Atomic Energy Community (EAEC or Euratom). As the three communities were managed by common institutions they were collectively referred to as the European Community (EC), and this term came to replace the term European Economic Community.

Membership of such a large economic community opened up enormous opportunities for indigenous Irish companies to develop Continental European markets and thus reduce reliance on UK markets. In addition, membership of the EC became a highly significant selling point for the IDA when promoting Ireland as an investment location, particularly in the USA. Ireland could now be sold as a European base for foreign multinational corporations (MNCs) to enter the European market. For farmers, the Common Agricultural Policy (CAP) heralded the end of their reliance on the UK market.

Membership of the EC had significant benefits in relation to state aid programmes; however, the EC Commission was required to control state aid by member states in order to avoid competitive advantage based on national interest. EC state aid policy is laid down in Article 87.1 of the Treaty of Rome, which provides that state aid is, in principle, incompatible with the common market. Under Article 88, the EC Commission is given the task of controlling state aid. This article requires member states to inform the Commission in advance of any plan to grant state aid.

Ireland received monetary transfers under both the European Social Fund and the Regional Development Fund (programmes designed to assist countries, particularly those in peripheral locations) throughout the 1970s and, by 1980, had been funded the equivalent of 5 per cent of national income. In later years, Ireland continued to receive funds through the Structural and Cohesion Funds, which greatly assisted the development of Irish infrastructure. From 1973 Irish reliance on UK markets declined substantially and by 1981 almost a third of exports were destined for other EC countries. The reduction in the share of Irish exports to the UK paved the way for Ireland's membership of the European Monetary System (EMS), whereby the direct link with sterling was eliminated. The structure of the Irish economy had undergone a significant change in this regard, especially when compared to the post-1922 era of UK dependence.

During the 1970s additional foreign investment was attracted to Ireland, particularly from the USA. By 1979 Ireland received 2.5 per cent of US manufacturing investment in the EC, while Irish GNP amounted to only 0.7 per cent of the EC total.[21] In 1978 the government abolished export profit tax relief and introduced a 10 per cent rate of corporation tax for all manufacturing from 1981 to 2000. The IDA strategy at this time involved a direct marketing approach targeting electronics, pharmaceutical and chemicals companies. Companies investing in Ireland in the early 1970s included Snia Viscosa, Asahi, Courtaulds (Northern Ireland), Gillette-Braun, Syntex, Merck Sharp & Dohme and Warner–Lambert.

However, the first oil crisis of 1973 severely hampered investment in Ireland as companies became more risk-averse, and the numbers locating in Ireland dropped from 80 in 1973 to 45 in 1975. But the late 1970s saw the arrival of Mostek, Wang Laboratories, Verbatim and Apple Computers. In 1979 the IDA approved 105 new projects, 40 of which were American.[22] Bausch & Lomb in Waterford, IMED in Letterkenny, Kostal in Limerick and Fujitsu in Tallaght followed in early 1980. This, however, was the last wave of investment before deepening recession changed industry fortunes.

While the 1970s marked a period of significant foreign investment, indigenous industry failed to make significant advances. Of the net increase in industrial jobs (27,000 during the period 1973–80) just 5,000 were in the indigenous sector, which failed to increase its share of output or significantly reduce its reliance on the UK market (see Management Focus 2.5).

During the 1970s Irish economic growth was dampened by the two oil crises, and the rate of growth of GDP for 1973–81 was 0.5 per cent below that for the preceding 12 years. However, in the late 1970s the Irish economy grew faster than the EC average, for two main reasons: first, the positive inflow of US FDI; and second, the increase in spending through external borrowing by the public sector from 1977 onwards. This development created an expansionary stimulus for the domestic economy, which led to increased output but deterioration in the trade deficit. In 1979, debt rose from €377.1 million to €1,382 million. The deficit in the balance of payments increased from 2.4 per cent of GNP in 1978 to 10.1 per cent in 1979.[23]

Management Focus 2.5 Indigenous Irish companies in the 1970s

The industrial legacy of the 1930s was characterised by small domestic market-focused companies without the capital, experience or skills to expand and develop international markets. The transformation of farmers' co-operatives into major food companies was at an early stage of development and actually involved significant job losses and increased capitalisation in the food industry. Irish-owned industry across many sectors contracted, with job losses occurring in the traditional manufacturing sector. The employment increases secured by companies in the modern manufacturing sector (most of which were foreign) did little to keep pace with the overall losses. IDA policies were focused on grants for the acquisition of new capital equipment, as obsolete equipment was perceived to be the major weakness of indigenous companies. However, the response by the IDA to the domestic industry situation was, with the benefit of hindsight, unimaginative and concentrated too heavily on the capital equipment needs of industry.

2.7 Recession and recovery (1980–93)

The situation continued to deteriorate until 1981 when the debt/GNP ratio stood at 94 per cent and the balance of payments deficit was 12.5 per cent. This represented a growing crisis, which demanded immediate action. The Fine Gael–Labour coalition (1982–87) pursued a strategy of increasing taxation to reduce government borrowing and the level of debt. Unemployment increased from 7.3 per cent in 1980 to 17.7 per cent in 1985. Emigration resumed and economic growth did not materialise. Despite the fact that Ireland had received a positive inflow of funds from the EC, employment numbers had increased by only 4 per cent since 1973. Between 1980 and 1986 employment fell by 76,000.

The FDI effort was hampered by the deepening recession in the USA, which resulted in a sharp drop in US inward investment. Another possible explanation for the timing of the slow-down was that the pace of US FDI in the 1970s was a one-off adjustment to Ireland's EC membership and that this had levelled off by 1980. In addition, other countries provided favourable packages designed to induce companies to establish operations with them. The IDA increasingly found that the business of attracting foreign companies was becoming cut-throat.

In January 1981 the government extended the 10 per cent tax on profits for foreign companies until 2010. This was soon followed by the launch of the IDA's Strategic Plan (1982–92). The focus of the IDA's new strategy concentrated on attracting companies with high output, using the best available technology while spending significant amounts on Irish materials and services. In this way, it was envisaged that these companies would not only generate jobs in their own areas, but would also feed demand for related services and raw materials, which would lead to increased employment. This was a reversal of the former IDA policy of attracting the most labour-intensive industries. The industrial sectors targeted for promotion included biotechnology, healthcare, software and electronics.

Promotional strategies also changed in the 1980s. The focus of promotion moved from financial grants and incentives towards the importance of human capital. Ireland's young educated workforce became a huge selling point for the IDA, and its change of focus was reflected in a new advertising campaign entitled 'We are the young Europeans'. Despite the recession, some companies, including Fruit of the Loom (1985) and Yamanouchi (1985), decided to locate in Ireland during this period. However, there were losses in the foreign sector: in 1983, Telectron (owned by AT&T) and Black & Decker both announced they were to close, with the loss of 1,000 jobs.

Focusing on the service sector, a new International Services Programme was launched, which was designed to attract service companies. It was recognised that such companies would require a different set of financial incentives, and the Industrial Development (No. 2) Act No. 2 1981 gave the IDA the power to award employment grants unrelated to investment in capital goods. The programme saw many companies setting up premises in Ireland, including IBM (1983), Lotus (1984) and Microsoft (1985). This highly significant development helped to further the concept of Ireland as a world-class centre for software.

This period was also marked by a growing concern that indigenous Irish companies had failed to develop. It had originally been hoped that Irish industry would develop alongside a thriving foreign sector, supplying it with raw materials and related services. However, by the early 1980s it had become clear that this would not be the case. In response, a report to evaluate industrial policy was commissioned by the government: see Management Focus 2.6.

Management Focus 2.6 The Telesis Report (1982)

The Telesis Report (1982) criticised industrial policy for allowing a situation to arise in which there was an over-reliance on the foreign sector, rather than a more even balance between foreign and indigenous industry. The report was never implemented in full and it was not until the early 1990s that the challenge posed by Telesis was taken up. However, debate continued in relation to the failure of an Irish enterprise sector to develop. Joseph Lee offers an explanation: he argues that societies can be shaped or founded on two different principles – the performer versus the possessor. Where the possessor principle is dominant, Lee argues, a person is judged in life by what they possess, whereas the performance principle means that a person is judged on their performance. He further argues that due to our mainly agrarian society until the 1950s, Ireland had a predominance of the possessor principle well into the second half of the twentieth century. Consequently, Lee states, there was little real incentive to achieve or to become an entrepreneur.

Source: Lee, J. (1989) *Ireland 1912–1985: Politics and Society*. Cambridge: Cambridge University Press.

In 1987 a political consensus on fiscal policy started to emerge, largely as a result of the publication by the National Economic and Social Council (NESC) of *Strategy and Development 1986–1990*. This document argued that the national debt had to be reduced, as a matter of urgency, through public spending cuts. The NESC document was widely welcomed by trade unions, farmers' organisations, employers and the opposition. The main opposition party, led by Alan Dukes, agreed to support the minority government as it pushed through measures that were in the country's best interests. Such a bold and daring strategy reflected the growing concerns of all involved.

The development of the social partnership model in 1987 laid the foundations for recovery. The Programme for National Recovery (PNR) of 1987 was the first of four highly successful centralised agreements, and this was the first time that an agreement on wages was tied to agreement on a range of economic and social policy issues underpinned by political consensus. Under the PNR the government agreed to reduce income tax (to increase the real take-home pay of workers) in return for moderate pay increases (to increase competitiveness and employment in Irish industry). The most important feature of the agreement was the fact that it was the product of a social partnership in which all parties – government, unions, employers and farmers – had a role in aspects of economic policy, denoting a greater sense of realism by all involved.

By 1990, as the PNR came to a close, the budget deficit had fallen to 0.7 per cent of GNP, down from 8.3 per cent in 1986. This period also witnessed changes to the tax incentives for business. The government concluded that the tax incentives were too generous and that the high relief available encouraged investment in fixed assets rather than job creation. The 1988 budget introduced a broader tax base with fewer reliefs. This marked the first step on the road to the reform of corporation tax.

Throughout the late 1980s the IDA capitalised on the pace of recovery in its FDI promotion. Motorola, Teradata, Intel, Stratus, EDS and Sandoz all established facilities in Ireland during this period. The Intel investment was seen as particularly significant, reinforcing the important role Ireland had come to play in the international electronics sector. At the end of 1991 indigenous industry employed 120,000 people while foreign industry accounted for 94,000.[24] In 1991 the Maastricht Treaty was signed by EC member states, which committed them to the establishment of a common currency – European Monetary Union (EMU) – by the end of 1999 at the latest. In order to qualify for membership in the first round countries had to meet stringent convergence criteria, which included: no devaluation of currency for at least two years prior to entry; low inflation; and strict budget deficit/GDP and debt/GDP ratios.

As a result there was a change in focus by the government, away from a preoccupation with public finances to making sure that the economy could meet the convergence criteria. The social partnership model developed with the PNR was continued with the second centralised agreement, the Programme for Economic and Social Progress (PESP) (1991). The PESP, which covered the years 1991 to 1993, broadly followed the same concepts developed under the PNR. Wage moderation was guaranteed in return for tax concessions to boost competitiveness and growth. Fiscal targets in the PESP were designed to ensure qualification for EMU membership.

In 1991 the Minster for Industry and Commerce commissioned a further review of industrial policy. The Industrial Policy Review Group (chaired by Jim Culliton) firmly believed that growth in output was the key to employment growth. Growth in output could only be achieved by increased efficiency and competitiveness. This underlying premise guided the findings and recommendations of the Culliton Report, as it came to be known. The report, published in 1992, argued that a much broader approach was required in formulating and evaluating industrial policy.[25] The report recommended the establishment of a task force that would report to the Taoiseach on how the report should be implemented. The Moriarty Task Force Report subsequently reported to the government on how the Culliton Report could be implemented.[26] Throughout the decade the recommendations of the Culliton report were gradually put into place.

2.8 The Celtic Tiger (1993–2007)

Government taxation policy changed significantly with the new Labour–Fianna Fáil coalition government. The emphasis was now firmly placed on broadening the tax bands and allowances to help lower income earners. The Programme for Competitiveness and Work (PCW) was agreed in 1994 and, like its two predecessors, it involved a trade-off between pay moderation and tax concessions that were designed to increase after-tax income and employment levels. In addition, to encourage employers to recruit more lower-paid staff, employers' payroll costs were reduced, with a 9 per cent employer PRSI levy on income introduced on incomes below €11,428.

In December 1994 the standard rate of corporation tax was cut to 12.5 per cent. The economy grew by 9 per cent in 1995 and 6 per cent in 1996. In 1995, 11,254 new jobs were created by IDA-supported companies, a record level, with total employment up by 7.9 per cent between 1994 and 1995. The destination of manufacturing exports changed markedly between 1970 and 1995, with greater reliance on the European Union (EU). (From November 1993 the term EU replaced the older EC.) The increasing importance of the pharmaceutical and electronics sectors was becoming evident.

The emphasis on broadening tax bands and allowances continued and the government was in a position to finance tax cuts without resorting to borrowing or inflation. They also benefited significantly from Structural Funds received from the EU. The scale of recovery in the early 1990s was due partly to the influx of funds received under two rounds of Structural Funds amounting to €9.52 billion 1989–2000. In particular, the 'Delors 1' round (1989–93) helped to finance much infrastructural development. Another significant development on the European front during this period was the launch of the EU common currency, the euro. In January 2002 the euro replaced the individual currencies of those EU member states that had signed up for membership of the single currency.

Partnership 2000, covering the years 1997–99, followed the same guidelines as the first three programmes, and included additional measures at the enterprise level to reduce unemployment. In 1997, after the change of government, there was a move back to reducing tax rates. The 1999 budget marked a new departure, with the introduction of a tax credit system which brought greater equity to the system by providing a standard rating to personal allowances. This ensured that any increases in allowances amounted to the same value to all taxpayers irrespective of their income. For an economy experiencing rapid growth coupled with labour shortages, and therefore running the risk of wage inflation, the move to a tax credit system was appropriate.[27] Easing the tax burden helped to increase the supply of labour, as it meant that people were better off working than receiving benefits.

Another measure that increased confidence in the business community was the decision to reduce capital gains tax (CGT) from 40 per cent to 20 per cent in 1998. This stimulated a more productive use of assets and at the same time increased revenues for the government.

The Irish economy had experienced remarkable levels of growth to emerge as the Celtic Tiger. Between 1994 and 1999 the country reported growth levels in the region of 9 per cent per annum, significantly higher than any of our EU counterparts. The budget deficit of €1.77 billion in 1986 had been transformed into a surplus of €2.53 billion by 1998. During this period there was net inward immigration of 38,000 between 1996 and 1998. Exports continued to outstrip imports by €56.8 million to €39.4 million in 1998. Overall permanent full-time employment (for manufacturing, internationally traded and financial services, and other activities supported by the IDA agencies) increased by 35.2 per cent over the 10-year period from 1990 to 1999. Over the same period permanent full-time employment in foreign-owned companies grew by 54 per cent, with employment in Irish-owned companies increasing by 19.7 per cent. By the end of the decade permanent full-time employment in foreign-owned companies accounted for 50.9 per cent of total employment in manufacturing, internationally traded and financial services, and other agency-supported activities, compared to 50.2 per cent in 1998 and 44.5 per cent in 1990.[28]

During the decade permanent full-time manufacturing employment rose by 18 per cent, although this was experienced in modern manufacturing industries rather than the more traditional industries. Permanent full-time employment in internationally traded and financial services displayed consistent year-on-year growth from 10,788 in 1990 to 49,206 by 1999, a jump of 356 per cent.[29] Such trends were in line with overall industry patterns away from traditional manufacturing to a post-manufacturing knowledge-based industry. These developments posed problems in relation to an adequate labour supply and reskilling for the future.

In 2000 a new social partnership agreement – the Programme for Prosperity and Fairness (PPF) –was put in place. This programme carried on many of the key initiatives of previous partnership agreements. It focused on achieving a balance between distributing the benefits of economic growth and improving social inclusion in Ireland, and maintaining Ireland's competitiveness and economic prosperity was another key goal. IDA Ireland focused on the quality rather than quantity of jobs created, and in 1999 for the first time in its history revised downwards its target for new job creation (see Management Focus 2.7).

Management Focus 2.7 The new IDA policy of the 1990s

The IDA's policy in the 1990s reflected the changing profile of Irish industry away from manufacturing to more modern sectors, such as medical technologies and information and communications technology (ICT). The closure of traditional textile companies, such as Fruit of the Loom in Co. Donegal in the late 1990s, was a typical symptom of the decline in manufacturing. The shift in IDA strategy was indicative of the urgent need for consensus on the need to balance economic growth and development against the need for infrastructural development in roads, communications, electrical power generation and distribution, the mobile telephony and waste and management services. Labour shortages in key areas and the resultant increase in labour costs made the FDI process more demanding and challenging.

The 1990s brought enormous changes for the Irish economy, with gains in economic growth, employment and the overall state of the country's finances. Ireland's economic growth was eagerly studied and examined by other countries hoping to emulate the success of the Irish economy. From the mid-1990s until early 2000 Ireland's growth has been described as a 'catching-up' period, during which Ireland rapidly converged with the world's most successful economies after years of lagging behind. There was a slowdown in economic growth in the immediate aftermath of 9/11 in the USA – in fact there had been signs of a slowdown before 9/11, but this accelerated the move towards a slump. In early 2001, the Irish economy was affected by an outbreak of foot and mouth disease in the UK, and a confirmed case in Ireland, which, together with 9/11, had a knock-on effect on travel, tourism and markets.

The dizzy growth rates of the 1990s were replaced by more steady rates in the 2000s. From 2002 to 2007 Ireland still continued to experience comparatively high growth rates, but the basis of this growth changed dramatically. It was now predicated on an expansion of cheap credit and increased personal debt. This was fuelled by increasing property prices and people's willingness to engage in property speculation. Construction as a share of the economy started to grow disproportionately. This was to have a significant impact on the economy after 2008.

2.9 Financial crisis and the end of the Celtic Tiger (2008–)

Early warning signs of the impending financial crisis can be found in the USA from 2007, when a number of financial institutions ran into trouble in the sub-prime mortgage market. These sub-prime lenders gave mortgage loans to customers who traditionally experienced difficulty in getting loans, and who were perceived to be a high risk due to, for example, irregular income or unverifiable sources of income. Staff working for sub-prime lenders were monetarily incentivised to sell their products. While interest rates remained low (just 1 per cent in 2004[30]) these customers were able to make repayments on their loans. However, after 2005, when interest rates started to rise steadily, so too did the mortgage repayments, which overstretched many borrowers. House prices also started to fall, leaving many sub-prime mortgage holders in the USA in negative equity. Many customers began to default on their mortgage payments. This had a knock-on effect on the lending institutions in the USA, but also had far-reaching effects on global financial markets due to complex arrangements that the banks had entered into with one another. It was these connections that ensured that a localised problem (sub-prime defaults in the USA) led to a global economic meltdown.

The connections between the world's largest banks took the form of securitisation; the banks grouped together bundles of mortgage loans and then sold them on to other investors. The banks were paid cash for these bundles of loans and the mortgage repayments would then be channelled to the new investor. In many instances these bundles were resold and a very complex web of transactions was created, which in effect spread the risk across the world. This worked while the mortgage repayments were made, but by 2007 there was a growing default problem in the US market. In July 2007 Bear Stearns, a US bank that was heavily exposed to sub-prime losses, went out of business. Financial institutions started to become wary of lending to each other and investors became very concerned.

In autumn 2007, the UK bank Northern Rock ran into difficulty when the international money markets stopped lending it money as a result of the unfolding financial crisis in the US sub-prime market. The bank was forced to approach the Bank of England for a loan facility, news of which caused panic among investors, leading to a run on the bank.[31] The UK government stepped in to guarantee savings, and Northern Rock was taken into state ownership in 2008 and eventually sold to Virgin Money in 2012.[32] What had started as a problem in a mortgage segment of the USA had now become a European problem. As banks were refusing to lend to each other, central banks had to step in and inject much-needed funds. By early 2008 the crisis had started to spread to other banking sectors such as commercial property and loans to business. By the summer of that year the US government had stepped in to support two major mortgage lenders, Fannie Mae and Freddie Mac. By autumn the resulting credit crisis had spiralled, with stock markets falling and unemployment levels starting to rise. Tens of millions of people, mainly in North America and Europe, lost their jobs. The banking sector was rocked by the collapse in September 2008 of Lehman Brothers, a major US bank, which was followed by the Bank of America takeover of Merrill Lynch[33] and, in the UK, Lloyds/TSB's rescue of HBOS.[34] By the end of 2008 the world had entered into the greatest financial crisis since the 1930s.

As we have seen, in Ireland the period 2002–7 was characterised by a credit-fuelled property bubble. Increased bank lending, borrowing and investment all led to increased GDP growth in Ireland over this period, as shown in Figure 2.1.

FIGURE 2.1 ANNUAL GROWTH IN REAL GDP AND REAL GNP 2000–11

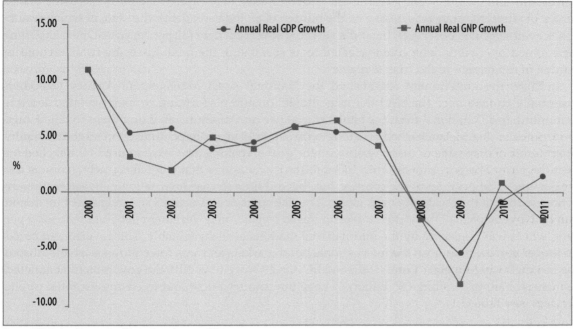

Source: CSO, National Income and Expenditure Accounts 2011.

As more people acquired property there was an increase in bank lending to support it, in the Irish case mostly from French and German banks to Irish banks. Traditionally the banks had relied on their deposit base to lend to customers, but they now turned to the wholesale money markets based abroad to fund loans. The lending practices of the banks became increasingly risky, with people acquiring 100 per cent mortgages and speculating on buy to let properties in Ireland and overseas. These loans could be serviced while people had jobs and could rent additional properties but became untenable with the onset of recession. Banks engaged in what is referred to as 'light touch' oversight and control, where risks were not identified or acted on.[35] Tax revenues were increasingly linked to the property sector, with large increases in stamp duty and capital gains tax. There was a slippage in competitiveness throughout the noughties with the cost base (wages and prices) increasing, driven by increased consumer spending and a spiralling property bubble – all caused by cheap credit.[36]

As a result of their excessive overseas borrowings to fund the property bubble, when the international financial crisis developed in late 2007 Irish banks were exposed. Interbank funding dried up in late 2008. This made funding of day-to-day banking extremely difficult for the most vulnerable Irish banks. As property prices began to fall the banks started to make losses on their loans. By 2008 Ireland had entered a severe recession. At the same time short-term interbank lending, normally used to cover temporary shortfalls, became difficult to access. By September 2008, despite reassurances from the Financial Regulator that the Irish banks were well capitalised, confidence began to ebb and an outflow of deposits began.[37] The government responded on 29 September by issuing a blanket guarantee on all of the deposits and debts of the six largest banks in the country: Bank of Ireland; Allied Irish Bank; Anglo Irish Bank; Irish Nationwide; Irish Life and Permanent; and the EBS.[38] The government also committed to re-capitalising the banks using public funds. In effect, the state was to take on the burden of all the bank debts, the scale of which was to shock even seasoned observers. Ireland's very low sovereign debt (32 per cent of GDP in 2007) was now joined by a bank debt, often referred to as socialising the bank losses by transferring the burden of repayment to the Irish taxpayer.

In 2009, the government established the National Asset Management Agency (NAMA), essentially to take over (or buy) the large 'toxic' or non-performing property-related loans – amounting to €77 billion – from the banks at a 30 per cent discount, enabling them to deleverage more quickly.[39] NAMA embarked on a long-term (up to 10 years, depending on market conditions) programme of disposing of these assets with the goal of making a positive return to the exchequer over the term. The government introduced austerity measures that were designed to combat the weakening fiscal position of the country, but this did little to ease international investors already concerned about the escalating bank losses. The risk spreads on Ireland's sovereign debt increased and by November 2010 the yields/interest rates to be paid on government debt had reached 9 per cent, which was perceived by the international markets as unsustainable. The government could no longer borrow money on the international bond markets and was forced to seek a bailout from the International Monetary Fund (IMF) and EU. On 29 November 2010 the government negotiated a financial bailout totalling €85 billion to keep the country afloat and to ensure essential public services (see Table 2.1).[40]

TABLE 2.1 EU–IMF FINANCIAL ASSISTANCE PROGRAMME

	Amount (€ billion)	Indicative Interest Rate
IMF	22.5	4.8
EU of which:	45.0	
European Financial Stability Mechanism (EFSM)	22.5	2.9
European Financial Stability Facility (EFSF)	17.5	3.1
Bilateral loans (UK, Denmark, Sweden)	4.8	
Total external support	67.5	
Irish National Pension Reserve Fund	17.5	
Total package	**85.0**	

Source: http://ec.europa.eu/ireland/economy/irelands_economic-crisis/index-en.htm.

Apart from the financial bailout, the EU/IMF financial assistance programme includes three additional elements:

1 **Banking sector reform.** Bank mergers and reconstituted bank boards.

2   **Fiscal consolidation**. Target of a budget deficit below 3 per cent by 2015.
3   **Structural reforms.** Reforming the framework of sectoral labour market agreements.[41]

Ireland was not the only country to find itself in financial difficulties. Greece, Spain, Italy and Portugal all experienced negative consequences associated with recession. However, the level of bank debt in Ireland is a differentiating factor. By 18 April 2012, according to the then Minister for Finance, Michael Noonan, the government had injected €62.8 billion into the banking system since the beginning of the crisis in 2008, the costliest banking crisis of any advanced economy since the Great Depression. It is estimated that €34.7 billion had been put into the institutions (Anglo Irish Bank and Irish Nationwide) that comprise the Irish Bank Resolution Corporation (IBRC), while €28.1 billion had been spent recapitalising and acquiring full ownership of AIB/EBS and Irish Life and Permanent, and acquiring preference shares and a minority ordinary shareholding in Bank of Ireland.[42] NAMA has acquired loans with a face value of €74 billion since its establishment in 2009. Figure 2.2 illustrates that between 2000 and 2007 the levels of Irish public debt were low; national debt fell from 34 per cent of GDP in 2000 to 20 per cent of GDP in 2007, and general government debt fell from 38 per cent of GDP in 2000 to 25 per cent of GDP in 2007.[43] The recession, combined with significant amounts of public money injected into the Irish banking system between 2009/2011, saw the level of public debt soar. National debt increased from 20 per cent of GDP in 2007 to 75 per cent of GDP in 2011, and the general government debt increased from 25 per cent of GDP in 2007 to 107 per cent of GDP in 2011.

FIGURE 2.2 GOVERNMENT DEBT 2000–11

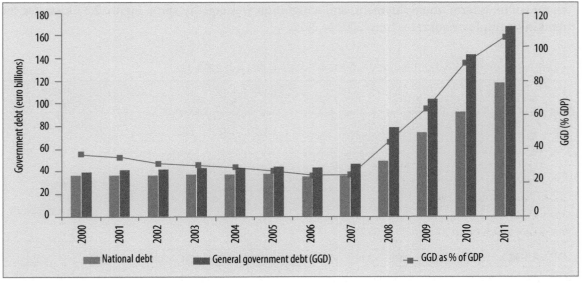

Source: NTMA, Department of Finance

It is well known that the Irish state has taken on huge debts by taking over liabilities previously owed by privately owned banks. The majority of this cost relates to Anglo Irish Bank and Irish Nationwide Building Society, which have been merged to form IBRC. The total cost of taking on these liabilities has been about €35 billion, or 22 per cent of Ireland's nominal gross domestic product in 2011. Without this cost, Ireland's debt–GDP ratio in 2011 could have been 85 per cent, roughly in line with the Eurozone average, rather than the 107 per cent that was recorded. It is possible that without the cost of absorbing the IBRC's liabilities, Ireland could have maintained access to sovereign bond markets and thus avoided an EU–IMF programme.[44]

The total government outlay in 'fixing' the broken banking system can be broken down as follows:[45]

- €30.7 billion in promissory notes, of which two instalment payments have been made. In February 2012, the government wound up IBRC into NAMA, and replaced the remainder of the promissory notes with long-dated sovereign debt. This means that €28 billion worth of costly IOUs from the nationalisation of Anglo Irish Bank were swapped for long-term sovereign bonds.[46]
- €20.7 billion from the National Pension Reserve Fund (NPRF) has been invested in acquiring ownership stakes in AIB and Bank of Ireland.
- €11.4 billion of additional exchequer resources have been spent on IBRC, AIB and ILP.

The financial crisis has severely affected Ireland's economic growth, employment and emigration levels. Between 2000 and 2007, the annual average growth in real GDP and real GNP was 5.8 per cent and 5.2 per cent respectively. However, with the onset of the global financial crisis, and the resulting collapse of the construction and banking sectors, the Irish economy entered a very deep recession in 2008. Between 2008 and 2011 real GDP declined by 4.8 per cent, while real GNP declined by 9.5 per cent (see Figure 2.1). By 2012 Ireland was officially out of recession and in a 'bumpy recovery', according to the IMF.[47] The effect of the crisis on employment levels, in particular the rate of long-term unemployment, and emigration was equally stark. Figure 2.3 illustrates the trend in unemployment rates from 2002 to 2012.

FIGURE 2.3 SEASONALLY ADJUSTED UNEMPLOYMENT RATES IN IRELAND 2002–12

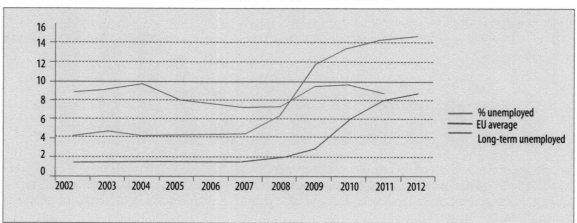

Source: CSO Irish Labour Market Statistics 2012
(www.cso.ie/en/statistics/labourmarket/principalstatistics/seasonallyadjusted/).

Losses, however, were not evenly borne by every sector, as illustrated in Figure 2.4, which shows the huge losses experienced by the construction sector over the period.

FIGURE 2.4 EMPLOYMENT TRENDS BY SECTOR 2005–12 (000s)

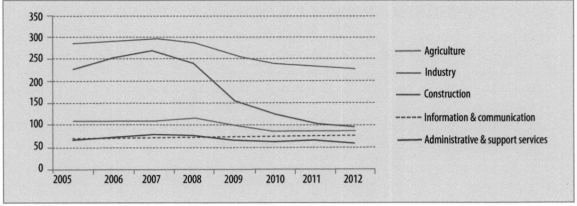

Emigration from Ireland in the 12 months to April 2012 is estimated to have increased to 87,100 from 80,600 in the year to April 2011, while the number of immigrants is estimated to have fallen marginally to 52,700 from 53,300 over the same period. Of the 87,100 people who emigrated in the year to April 2012, Irish nationals were the largest group, accounting for 46,500 or 53 per cent.[48]

The political fallout from the Irish banking crises of 2008 saw a change of government at the general election of 28 February 2011. With Ireland's sovereignty effectively forfeited by the acceptance of the EU/European Central Bank (ECB)/IMF ('Troika') bailout, the new Fine Gael/ Labour government immediately set about implementing their programme for recovery and reform of the Irish economy entitled 'NewERA'. This had been originally devised by Fine Gael in 2009, well in advance of the November 2011 bailout, the terms of which had not been anticipated at the time. These terms were not only onerous but also critically focused on fiscal rectitude, to the detriment of the recovery of the Irish economy, and homed in on the requirement to realise a 3 per cent budget deficit by 2015. NewERA's funding plans were thus severely compromised.

2.10 Future prospects

The recession and financial crisis have had a severe impact on business in Ireland. (See Appendix 1 at the end of this chapter for a summary of the key business sectors operating in Ireland.) In the immediate aftermath many companies went out of business, such as Waterford Crystal, Vita Cortex and Game, further increasing unemployment levels; and Dell in Limerick moved its manufacturing operations to Poland in January 2009.[49] For those remaining in business, lines of credit from the banks tightened, making operations difficult to fund. While there have been some good stories from this period, there remain many significant challenges for Irish businesses in the years ahead. Global competitiveness and economic growth are critical to Ireland's recovery. The *Global Competitiveness Report (2012–2013)*, compiled by the World Economic Forum (WEF) ranked Ireland

27th (up from 29th the previous year) in its worldwide ranking of competitive economies. The top 30 ranked countries are shown in Table 2.2.

TABLE 2.2 THE GLOBAL COMPETITIVENESS REPORT 2012–13: TOP 30 COUNTRIES

Rank	Country	Score (1–7)
1	Switzerland	5.72
2	Singapore	5.67
3	Finland	5.33
4	Sweden	5.53
5	Netherlands	5.5
6	Germany	5.48
7	United States	5.47
8	United Kingdom	5.45
9	Hong Kong SAR	5.41
10	Japan	5.40
11	Qatar	5.38
12	Denmark	5.29
13	Taiwan, China	5.28
14	Canada	5.27
15	Norway	5.27
16	Austria	5.22
17	Belgium	5.21
18	Saudi Arabia	5.19
19	Korea, Rep.	5.12
20	Australia	5.12
21	France	5.11
22	Luxembourg	5.09
23	New Zealand	5.09
24	United Arab Emirates	5.07
25	Malaysia	5.06
26	Israel	5.02
27	Ireland	4.91
28	Brunei Darussalam	4.87
29	China	4.83
30	Iceland	4.74

Source: World Economic Forum *Global Competitiveness Report 2012–2013.* Geneva: World Economic Forum. Available at http://reports.weforum.org/global-competitiveness-report-2012-2013/. Accessed 23 October 2012.

Switzerland tops the ranking for the fourth year in a row, while Europe remains in a strong position with five other entries in the top 10. At 29, China is the highest ranking of the BRICs (Brazil, Russia, India, China and South Africa), with Brazil at 48, South Africa at 52, India at 59 and Russia lowest at 67.

Among the positives in relation to Ireland are the following rankings:

- judicial independence – 4th
- health and primary education – 12th
- strength of investor protection – 5th
- business sophistication – 18th
- technological readiness – 4th
- exports as a percentage of GDP – 5th.

However, Ireland received a score of 131 for its overall macroeconomic environment:

- government budget balance – 141st
- gross national savings – 124th
- general government debt – 137th
- country credit rating – 66th.

These scores reflect concerns about Ireland's growing debt, high debt to GDP ratio and its economy's ability to recover from the recession. Also of concern is Ireland's financial market ranking of 108th, reflecting uncertainty regarding the financial markets, and the difficulty businesses experience in accessing finance. There is little doubt that Ireland has slipped on the scale of global competitiveness, but it remains an attractive location for FDI, particularly from the USA. The low corporate tax rate, access to EU markets and an English-speaking workforce continue to make Ireland appealing for overseas investment (see Management Focus 2.8).

Many US companies are taking advantage of lower costs (unit labour costs have been declining since 2009) and new investment opportunities. While Dell closed its manufacturing facilities in Limerick in 2009, it has continued to grow its presence in Ireland and currently employs 2,300 people between Dublin and Limerick, with its focus currently on moving to higher-end value-adding activities. Dell provides sales, marketing and high-end support for enterprise-level customers from its Dublin plant, while Limerick is one of its 12 software solutions centres worldwide. A large part of Ireland's attractiveness for a company like Dell is its corporate tax rate.[50]

Management Focus 2.8 Why are US companies moving to Ireland?

PayPal, Google, Yelp, LinkedIn and Facebook have all looked to expand their presence in Ireland. Over 40 per cent of the offices leased or bought in 2011 were done so by US companies, who have noticed that the financial crisis has reduced commercial property rents and labour costs. Ireland was the fifth most expensive location in the world for office accommodation in 2007, but by 2012 it was down to 45th. The IDA is already looking for the next opening in Ireland. In 2010 it set up a new unit targeting companies with less than $30 million a year in revenue. By 2012 35 of them had set up facilities in Ireland.

Source: Irish Times (2012) 'Why US Firms are Moving to Ireland' [online]. Available at www.irishtimes.com /newspaper/breaking/2012/0221/breaking30.html.

Intel, regarded by many as the jewel in the crown of Irish FDI, has also continued to invest and in January 2011 announced a $500 investment in developing a new product at its plant in Leixlip, Co. Kildare. (The plan has since been delayed, however.[51]) While the company does set up bases in emerging markets with lower cost structures than Ireland, it doesn't make investment decisions on cost alone. One of the big advantages that Ireland has is its benign business environment, with a low corporate tax rate and a proactive industrial development policy. The availability of a highly skilled and technical workforce, coupled with a good education system, also makes Ireland attractive to Intel. According to Eamon Sinnott, General Manager of Intel Ireland, 'In Ireland we have built up skills and experience in advanced manufacturing that is a national asset'.[52]

Ireland continues to face competition from the UK for FDI. While the UK corporation tax rate stands at 21 per cent, from April 2013 companies based in the UK will be charged 10 per cent on income from royalties and patents,[53] compared to 12.5 per cent in Ireland. However, the future of FDI in Ireland centres on its comparatively low corporation tax and benign business environment. The more jobs that can be generated, the greater the tax bounce to the exchequer. As long as there are no major changes to this scenario Ireland should continue to attract FDI.

Central to the future prospects for business in Ireland is the government's NewERA programme, an ambitious economic stimulus investment of €18 billion to restructure the key infrastructural areas in Ireland, as shown in Figure 2.5. The areas covered include:

- communications: Broadband 21
- energy: Smart Grid, which will integrate all the energy utilities, including renewables; GasLink, linking Bord Gáis's gas grid with Northern Ireland
- Bio-energy & Forestry Ireland
- water: Irish Water, which will restructure and manage the provision of water services in Ireland.

All of this is to be part funded by the NPRF, a new state-owned 'strategic investment bank' (National Recovery Wholesale Bank) and the sale of 'non- strategic state assets' (Bord Gais's retail business, some electricity generation assets and the National Lottery licence).[54]

FIGURE 2.5 A RESTRUCTURED SEMI-STATE SECTOR

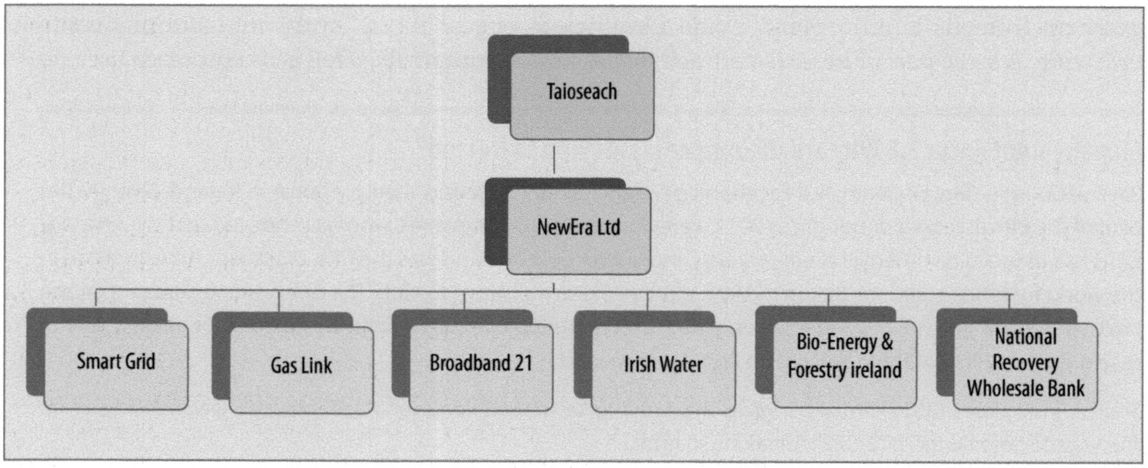

Source: Fine Gael (2009) *NewERA*.

The plan pins hope for the recovery of the Irish economy on a radical restructuring of the successful commercial semi-state sector originally established from the 1920s onwards. It promises the creation of 105,000 new jobs and far-reaching improvements in the national energy, communications and water infrastructure, sometimes criticised by prospective FDI companies as an impediment to setting up in Ireland. Although NewERA has been well received in principle, in practice the government is facing some serious difficulties in accessing the necessary funds to implement it.[55] There was a strong international interest in utilities; however, it was feared that Ireland's serious debt profile and pressure from the Troika might lead to a fire sale and that these non-strategic assets would not attract their real market value.[56] Therefore it was considered prudent to wait for an upturn in the global economy and a general improvement in the market for these assets. The other sources of funding earmarked for this project – public–private partnership (PPP) investment and National Recovery Bond issues – were also adversely affected by the global downturn. In November 2011 the government presented its Infrastructure and Capital Investment Framework (2012–16),[57] a €17 billion exchequer-funded plan for investment across four main areas, incorporating some of the NewERA plan:

- Economic infrastructure: transport networks, energy provision and telecommunications capacity.
- Investment in the productive sector and human capital: e.g. direct supports for enterprise development; science, technology and innovation advancement; supports for tourism, agriculture, fisheries and forestry; and capital investment in education infrastructure.
- Environmental infrastructure: including waste and water systems and investment for environmental sustainability.
- Critical social investment: including the health service and social housing programmes.

In July 2012 the government announced the details of an additional €2.25 billion stimulus package to boost economic growth and create 13,000 jobs. The Troika (ECB, EU and IMF) approved the package as long as spending limits were not breached.[58] Projects were identified in health, education, transport and the justice sectors, with the aim of increasing employment, particularly in construction. The funding for the programme (€1.4 billion in Phase 1) will come from loans from the European Investment Bank, the National Pensions Reserve Fund, domestic bank loans and other potential private investment sources. An additional €850 million is expected in the longer term from the sale of state assets and new licensing arrangements for the national Lottery.[59]

In 2012 the EU agreed to the expansion of the European Stability Mechanism (ESM), with the conditions that an EU banking supervisor would be appointed and that it would be applied to future problems only. This effectively means the appointment of a European Finance Minister, backed by Germany, with huge financial muscle and far-reaching powers over sovereign fiscal policies that would take over failed European banks and wind them up. This would socialise such bank debt across the eurozone, avoiding the danger of future sovereign defaults. While this was a positive development it did not cover Ireland's legacy bank debt. Despite the deal on bank debt agreed in February 2012 Ireland remains heavily burdened, with €64 billion in bank debt, as distinct from sovereign debt, which will have to be covered, albeit over a longer time period. This clearly underscores the downside of ceding fiscal sovereignty. Even if Ireland meets the terms to exit the Troika bailout by 2015 and returns to the bond markets, there will be no relief from the terms of the remaining legacy bank debt. Although recent indications from the bond markets are encouraging with respect to a 2015 re-entry for Ireland, the burden of the terms of the combined sovereign and bank debts may just prove too much and a breaking point may well be reached before then. Coming to the end of 2012, with Ireland facing its sixth austerity budget in a row the prospect for recovery is mixed. To meet the terms of the financial bailout, the government took €3.5 billion out of the economy in spending cuts and additional taxes in the 2013 budget followed by a further €1 billion in 2014 and €500 million in 2015.

The future prospects for further expansion of Irish FDI hinges on Ireland's ability to maintain a low rate of corporation tax and a benign business environment. As long as this is the case we will remain an attractive overseas location. However, competition for FDI is becoming more intense and it will require substantial efforts to secure investment. Ireland needs to be economically competitive with dynamic emerging economies. On the indigenous front, the recently announced infrastructure and capital investment stimulus package, coupled with the NewERA programme, should promote growth and jobs. Continued support and reward for the innovator will prove to be the critical success factor in years to come. It is hoped that the culture of corruption and greed that crept in during the Celtic Tiger years will be replaced by a new set of values offering the prospect of a fairer and more sustainable future to the next generation.

2.11 Summary of key propositions

- With the establishment of the Free State in 1922 a conservative approach was taken to the development of industry, with little state involvement. The development of agriculture was prioritised during the period.
- From 1932 to 1958 a policy of self-sufficiency and protectionism was pursued, which was motivated by both economic and political factors. Protectionism meant that Irish companies were protected from external competition by the imposition of high tariffs on imported goods. Such tariffs ensured that foreign imports were more expensive than Irish goods.
- In 1958 Whitaker produced a document called *Economic Development*, which altered the course of industrial development. The document advocated a move to free trade and a policy of FDI, and was later translated into the First Programme for Economic Expansion.
- In 1969 the IDA was restructured under the Industrial Development Act. As a result of the changes the IDA assumed sole responsibility for the development of industry, both indigenous and foreign.
- In 1973 Ireland joined the EEC. Membership of the EEC became a highly significant selling point for the IDA, when promoting Ireland as an investment location, particularly in the USA. Ireland could now be sold as a European base for foreign MNCs that could serve the European market. It also opened up a market for Irish indigenous companies of 250 million people.
- The recession of the early 1980s forced the IDA to rethink its strategy. The main thrust of the new approach was to concentrate on attracting companies with high output using the best technology while spending significant amounts on Irish materials and related services. The IDA introduced a new International Services Programme and changed its promotional efforts from offering financial grants to emphasising the importance of human capital in Ireland.
- The Telesis Report, published in 1982, heavily criticised industrial policy for its over-reliance on the foreign sector at the expense of Irish indigenous companies. The report argued that there should be a better balance between the two sectors.

- The period from 1987 onwards was characterised by economic and industrial recovery through social partnership and fiscal rectitude. Under the PNR (1987), wage moderation was agreed in return for significant cuts in taxation. The PNR was followed by the PESP (1991), the PCW (1994), Partnership 2000 (1997) and the Programme for Prosperity and Fairness (PPF) (2000). All of these centralised deals marked a greater degree of involvement and realism among the social partners.
- Economic policies of the early 1990s were heavily influenced by events in Europe. The Maastricht Treaty (1991) signalled the intent to establish a common currency by 1999. In order to gain membership, states had to meet strict criteria.
- Between 1987 and 2000 the economy underwent a recovery. Budget deficits were converted into surpluses, emigration became immigration, employment increased and inflation was kept at a manageable level.
- In 2008 Ireland experienced a financial crisis and entered recession. Sovereign debt, coupled with growing bank debt, resulted in a very severe financial crisis, which led to the EU/IMF bailout in November 2009.
- The key business sectors in Ireland are: life sciences (pharmaceutical and medical technologies); financial services; cloud computing; industrial products and services; ICT; entertainment and media; clean technologies; consumer products and service providers; and business services.

Discussion Questions

1   Explain the pattern of early industrial development in Ireland before 1958.
2   Explain the significance of Whitaker's *Economic Development* document for the subsequent move to free trade and FDI.
3   How did membership of the EEC in 1973 affect industrial policy performance?
4   Why were the changes that were introduced to the educational system in the late 1960s and early 1970s so important in later years?
5   What were the main strategies pursued by the IDA during the period 1980–86? Critically evaluate their success.
6   Why was the move to a social partnership model so important for economic and industrial recovery?
7   How did EU membership affect economic and industrial policy during the 1980s and 1990s?
8   Account for Ireland's economic recovery from 1994 onwards.
9   What lessons can be learned from the financial crisis that began in 2007/8? What future direction should Irish industrial policy take?

Concluding Case: The International Financial Services Centre (IFSC) – looking for direction?

The IFSC, which is located in Dublin, refers to Ireland's internationally traded financial services industry. It has made a critically important contribution to the Irish economy over the years since its inception. It consists of 450 internationally and Irish-owned cross-border financial services businesses involved in banking, asset financing, fund management, corporate treasury management, investment management, custody and administration and specialised insurance operations. It employs an estimated 32,700 people and pays about €1 billion in corporate taxes each year, with a further €1 billion going to the exchequer in payroll taxes. In addition, indirect IFSC employment stands at over 6,000 in professional services and market infrastructure (service provider) companies. It has become one of the leading hedge fund service centres in Europe, with many of the world's most important financial institutions having a presence in the IFSC. A sophisticated support network, of software development, shared services centres, and legal and accountancy companies, has also developed around the IFSC.

Key facts and figures

- More than 50 per cent of the world's leading financial services firms have subsidiaries in the IFSC. These include Sumitomo Bank, ABN AMRO, Citibank, AIG, JPMorgan Chase, BNP Paribas and EMRO.
- Half of the world's fleet of leased aircraft are managed from the IFSC.
- The investment fund industry represented 11 per cent of total shares/units in issue by euro area funds (31 March 2011).
- The IFSC is the largest provider of cross-border insurance in the EU with €16.4 billion in premiums in 2009.
- €1.9 trillion in funds was administered in its investment funds sector (December 2010).

In 1987 the government established the International Financial Services Sector in the Customs House Docks area of Dublin. Prior to this the idea of establishing a world-class international financial services centre in Dublin seemed an impossible dream. In terms of financial markets and mere presence in the financial services sector, Dublin was completely overshadowed by London. As London was the third largest financial centre in the world, the thought of building up a presence in the market must have appeared daunting. However, in the late 1980s four factors emerged that presented Ireland with the opportunity to become a player in the industry. Financial markets became global and increasingly interdependent. Invested funds could be easily traded around the world; multinational corporations were trading on stock exchanges around the world, and international financial instruments developed. In addition, operations were now conducted round the clock. Technological advances had led to the emergence of an electronic marketplace for financial services, which offered enormous opportunities for companies. The global deregulation of financial services meant that companies could now offer products outside their traditional markets, thereby increasing the range of financial services available on an international basis. There was also a rapid growth in the financial services sector worldwide at the end of the 1980s.

The original concept of developing a specialised centre for international financial services can be traced back to Dermot Desmond (NCB Stockbrokers), who argued that the international financial services sector presented a great opportunity for Ireland. A feasibility study of the concept that was undertaken in 1986 concluded that the project had enormous potential. Chief among the critical success factors possessed by Ireland was lower operating costs when compared to London, a plentiful supply of educated young people, a modern digital-based telecommunications network, the English language and presence in the same time zone as London. All of these factors conspired to produce an opportunity ripe for the taking.

A licensing mechanism was quickly established which was designed to ensure that only the most desirable projects were chosen, ones from which jobs and economic activity would result. Unlike previous developments no cash grants were given for investment in the IFSC. A 10 per cent corporation tax rate was given to all licensed companies establishing facilities and this was included in the 1987 Finance Act. Irish companies were encouraged to set up in the centre provided that they generated business and jobs. The Central Bank agreed to supervise activities in the centre and strove for integrity.

By the end of 1987 the IDA had granted approval for 18 projects to set up facilities in the IFSC. Despite such early success the government decided to change the promotional approach by establishing a Government Representative Group to market the IFSC to the highest levels internationally. The government group consisted of three high-profile men, Tomas O'Cofaigh (former Governor of the Central Bank), Seamus Páircéir (former Chairman of the Revenue Commissioners) and John Hogan (former Second Secretary at the Department of Finance), who became known as the 'wise men'. This group was to be highly successful in its promotion of the IFSC, particularly given their financial backgrounds. They were responsible for attracting the Dutch Rabobank and ABN AMRO, and the German Dresdner Bank to locate in the IFSC. By April 1989 60 projects had been approved and the group retired.

From 1 January 2008 all companies operating in the IFSC have been subject to a corporation tax rate of 12.5 per cent. The special IFSC rate ended in accordance with agreements between Ireland and the EU on state aid rules. The 12.5 per cent is still below the corporation tax rate of many of Ireland's European competitors, but several new EU member countries from eastern and central Europe have also slashed their corporation tax rates to emulate Ireland's achievements in attracting FDI.

In the aftermath of the financial crisis there have been calls for stricter EU regulation of the entire financial services sector. Much of the success of the IFSC has been built on having a proactive financial regulator, often referred to as a 'light touch' regulator. This is a model which has come under severe criticism in recent years. But a tightening of regulation could undermine Ireland's efforts to attract international firms to the IFSC. There are no plans currently under discussion in the EU to bring about this state of affairs about; however, there could be a domestic regulatory backlash that could potentially affect the IFSC.

Competition has also increased in recent years from other international locations, particularly in the Middle East and Asia. Countries within these regions are looking to challenge the IFSC's position as a centre of funds administration excellence. While the tax regime remains very attractive, the cost base in Ireland has increased steadily. Despite this the IFSC remains an appealing location due to the body of expertise that has been built up. The government has stated its strong desire to move up the value chain into higher value-added activities such as front office activities. However, this has proved difficult, particularly in the hedge fund business, as Dublin's size works against it. There is no currency or derivatives market and with only 40 companies listed on the Irish Stock Exchange, it's hard to compete with locations such as London.

Kieran Donoghue, Executive Vice President of International Financial Services, IDA Ireland, believes that the sector offers plenty of opportunity for future development including incremental business related to the existing core activities:

> We also need to look at new areas of opportunity in existing areas of capability that have potential for further development. These would include the application of existing skills sets to new areas like green finance emissions trading, development of intellectual property, but also financial technology, customer and technical support, data and analytics, services innovation and R&D.

There is considerable experience and skills within the international financial services sector in Ireland which can be leveraged to ensure a strong presence in the post-financial crisis industry. However, a shared vision and appropriate regulatory regime will be critically important for future development.

Keep up to date
www.ifsc.ie

Sources: Finance Dublin [website] 'The IFSC Story' www.financedublin.com/the_ifsc_story.php; IFSC [website] 'About the IFSC' www.ifsc.ie/page.aspx?idpge=6; Walsh, J. (2009) 'IFSC – Looking for Direction', *Business and Finance* [online] www.businessandfinance.ie/index.jsp?p=553&n=559&a=2510; White, P. (2000) 'The Evolution of the IDA', in R. MacSharry and P. White, *The Making of the Celtic Tiger: The Inside Story of Ireland's Boom Economy*. Dublin: Mercier.

Case Questions
1   Account for the success of the IFSC.
2   How does the strategy for developing the IFSC fit into the overall industrial development policy in Ireland?
3   What does the future hold for the IFSC?

Notes and References

1   The authors would like to thank the following people for their help on earlier drafts of this chapter: Mr Kevin Kelly, Dr Stephen Kinsella (University of Limerick) and Dr Donal Palcic (University of Limerick). The opinions expressed, and any errors, are the authors'.

2   O'Malley, E. (1980) *Industrial Policy and Development: A Survey of the Literature from the Early 1960s*. Dublin: National Economic and Social Council.

3   Fitzpatrick, M. (2000) 'A Century of Irish Business', *Sunday Independent* 2 January, 18L–19L.

4   Ibid.

5   Ibid.

6   O'Malley, *op. cit.*

7   Fitzpatrick, *op. cit.*

8   Fitzpatrick, *op. cit.*

9   Lee, J. (1989) *Ireland 1912–1985: Politics and Society.* Cambridge: Cambridge University Press.

10 Kennedy, K. (1998) *From Famine to Feast: Economic and Social Change in Ireland 1847–1997.* Dublin: Institute of Public Administration.

11 MacSharry, R. and White, P. (2000) *The Making of the Celtic Tiger: The Inside Story of Ireland's Boom Economy.* Dublin: Mercier.

12 IDA (1970–1997) *Annual Reports.* Dublin: IDA.

13 Fitzgerald, G. (1968) *Planning in Ireland.* Dublin: Institute of Public Administration.

14 Fitzpatrick, *op. cit.*

15 Fitzpatrick, *op. cit.*

16 Lee, *op. cit.*

17 An Foras Forbartha (1973) *Regional Development and Industrial Location in Ireland.* Dublin: An Foras Forbartha.

18 Lee, *op. cit.*

19 Lee, *op. cit.*

20 Cooper, C. and Whelan, N. (1973) *Science, Technology and Industry in Ireland. Report to the National Science Council.* Dublin: Stationery Office.

21 Haughton, J. (1987) 'The Historical Background' in J. O'Hagan (ed.) *The Economy of Ireland: Policy and Performance* (5th edn). Dublin: Irish Management Institute.

22 IDA *Annual Report 1979.* Dublin: IDA.

23 Lee, *op. cit.*

24 IDA *Annual Report 1992.* Dublin: IDA.

25 Culliton, J. (1992) *A Time for Change: Industrial Policy for the 1990s.* Report of the Industrial Policy Review Group (Culliton Report). Dublin: Stationery Office.

26 Moriarty, P. (1993) *Employment through Enterprise: The Response of the Government to the Moriarty Task Force on the Implementation of the Culliton Report.* Dublin: Stationery Office.

27 MacSharry and White, *op. cit.*

28 IDA *Annual Report 2004.* Dublin: IDA.

29 Forfás *Annual Report and Accounts 1999.* Dublin: Forfás.

30 Federal Reserve Statistical Release (2004) Selected Interest Rates [online]. Available at www.federalreserve.gov/releases/h15/20040628/. Accessed 12 December 2012.

31 BBC News (2007) 'Rush on Northern Rock Continues' [online]. Available at http://news.bbc.co.uk/2/hi/6996136.stm. Accessed 12 December 2012.

32 BBC News (2011) 'Northern Rock Sold to Virgin Money' [online]. Available at www.bbc.co.uk/news/business-15769886. Accessed 12 December 2012.

33 CNBC (2008) 'Bank of America to Buy Merrill Lynch for $50 Billion' [online]. Available at www.cnbc.com/id/26708319/. Accessed 12 December 2012.

34 Reuters (2008) 'Lloyds Rescues HBOS in $22 Billion Deal' [online]. Available at www.reuters.com/article/2008/09/18/us-lloyds-hbos-idUSLI31193420080918. Accessed 12 December 2012.

35 *Irish Examiner* (2011) 'Catalogue of Failures in Irish Banking' [online]. Available at www.irishexaminer.com/ireland/kfojkfsnidmh/rss2/. Accessed 12 December 2012.

36 EC, 'Ireland's Economic Crisis: How did it Happen and What is Being Done About It?' [online]. Available at http://ec.europa.eu/ireland/economy/irelands_economic_crisis/index-en.htm. Accessed 23 November 2012.

37 *The Economist* (2011) 'A Very Short History of the Crisis' [online]. Available at www.economist.com/node/21536871. Accessed 19 November 2012.

38 RTÉ (2008) 'Bank Guarantee Bolsters Irish Market' [online]. Available at www.rte.ie/news/2008/0930/economy.html. Accessed 12 December 2012.

39 RTÉ (2009) 'NAMA to Pay €54 billion for Bank Loans' [online]. Available at www.rte.ie/news/2009/0916/banks.html. Accessed 12 December 2012.

40 *Irish Times* (2010) 'Ireland to Receive €85 billion Bailout at 5.8%' [online]. Available at www.irishtimes.com/newspaper/breaking/2010/1128/breaking1.html. Accessed 12 December 2012.

41 For further discussion see Kinsella, S. (2011) 'Is Ireland Really the Role Model for Austerity?', *Cambridge Journal of Economics* 36(1), 223–35. Available at http://ssrn.com/abstract=1929545.

42 Whelan, K. (2012a) 'What is Ireland's Bank Debt and What can be Done About it?' [online]. Available at http://karlwhelan.com/blog/?p=471. Accessed 13 November 2012.

43 ESRI (2012) 'The Irish Economy' [online]. Available at www.esri.ie/irish_economy/. Accessed 23 October 2012.

44 Whelan, *op. cit.*

45 Whelan (2012b) 'Briefing Paper on IBRC, ELA and Promissory Notes to Oirechtais Joint Committee on Finance, Public Expenditure and Reform' [online]. Available at www.karlwhelan.com/IrishEconomy/Oireachtas-Feb-2012.pdf. Accessed 13 November 2012.

46 See more at www.independent.ie/irish-news/kenny-hails-benefits-of-debt-deal29053488.html#sthash.15fPLvjo.dpuf.

47 Flanagan, P. (2012) 'Only Irish Will Post Growth this Year – IMF' [online]. Available at www.independent.ie/business/irish/only-irish-will-post-growth-this-year-imf-28891190.html.

48 ESRI (2012) *The Irish Economy* [online]. Available at www.esri.ie/irish_economy/. Accessed 23 October 2012.

49 BBC News (2009) 'Lean Times in Limerick' [online]. Available at http://news.bbc.co.uk/2/hi/programmes/from_our_own_correspondent/7897725.stm. Accessed 12 December 2012.

50 Walsh, J. (2012a) 'Technology: Dell of a Time', *Business and Finance* [online]. Available at www.businessandfinance.ie/bf/2011/6/intsfeatsmayissue/coversotryintelssecretrecipe./. Accessed 23 October 2012.

51 *Business World* (2012) 'Intel's Irish Business Future' [online]. Available at www.businessworld.ie/livenews.htm?a=3003930;s=rollingnews.htm. Accessed 12 December 2012.

52 Walsh, J. (2012b) 'Intel's Secret Recipe', *Business and Finance* [online]. Available at www.businessandfinance.ie/bf/2011/5/intsfeatsjune2011/technologydellofatime./. Accessed October 2012.

53 *Irish Times* (2012) 'UK Regime Change Taxing for Ireland' [online]. Available at www.irishtimes.com/newspaper/finance/2012/1217/1224327921892.html. Accessed 17 December 2012.

54 McGee, H. (2012) 'Government to Dispose of up to €3 billion in Assets over Two Years', *Irish Times* 23 February 23 [online]. Available at www.irishtimes.com/newspaper/finance/2012/0223/1224312241.

55 For a fuller discussion, see: Palcic, D. and Reeves, E. (2011) 'Is this a New Era for the State-owned Sector or a False Dawn?' *Irish Times* 16 December [online], available at www.irishtimes.com/newspaper/finance/2011/1216/1224309145; *Irish Independent* (2010) 'Fine Gael will Back Sale of State Assets' [online], available at www.independent.ie/national-news/fine-gael-will-back-sale-of-state-assets-2280618.html, accessed 12 December 2012; Mc Manus, J. (2012) 'Was NewERA Only a Fig Leaf for the Sale of State Assets?', *Irish Times* 5 November [online], available at www.irishtimes.com/newspaper/finance/2012/1105/1224326141.

56 *Irish Times* (2011) 'Tanaiste Rejects Fire Sale Claim' [online]. Available at www.irishtimes.com/newspaper/ireland/2011/0930/1224305001640.html. Accessed 12 December 2012.

57 Department of Public Expenditure and Reform (2012) *Infrastructure and Capital Investment 2012–16: Medium Term Exchequer Framework* [online]. Available at http://per.gov.ie/wp-content/uploads/Infrastructure-and-Capital-Investment-2012-16.pdf. Accessed 12 December 2012.

58 *Financial Times* (2012) 'Ireland to Unveil Stimulus Package' [online]. Available at www.ft.com/cms/s/0/08f3c34e-cb7a-11e1-911e-00144feabdc0.html#axzz2EpdnVtsg. Accessed 12 December 2012.

59 BBC News (2012) 'Ireland Stimulus Package Aims to Create 13,000 Jobs' [online]. Available at www.bbc.co.uk/news/world-europe-18878041. Accessed 12 December 2012.

Appendix 1
The structure of Irish business following the Celtic Tiger era

The top 25 companies in Ireland by turnover in 2011 are shown in Table A1.

TABLE A1 TOP 25 COMPANIES IN IRELAND 2011 (BY TURNOVER)

Name	Industry	Turnover (€ billion)
1 CRH	Construction	18.1
2 Microsoft Ireland	Consumer technology	13.4
3 Google	Consumer technology	12.5
4 DCC	Energy	10.7
5 Dell	Consumer technology	9.9
6 Smurfit Kappa	Manufacturing	7.4
7 Pfizer Global Supply	Health	6.9
8 Oracle	Business technology	5.6
9 Kerry Group	Food	5.3
10 Musgrave Group	Retailing	4.5
11 Ryanair	Transport	4.3
12 Cooper Industries	Energy	4.2
13 Boston Scientific	Health	4
14 Dunne's	Retailing	3.5–4
15 Penney's	Retailing	3.6
16 Apple	Consumer technology	3.5
17 Kingston	Consumer technology	3.2
18 Sandisk	Consumer technology	3.1
19 Tesco	Retailing	3.1
20 ESB	Energy	2.9
21 Peninsula Petroleum	Resources	2.9
22 Topaz	Energy	2.8
23 Glanbia	Agribusiness	2.7
24 CMC	Energy	2.7
25 Total Produce	Agribusiness	2.5

Source: Irish Times (2012) Top 1000. www.top1000.ie.

All the leading companies have an international presence in many markets, adopting a portfolio approach so that if one geographical sector performs badly other sectors can compensate. The largest company by turnover is Cement Roadstone Holdings (CRH), the building products group, which reported pre-tax profits of over €711 billion in 2011. It employs approximately 76,000 people at 3,600 operating locations in 36 countries. The group was formed by the merger in 1970 of two leading Irish public companies, Cement Ltd (established in 1936) and Roadstone Ltd (1949). Microsoft, Dell and Google all feature in the top five, which illustrates the strength of the consumer technology area. The importance of agribusiness in the Irish economy is also evident, with companies such as Glanbia, Kerry Group and Total Produce performing well. Musgrave's, Dunne's, Penney's and Tesco, representing the retail sector, all make the top 25 by turnover.

The key business sectors in Ireland

The key sectors in Irish business are discussed in detail below. The sectors have been chosen on the basis of their contribution to economic growth.

1 Business services incorporates a range of activities such as shared services centres, customer contact centres, European headquarters and regional operations centres providing essential business services. Shared services involves the provision of a service in one part of an organisation or group where previously the service would have been duplicated across areas. In this sense one unit of the organisation/group produces the services and shares with the others. This differs from outsourcing, which is normally to a third party. The business services sector is well represented in Ireland, with a broad range of global brands running services out of Ireland. The key players in this sector are listed in Table A2.

TABLE A2 BUSINESS SERVICES: SOME EXAMPLES

Company Name	Nature of Business	Company Website
Accenture	US-based provider of management consultancy and technology services with over 100,000 employees in 48 countries. Accenture in Ireland delivers added services in consulting, technology and outsourcing. The company employs over 1,000 people serving a client base including Irish blue chip companies, local subsidiaries of multinational corporations and various government departments and agencies.	www.accenture.com
Arvato	Wholly owned subsidiary of German company Bertelsman AG, Europe's largest media group employing over 100,000 people worldwide.	www.arvato.ie
Perot Systems	Globally focused management consulting, technology services and outsourcing enterprise. It operates in 16 countries and employs over 23,000 people. The company has two operations in Ireland (in Limerick and Dublin), providing software design, test and maintenance.	www.perotsystems.com
United Parcel Service (UPS)	The world's largest package delivery company and a leading global provider of specialised transportation and logistics services. UPS Inc. established UPS CSTC Ireland Ltd in 1995, which comprises a multilingual customer service contact centre based in Tallaght and a back-office data-processing facility in Ballymount.	www.ups.com

Source: IDA Ireland (www.idaireland.com/business-in-ireland/professional-business-ser/). Accessed 28 November 2012.

2 Consumer products and service providers include fashion, food, hospitality and cosmetics enterprises. These companies carry out a variety of activities including supply chain management, marketing, manufacturing, demand fulfilment, finance and innovation. Ireland has developed a world-class environment in which to support and grow a variety of consumer product businesses, from online retail to fast-moving consumer goods.

TABLE A3 CONSUMER PRODUCTS AND SERVICE PROVIDERS: SOME EXAMPLES

Company Name	Nature of Business	Company Website
Kellogg's	Kellogg's (EMEA HQ – marketing, supply chain management and innovation, finance) established its European headquarters in Dublin in 2004. The operation supports Kellogg's manufacturing and distribution operations across Europe through supply chain, finance and marketing groups. Kellogg's Ireland co-ordinates business setting strategy, business priorities and goals and is responsible for the efficient operation of manufacturing and distribution.	www.kelloggs.ie
Amazon	Amazon's centre in Cork handles both internet and telephone customer queries for Amazon's UK and French websites. As well as multilingual customer support it is also involved in hosting and software development. The availability of experienced, multilingual personnel in the southwest region was a strong factor in Amazon's decision to locate its centre in Cork. Amazon also has a development centre in Dublin.	www.amazon.com www.amazon.co.uk
Bose	Leaders in the fields of speaker design and psychoacoustics (the human perception of sound). You can hear Bose wherever quality sound is important, from the Olympic Games to the Sistine Chapel. Bose established its first Irish operation 27 years ago and its first Irish employee, John Coleman, is now the President and CEO of the Bose Corporation.	www.bose.ie

Source: IDA Ireland (www.idaireland.com/business-in-ireland/consumer-products/). Accessed 28 November 2012.

3 Clean technologies companies have been attracted to Ireland because of the potential of natural resources, a government commitment to renewable energy development and deployment and internationally proven relevant expertise. Many of the 1,000 multinational companies already operating in Ireland are diversifying into this sector and taking advantage of their local know-how and technology development expertise to explore new technologies and energy efficiencies. Ireland also has a growing indigenous clean technology industry with companies like Wavebob and Ocean Energy developing and testing ocean energy prototypes around Ireland.

TABLE A4 CLEAN TECHNOLOGIES: SOME EXAMPLES

Company Name	Nature of Business	Company Website
AirTricity	AirTricity is a world leading renewable energy company developing and operating wind farms across Europe.	www.airtricity.com
Wavebob	Develops and tests ocean energy prototypes around Ireland.	www.wavebob.com
Ocean Energy	Develops and tests ocean energy prototypes around Ireland.	www.oceanenergy.ie

Source: IDA Ireland (www.idaireland.com/business-in-ireland/clean-technology/). Accessed 28 November 2012.

4 The entertainment and media sector includes R&D, supply chain management, shared services, customer support, technical support, software development and data hosting. Entertainment and media comprises a number of fast-growing sub-sectors; digital media, social networking, search engines, integrated telecommunications, electronic games, film and TV, and intellectual property management and distribution. IDA Ireland has attracted a diverse range of companies operating in these sectors to locate their European and global operations here.

TABLE A5 ENTERTAINMENT AND MEDIA: SOME EXAMPLES

Company Name	Nature of Business	Company Website
Google	Google was founded in 1998 by Stanford University PhD students Larry Page and Sergey Brin. Its mission is to organise the world's information and make it universally accessible and useful.	www.google.com
eBay	The world's leading online marketplace for the sale of goods and services by individuals and businesses. In 2004 eBay announced that it would locate its second European Customer Support Centre in Dublin. The presence of a company such as eBay in Dublin confirms Ireland's position as a leading location in Europe for the digital business sector.	www.ebay.ie
PayPal	The market leader and provider of secure payment services used in online transactions, PayPal opened its international HQ in Dublin in 2004. PayPal recently cemented its long-term commitment to Ireland with an investment of more than €15 million and the opening of a new European Centre for Operational Excellence, which will result in the creation of up to 35 highly skilled jobs in operational excellence and business analytics at its Dublin facility.	www.paypal.com
GOA	GOA, the online games division of Orange, announced in 2008 the establishment of its Multilingual Customer and Operations Support Centre in Dublin. In 2006 GOA signed an exclusive contract with Mythic Entertainment, a leading developer of online computer games including *Warhammer Online: Age of Reckoning* (*WAR*). GOA's office in Dublin will support *WAR* and its portfolio of other games in five languages across the whole of Europe.	

Source: IDA Ireland (www.idaireland.com/business-in-ireland/media-and-entertainment/). Accessed 28 November 2012.

5 The industrial products and services sector in Ireland ranges from companies in the automotive sector and aerospace industry to those operating in mechanical and electrical engineering, fluid components, process equipment and materials handling. Activities carried out at these operations include high-value manufacturing, supply chain management, R&D and intellectual property management. Industrial products and services incorporates IDA's traditional engineering portfolio client companies. This sector, together with consumer products and general services companies, reflects the longest-established and most diverse nature of foreign direct investors in Ireland. Siemens and Cameron are among the high-profile companies that have chosen Ireland as a base for overseas operations.

TABLE A6 INDUSTRIAL PRODUCTS AND SERVICES: SOME EXAMPLES

Company Name	Nature of Business	Company Website
Valeo	Valeo is one of the world's leading automotive suppliers. It designs and manufactures components and systems for cars and trucks. The group has 124 production sites, 21 research centres, 39 development centres and 10 distribution platforms and employs 61,400 people in 28 countries worldwide.	www.valeo.com
Liebherr	The Liebherr Group is a German, diversified, family-owned company. A world-leading manufacturer of construction machinery, it also produces domestic appliances, machine tools and aviation and rail systems	www.liebherr.com
Ingersoll Rand	Ingersoll Rand's operations in Ireland focus on high-value manufacturing and HQ activities. The manufacturing operation came about as a result of the acquisition of ThermoKing, an Irish company producing transport refrigerators. Following this acquisition, further investment by Ingersoll Rand has resulted in expansion of the facility. Ingersoll Rand (IRI) is responsible for global export sales and activities.	www.ingersollrand.com
Siemens	Siemens is a global electronics and electrical engineering company providing products, systems, services and solutions for the industry, energy and healthcare sectors. Siemens has a long-standing tradition of delivering key infrastructure projects in Ireland. It recently completed Ireland's largest onshore wind farm for AirTricity and supplied the world's most advanced CT scanner to the Mater Private Hospital.	www.siemens.ie

Source: IDA Ireland (www.idaireland.com/business-in-ireland/industrial-products-and-s/). Accessed 28 November 2012.

TABLE A7 THE ICT SECTOR: SOME EXAMPLES

Company Name	Nature of Business	Company Website
Analog Devices	Founded in 1965, Analog Devices Inc. is a world leader in high-performance signal processing and is synonymous with high performance and innovation among electronics manufacturers. Its diverse product portfolio covers entertainment and media, industry and aerospace, medical technology, wireless and automobile applications.	www.analog.com
Intel	Intel is the world's largest semiconductor chip maker and has a 75% share of the microprocessor market. The company's largest customers are Dell and Hewlett-Packard. Worldwide, Intel employs 94,000 people and includes wafer fabrication facilities in Ireland, Arizona, Oregon, New Mexico, California, Massachusetts and a Chinese operation currently under construction.	www.intel.com
SAP	Founded in 1972, SAP is the world's leading provider of business software and is an industry leader with a rich history of innovation and growth. SAP's vision is for companies of all sizes to become the best run in business. The company has sales and development locations in 50 countries and services customers in 120 countries worldwide.	www.sap.com
Hewlett-Packard	Hewlett-Packard is a major presence in Ireland, employing over 4,000 people in a variety of activities – manufacturing, software development, R&D, sales and marketing. The Inkjet Manufacturing Operation (DIMO) is one of three inkjet manufacturing facilities worldwide for Hewlett-Packard's Imaging and Printing Group.	www.hp.com

Source: IDA Ireland (www.idaireland.com/business-in-ireland/information-communication/). Accessed 28 November 2012.

6 The ICT sector in Ireland (see Table A7) incorporates the full range of high-tech activities including R&D, high-value manufacturing, shared services, supply chain management, software development and technical support operating in areas from computers to chips, telecommunications to software and components to copiers. Seven of the world's top 10 ICT companies have operations in Ireland, along with many other leading names in the sector.

7 The cloud computing sector in Ireland is capturing more than its fair share of global cloud investments. The country has been steadily growing an ecosystem of major cloud computing brands – from both existing multinationals based in Ireland since the 1980s and 1990s, and new start-ups emerging from Silicon Valley. There are many reasons for this: Ireland has the infrastructure in terms of data centres and electricity, as well as the skills needed to grow cloud computing businesses.

TABLE A8 CLOUD COMPUTING: SOME EXAMPLES

Company Name	Nature of Business	Company Website
Dell	Dell has been one of the world's leading computing and IT companies since its foundation in 1984, so it's no surprise to see it leading the way in one of the most revolutionary and innovative technologies. Ireland is home to the company's cloud research and development centre, where engineers are developing the company's next generation of cloud computing architectures.	www.dell.ie
Microsoft	Since 2009, Microsoft has located its 'mega data centre' in Dublin. Representing a key element of the company's cloud portfolio, the sprawling facility of 303,000 square feet involved an investment of $500m. In a highly competitive process, Ireland was chosen as the location for the centre after a comprehensive global analysis. The centre supports Microsoft's EMEA online, live and cloud services.	www.microsoft.ie
Google	In September 2011, Google announced that it would be bringing its cloud technology operations to Ireland. Irish computer technicians, electrical and mechanical engineers will eventually work in the energy-efficient, air-cooled datacentre in Dublin, which joins a second Google data centre in the capital.	www.google.com
Hewlett- Packard	HP is one of the original Palo Alto tech-set, and like its competitors has also seen the benefits of locating its cloud computing operations in Ireland. Located in HP's Galway software development centre, the global centre of competency for cloud computing is a key element of HPs cloud application delivery. From here, HP powers a generation of solutions that reduce errors, increase efficiencies, and cut costs for its customers.	www.hp.com

Source: IDA Ireland (www.idaireland.com/business-in-ireland/cloud-computing/). Accessed 28 November 2012.

8 The financial services sector in Ireland carries out a number of different activities including shared services, R&D and contract centres. The main sub-sectors in international financial services companies include mutual funds, banking/asset financing, asset management, corporate treasury, life assurance and pensions.

TABLE A9 FINANCIAL SERVICES: SOME EXAMPLES

Company Name	Nature of Business	Company Website
Citi	Citi is an international financial conglomerate with operations in consumer, corporate and investment banking and insurance. They are a pre-eminent financial services company, with some 200 million customer accounts in more than 100 countries.	www.citigroup.com
Pramerica	Pramerica Systems Ireland, the wholly owned subsidiary of Prudential Financial Inc., is based in the northwest of Ireland, where it operates in software development and testing operations, call centre and financial services to its parent company. Due to the high level of success experienced here, Pramerica has expanded its Irish business activities.	www.pramerica.ie
Zurich	Zurich Financial Services Group (Zurich) is an insurance-based financial services provider with offices in North America, Europe, the Asia Pacific, Latin America and other markets. Founded in 1872, Zurich has 60,000 employees and operates in 170 countries.	www.zurich.ie

Source: IDA Ireland (www.idaireland.com/business-in-ireland/international-financial-s/). Accessed 28 November 2012.

9 Life sciences – medical technologies activities include R&D, high-value manufacturing, globally traded services, IP management and supply chain management in the cardiovascular and cardiac rhythm management, orthopaedic, diagnostic and ophthalmic sectors. With its focus on high-value activities, this sector fits well with the IDA Ireland transformation policy of moving Ireland up the value chain, including companies who have existing operations in Ireland and potential new investors. This variety of activities is testament to a flexible, skilled and adaptable workforce and ensures that many companies expand their activities beyond their initial presence.

TABLE A10 LIFE SCIENCES – MEDICAL TECHNOLOGIES: SOME EXAMPLES

Company Name	Nature of Business	Company Website
Boston Scientific	Boston Scientific is a leading worldwide developer, manufacturer and marketer of medical devices. Its Galway site is its largest manufacturing site with over 3,000 people employed in the R&D and manufacture of cardiology and peripheral vascular products.	www.bostonscientific.com
Johnson & Johnson	Johnson & Johnson, the world's most comprehensive and broad-based manufacturer of healthcare products, has a long history of foreign investment in Ireland. It currently has six IDA-supported operations in Ireland, two of which are in the high-value manufacture of medtech products.	www.jnj.com
KCI	In 2007 Kinetic Concepts Inc. (KCI), a global medical technology company, announced that it would establish a global manufacturing centre of excellence in Athlone, Co. Westmeath, further adding to Ireland's BMW medtech cluster. KCI's proprietary products include advanced wound care systems and therapeutic surfaces.	www.kci-medical.ie

Source: IDA Ireland (www.idaireland.com/business-in-ireland/life-sciences-medical-tec/). Accessed 28 November 2012.

10 Life sciences – pharmaceutical. The main activities carried out in Ireland are R&D, global business service centres, high-value manufacturing, headquarters and IP management and supply chain management. Biotechnology encompasses all aspects of the industrial application of living organisms and/or biological techniques. It is a collection of technologies that capitalise on the attributes of cells and biological molecules, such as DNA, to work for us. The primary biotechnology activity carried out in Ireland is R&D. Ireland has experienced massive growth in the biotechnology sector in the last decade.

TABLE A11 LIFE SCIENCES – PHARMACEUTICAL: SOME EXAMPLES

Company Name	Nature of Business	Company Website
GlaxoSmithKline (GSK)	GSK is the world's second largest pharmaceutical company and a world leader in the areas of anti-infectives, central nervous system and respiratory. GSK established a manufacturing facility in Cork in 1974 to develop and produce bulk pharmaceuticals.	www.gsk.ie
Merck	Merck & Co. Inc. is a global healthcare company ranked eighth in the world for pharmaceutical sales. It is a research-driven pharmaceutical company dedicated to putting patients first. Established in 1891, Merck currently discovers, develops, manufactures and markets vaccines and medicines to address unmet medical needs.	www.msd.ie
Pfizer	Pfizer is the largest pharmaceutical company in the world and produces human and animal medicines and consumer healthcare products. Pfizer has eight operations in Ireland employing over 2,000 people in both high-end manufacturing and R&D.	www.pfizer.ie
Genzyme	Genzyme Corporation is the fourth largest independent pharmaceutical biotechnology business in the world. In 2001 it announced the establishment of a new multi-phase manufacturing facility on a 31-acre site in Waterford. In 2007 Genzyme Ireland Ltd was approved an R&D grant of €3.9 million in support of a major new R&D investment of €19.5 million in facilities and R&D projects involving four platform technologies.	www.genzyme.ie

Source: IDA Ireland (www.idaireland.com/business-in-ireland/life-sciences-pharmaceuti/). Accessed 28 November 2012.

CHAPTER 3

The Global Business Environment

- To understand what comprises the global external business environment and why it is important for an organisation to be aware of components and developments.
- To understand the term 'globalisation' and its impact on an organisation. To appreciate the difference between the globalisation of production, which is commonplace, and the globalisation of markets, which is less so.
- To understand global trade, regional trading alliances and their role in global competition.
- To understand the shifting balance in global economic power and the role played by the BRIC nations (Brazil, Russia, India and China); and to understand likely future trends and developments in global competitiveness.
- To understand that the global business environment comprises both a macro and a competitive environment. Factors in the global macro environment include the political/legal, economic, technological and socio-cultural contexts.
- To appreciate that all of these factors are forcing change for organisations by increasing competitiveness and complexity.
- To understand that the competitive environment is the immediate environment facing the organisation. Factors included in the competitive environment are competitors, suppliers, customers, new entrants and substitutes.
- To conduct a competitive analysis on an industry sector. As the current business environment has become increasingly competitive, organisations need to undertake competitive analyses of their industry to work out how they can achieve a competitive advantage.
- To understand that favourable competitive environments are high-growth industries with few competitors, high barriers to entry, few substitute products and services, and suppliers and customers with little power over the organisation; and that unfavourable competitive environments are low-growth industries with many competitors, few barriers to entry, many substitute products and services, and customers and suppliers with strong power over the organisation.
- To understand key decisions involved in the internationalisation process.

3.1 Introduction

This chapter analyses the global business environment within which all organisations operate. It considers the growth and spread of globalisation and its impact on economic competitiveness, and analyses the BRIC nations and other emerging economies. It is possible to consider the external global business environment from two points of view: the macro global environment; and the competitive environment. Competitive analysis can be undertaken to determine the degree of competition in the marketplace and to assess whether the environment is favourable or unfavourable. Based on this analysis, the organisation can then make decisions in relation to market entry and future strategies.

3.2 Understanding the global business environment

Organisations, regardless of their size, and whether they are public or private enterprises, domestic or international, all operate within the context of an external global environment. The external global business environment includes all factors that affect the organisation yet that lie outside the organisation's boundary; that is, all factors that are external to the organisation. In order to fully understand the challenge faced by managers it is important to come to terms with the relationship between an organisation and its external environment.

Systems theory, which was introduced and discussed in Chapter 1, highlighted the importance of the external environment in viewing an organisation as an open system. All organisations must have inputs (people, money, information and materials) from their external environment and in turn exchange the finished goods and services they produce to provide energy for continued existence. Managerial performance is often dependent on knowing how the organisation influences, and is influenced by, its external environment. No organisation can be viewed as having enough power and influence to enable it to ignore environmental pressures.

Factors contained in the external environment are essentially uncontrollable from an organisation's point of view. For example, there is very little an organisation can do to prevent the onset of a recession. However, this does not mean that an organisation can ignore such factors. We saw in Chapter 2 that many Irish organisations have been severely affected by the recent financial crisis.

To survive in the current business environment the organisation needs to be able to manage its environment by being constantly aware of developments, and, where possible, anticipating future developments, to ensure a speedy and accurate response to the situation at hand. Even small companies operating in local markets have become exposed to external competition and are affected by developments in other parts of the global environment. All organisations should be aware of developments on the international front, in order to facilitate future decisions on international expansion and to keep abreast of developments that may lead to new entrants in the domestic market. All of these developments have been augmented by the spread of globalisation.

3.2.1 Globalisation

Globalisation refers to the increasing and deepening interactions and connections between individuals, groups and organisations across the world. Thomas Friedman has described the world as 'being tied together into a single globalised marketplace driven by the spread of free market capitalism to virtually every country in the world'.[1] Such connections mean that events in any part of the world have an immediate impact on other areas. The financial crisis of 2007/8 illustrates how events (sub-prime mortgage defaults) which started in the USA had soon far-reaching effects (global recession) across the entire world.

The world is undergoing changes in the global economic order, which are as significant for the world economy and international relations as the end of the Cold War in the mid-1980s. Globalisation and economic integration are accelerating, propelled by growing trade and capital flows, deepening financial markets, falling transportation costs, and the revolution in information and communications technology (ICT). As with all such developments, there are huge opportunities, but these are accompanied by threats and risks for organisations, along with pressures on natural resources, climate, and traditional industries and livelihoods. There is little doubt that old certainties can no longer be relied upon, which has aroused new fears. However, the extent to which the world has become fully globalised is in dispute. At one extreme it can be argued that we are all converging towards a common global system, often referred to as 'hyperglobalisation'. On the other hand, it can be argued that globalisation has been exaggerated and that markets and organisations function more along national and regional lines. Somewhere in between the two we find a more moderate approach arguing that global processes are taking place but proceeding more rapidly in some places than others and also differing in their intensity and effects.

The globalisation of production has been significant. It has allowed companies to break down the manufacturing process into separate stages, and to locate each stage in the most advantageous location available. Global supply chains are therefore changing as organisations outsource production and related service to lower-cost economies. For example, India's IT capacity has attracted global companies to outsource IT and related services there. China's source of cheap labour has allowed mass production manufacturing to flourish. It is increasingly common to find that elements of a single product are sourced in a range of countries, replacing traditional trade in finished goods. The globalisation of markets has seen a more mixed pattern of development. Levitt predicted that there would be a single global market where standardised products would be sold everywhere.[2] Tastes and preferences would be homogenised across the world. The global spread of McDonald's, particularly during the 1990s when it first opened outlets in Moscow, would seem to lend weight to this argument. Many industry sectors have become dominated by big global brands, from hotel chains (Holiday Inn, Clarion, Radisson Blu, Best Western, Sheraton) to petrol companies (Shell, BP).

What does globalisation mean to the consumer? In general terms, globalisation has meant more choice for the consumer. Where previously a domestic marketplace was served by one or two small national firms, the market has now opened up to international competition. Increased competition normally results in lower prices. Large global multinational corporations (MNCs) also benefit from economies of scale and scope, giving opportunities for lower prices. The national identity of brands has become increasingly blurred. MNCs also affect career choice and progression, with many people continuing to work for the same MNC throughout their career, although perhaps in different geographical locations. However, many markets worldwide have remained diverse and far from homogenous in terms of consumers' tastes and preferences. Markets for consumer products in which tastes and preferences are influenced by culture have not become as homogenised. Food and drinks markets are a case in point. Tastes vary hugely, and even drinks such as Coca-Cola and Fanta, which are apparently the same the world over, are made in different colours and with different proportions of sugar according to local market preferences. Globalisation of markets is most pronounced in sectors that rely on standardised products/services, such as microchips and engine components, for all consumers. Even the car manufacturing industry responds to local market preferences (see Management Focus 3.1). So despite moves towards a global market there remain fundamental differences based on geography and culture.

Management Focus 3.1 Appealing to the Chinese customer

China emerged as the world's top car market in 2009, and though the sector stalled in 2010, with sales rising just 2.5 per cent to 18.51 million, car makers are convinced it is where the industry's future lies. Manufacturers such as Nissan have started to include features that appeal to the Chinese consumer, from large grilles and highly visible chrome fittings to luxury back seats for the in-laws.

Source: *Daily News America* [online]
http://articles.nydailynews.com/2012-05-01/news/31523710-1-chinese-market-freder.

There is no doubt that more countries than ever before are seizing the opportunities presented by globalisation. In the second half of the twentieth century, the USA, Europe and Japan drove the global economy. Today they are being joined by increasingly open and expanding economies, in particular China and India, but also Brazil, Russia and others. China is already the third largest exporter and likely to become the second largest national economy in a few years from now. Within the same time frame, India could become the sixth largest. The nature of global trade is changing as a result of these changes.

Globalisation has offered huge opportunities for firms to expand into new international markets. However, many smaller domestic markets have been opened up to competition from large global MNCs. It can be argued that globalisation enhances the monopoly power of large MNCs, but on the other hand small local companies remain strong competitors and have a role to play in the global economy. Successful firms, large and small, are able to source components globally and deliver finished products to diverse markets, providing customers in each market with products adapted to their tastes at competitive prices.

3.2.2 Regional trading alliances

Global competition is further shaped by regional trading blocs or alliances, which are largely driven by geographical location. The main trading blocs and regional trading agreements include the enlarged European Union (EU), North American Free Trade Agreement (NAFTA), Mercosur (South America) and the Association of Southeast Asian Nations (ASEAN). There are other trading blocs in different parts of the world, including CARICOM (the Caribbean Community), which has seen the development of a single market and economy.

EU

The EU has undergone significant change since 1992 to emerge as the world's largest economy with a per capita gross domestic product (GDP) of €25,000 for its 500 million consumers. This represents a €12.6 trillion economy, and only the United States (€11.5 trillion) is in the same league; even China (€4.6 trillion) and Japan (€4.2 trillion) are considerably smaller.[3] It has the third largest population in the world (just under 500 million) after China and India.[4] The EU's trade with the rest of the world accounts for around 20 per cent of global exports and imports, and it is the world's biggest exporter and the second biggest importer. In the region of two-thirds of EU countries' total trade is done with other EU countries. The USA is the EU's most important trading partner, followed by China.[5]

In 1992, the member states of the EU (then 15 countries) integrated economically to form the largest market in the world. Economic integration resulted in the elimination of trade barriers between member countries, allowing goods, people and money to flow freely within the EU. Trade between EU member states has increased, as has trade between the EU and other global trading partners. Between 1990 and 2000, the EU's total trade with the rest of the world doubled in value. Trade between EU countries has become much easier and cheaper as a result of the removal of tariff barriers and customs duties. As the EU member states removed tariffs on trade between each other, they unified all tariffs on goods imported from outside the EU. The harmonisation of this common external tariff (CET) meant that EU countries had to participate in multilateral international trade negotiations. External trade therefore became one of the first elements of European integration in which member states had to pool their sovereignty. In 2002, the common currency (the euro) was introduced and 17 out of the current 27 EU members use the currency. Only the UK, Sweden and Denmark have opted to remain outside the euro.

FIGURE 3.1 AN ENLARGED EUROPE: EU27

The EU has gone through a period of significant enlargement. Denmark, Ireland and the UK joined in 1973, followed by Greece in 1981. Portugal and Spain joined in 1986, with Austria, Finland and Sweden following in 1995. Ten new countries joined the EU on 1 May 2004; Cyprus, the Czech Republic, Estonia, Hungary, Latvia, Lithuania, Malta, Poland, Slovakia and Slovenia. This enlargement from 15 to 25, the biggest in EU history, owed its origins to the collapse of communism and the fall of the Berlin Wall in 1989, which offered an unprecedented opportunity to integrate Central and Eastern Europe. Romania and Bulgaria were admitted in 2007. Turkey, Macedonia and Croatia have applied for EU membership. The new enlarged EU 27 is shown in Figure 3.1.

Management in Focus 3.2 EU–South Korea free trade agreement

In July 2011 a new free trade agreement between the EU and South Korea came into force. It is a ground-breaking agreement that covers a huge range of subjects, from border barriers to the more complex regulatory and administrative measures that can present hurdles to international trade. It also links the EU with its fourth largest partner outside Europe. It will have a significant positive impact on the EU's economy and will change the conditions of competition in important markets. It is a testament to Europe's ability to move forward on trade that this agreement moved swiftly through Europe's approval procedure despite considerable political pressure from economic sectors concerned about its impact. Negotiations were opened in May 2007 and the agreement entered into force four years later. By contrast, the negotiations between Korea and the USA began in February 2006 with agreement only coming into force in March 2012, six years later.

Source: European Commission (2013) 'The EU's Free Trade Agreements – Where Are We?' [online] http://trade.ec.europa.eu/doclib/docs/2012/november/tradoc_150129.pdf

One of the outcomes of recent EU enlargement has been the problems inherent in effectively managing a much larger entity: managing a union of 27 members is far more complex than running one of 15 members. With this in mind, the Lisbon Treaty (2009) changed the structural workings of the EU with the aim of making it more democratic and responsive to individual members. It strengthened the role of the European Parliament and allowed a greater involvement on the part of national parliaments. Lisbon also simplified working methods and voting rules, and introduced a Charter of Fundamental Rights into European primary law, providing for new solidarity mechanisms and ensuring better protection of European citizens. Underlying the treaty was the belief that an open market, with effective and enforced internal rules in areas such as competition, innovation, education, research and development (R&D), employment, social and cohesion policy is essential in helping European companies compete globally. The treaty entered into force on 1 December 2009.[6] EU policy has therefore concentrated on liberalising trade and opening up markets to allow EU firms to grow and expand. The Global Europe Strategy (2006) facilitated a new generation of free trade agreements (FTAs) with Asian markets and heightened European focus in areas such as intellectual property and access to raw materials.[7]

Recently approved agreements include an Economic Partnership Agreement with Caribbean countries and an agreement liberalising trade in agricultural and fisheries products with Morocco. In 2012 the EU also signed agreements with Columbia, Peru, Central America and South Korea (see Management Focus 3.2).

In the ASEAN region, the EU is currently also negotiating an FTA with Malaysia (launched in May 2010) and Vietnam (launched in June 2012). Singapore is currently the EU's largest trading partner in the ASEAN group (€65 billion) and the EU's main investment partner in ASEAN, accounting for 80 per cent of the investment stock between the regions. Therefore an FTA with Singapore would be a gateway into the Asian region, offering opportunities for European business expansion there. Economic partnership agreements (EPAs), which are trade and development partnerships, have been signed between the EU and African, Caribbean and Pacific countries (ACP), based on the Cotonou Agreement (2000).[8]

NAFTA

The Americas have also moved further towards more co-operative arrangements in relation to trade. Canada, the USA and Mexico signed the North American Free Trade Agreement (NAFTA) in 1994, linking them in an economic alliance. All remaining duties and quantitative restrictions were eliminated, as scheduled, on 1 January 2008. NAFTA has created one of the world's largest free trade areas, now comprising 450 million people producing $17 trillion worth of goods and services. Trade between the USA and its NAFTA partners has increased since the agreement entered into force, and in 2009 US goods and services trade with NAFTA totalled $1.6 trillion (the most recent data available for goods and services trade combined).[9] Despite the difficulties that emerged during the course of negotiations between the various countries, the agreement marked the first stage in the establishment of an American economic community. The Free Trade Area of the Americas (FTAA) is a proposed agreement to reduce and possibly eliminate all trade barriers between countries on the American continent, and is closely modelled on NAFTA.

Mercosur

Mercosur, the main trading bloc in South America, is known as the Common Market of the South. It was set up in March 1991 by Argentina, Brazil, Paraguay and Uruguay under the Treaty of Asunción. The 1994 Treaty of Ouro Preto gave the body a wider international status and formalised a customs union. Bolivia, Chile, Colombia, Ecuador and Peru are associate members, meaning that while they can join FTAs, they remain outside the bloc's customs union. Moves to include Chile as a full member were suspended after the country signed a free trade deal with the USA in 2002. The bloc's combined market encompasses more than 250 million people and accounts for more than three-quarters of the economic activity on the continent. Mercosur tariff policies regulate imports and exports and the bloc can arbitrate in trade disputes between its members. In the longer term, Mercosur aims to create a continent-wide free trade area, and the creation of a Mercosur development bank has been mooted. There have been many disputes within Mercosur (see Management in Focus 3.3), and the issue of Venezuela's membership is still a problem. The country was accepted as a full member in July 2006, pending ratification by the other member states, but four years later its status remained in limbo as Paraguay had not yet officially approved the decision. This was mainly on account of objections raised by the Paraguayan senate, which expressed doubts over the democratic credentials of the late Venezuelan President Hugo Chavez.[10] This may change with time but will be dependent on developments in Venezuela in the post-Chavez era.

Management Focus 3.3 Mercosur disagreements

- When Brazil's car industry became increasingly competitive, aided by the devaluation of its currency in 1999, Argentina responded by imposing tariffs on Brazilian steel imports. The spat was resolved in December 2000 when the two countries signed a bilateral agreement to end the crisis.
- In 2006 Argentina and the bloc's smallest country, Uruguay, clashed over plans to build two large pulp mills along the border – the biggest foreign investments Uruguay had ever attracted. Argentina said it feared pollution and the impact on tourism and fishing. The matter went to the International Court of Justice (ICJ), which ruled in favour of Uruguay. Argentina pledged to continue its fight against the mills.

- The bloc's smaller members, Paraguay and Uruguay, complain of restricted access to markets in Argentina and Brazil and have sought to set up bilateral trade deals outside Mercosur. The organisation's rules forbid this.

Source: BBC News, 'Profile: Mercosur – Common Market of the South' (www.bbc.co.uk/2/hi/americas/5195834.stm).

Critics have accused Mercosur of becoming politicised and moving away from its free trade origins. Talks to secure a trade accord with the EU began in 1999 but were suspended in 2004, with subsidies for European farmers and tariffs on industrial goods being among the stumbling blocks. The two blocs agreed to resume negotiations on a free trade agreement at talks in Madrid in May 2010, despite opposition from several key European nations including France. Negotiations on a planned, US-backed FTAA are similarly mired, with some Mercosur leaders rejecting US free market policies.[11]

ASEAN

The Association of Southeast Asian Nations (ASEAN) is a trading bloc consisting of ten countries: Brunei, Cambodia, Indonesia, Laos, Malaysia, Myanmar (Burma), Philippines, Singapore, Thailand and Vietnam (see Figure 3.2). With a population of approximately 620 million and a combined GDP of over $2.2 trillion, ASEAN is the USA's fourth largest export market and fifth largest trade partner overall (2011).[12]

Trade issues have also been discussed between what is termed ASEAN+3 (all members of ASEAN plus China, Japan and South Korea). A Framework Agreement on Comprehensive Economic Cooperation between ASEAN and China was signed by all the ASEAN member states and the People's Republic of China on 4 November 2002. This agreement provided the legal basis for ASEAN and China to negotiate, and ultimately led to the creation of the *ASEAN–China Free Trade Area (ACFTA)* on 1 January 2010. China is currently the third largest trading partner of ASEAN, after Japan and the EU, with a trade value of US$192 billion in 2008. This makes up 11 per cent of ASEAN's total trade with external parties. The ACFTA is a market of 1.91 billion consumers with a combined GDP of about US$5.83 trillion (2008). In terms of consumer market size, the ACFTA is the biggest FTA in the world.[13]

The ASEAN–Japan Comprehensive Economic Partnership (AJCEP) Agreement signed in April 2008 covers areas such as

FGURE 3.2 THE ASEAN TRADING BLOC

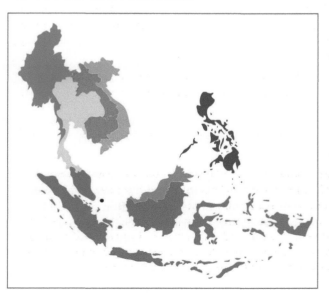

trade in goods, trade in services, investment, and economic co-operation. ASEAN and Japan have a combined gross domestic product of US$6.4 trillion (2008). The total value of bilateral trade between ASEAN and Japan has reached US$211.7 billion, making Japan ASEAN's top trading partner in 2008. South Korea is the second partner with which ASEAN has forged an FTA. In 2005, ASEAN and South Korea signed the Framework Agreement on Comprehensive Economic Co-operation, and subsequently signed four more agreements that form the legal instruments for establishing the ASEAN–Korea Free Trade Area (AKFTA).[14]

Africa

The African continent offers the potential for long-term growth. Many areas are rich in natural resources and could emulate the success of post-apartheid South Africa, which has experienced economic recovery and attracted significant overseas investment. In 2011 an initial agreement was reached to secure an FTA between the 26 member countries of the combined Southern African Development Community (SADC), the East African Community (EAC) and the Common Market for Eastern and Southern Africa (COMESA). The agreement centres on creating the continent's biggest free trade bloc to create a single continent-wide market estimated to be worth US$1 trillion in 2013. The countries involved have an aggregate GDP of US$860 billion and a combined population of 590 million. Figure 3.3 illustrates the geographical extent of the FTA. The entire area in blue will be part of the proposed new free trade region.

FIGURE 3.3 PROPOSED AFRICAN FREE TRADE AREA

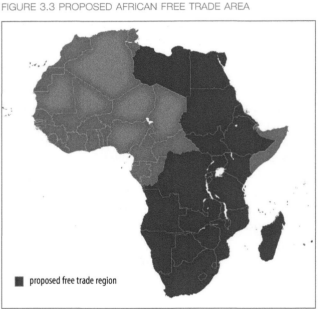

proposed free trade region

Source: How we Made it in Africa: 'Africa's Grand Free Trade Area and What it will Mean for Business' (www.howwemadeitin africa.com/africas-grand-free-trade-area-and-what-it-will-mean-for-business/11172/).

While Africa represents a growing opportunity and is experiencing the third fastest growth in the world (behind China and India), a mere 10 per cent of Africa's trade is between African countries. The continent's poor infrastructure is a key developmental priority, and the problems relating to infrastructure are most acute for landlocked countries, which are heavily reliant on neighbouring states to reach international export markets. The World Bank has estimated that upgrading road linkages between the Central African Republic and the Democratic Republic of the Congo (DRC) could increase intra-African trade by between $10 billion and $30 billion a year.[15] Other challenges that need to be addressed include non-tariff trade barriers, such as corruption and bureaucratic delays at ports. The next step will be to include West African countries in the free trade negotiations.

The trend towards the formation of regional trading blocs is clearly still very active; and countries continue to group together to gain the benefits of a common economic and trading entity.

3.2.3 The BRICs and other emerging economies

The term 'BRICs' refers to the four large emerging economies of Brazil, Russia, India and China. It was coined in 2001 by Jim O'Neil of Goldman Sachs in a paper entitled 'The World Needs Better Economic BRICs'. The BRIC countries have since gone on to experience high growth rates, leading to a shift in the balance of global economic power away from the more established G7 economies of the UK, USA, Japan, Italy, France, Canada and Germany. The population size of these four geographical regions, coupled with their economic potential, marked them out as different from other emerging economies. Collectively the four BRICs are home to more than 2.8 billion people or 40 per cent of the world's population, cover more than a quarter of the world's land area over three continents, and account for more than 25 per cent of global GDP. The size of a country's population has a direct effect on the size of its economy and on its potential for economic growth. The growth rates in GDP from 2004 to 2011 for the BRICs, the USA and the EU are illustrated in Figure 3.4.

FIGURE 3.4 BRICS, USA AND EU REAL GDP GROWTH RATES 2004–11

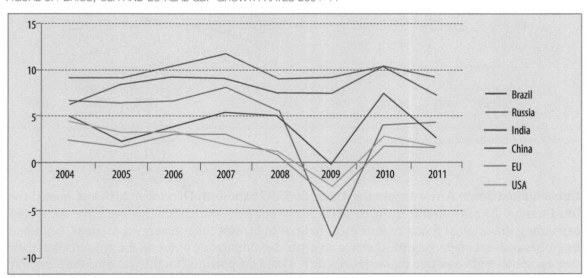

Source: compiled from data available at www.indexmundi.com/g/.aspx?c=br&v=66.

We can see quite clearly that India and China have experienced strong and steady growth rates over the period. The performance of China has, however, been significantly ahead of the average BRIC growth rate. Brazil and Russia enjoyed high growth rates until 2009 but have both experienced dips in growth, although the Russian experience is more extreme. Overall growth rates for the BRIC economies is significantly higher than that experienced by the USA and EU, leading to the term 'Sicks' to describe unhealthy economies. As early as 2003, Goldman Sachs forecast that China and India would become the first and third largest economies by 2050, with Brazil and Russia capturing the fifth and sixth spots. Currently the countries/regions predicted to be the top six economies in the world by 2050 are China, the USA, India, the EU, Brazil and Russia respectively.

The rapid economic growth experienced by the BRICs has led to the emergence of a large middle class in all of these nations, with increasing disposable incomes that have fuelled consumption and consequently economic growth. The expansion of the middle classes is illustrated in Figure 3.5. The increase in the middle-class population of the BRIC countries is forecast to more than double that of the developed G7 economies.

FIGURE 3.5 THE EXPANDING MIDDLE CLASSES

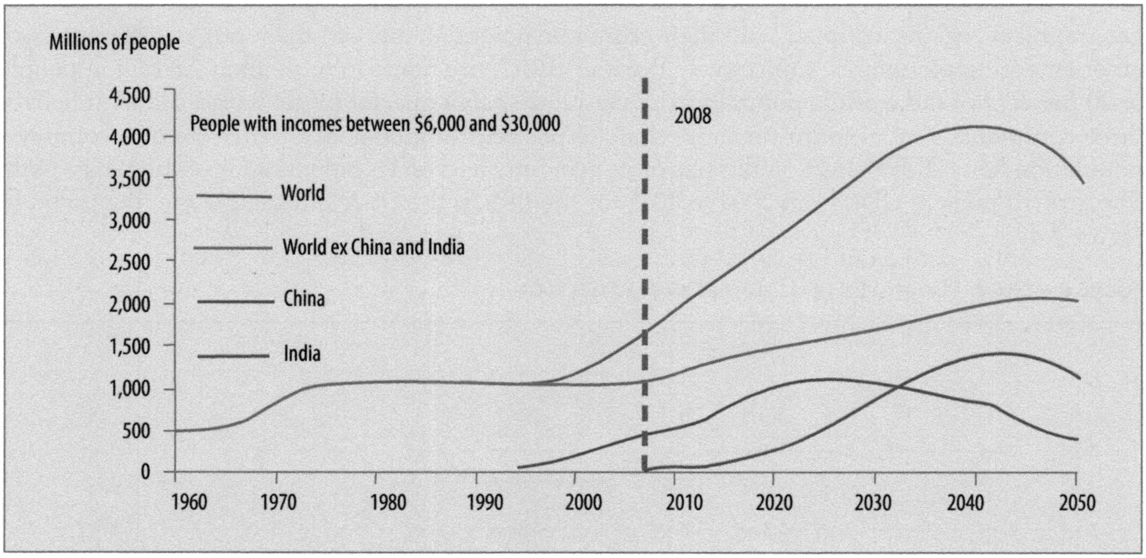

Source: www.globalsherpa.org/bric-countries-brics.

China invited South Africa to join the group of BRIC nations in December 2010 and hosted the third annual BRICs summit in April 2011. Many analysts and commentators have suggested expanding the original group of four BRIC nations to include other emerging markets. Goldman Sachs has resisted conferring BRIC status on other developing countries on the grounds that their demographics and economic characteristics do not hold the potential for them to rival the economic size or influence of the BRIC countries or today's leading economies (e.g. the USA and Japan). The term MIKT has been coined to reflect the future potential of Mexico, Indonesia, South Korea and Turkey. Goldman Sachs identified another group of economically dynamic and promising developing countries creatively labelled the 'Next 11': Bangladesh, Egypt, Indonesia, Iran, Mexico, Nigeria, Pakistan, Philippines, South Korea, Turkey and Vietnam.[16]

However, as we saw in Figure 3.4, the BRICs have been affected by the weakened position of western economies, and arguments that the BRICs were decoupled from the west may have been premature. In addition, all the BRICs have found that corruption still has a role to play in their political systems. China's rate of growth is slowing and this will have a knock-on effect on the remaining BRICs because it is the largest trading partner for Brazil, India and South Africa. The Brazilian economy has experienced a significant drop-off in growth, but has both the FIFA World

Cup (2014) and Olympics (2016) to boost growth potential. India too has witnessed a fall-off in growth, and infrastructural shortcomings were evident in the blackout of 2012, which left 600 million people without electricity. Russia too has experienced problems. Putin's return to power was met with protests and the twin pillars of the Putin system – revenues from oil and gas and an acquiescent middle class – have both shown signs of weakening. South Africa has witnessed strikes in the mining sector and political tensions. Notwithstanding these difficulties there is little doubt that the BRICs will continue to outpace the 'Sicks' for many years to come.[17]

3.3 Managing the global business environment

The external business environment consists of two main elements. First, the organisation operates within a macro environment, which is the most general part of the environment, containing, for example, the political and economic contexts and other fundamental factors that generally affect all organisations. Second, the organisation also operates within a more specific competitive environment, which includes competitors, suppliers and customers, all of whom interact with the organisation. Figure 3.6 illustrates the external global environment facing organisations.

FIGURE 3.6 THE GLOBAL MACRO BUSINESS ENVIRONMENT

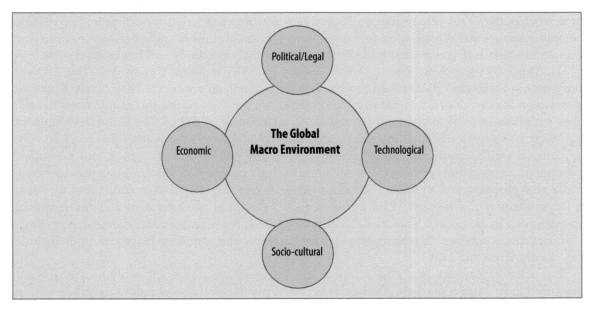

The global macro environment within which an organisation operates contains general factors that affect all organisations and includes the political–legal, economic, technological and socio-cultural contexts. The macro environment is quite similar for most organisations, given the general nature of the various factors. For example, economic developments affect most organisations. How organisations perceive and react to these factors, however, accounts for the variations in organisational performance in relation to the external environment. Each of the elements of the macro environment will be discussed below (this is often referred to as a PEST analysis).

3.3.1 The political–legal context

The political–legal context is shaped by the activities of governments at both national and international level. Governments of different countries can have an enormous impact on the business environment in terms of economic policies, international trade policies and tax laws. The economic environment (which will be discussed in the next section) is also shaped by government activities. On a national level, a government can affect business through its policies in relation to industrial/services development and in particular by the tax incentives, capital grants and expansion schemes available. On an international level, the political environment influences business through policies in relation to international trade, deregulation/liberalisation and, more important for firms seeking to internationalise, through host country political systems and policies. One of the main ways in which individual governments seek to influence international trade is through their input into the World Trade Organisation (WTO) and its predecessor, the General Agreement on Trade and Tariffs (GATT). Both past and present bodies recognise the right of governments to levy duties to offset export subsidies or dumping (selling goods and services at less than a fair value). The last fully completed round of GATT negotiations, known as the Uruguay Round, took place over the period 1986–94. The aim of these rounds, which are now held in the framework of the WTO, is to reduce tariffs and remove other barriers to world trade. The WTO is the only international organisation that deals with the global rules of trade between nations and its main function is to ensure that trade flows as smoothly, predictably and freely as possible.[18]

The Doha Development Round, which began in 2001, remains incomplete. The Cancun conference in September 2003 failed to reach agreement due to an unexpected gap that had opened up between the developed and developing countries on several issues concerning access to each other's markets and the long-running question of agricultural subsidies. The Doha Development Agenda remains a priority and the work programme includes negotiations and other work on non-agricultural tariffs, trade and environment, WTO rules such as anti-dumping and subsidies, investment, competition policy, trade facilitation, transparency in government procurement, intellectual property, and a range of issues raised by developing countries as difficulties they face in implementing the present WTO agreements.[19] Individual governments and international agencies such as the United Nations (UN) can also impose trade embargoes or sanctions on trade with particular countries. Examples of countries that have had sanctions placed on trade include Iraq, South Africa and Libya.

The political context has also affected the business environment, with moves toward deregulation in certain markets. Deregulation attempts to remove restrictions on trade within particular industries. Recent developments in the EU have seen moves toward the deregulation of financial markets, public utilities and the airline industry, with the aim of removing protective restrictions on operations in order to allow greater competition. Moves toward deregulation have opened up market opportunities for other companies. (See Management Focus 3.4.)

Management Focus 3.4 The 'Big Switch'

The Commission for Energy Regulation (CER) in Ireland has overseen the gradual liberalisation of the electricity supply market, which culminated in full market opening in February 2005. The regulatory framework created the right environment for competition to develop and since then competition has increased in the business and domestic markets. In 2010, the CER published its *Roadmap to Deregulation*, which set out the milestones for the end of price regulation. All business markets were deregulated from 1 October 2010. From April 2011, the domestic market was deregulated and all suppliers are now free to set their own tariffs. The market now consists of Electric Ireland (formerly the ESB), Bord Gáis and AirTricity. Competition between suppliers has increased significantly, with 20 per cent of customers switching supplier in 2009 alone.
Source: www.cer.ie/en/electricity-retail-market-overview.aspx.

When firms expand internationally they are exposed to the political context of the host nation. In addition to managing the political context in their home environment, firms are now opened up to a range of political environments that requirement effective management. Political constraints and political risk are part and parcel of conducting business across national boundaries. There are a number of key questions a firm needs to ask before making a significant investment abroad.

- Who runs the government? Who is the president? What type of government is it? Democratic? Left or right?
- Who are the opposition parties and what role do they play?
- Is the system stable and what is the recent political history?
- What relationships exist with other countries?
- Who do they trade with? Are they members of free trade groups?
- What are the government's policies for business?
- What is the level of political risk?
- What are accepted political behaviours?

It can take time for a firm to become familiar with how to operate under a different political system. Figure 3.7 outlines the main differences between democratic and authoritarian systems.

FIGURE 3.7 FEATURES OF AUTHORITARIANISM VS. DEMOCRACY

Authoritarianism	Feature	Democracy
• Power determines law	• Rule of law	• Constitutional framework, equality
• Few rights	• Civil rights	• Right to a fair trial
• Restrictions	• Political rights	• Right to vote, stand for office, etc.
• Few candidates, little choice	• Elections	• Regular and free elections
• Administrative arm of government	• Courts	• Independent judiciary, transparent process
• Press controlled by state	• Freedom of the press	• Editorial and reporting independence from state

However, political processes also offer opportunities for firms. Government incentives, preferential subsidies and other political acts alter the transaction costs for MNCs and influence strategic decision making. (For example, high import tariffs may result in a firm deciding to set up a new facility to avoid tariffs.) Firms doing business abroad need to be politically astute and effectively manage their relationship with both the host and home government. Evaluating the political risk associated with any investment is crucial for any firm, and as their investment commitment increases the risks become greater. There are two main risks:[20]

1   **Expropriation risk**: the risk that the host government could seize the firm's assets. Firms could be forced to reduce their stake by sharing ownership with local firms. For example, Venezuela has in the past re-nationalised foreign-owned investments.
2   **Policy risk:** the risk that the host government could discriminatorily change the laws, regulations, or contracts governing an investment.

In attempting to establish a favourable trade and investment climate, firms will have to weigh up the advantages and risks associated with making an investment overseas. Countries deemed to have a high political risk in 2009 included Zimbabwe, the Congo, Cambodia, Sudan, Iraq, Syria and Egypt. Firms can minimise political risk by avoiding risky locations or by reducing their exposure where investment is necessary in risky environments. They can team up with a local partner, source both finance and raw materials locally to demonstrate commitment to the country and slowly build up political support.

Firms are also presented with challenges when dealing with an unfamiliar legal system. Legal systems determine a country's legislative framework and institutional arrangements. There are three main types of legal system commonly in use:

1   **Common law system:** an independent judiciary is the basis of law, which relies on case precedents. Examples: UK, USA.
2   **Civil law:** relies on a legal code that is applied universally. Example: Europe.
3   **Theocratic law:** based on an accepted religious code. Examples: Iran, Saudi Arabia.

Firms need to be familiar with differences in law that are likely to impact on their operations. Laws in relation to competition, patent filing, employment, safety, environmental protection, marketing and product liability will all vary in different countries. Firms must also be aware of the degree of judicial independence and the extent of legal enforcement.

Firms all operate within a political context, including both home and host country political systems; they therefore need to be fully aware of and manage the political context to enable them to compete effectively.

3.3.2 The economic context

The economic context is shaped by the general state of individual economies, by the economic policies pursued by government (as seen in Chapter 2), and by the position of the economy in relation to others, particularly those of their trading partners. In effect, the economic context consists of complex interconnections between the economies of different countries.

Governments pursue different economic policies, which affect key areas like inflation (changes in prices levels from one year to the next), interest rates (the cost of borrowing money) and wage rates (levels of pay). Variations in these key areas have important effects on the business environment. Interest rates determine the extent of an organisation's loans and investments. In general, high interest rates deter organisations from heavy investment. Inflation and wage rates can be considered together. Increased inflation is usually followed by demands for higher wages on the part of the workforce, the reason being that as inflation increases the purchasing power of the consumer declines: in other words, the same wages will buy fewer products and services. Wage levels affect an organisation's cost structure: high wages mean high costs; and they also determine the amount of disposable income – the amount customers can spend on goods and services – which affects demand for the organisation's product.

Exchange rates have a huge impact on organisations that export much of their produce and/or import large quantities of raw materials. When the value of the home country's currency rises in relation to that of the country to which they export, an organisation's goods and services become more expensive, thereby reducing its competitiveness. Therefore, variations in these areas greatly affect the business environment within which organisations operate.

As we saw in section 3.2 on globalisation, one of the most important developments in relation to the economic context has been the emergence of global interdependencies between different economies. This development is particularly important given that Ireland is a small open economy. National economies no longer operate in isolation; today they share an interdependence with other national economies. In other words, events in one economy impact on other economies.

Therefore, developments in one economy have enormous implications for others, which means that organisations have to keep up to date on growth and recession, both domestically and internationally. Organisations that operate in a number of countries must be aware of the economic conditions in both parent and host nations. The main result of growing interdependencies between economies is that the complexity of conducting business increases.

3.3.3 The technological context

The technological context is concerned with technological developments and the pace of these developments. It is a critically important part of the macro environment: no organisation is immune to the effects of technological developments.

Technology generally affects organisations in three ways.

First, **technological innovation**, such as the development of the Apple suite of products (iPod, iPad and iPhone), leads to the creation of new industries, markets and competitive niches. Therefore, the advent of new technology can create a whole new industry, as the personal computer (PC), compact disk (CD), digital versatile disk (DVD) and MP3 players did in the past. Technological innovation is now faster than ever, and this has an enormous impact on markets and whole industries. The lead times associated with such innovation are also decreasing. (Lead time refers to the amount of time between the inception of the idea and its final production.) One of the key results of the increase in the pace of technological change is that organisations can no longer rely on a technological innovation to provide them with long-term success. Due to the increased pace of change, competitor organisations can quickly imitate the innovation, thereby eliminating any advantage the innovating organisation had. Therefore, organisations have to stay at the leading edge of technological change in order to enjoy long-term success.

Second, technology affects **production techniques**. For example, technological innovations in the use of computers have resulted in computers being increasingly used for product design and manufacturing. Computer-aided design (CAD) involves using computer graphics for product design; computer-aided manufacturing (CAM) uses computers to assist in the manufacture of goods and services. Both CAD and CAM techniques are widely used in the automotive and electronics industries. Guinness has replaced its older brewing equipment with state-of-the-art technology that has enabled the complete automation of the brewing production process. Self-checkout systems are becoming increasingly common in retail outlets: these systems use simple technology such as touch-screen menus and automated voice instructions to help customers through the process. The U-Scan machine manufactured by Fujitsu has reduced costs by as much as 120–150 employee hours per week.[21]

Third, technology affects how an organisation is **managed** and how **communications** take place in the organisation. The more sophisticated the technology, the easier it is to communicate and thus manage large organisations. Systems such as financial information systems (FIS) and management information systems (MIS) mean that information can be acquired at the push of a button rather than by sifting through mounds of paper and allow calculations to be computed on the data, something which previously took a long time to achieve. E-business and online sales have continued to grow and evolve. E-business can be defined as the interchange of goods, services or property of any kind through an electronic medium.[22] Selling books, airline tickets and concert tickets are a few of the many areas that have been revolutionised by online direct sales activity. E-commerce remains one of the fastest growing markets in Europe: the total market was worth €200.52 billion in 2011 – up from €169.63 billion in 2010. Online retailers in only three countries – UK, Germany and France – accounted for 71 per cent of European online sales.[23] Details of the online share of total retail sales are shown in Figure 3.8.

FIGURE 3.8 ONLINE SHARE OF RETAIL TRADE IN EUROPE (2011)

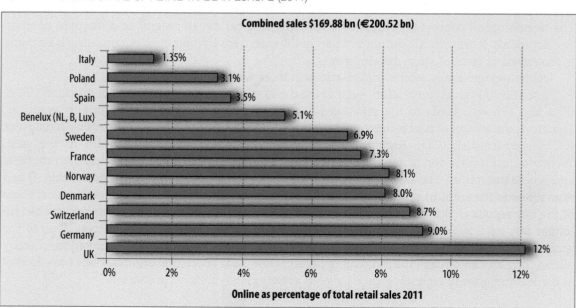

Source: Centre for Retail Research (www.retailresearch.org/onlineretailing.php).

Irish internet usage has grown steadily over recent years, as shown in Figure 3.9. In 2010, according to a survey by the International Telecommunication Union, 3,229,108 people in Ireland (68.9 per cent of the population) subscribed to the internet. This figure has certainly grown since then, with more and more people accessing the internet via mobile devices such as smartphones, iPhones, iPads and android devices. Despite this, Irish businesses have been slow to cash in on this huge customer base: only 66 per cent of Irish businesses have a website and only 21 per cent have e-commerce facilities.[24]

FIGURE 3.9 GROWTH OF THE INTERNET IN IRELAND 1994–2010

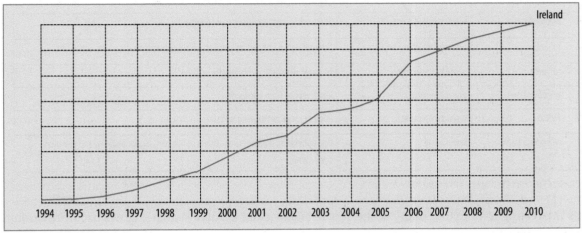

Ireland

1994 1995 1996 1997 1998 1999 2000 2001 2002 2003 2004 2005 2006 2007 2008 2009 2010

Source: NuaSoft (www.nua.ie/surveys/).

Online sales from global retailers doubled between 2011 and 2012, placing the Irish market 1 per cent behind the USA and the UK, where 44 per cent of the same retailers deliver goods. In the past, the lack of a postcode system may have impeded delivery of goods bought online; however, retailers like Debenhams and Marks and Spencer have overcome this and use advanced logistics networks with the UK and Europe to improve their platform. Only 40 per cent of the global retailers delivering goods to Ireland had a store in the Irish market, and with prime rents on the high streets and in key shopping centres throughout Ireland at a much more competitive level, there is real potential for some retailers who had tested the Irish market online to establish a physical presence here.[25] However, some of the established players in the Irish retail market have announced plans to close stores in a bid to increase online sales (see Management Focus 3.5).

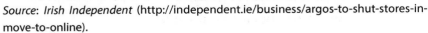

Management Focus 3.5 Argos goes online

Retailer Argos is to get a digital overhaul that will see its catalogue take a back seat and at least 75 stores closed or relocated over the next five years. Parent company Home Retail Group said it would reduce the circulation of the traditional catalogue, launched in 1973, as it refocuses the chain as a digital-led online sales retailer.

Source: Irish Independent (http://independent.ie/business/argos-to-shut-stores-in-move-to-online).

The top 10 most visited sites in Ireland are listed in Table 3.1.

TABLE 3.1 THE TOP 10 MOST VISITED WEBSITES IN IRELAND

Rank	Website	Comments
1 Google	www.google.ie	Irish version of Google's search engine, giving preference to Irish search results
2 Google	www.google.com	International version of Google
3 Facebook	www.facebook.com	Social media giant
4 YouTube	www.youtube.com	Video upload website. Owned by Google, meaning that three out of the top four most popular websites in Ireland are Google properties
5 Wikipedia	www.wikipedia.org	The world's most popular encyclopaedia
6 Yahoo!	www.yahoo.com	Internet portal and service provider offering search results, news, email, etc.
7 LinkedIn	www.linkedin.com	Business networking community website
8 Windows Live	www.live.com	Email service from Microsoft
9 Twitter	www.twitter.com	Popular social networking website
10 Allied Irish Bank	www.aib.ie	One of Ireland's leading banks. Offers online banking for business and personal customers

Source: NuaSoft (www.nua.ie/surveys/).

It's interesting to note that many of the Top 10 sites visited involve search engines or information exchange. Further illustrating this point, the traditional media sector in Ireland has been strongly affected by the migration to online content, as outlined in Management Focus 3.6.

Management Focus 3.6 The new online media market

One of the biggest issues for newspapers is that news is migrating online.
- Independent News and Media has launched a number of websites in Ireland to build on local content (LoadzaJobs.ie, LoadzaCars.ie, YourLocal.ie and TheMeetingPoint.ie) and has also launched a number of apps and an e-paper for the iPad tablet.
- The *Irish Times* spent €3 million on a new website in 2008 and has launched a paper and iPhone app.
- The *Limerick Post* has worked hard to ensure that its online presence can increase circulation and provide increased value to customers with its iPhone app, which has been downloaded more than 5,000 times.

The real challenge for all newspapers is to produce a revenue stream from online advertising in the same way that print has been leveraged.
Source: *Business and Finance* (www.businessandfinance.ie.bf/2011/4/intsfeatsapril2011/mediadrowning inonlineslipstream).

As a result of all of these changes, the technological context is becoming increasingly complex and organisations need to keep up to date with developments, and as the pace of technological change increases, they need to be aware of the leading role of technology. In the current business environment organisations must incorporate technology into their strategies to ensure survival. This is especially important for organisations involved in technological industries, but it also has implications for all organisations in relation to production and sales techniques and communications.

3.3.4 The socio-cultural context

The socio-cultural context is concerned with demographics, and with the attitudes and behaviour of the members of society. Demographics is concerned with identifying the characteristics of the people making up the social units of society. Demographic groups include work groups, organisations, countries, markets and societies, and can be measured in terms of age, gender, family size, education and occupation. These are the measures that are normally used in a population census.

Demographics impact on the business environment in two important ways: through the workforce employed by organisations and the consumers who purchase final goods and services. Organisations must be aware of the workforce demographics when formulating plans for the recruitment, selection, training and motivation of staff. The shortage of skilled labour in some industrial sectors means that the labour market is a seller's market, and as a result, organisations need to focus very clearly on staffing requirements and how to satisfy demand.

Consumer demands are largely a function of the demographics of a society. Larger numbers of lone-parent and dual-income families with children have led to the establishment of crèche facilities, and disposable nappies and ready-made baby foods are commonplace. Demographics also affects demand for services such as radio stations like 98FM and FM104, which specifically cater for the musical tastes of the large proportion of the population who grew up in the 1960s and 1970s. During the Celtic Tiger years Ireland witnessed a large flow of immigrants, largely from the EU accession states but also from countries in Africa. This led to an increase in demand for 'ethnic' foods and to more shops catering to this demand. Supermarkets also responded, and many now stock these foods. All these changes have been driven by shifting demographic patterns. Therefore, demographics affect human resource policies and the nature of the products and services available.

Developments in the wider social environment that affect people's attitudes and behaviour are also critically important for organisations. As with demographics, developments in the social environment have implications for organisations in two main areas: the attitudes and behaviour of the workforce; and the attitudes and behaviour of consumers. In relation to the workforce, the major social change has been the emergence over the last two decades of a large number of mothers working outside the home. This has meant that organisations have had to introduce supportive policies regarding maternal and paternal leave, flexible working hours and childcare. In 1994, for example, paternal leave became compulsory in Sweden for working fathers. In Ireland, additional unpaid parental leave is now available for new parents.

Social changes in relation to consumer demand have been equally important. Among the main developments has been the emergence of a more environmentally aware and health-conscious consumer. This has led to the development of whole new industry sectors such as organic foods and health food stores such as Holland and Barrett and to the emergence of locally based farmers' markets. In 2008 the sale of organic foods in Ireland was worth €104 million, marking an 82 per cent rise since 2006.[26] Customers are more vocal in their demands for information about the nutritional content of food and drink products: in the USA and Australia it is a legal requirement that all restaurants provide the calorie content of food; nutritional details are listed on most of the items purchased in an average weekly shop; and low-fat and fat-free versions of many products have become available. Organisations have also been forced to become more environmentally aware by using recyclable materials, particularly for packaging.

The cultural element of the socio-cultural context is most significant when a firm expands internationally and has to deal with a very different set of cultural norms. This has implications for individuals both as customers and as employees. Understanding cultural difference is critically important for international business. Culture refers to the values and beliefs that are held by groups of individuals and that largely determine behavioural norms. A country can have a broadly common set of cultural values; but even within one country (for example Belgium) there are groups with very different cultural backgrounds.

One of the earliest attempts at classifying cultural differences between countries was undertaken by Geert Hofstede, who studied over 100,000 IBM employees worldwide.[27] Based on his initial findings, and further studies,[28] he identified five underlying cultural dimensions.

1. **Power distance (PD):** the extent to which hierarchical differences are accepted in society. Cultures with a high PD score display a strong deference to authority. In a work context, countries with a high PD score have tall hierarchies, high centralisation, more supervisory staff and larger wage differentials.

2. **Uncertainty avoidance (UA):** the extent to which uncertainty and ambiguity are tolerated. Countries with a high score try to avoid uncertainty by standardising behaviour and rules. In contrast, those with a lower score display less ritualistic behaviour and are more likely to take risks. This is probably the most critical dimension for foreign direct investment (FDI) because of its implication for risk taking. MNCs from cultures high in UA are more likely to take an incremental approach to internationalisation.

3. **Individualism (IND):** the extent to which the self or group constitutes the centre point of identification for the person. High collectivism means that the pursuit is conducted within acceptable group frameworks with group norms guiding individual behaviour with group harmony. High scores in collectivism mean that the organisation treats employees like family members and is more likely to adopt a paternalistic approach to work. The USA had the highest score on individualism.

4. **Masculinity (MAS):** the extent to which traditional 'masculine' values such as aggression and assertiveness are emphasised, as opposed to nurturing and concern for others, which are more traditionally associated with females. Organisations from cultures high in masculinity typically reward competition and aggressive behaviours more than 'softer', more intuitive skills.

5. **Long-term orientation (LTO):** cultural attitudes to time/the future. A high LTO score means a pragmatic, future-oriented perspective. Cultures high in LTO are likely to adopt a longer planning horizon, with individuals ready to delay gratification. Organisations high on LTO are more willing to defer on investment for a long time.

A summary of Hofstede's classification and some country comparisons are shown in Figure 3.10, and Hofstede's score for Ireland, along with the comparator scores for the BRICs, are presented in Figure 3.11.

FIGURE 3.10 HOFSTEDE'S FIVE DIMENSIONS OF NATIONAL CULTURE

High Power Distance	Low Power Distance
Mexico, Brazil	Sweden, Norway
High Uncertainty Avoidance	Low Uncertainty Avoidance
Greece, Japan	USA, UK
Individualistic	Collectivist
USA, Australia	China, Mexico
High Masculinity	Low Masculinity
Italy, Japan	Sweden, Denmark
High Long-term Orientation	Low Long-term Orientation
China, Taiwan	USA, Germany

FIGURE 3.11 HOFSTEDE'S SCORES FOR IRELAND, AND COMPARATOR SCORES FOR THE BRIC COUNTRIES

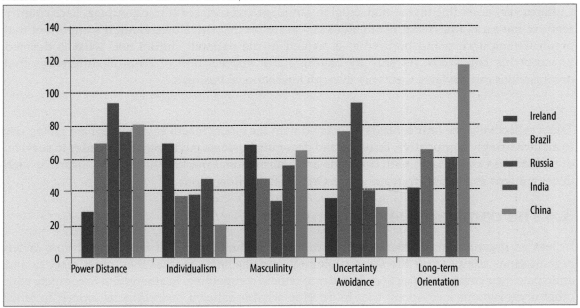

Source: Hofstede Centre, 'National Culture: Ireland' (http://geert-hofstede.com/ireland.html).

How does Ireland score on Hofstede's cultural comparisons?

- **Power distance:** Ireland scores lower on PD than the other countries. In Irish organisations, hierarchy is established for convenience, superiors are always accessible and managers rely on individual employees and teams for their expertise. Both managers and employees expect to be consulted and information is shared frequently. At the same time, communication is informal, direct and participative.

- **Individualism:** Ireland scores high on individualism with a score of 70. In the business world, employees are expected to be self-reliant and to display initiative. Hiring and promotion decisions are based on merit or evidence of what one has done or can do.

- **Masculinity:** with a score of 68, Ireland is a masculine society that emphasises success. Behaviour in school, work and play are based on the shared values that people should 'strive to be the best they can be' and that 'the winner takes all'. The Irish are proud of their successes and achievements in life, and this offers a basis for hiring and promotion decisions in the workplace. Conflicts are resolved at the individual level and the goal is to win.

- **Uncertainty avoidance:** at 35 Ireland has a low score on uncertainty avoidance. Ideas are important, and being imaginative is appreciated. Irish businesses embrace creativity and are always looking for new ways to approach problems.

- **Long-term orientation:** a score of 43 suggests that Ireland is a short term-oriented society that has a great respect for history and tradition as well as a focus on quick results in the future. Planning horizons tend to be short and business particularly is very focused on short-term quarterly goals and quick results. The notion of giving up something today for the promise of something bigger in the future is not widely held.

Source: Hofstede Centre, 'National Culture: Ireland' (http://geert-hofstede.com/ireland.html).

Cultures vary according to tradition, religion, language and social or ethnic grouping. Each country tends to have a unique mixture of values and attitudes that drive behaviour. It's important that organisations understand both what is valued in the national culture and what is deemed unacceptable behaviour. Its only by having a full appreciation of cultural differences that organisations can navigate their way through international business.

Taken collectively, the four contexts associated with the global macro environment are giving rise to an increasingly competitive, complex and changing business environment. In order to survive, organisations operating in both domestic and international markets need to be aware of such developments and adopt strategies that reflect these considerations.

3.4 The competitive environment

Unless an organisation is operating in a monopoly situation, it will face competition. When organisations compete for the same customers and the same market they must react to and anticipate their competitors' actions in order to remain competitive. In attempting to compete with other organisations a company tries to develop what is called a *competitive advantage*. In other words, it must find some form of advantage over its rivals. Michael Porter explains the concept of competitive advantage thus:

> Competitive advantage grows fundamentally out of the value a firm is able to create for its buyers that exceeds the firm's cost of creating it. Value is what buyers are willing to pay, and superior value stems from offering lower prices than competitors for equivalent benefits or providing unique benefits that more than offset a higher price.[29]

Therefore, to achieve competitive advantage, an organisation must either provide equal product value but operate more efficiently than rivals, which will enable it to charge a lower cost – this is called *cost leadership* (e.g. Ryanair, Lidl and Aldi) – or operate in a unique manner that creates greater product value, which in turn commands a premium price – this is *differentiation* (e.g. Emirates, Marks & Spencer). Organisations that are unable to develop competitive advantage through either cost leadership or differentiation will find that the law of the marketplace dictates that they will either have to change their product line or risk going out of business.

In order to compete effectively in a product market and develop a sustainable competitive advantage, an organisation clearly has to analyse its competitive environment. The most widely used technique for analysing the competitive environment was developed by Michael Porter in his famous books *Competitive Strategy: Techniques for Analysing Industries and Competitors* (1980) and *Competitive Advantage: Creating and Sustaining Superior Performance* (1985). Porter, a professor at Harvard Business School, has had a phenomenal impact on management thinking and practice in the past three decades. Porter believes that the most important thing for an organisation to consider when formulating strategy is how to deal with the competition, and he argues that five forces shape the degree of market competition operating within an organisation's competitive environment:

1. the degree of rivalry among existing competitors
2. the threat of substitute products and services
3. the threat of new entrants into the market
4. the bargaining power of suppliers
5. the bargaining power of buyers / customers.

The combined power of these five forces determines the profit potential of an industry by shaping the price an organisation can charge and the costs and investment required to compete. Figure 3.12 illustrates Porter's five forces model for competitive analysis.

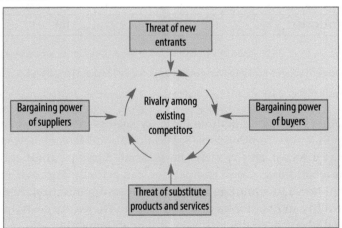

FIGURE 3.12 THE FIVE COMPETITIVE FORCES THAT DETERMINE INDUSTRY PROFITABILITY

Source: Porter, M. (1985) *Competitive Advantage: Creating and Sustaining Superior Performance*. New York: Free Press.

3.4.1 Rivalry among existing firms

Organisations in direct competition with each other use tactics such as price competition, advertising campaigns, new product launches and better customer service or warranties to gain an advantage over rivals. Rivalry occurs because at least one competitor comes under pressure or feels that there is an opportunity to gain market share. Competition and rivalry are most intense when there are many direct competitors (domestic or international) and when the industry is a slow-growth industry. New high-growth industries offer organisations the opportunity to make good profits. However, as an industry matures the excess profits attract new entrants, thereby making the industry more competitive. As the industry reaches maturity the intense competition causes an industry shakeout, whereby weaker companies are eliminated and the stronger ones survive.

In industries characterised by a high degree of rivalry, market actions by one competitor provoke countermoves by others. In Ireland, an example of a highly competitive industry is the supermarket sector, in which the main players are engaged in intense rivalry. Price wars have been a constant feature of this industry sector, with each competitor attempting to match price reductions by their rivals. Table 3.2 shows the main competitors in the sector. Tesco, Dunnes and Supervalu together control a little over 70 per cent of the market, with Aldi and Lidl controlling over a further 11 per cent.

TABLE 3.2 THE IRISH SUPERMARKET SECTOR: THE MAIN PLAYERS

Name	Market Share January 2012 (%)	Market Share January 2013 (%)
Tesco	28.1	27.6
Dunnes Stores	23.4	24.3
Supervalu	20.0	19.8
Lidl	5.7	5.7
Aldi	4.6	5.9
Superquinn	5.6	5.3
Other outlets*	12.6	11.4

*Other outlets include M&S, Boots, Spar, Centra, greengrocers, butchers and cross-border shops.

Source: 'Promotions Help Dunnes Stores Boost its Market Share by 4.6 per cent', *Irish Independent* Business section, 5 February 2013, 29.

Other highly competitive industry sectors include mobile phones (Apple, Samsung and Nokia), mobile service providers (3, Vodafone and Meteor), newspapers and magazines, and cars.

However, rivalry – and its associated intense competition – should not necessarily be viewed as a bad thing. Good competition can actually improve an organisation's performance because it can serve to stimulate and motivate an organisation. For example, an organisation faced with a healthy competitor has a strong impetus to reduce costs, improve the quality of goods and services and keep pace with technological developments.

3.4.2 The threat of substitutes

Organisations compete not only with other organisations providing similar products and services but also with those that produce *substitute* products and services. For example, shipping companies like Irish Ferries and Stena Line compete directly with each other and also with organisations involved in other forms of transport, such as airlines.

The availability of substitutes can severely limit an industry's potential, unless organisations become involved in aggressive marketing campaigns and continue to improve product quality. For example, butter manufacturers such as Kerrygold and Mitchelstown have to compete directly with substitute products such as alternative dairy spreads and Flora. Since their introduction the market share of dairy spreads has increased significantly at the expense of butter. In order to compete more effectively the butter manufacturers have run successful advertising campaigns to promote the sale of butter.

Management Focus 3.7 Nintendo squeezed by substitutes

The creator of the famous Super Mario franchise has dominated the video games industry for years with its DS handheld devices and its Wii home console. However, in 2011 the Japanese company's profits took a tumble. Poor sales of the much-awaited Nintendo 3DS led to price reductions and sales projections for the ageing Wii console were cut. The main problem for Nintendo in the handheld devices market is the availability of new substitute products in the form of smartphones (iPhone/Samsung) and tablets, both of which feature games.

Source: Sky News (2012) [online] http://news.sky.com/story/965259/nintendo-reports-loss-after-3ds-price-slash.

3.4.3 The threat of new entrants

When new entrants enter an industry segment they compete directly with existing organisations. If many factors prevent new companies from entering the industry the threat to established organisations is less serious. However, if there are few barriers to entry, the threat of new entrants can become significant.

The government can limit or prevent new entrants from entering a particular industry. This is most notable in the airline industry. However, deregulation has significantly changed this. Capital requirements for certain industries can be so high that organisations will be unable to raise sufficient capital to finance set-up costs. Airlines typically experience high start-up costs, although recent trends toward leasing and franchising are making this less of a problem. Another barrier to entry is brand identification, which means that new organisations would have to spend a considerable amount of money on advertising to develop customer loyalty. For example, because the brand name Apple is synonymous with technological innovation and impeccable design, Apple defied the sceptics who predicted that competition would erode the iPod's dominant market position.[30] Cost advantages also act as a barrier to entry: existing organisations may have favourable locations or existing assets that give them a cost advantage over newer rivals. Finally, distribution channels act as a barrier to entry for new entrants in getting their products and services to customers. For example, existing supermarket products are allocated a certain shelf space and position and if a new entrant is to make headway it will have to undertake promotions, price cuts and intensive selling to displace existing products.

If an organisation can overcome the barriers to entry and break into a market, the result is normally an increase in the supply of the product, with the new entrant using considerable resources to gain market share. As a result, market prices usually fall and this has a negative impact on the profitability of all organisations, serving to further increase competition.

3.4.4 The bargaining power of suppliers

In line with systems theory, organisations obtain inputs from the external environment and convert these into products and services to be sold. Suppliers provide the sources of raw materials, for example schools and universities (people), banks and other lending agencies (capital) and producers, wholesalers and distributors (inputs required for the manufacturing process). Therefore, organisations are extremely dependent on the suppliers of raw materials, who form an integral part of the competitive environment. Choosing suppliers is a critically important decision for any organisation. Favourable supplier relations can lead to improved quality, better shipping arrangements, improved manufacturing time, early warning of price changes and information about developments in the marketplace.

As discussed earlier, e-business has changed relationships within the supply chain as companies can now purchase online, thereby saving time and money. The advent of e-business also facilitates disintermediation – the elimination of intermediaries in the value chain. This has serious consequences for suppliers in the middle of the value chain, who face the prospect of losing business.

Individual sectors are also experiencing change. In the retail sector worldwide there is a trend toward increasing the control of retailers over the supply chain through centralised distribution. Suppliers face the challenge of forming links with other suppliers from different sectors to provide a value-added package to retailers and to consider the potential for international cross-group sales. Suppliers are critically important to the organisation because of the resources they supply. Suppliers can exert power on an organisation by threatening to raise prices or to reduce product quality. In relation to price increases, if the organisation is unable to recover the increased costs through price increases on its own products, its long-term profitability will suffer, making it all the more difficult to compete.

An organisation is at an extreme disadvantage if it is over-dependent on one supplier. In contrast, the supplier is in a powerful situation if the organisation has few sources of supply or if the supplier has many other customers. It is also very powerful if it has built up switching costs – these are fixed costs that organisations face if they change supplier. For example, if a company is used to purchasing and operating a particular brand of computer, changing to another type may involve switching costs if the existing software packages also have to be changed.

However, organisations can be in a strong position if they are the dominant customer for a supplier. In situations like this the organisation can demand credit arrangements and that the supplier goes through inspection and education processes to ensure that the supplies are of acceptable quality. Some suppliers may find themselves in a weak position if there are many suppliers in the market, all seeking market share. The market concentration in the supermarket sector leads to decreased bargaining power on the part of small local suppliers.

The emergence of e-business has given some companies the opportunity to seriously weaken the bargaining power of their suppliers. By moving their purchasing operations online, some of the larger car companies in the USA are reported to have saved thousands of dollars on the cost of each car they produce. E-business also allows companies to compare prices on alternative suppliers and streamline stock control processes.

3.4.5 The bargaining power of buyers

Customers are the people who buy the product or service produced by the organisation and consequently are a critically important element of the competitive environment. Final customers are those who purchase a final product such as a car or a meal. Intermediate customers buy wholesale products and then sell to a final customer, for example a clothes wholesaler who buys from the manufacturer and sells to specific clothes outlets. However, the trend toward disintermediation mentioned above, particularly in the clothing sector, will eliminate the layers of potential customers. The internet, which enhances price transparency, is further contributing to this development.

In competitive markets, organisations realise that giving the customer a top-quality service is critically important if the organisation is to get repeat trade. Providing a quality customer service includes filling and delivering the order speedily, being willing to meet emergency requests, delivering products in good condition, being willing to rectify faults quickly and offering a repair and/or spare parts service. In order to develop customer loyalty the organisation needs to be fully aware of who the customers are and what products and services they need.

Many organisations are turning to customer groups themselves to find answers. A key example of an Irish organisation with a strong customer focus is Superquinn. In striving to improve the quality of the product and service, customer groups are frequently interviewed and asked for their suggestions. Buyers or customers are extremely important for an organisation's success because without a market organisations go out of business. Customers can put pressure on organisations by demanding lower prices, higher quality or additional services. Customers can also play off competitors against one another. For example, when purchasing durable goods of a high cost (a car, for example), a buyer can collect different offers and negotiate for the best possible deal.

Organisations have problems if they depend on a few strong customers. Customers are powerful if they make large purchases of the product either in monetary or volume terms, or if they can easily find alternatives. When the customer is powerful s/he can exert pressure on an organisation and is more likely to be able to negotiate a better deal than a minor customer. When there are many customers who purchase small amounts of the product, the organisation has strong bargaining power. In the mobile phone industry, for example, customers exert little power over the price and in this respect have little bargaining power over companies like Vodafone, 3 or Meteor.

3.4.6 Identifying favourable and unfavourable business environments

Analysing the five environmental factors described above enables an organisation to identify its competitive strengths and weaknesses in relation to the external environment and to understand the nature of the competitive environment in which it is located. A competitive analysis helps to guide strategic decisions, such as whether to acquire a company in another industry or whether to divest a particular business interest. It also facilitates an evaluation of the potential for different business ventures by assessing their competitive environment.

Based on this analysis, it is possible to identify favourable and unfavourable competitive business environments that may confront organisations. Figure 3.13 outlines the characteristic features of each type of environment. It should be noted that an organisation's competitive environment will often contain elements of both favourable and unfavourable environments and consequently the organisation will have to make sound decisions on future direction. However, the classification serves as a useful guideline.

FIGURE 3.13 FAVOURABLE AND UNFAVOURABLE COMPETITIVE ENVIRONMENTS

Factor	Favourable	Unfavourable
1 Competitors	Few; high-growth industry	Many; low-growth industry
2 Threat of entrants	Low threat, many barriers	High threat, few barriers
3 Substitutes	Few	Many
4 Power of suppliers	Many, low bargaining power	Few, high bargaining power
5 Power of customers	Many, low bargaining power	Few, high bargaining power

Source: Porter, M. (1985) *Competitive Advantage: Creating and Sustaining Superior Performance*. New York: Free Press.

Porter concludes that when formulating strategies based on competitive analysis, organisations should consider moving into industries with limited competition and many customers and suppliers. Organisations should similarly avoid industries in more difficult or unfavourable competitive environments.

3.5 Entering international markets

In meeting the opportunities and threats that a PEST and/or a competitive analysis should identify, an organisation can choose to expand internationally. International expansion is a far more complex task than simply replicating an existing national strategy and enlarging its existing structure. As we have seen above, a host of factors, such as the political/legal and cultural environments, become relevant. The decision to expand abroad can be either proactive or reactive. A proactive decision tends to be future-directed and occurs when an organisation identifies an opportunity for expansion and making a profit. In a reactive situation the organisation is responding to deterioration in its competitive position, possibly from declining sales and market saturation. When considering whether to expand abroad the organisation is typically faced with three major decisions, as shown in Figure 3.14.

The first big area for decision concerns the location of any proposed expansion. Different locations have different business environments and vary in their receptiveness to expansion by overseas firms. Industrial policies and incentives offered to firms will also differ. A PEST analysis will provide the firm with a basis from which further information can be gathered and decisions made. More detailed analyses of the potential host environment, such as market conditions and production potential, may also require consideration. Many firms have expanded abroad to meet

FIGURE 3.14 KEY DECISIONS FOR FIRMS BEFORE INTERNATIONALISING

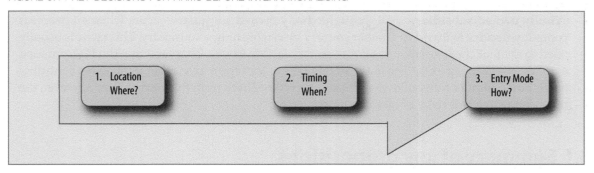

an increased market demand. The growth of the middle classes, particularly in the BRIC economies, has been viewed as a huge market opportunity by many firms, evidenced for example by B&Q's decision to enter the Chinese market.

Another key decision centres on the timing of any move in relation to overseas competitors. 'Early mover advantages' against later entrants include developing market share and power, and greater pre-emptive opportunities. However, early movers are also exposed to more environmental uncertainty and more risks associated with early market penetration.

The final decision area concerns how to enter the market. There are a variety of different entry modes open to organisation and much will depend on costs, risk, expected returns, control and the level of commitment the organisation is willing to invest.

1 **Exporting.** This is the most basic type of international business. Direct exporting involves producing a product/service in a domestic market and then selling it to another country. It requires in-house expertise to develop contacts, undertake market research, and prepare documentation. Indirect exporting allows the exporting function to be outsourced to intermediaries who prepare the export documentation, take responsibility for the physical distribution of goods and set up sales and distribution channels in the foreign market. As a first step to international business this strategy offers small cash outlay, low risk, gradual exposure and good use of existing facilities. On the negative side, it can incur high transportation costs, and tariffs and duties may be imposed.

2 **Franchising/licensing.** Franchising is another strategy often pursued and involves getting another organisation in an overseas country to produce the product/service under a special arrangement. This effectively allows another organisation to use the original organisation's brand name, trademark and technology. The franchisee pays a fee for this arrangement. Licensing involves an outsourcing arrangement where the production of goods subject to patent, brand or other intellectual property rights is contracted out to another firm under terms and conditions agreed with the owner. It is a quick and easy way to enter a market, but there can be problems with technology spillover.

3 **Joint ventures/alliances.** Strategic alliances or joint ventures have become increasingly popular for international business. A strategic alliance is an agreement between two or more organisations to co-operate to achieve specific goals in order to prosper. No equity is involved in this type of arrangement. Strategic alliances are very common in the airline industry, the three largest being Oneworld, Skyteam and Star Alliance. Joint ventures, on the other hand,

involve joint ownership of a project, and both partners share the costs and rewards. This type of shared ownership limits overall control held by any one party.

4 **Wholly owned subsidiary.** FDI through wholly owned subsidiary occurs when an overseas company decides to invest in another country by establishing a subsidiary. This tactic is usually used to avail of cheaper labour and raw materials. (We saw in Chapter 2 that the IDA pursued a policy of attracting FDI.) The main advantages of this approach is that it increases control of assets and operations and allows quick and direct feedback from the market. It is, however, the most expensive and risky of all the options.

3.6 Summary of key propositions

- All organisations operate in an external global business environment, which is a critically important area to consider. The external environment has two main components: a macro environment and a competitive environment.
- Globalisation refers to the increasing and deepening interactions and connections between individuals, groups and organisations across the world. The world is undergoing changes in the global economic order, which are as significant for the world economy and international relations as the end of the Cold War in the mid-1980s.
- Globalisation and economic integration is accelerating, propelled by growing trade and capital flows, deepening financial markets, falling transportation costs, and the revolution in ICT. Production is more globalised than markets.
- Global competition is further shaped by the existence of regional trading blocs or alliances, which are largely driven by geographical location. The main trading blocks and regional trading agreements are the enlarged EU, NAFTA, Mercosur and ASEAN.
- The term 'BRICs' refers to the four large emerging economies of Brazil, Russia, India and China. The BRIC countries have experienced high growth rates, leading to a shift in the balance of global economic power away from the more established G7 economies of the UK, USA, Japan, Italy, France, Canada and Germany.
- The macro global environment is made up of factors that affect all organisations and in this sense is very broad. Factors included are the political–legal, economic, technological and socio-cultural contexts. All of these factors are forcing change for organisations by increasing competitiveness and complexity.
- The competitive environment is the immediate environment facing the organisation.
- Factors included in the competitive environment are competitors, suppliers, customers, new entrants and substitutes.
- As the current business environment has become increasingly competitive, organisations need to undertake a competitive analysis of their industry to work out how they can achieve a competitive advantage.
- Favourable competitive environments are high-growth industries that have few competitors, high barriers to entry, few substitute products and services and suppliers and customers with little power over the organisation.

- Unfavourable competitive environments are low-growth industries that have many competitors, few barriers to entry, many substitute products and services, and customers and suppliers with strong power over the organisation.
- When expanding internationally, organisations need to decide the location, timing and mode of entry. The alternatives vary depending on the level of control, risk and costs.

Discussion Questions

1   What do you understand by the term 'global business environment' and why is it important for organisations to consider it?
2   Explain the term 'globalisation' and how globalisation has evolved.
3   How important are regional trading alliances for promoting international trade?
4   Explain the growth of the BRIC economies and evaluate their future prospects.
5   Explain the difference between the macro and the competitive environments.
6   Select a company that you are familiar with and undertake a PEST analysis.
7   Why are competitors so important for organisations to consider?
8   Apply Porter's five forces model of competitive analysis to any Irish organisation/industry.
9   Consider the soft drinks market in Ireland. Evaluate whether the current competitive environment is favourable or unfavourable.
10 You are considering setting up your own pizza restaurant in your home town. Undertake a competitive analysis of the industry in the locality and examine whether you would establish a business there or not, based on your analysis.
11 Overall, how would you describe the external business environment affecting Irish organisations operating domestically or internationally?
12 How can organisations approach internationalisation?

Concluding Case: The Irish airline industry – the Dublin–London route

The global airline industry consists of 1,629 airlines operating more than 27,271 commercial aircraft to over 3,733 airports. In 2010 2.7 billion passengers travelled by air, generating revenues in excess of $547 billion (International Air Transport Association (IATA)). Strategically the airline industry has an important global role to play: it is the bedrock of the leisure and tourism industry; the conduct of business depends on the ability to travel; and it generates one in 15 jobs globally and drives 12 per cent of the global economy. Domestic and international business depends on air travel.

Unlike other industry sectors, it has experienced unprecedented and sustained levels of growth. Exceptions to this include the 1986 Libyan crisis, the two Gulf Wars, 9/11 and the most recent recession, which saw demand fall to -2 per cent. In the 1990s the industry grew by 7–8 per cent which, while lower than the 1960s' 14 per cent rate, was still high by industry standards. Current predictions are that the industry will continue to grow by 5 per cent per annum (IATA 2012).

Yet despite such growth, profitability has remained marginal and represents one of the apparent contradictions in the industry. The global airline industry reported a $2.8 billion loss in 2009 as demand for air travel plummeted in the wake of the financial crisis. Profitability, like growth, is highly cyclical in the airline industry, due partly to instabilities in the industry. Demand for the product is derived and, in this sense, dependent on, demand for related activities (e.g. holidays and business); it is instantly perishable, and demand is seasonal in nature. There are high fixed costs relative to variable costs, so volume is crucial. The industry is also susceptible to environmental influences. Increased global terrorism in the wake of 9/11, wars, natural disasters (volcanic ash), and diseases (avian flu, SARS and foot and mouth) have all impacted on demand for air travel. Competition from other modes of transport is an ever-present threat to short-haul operations.

Competition in the airline industry has been transformed since the mid-1990s, leading to the emergence of a variety of new entrants. As a result, restrictions on the provision of low fares have been removed, and legislation has helped the proliferation of new-entrant, low-cost carriers (LCCs), and fuelled competition. The advances made by Ryanair, Air Berlin and easyJet (EU), JetBlue and Spirit (USA) have highlighted the emerging role for a no-frills type of service. Globally LCCs account for between 22 per cent (OAG) and 24 per cent (IATA) of airline traffic. The biggest growth has come from Europe where the market share has grown from 9 per cent to 39 per cent in the last decade.

The Irish airline industry has also enjoyed strong growth over the same period. The UK market from Dublin airport remains the single biggest market, accounting for 7.6 million passengers in 2009. The London route is the most important route, with 19 per cent of all passengers departing from Dublin (see Figure 3.15). Heathrow remains the most important onward connecting airport for long-haul travel.

FIGURE 3.15 PASSENGER TRAFFIC FROM DUBLIN AIRPORT BY REGION (2009)

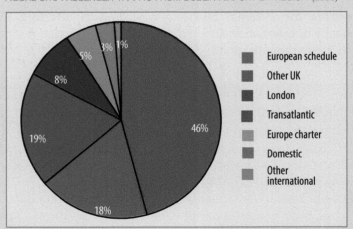

Source: Dublin Airport Authority (DAA)

The Dublin–London route is currently Europe's busiest international city pair. In 1991, 1.7 million passengers travelled between Dublin and London; in 2011 the figure was 3.7 million. The market is one of the most competitive in Europe and one of the most keenly contested. The Dublin–London route is served directly by four competitors: Aer Lingus; Ryanair; British Airways (BA); and Air France/Cityjet.

BA has joined the market once again after a 20-year absence; and following the acquisition of bmi by International Airline Group (IAG), BA now operates eight return flights per day, offering 2,000 seats per week. Commenting on the announcement, Simon Daly, British Airways' Sales Manager Ireland, said:

> I am delighted to see the British Airways colours back in Dublin after an absence of 20 years. We appreciate the importance of air links to London and are pleased to announce that less than two months after taking over this route, we are now able to respond to customer demand and increase capacity. Our improved schedule also sees us adding a new early morning departure

time from Dublin which will mean that passengers will be able to extend their working day should they need to. In addition, it offers both business and leisure passengers greater choice in terms of connections to our extensive global network at London Heathrow, bringing destinations on the world map closer to Ireland, benefiting Irish businesses, tourism and Ireland as a whole.

All of these airlines are fiercely competitive in the battle to achieve market share on the key Dublin–London route. The airports served by each of the main competitive rivals are shown in Table 3.3.

TABLE 3.3 AIRPORTS SERVED BY COMPETITIVE RIVALS ON THE DUBLIN–LONDON ROUTE

Airline	Heathrow	Gatwick	Stansted	City	Luton
Aer Lingus	X	X			
Ryanair		X	X		X
Air France/Cityjet				X	
BA	X				

The intense competition and rivalry is mainly caused by the fact that airlines have high fixed costs for wages, fuel and insurance and this puts pressure on them to fill capacity on their flights. The main competitive strategies used by the airlines are price competition and product differentiation. All the airlines engage in price competition, offering many different types of fare on the Dublin–London route. Traditionally, Ryanair had concentrated on the leisure passenger and the other main rivals, most notably Aer Lingus and BA, had targeted the business traveller. However, all airlines are currently engaged in fierce price competition across the various routes. Ryanair pursues a no-frills type of service, offering lowest fares, a single fleet, online sales and ancillary revenues (charging for food on board), use of secondary airports and relentless cost reductions. The use of a cost-leadership strategy by Ryanair is evident in its low-fare offers shown in Table 3.4.

TABLE 3.4 SELECTED LOW-FARE OFFERS FROM LONDON TO DUBLIN (ONE WAY, TAXES INCLUDED)*

Airline	Heathrow	Gatwick	Stansted	City	Luton
Aer Lingus	€29.99	€29.99			
Ryanair		€19	€14.99		€14.99
Air France/Cityjet	·			€54	
BA	€55				

*Mid-week fare (Tuesday) excluding holiday periods and sporting events.</FN>

While Ryanair tends to be the cost leader, it has increased its range and extent of fees and charges over the years. Passengers are charged for web check-in, priority boarding, seat assignment and checked baggage. Aer Lingus has followed this lead and now charges for baggage and reserved seating; but it does not charge extra for web check-in and has a cheaper prepaid seat assignment option of €5 available. All passengers travelling with Aer Lingus will be assigned seats at the airport for no extra charge.

In recent years Aer Lingus has lowered fares but the airline's strategy remains a differentiated one, focusing on the idea of being a 'value carrier, offering additional services to the customer'. One way of differentiating itself has been the focus on connectivity and airline partnerships, allowing customers to book onward journeys with other airlines, which facilitates ease of travel for the customer. Flight frequency is another differentiating factor: for example, Aer Lingus has tried to differentiate its product by having regular hourly flights from Dublin to Heathrow, which has excellent connections and a fast rail network to the City of London. Aer Lingus also has a frequent flyer programme, the Gold Circle Club, which is designed to build up customer loyalty and rewards miles flown with frequent flyer points. Points can also be earned and redeemed with Aer Lingus partner airlines, such as JetBlue in the USA, and BA, Qantas and Cathay Pacific. With airlines engaging in both price competition and product/service differentiation strategies, competition between rivals is intense in this market. Aer Lingus now provides passengers with the option of adding on elements to their package. For example, for €25 customers can access the Gold Circle Lounge in Terminal 2 at Dublin Airport. They can also pre-pay and order meals online. Aer Lingus offers three fare classifications on the Dublin –London route (Table 3.5).

TABLE 3.5 AER LINGUS FARES, DUBLIN–LONDON

	Low	Plus	Flex
Time/date change	€40 + fare difference	€40 + fare difference	None
Late check-in fee	Available to purchase	Available to purchase	None
Refundability	No	No	Yes
Advance seat selection	Available to purchase	On selected flights	Yes
Seat assignment at check-in	Yes	Yes	Yes
Cabin bag <10kg	Yes	Yes	Yes
Free check-in	Yes	Yes	Yes
Checked bag <20kg	From €15	1 bag	2 bags
Lounge access	Available to purchase	Available to purchase	Yes
Gold Circle points	On eligible fare classes	Yes	Yes

Source: www.aerlingus.com.

The airlines are also engaged in competition with other modes of transport, including the services offered by road, rail and sea. On the Dublin–London travel route the airlines compete with Irish Ferries and Stena Line. The substitutability of the airline product depends very much on price. When Ryanair and Aer Lingus were engaged in strong price competition in 1986, the demand for sea travel declined significantly. The product offered by the substitute companies has one drawback – the length of time taken by the trip. It takes three hours just to cross the Irish Sea by normal ferry, or 1 hour 50 minutes with a faster sailing. Travelling by air gets the customer to their final destination – rather than either Fishguard or Holyhead, or en route to London – much more quickly. The ferry option is inappropriate for business travellers and is the least preferred choice for leisure travellers. As long as the additional cost of flying can be offset against the time saving, the power of alternative forms of travel is limited. The main advantage that sea travel has is the ability to bring a car. Car rental companies offer good deals on car rentals, which diminishes the advantage. However, increased security provisions, restrictions on baggage size, weight and contents associated with air travel have made it less appealing to some customers.

Increased liberalisation of the Ireland–UK market means that the route is open to the threat of new entrants. However, the barriers to entry into the airline industry are still very high by industry standards. There are a number of significant entry barriers, which would deter new entrants from entering the market.

First, the capital requirements of entry are extremely high and include the costs of acquiring aircraft, maintenance provisions, training crew and booking landing slots at airports. Ryanair has estimated that its start-up costs were in the region of €30 million.

Economies of scale represent another barrier to entry. Economies of scale refers to the advantages attached to large-scale organisation. Examples in the aviation industry include bulk discounts in purchasing fuel, maintenance and catering supplies. If organisations already within the industry exhibit economies of scale it will act as a deterrent to potential new entrants, forcing them to come in at a larger scale or to accept cost disadvantages. The final barrier to entry is brand identity. Organisations with established brand names or high levels of customer loyalty present a huge barrier to a new entrant. In effect, it means that the new entrant will have to invest heavily in advertising and promotion to develop the market. So, while deregulation is encouraging new entrants into the market, the barriers to entry are still extremely high.

Airlines operating the Dublin–London route have five main sources of supply: aircraft leasing companies; fuel suppliers; catering companies; airport management companies; and travel agents. Purchasing an aircraft and its related equipment is one means of acquiring an aircraft; the alternative is leasing. Many airlines now lease aircraft rather than purchasing them outright. There are many specialist companies involved in leasing, and individual airlines also engage in leasing. Overall, there are a large number of suppliers with little power. The power of suppliers of aviation fuel can be extremely high in times of oil shortages. Under normal conditions there is an abundant supply of distributors who do not wield significant power. However, the long-term supply of fuel and oil is becoming scarcer and is likely to increase the power of the oil suppliers. Catering companies are plentiful, offering a wide choice for the airlines. In addition, the switching costs are low.

Airport management companies can possess significant power in determining which airline flies into which airport. For example, slots at Heathrow are in great demand, which increases the power of airport management companies. The final source of supply for an airline is the travel agent, who has traditionally been the intermediary between the airline and the passenger. However, one of the most dramatic changes to this established relationship has been the emergence of online ticket sales. Passengers can now book their flight directly with the airline, thereby eliminating the travel agent's role. This should result in more control by the airline of their reservation systems. Traditional travel agents have been replaced by online variations including Expedia, Travelocity and E-bookers.

The buyers of the airline product tend to make small purchases and are large in number. As a result they do not engage in any form of bargaining on price or quality. The airlines servicing the Dublin–London route do not cater for the charter market, do not deal with much group travel, and therefore would not offer discounts of any nature. Executive travellers, however, have a higher degree of buying power if they have corporate accounts with airlines. Corporate accounts can play the different airlines off against one another in the hope of lowering the price or getting a better deal.

Keep up to date
www.aerlingus.com
www.ryanair.com
www.ba.com
www.airfrance.com

Sources: Aer Lingus (www.aerlingus.com); Ryanair (www.ryanair.com); BA (www.ba.com); Air France (www.airfrance.com); Global Travel Industry News (2012) 'British Airways doubles frequency between Dublin and London Heathrow' [online], available at www.eturbonews.com/30757/british-airways-doubles-frequency-between-dublin-and-london-heat; Hancock, C. (2012) 'BA to Double Dublin–Heathrow Flights', *Irish Times* 16 August, available at http://www.irishtimes.com/business/sectors/transport-and-tourism/ba-to-double-dublin-heathrow-flights-1.537651.

Case Questions
1 Prepare a competitive analysis of the Dublin–London airline industry.
2 Based on the above analysis, advise both Aer Lingus and Ryanair on their competitive positions in the industry.

Notes and References

1   Friedman, T. (2000) *The Lexus and the Olive Tree*. London: Harper Collins.
2   Levitt, T. (1984) 'The Globalisation of Markets', *McKinsey Quarterly*, Summer, 1–20.
3   http://trade.ec.europa.eu/doclib/docs/2006ecttradoc_130376.pdf 2012 [Online] Accessed 23 November 2012.
4   EC, 'Why the European Union is an Essential Trade Partner' [online] http://eeas.europa.eu/delegations/rwanda/documents/press_corner/news/20121003_en.pdf.
5   EU, 'Facts and Figures' [online] http://europa.eu/about-eu/facts-figures/.
6   Ibid.
7   EC, 'Trade Topics: European Competitiveness' [online] http://ec.europa.eu/trade/creating-opportunities/trade-topics/european-competitiveness/. Accessed 21 November 2012.
8   EC (2013), 'The EU's Free Trade Agreements – Where Are We?' [online] http://trade.ec.europa.eu/doclib/docs/2012/november/tradoc_150129.pdf. Accessed 21 November 2012.
9   Office of the United States Trade Representative, 'North American Free Trade Agreement' [online]. Available at www.ustr.gov/trade-agreements/free-trade-agreements/north-american-free-trade-agreement-nafta. Accessed 21 November 2012.

10   BBC News, 'Profile: Mercosur – Common Market of the South' [online]. Available at www.bbc.co.uk/2/hi/americas/5195834.stm. Accessed 21 November 2012.

11   Ibid.

12   US Department of State Fact Sheet 'The US–ASEAN Expanded Economic Engagement (E3) Initiative' [online]. Available at http://iipdigital.usembassy.gov/st/english/texttrans/2012/11/20121119138863.html#ixzz2E0RbJBQZ_2012. Accessed 21 November 2012.

13   ASEAN Fact Sheets [online]. Available at: www.asean.org/resources/fact-sheets. 2012. Accessed 17 November 2012.

14   Ibid.

15   How we Made it in Africa [website], 'Africa's Grand Free Trade Area and What it will Mean for Business' www.howwemadeitinafrica.com/africas-grand-free-trade-area-and-what-it-will-mean-for-business/11172/. Accessed 17 November 12.

16   Global Sherpa [online] www.globalsherpa.org/bric-countries-brics. Accessed 6 December 2012.

17   Lin, M. (2012) 'Bearish BRICs: Have the BRIC Nations Lived up to the Hype?', *Economy Watch*, 4 September [online]. Available at www.economywatch.com/economy-business-and-finance-news/have-the-BRICS-lived-up-to-the-hype.04-09.html.

18   WTO, 'The WTO ... In Brief' [online] www.wto.org/english/thewto_e/whatis_e/inbrief_e/inbr00_e.htm. 2012. Accessed 6 December 2012.

19   Ibid.

20   Henisz, J. and Zelner,B. (2010) 'The Hidden Risks in Emerging Markets', *Harvard Business Review* 88(4), 88–95.

21   O'Brien, M. (2005) 'Self Check-out System Set to Dominate Irish Retail Sector', *Sunday Business Post*, Retail Technology Special Report, 21 August, 18.

22   Kalakota, R. and Andrews, W. (1997) *Electronic Commerce: A Manager's Guide*. Reading, MA: Addison-Wesley.

23   Centre for Retail Research [website] www.retailresearch.org/onlineretailing.php.Accessed 6 December 2012.

24   NuaSoft (2012) 'Irish Internet Usage Statistics' [online]. Available at www.nua.ie/surveys/. Accessed 6 December 2012.

25   *Irish Times* (2012) 'More Retailers DeliverOnline to Ireland', 27 June.

26   Murphy, M. (2008) 'Organic Food Sales in Ireland Up by 82 per cent', *Epoch Times*, 24 September [online] www.theepochtimes.com/n2/ireland/organic-food-sales-in-ireland-up-by-82-per-cent-4683.html.

27   Hofstede, G. (1984) *Culture's Consequences: International Differences in Work-related Values*. London: Sage.

28   Hofstede, G. (2002) *Culture's Consequences: Comparing Values, Behaviours, Institutions, and Organizations across Nations*. London: Sage.

29   Porter, M. (1985) *Competitive Advantage: Creating and Sustaining Superior Performance*. New York: Free Press.

30   Goodfellow, C. (2011) 'Media: Drowning in Online's Slipstream', *Business and Finance*, April.

CHAPTER 4

Planning

CHAPTER LEARNING OBJECTIVES

- To appreciate why planning is an important function for all organisations, providing the framework for all subsequent management functions.
- To understand that planning takes place at various levels of the organisation and involves all managers to a greater or lesser degree. Strategic planning takes place at the top of the organisation, tactical planning at middle levels and operational planning at lower levels.
- To appreciate that in addition to the three main types of planning, organisations also engage in contingency planning. This involves generating alternative courses of action should unexpected events occur in the business environment.
- To understand that organisations can use a variety of different plans to guide future action, ranging from the most basic (the mission statement) to more precise and specific forms (such as budgets), all of which form a hierarchy of plans. Typical plans used by an organisation differ according to four criteria: degree of repetitiveness; time frame; scope; and the level at which the plan is directed.
- To understand the planning process: defining corporate objectives; internal and external analyses; revising corporate objectives; and formulating strategic, tactical and operational plans.
- To understand the concept of business-level strategies: the operation of a single business that produces a particular line of goods/services marketed to a clearly identifiable customer group.
- To understand the Miles and Snow typology identifying four different types of strategy undertaken by organisations at the business strategy level – prospector, defender, analyser, reactor – and Michael Porter's three generic strategies undertaken by organisations – differentiation, cost leadership and focus.
- To understand that organisations can also develop strategies at the corporate level and that these may extend across many industry sectors. At the corporate level the key strategic issue for an organisation is the extent of diversification. Organisations typically pursue one of two kinds of diversification strategy: related diversification means that the organisation produces a variety of products/services that are connected; unrelated diversification involves the production of diverse products/services across different markets with no logical connection.
- To understand why organisations have sought to manage their diversification strategies by using portfolio management techniques, the most famous of which is the BCG matrix.

4.1 Introduction

This chapter focuses on the first managerial function – planning. It considers the importance of planning for an organisation, the types of planning that can be undertaken and the various approaches that can be used to facilitate planning. Drawing all these factors together, the chapter outlines the planning process and the numerous stages that an organisation goes through in order to plan successfully. Corporate and business-level planning and strategies are then discussed in more detail, focusing on key strategies and management techniques.

4.2 The nature and importance of planning

Planning is perhaps the most basic of all management functions. It can be defined as the systematic development of action programmes aimed at reaching agreed business objectives by the process of analysing, evaluating and selecting among the opportunities which are foreseen.[1]

Planning is therefore the process of establishing aims and objectives and choosing a course of action to ensure that they are achieved. This process serves to bridge the gap between where an organisation currently is and where it would like to be. Consider the examples of planning outlined in Table 4.1.

TABLE 4.1 RECENT EXAMPLES OF PLANNING IN ORGANISATIONS IN IRELAND

New retail chain plans 200 jobs[2]	Danish fashion brand Only plans to open four stores initially including a flagship store on Grafton Street. Other outlets are planned in Limerick and Cork.
Jam maker spreads the good news with expansion plans[3]	Irish jam manufacturer Folláin plans to invest €1.7 million in a new plant. The company has grown from a small cottage industry to a busy enterprise employing 15 people in the west Cork Gaeltacht of Cúil Aodha.
Visitor car par planned for Burren[4]	The state is making a fresh attempt to put in place plans for car parking facilities in the Burren National Park. This comes a decade after initial plans had to be shelved.
Santos to invest €8m in firm with plans to drill in Ireland[5]	Australian exploration giant Santos plans to invest €8 million in Tamboran Resources, the company with controversial plans to drill for natural gas in Leitrim and Fermanagh.
Bus Éireann unveils cost-cutting plan[6]	Bus Éireann has announced plans to push ahead with a raft of cost-cutting measures aimed at addressing a projected €16 million hole in its annual cost base.

As we can see, some plans are aimed at expansion while others concentrate on cost savings. Some are controversial, while others illustrate that even the government needs to plan for the future – which is not always easy. Planning is undertaken by all managers, irrespective of their position in the hierarchy; it is one of the most important managerial functions. Planning generally precedes all other management functions. In other words, before an organisation can organise, staff, lead and control, it has to identify its objectives and how to achieve them. Only by planning can the organisation decide what form of organisational structure, what people, what form of leadership and what means of control will be most effective.

Planning seeks to reduce the degree of uncertainty faced by the organisation. While no organisation can predict future events with certainty, if it fails to plan it is leaving things to chance: 'an enterprise without a plan is like a ship sailing in dense fog without any navigational means – the only thing it can possibly be sure about is whether it is afloat or not.'[7] Organisations therefore need plans to guide future action.[8]

Planning sets up the skeleton around which the organisation's activities can be built. It sets the scene for the type of business that will be conducted and the strategy that will be pursued. If, for example, it is foreseen that demand for the organisation's present product range will remain buoyant, this will have a positive effect on the forecast of net income, profit and cash flow. It might also enable the organisation to pursue a strategy of diversification into product lines complementary to its existing portfolio.

It is important for managers to remember that planning should at all times be perceived as a means and not an end in itself. Organisations have on occasion become so involved in specific details of planning that they have failed to respond to critically important events in the business environment. This happens because the organisation becomes bureaucratic in nature, focusing on filling out forms and having all plans in a perfect condition. This is often referred to as 'paralysis by analysis' and essentially means that the organisation analyses too deeply and fails to take action.

4.3 Types of planning

There are three main types of planning undertaken by an organisation, as shown in Figure 4.1.

FIGURE 4.1 TYPES OF PLANNING

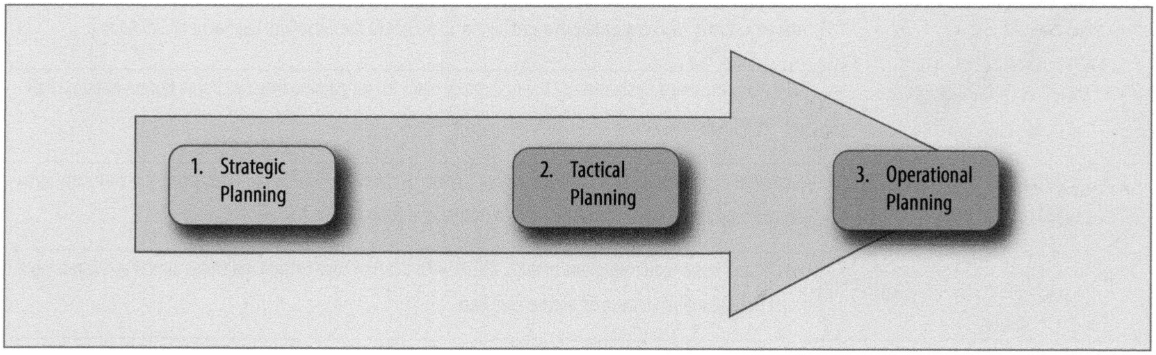

1. Strategic Planning
2. Tactical Planning
3. Operational Planning

1 **Strategic planning** involves issues of strategic direction and normally takes place at the top level of the organisation. Strategic planning therefore has a long-term orientation (greater than five years) and focuses on the organisation's basic mission, establishing organisational objectives, conducting internal analysis, assessing the external environment and developing strategic business plans. It serves to guide issues such as mergers, acquisitions, investment and divestiture, and areas for future expansion.

2 **Tactical planning** is concerned with the current operations of the component parts of the organisation and has a medium-term orientation (one to five years). This type of planning normally takes place at middle management levels. It involves interpreting the strategic plans

by formulating tactical plans to achieve strategic objectives, outlining functional roles and responsibilities and developing tactical responses to medium-term business problems facing the organisation, such as a decline in market share for a particular product.

3   **Operational planning** is concerned with short-term planning of day-to-day functions and serves to guide immediate action undertaken by the organisation. Consequently, it is undertaken by front-line supervisors who are in a position to make plans about short-term operations. Operational planning involves establishing short-term business unit or departmental targets, budgets and specific programmes of action geared toward achieving tactical plans.

An example of all three types of planning and the resultant plans for a small supermarket chain is shown in Figure 4.2.

FIGURE 4.2 STRATEGIC, TACTICAL AND OPERATIONAL PLANS FOR A SMALL CHAIN OF SUPERMARKETS

Mission
Our mission is to establish this chain of supermarkets as the best in the region, providing high-quality service at a reasonable price, with due care for the natural environment.

Strategic plans
- to increase market share
- to reduce costs and improve productivity of staff
- to provide an adequate return on investment—15%

Tactical plans
- to increase the number of retail outlets from five to nine over a period of four years
- to introduce a scanning system in all outlets within two years
- to increase outlet sales by 10% by the end of the year
- to embark on a long-term advertising and promotional campaign

Operational plans
- to investigate over the next three months other outlets where scanning facilities are already established
- to retrain staff in the area of customer service over six months
- to hire a new training manager with immediate effect to deal with the move to scanning techniques
- to establish a Facebook page and use social media for advertising

Most organisations use all three types of planning to guide their future actions. However, for these programmes to be successful, each level of planning must be strongly related. In other words, operational plans must be related to and reflect tactical plans. Similarly, tactical plans must reflect overall strategic plans.

All managers are involved in planning. However, as we have seen, the type of planning undertaken depends on the manager's position in the hierarchy. The amount of time spent on planning also varies depending on the manager's position. Top management has the overall responsibility for seeing that the planning function is carried out. They generally have time to devote to planning, usually have the best understanding of the organisational situation as a whole, and are therefore best equipped to make long-term strategic plans. Middle managers spend less of their time planning than top managers as they focus more on operational issues of the various business units. Middle managers have the best knowledge of the operations of the various areas and are therefore in a better position to make medium-term plans. Finally, lower-level front-line supervisors spend less time on planning than either top or middle managers because they have to focus on day-to-day operations. This focus means that they are best able to determine what can be achieved in the short term to achieve organisational objectives. Figure 4.3 shows the increase in time spent by managers on planning as one moves from front-line supervisors to top managers.

FIGURE 4.3 TIME SPENT PLANNING BY MANAGERS

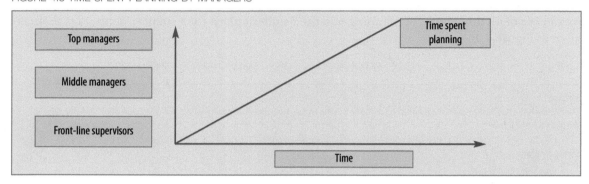

In addition to strategic, tactical and operational planning, organisations also undertake contingency planning. This involves generating alternative courses of action should unexpected events occur in the business environment.[9] Organisations usually develop different sets of plans depending on different economic forecasts: a plan for a recession scenario would be very different from that for a boom scenario. Contingency planning depends on the ability of the organisation to correctly identify and predict alternative scenarios.[10] If these are incorrectly generated, the contingency plans will have little practical use for the organisation.

In the current business environment, organisations typically have a number of different contingency plans which can be put into operation depending on the situation, thus ensuring that the organisation is prepared for all eventualities. Plans should therefore have an inbuilt flexibility, so that they can take account of unforeseen events, such as changes in the price of raw materials.

4.4 Types of plan

A plan is a statement of action to be undertaken by the organisation that is aimed at helping it achieve its objectives. Planning results in the formulation of statements of recommended courses of action, namely plans. As shown in Figure 4.4, plans have a number of important dimensions: repetitiveness; time; scope; and level.[11]

- **The repetitiveness** dimension concerns the extent to which a plan is used over and over again. Some plans apply to certain situations only, tend to have a short time frame and so are essentially non-repetitive. However, some plans apply to many situations and have a longer time frame. Such plans are repetitive by their very nature. This distinction is also referred to as single-use versus standard plans. Single-use plans are generally tailored to a specific situation and are usually strategic in nature. Standard plans are more routine and tend to be operational.

- The **time** dimension refers to the length of time associated with the plan. Some plans are short term and associated with operational planning, while others have a longer time frame and are associated with strategic planning.
- **Scope** refers to the elements of the organisation that are affected by the plan. Some plans have a broad nature and serve to guide the organisation as a whole. Others focus on particular functions or departments and therefore have a narrower scope.

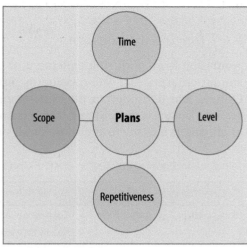

FGURE 4.4 DIMENSIONS OF PLANS

- The **level** dimension refers to the level of the organisation at which the plan is directed. Plans differ in the extent to which they focus on the top, middle or lower levels of the organisation. However, since plans are interdependent, most plans, irrespective of the level they are aimed at, will have an affect on all levels.

Organisations typically use a wide variety of plans to assist their planning process. Planning can be a difficult process when managers fail to recognise that there are a number of different types of plan, all of which have a future orientation.[12] There are generally considered to be eight different

FIGURE 4.5 THE HIERARCHY OF PLANS

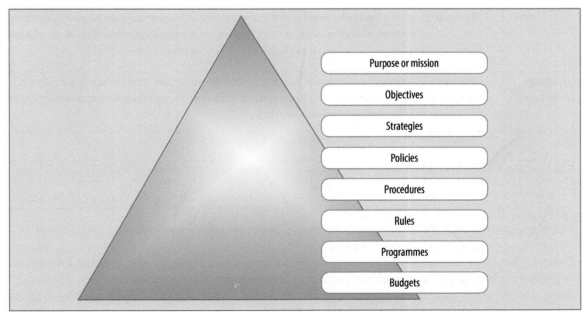

types of plan, which form a hierarchy (Figure 4.5). Each of the different types of plans is discussed below.

4.4.1 Purpose or mission

A mission is an enduring statement of purpose that distinguishes one organisation from other similar enterprises.[13] The mission or purpose is therefore the organisation's reason for existing. Only a clear definition of the mission and purpose of the organisation makes possible clear and realistic business objectives.[14] The mission is therefore the most fundamental organisational plan of all, and it lays the foundation for all subsequent plans.

TABLE 4.2 MISSION STATEMENTS: SOME EXAMPLES

Company name	Sector	Mission statement
Barnes & Noble	Retail: books	'Our mission is to operate the best specialty retail business in America, regardless of the product we sell. Because the product we sell is books, our aspirations must be consistent with the promise and the ideals of the volumes which line our shelves. To say that our mission exists independent of the product we sell is to demean the importance and the distinction of being booksellers. As booksellers we are determined to be the very best in our business, regardless of the size, pedigree or inclinations of our competitors. We will continue to bring our industry nuances of style and approaches to bookselling which are consistent with our evolving aspirations. Above all, we expect to be a credit to the communities we serve, a valuable resource to our customers, and a place where our dedicated booksellers can grow and prosper. Toward this end we will not only listen to our customers and booksellers but embrace the idea that the Company is at their service.'
Pfizer	Health/ pharmaceutical	'Pfizer's mission is to apply science and our global resources to improve health and well-being at every stage of life.'
Iarnród Éireann	Rail transport	'Working together we will renew and develop Ireland's rail transport system and progressively improve the standard of services we provide for our customers – so as to enhance people's quality of life. We will achieve this through investing in our people, processes and physical infrastructure.'
Irish Autism Action	Health/well-being promotion 'Irish Autism	Action's mission is to raise the quality of life of individuals and their families affected by autism through ensuring the provision of highest standards in education, care, support, employment and equality of living opportunities in partnership with families.'
Nike	Sportswear	'To bring inspiration and innovation to every athlete in the world.'
Ford Motor Company	Car manufacture	'We are a global family with a proud heritage passionately committed to providing personal mobility for people around the world.'

Sources: www.missionstatements.com/fortune_500_mission_statements.html; www.pfizer.ie; www.autismireland.ie.

Defining the organisation's mission or purpose involves looking at the scope of the business the organisation is involved in and the organisation's future direction. Consequently an organisation must decide what directions for growth are desirable, what market niches are sought, what pioneering aims are worthwhile and what synergies with other mission statements can be developed. In addition to a mission statement, some organisations prepare a vision statement, which outlines the organisation's fundamental values and ambitions. [15]

Table 4.2 shows some examples of the mission statements of a number of organisations, which outline their basic mission as an organisational entity. You will note that mission statements vary in their length and focus: Nike has a short and simple mission, while Barnes & Noble's is a much longer and more in-depth statement of purpose. Some statements, such as Ford's, refer to their history and heritage.

4.4.2 Objectives/goals

Objectives and *goals* are terms often used interchangeably to describe what must be undertaken by the organisation to achieve its basic mission or purpose. Objectives provide specific aims that the organisation is to achieve within the broader framework of its goals and usually involve a specific time frame. Objectives, therefore, outline more precisely how the organisation seeks to achieve its mission, breathing life into the mission by training the energies of each part of the organisation on what needs to be achieved.[16]

Objectives can be general, applied to the whole organisation (corporate objectives) or specific, focusing on one functional area. An example of a corporate objective would be 'to achieve a return on investment of 15 per cent at the end of the financial year'. An example of an objective specific to a production area would be 'to increase production by 50 per cent by 1 June 2015 without additional costs at the current level of quality'. There are a number of areas in which objectives and performance need to be set, including:

- market standing
- physical and financial resources
- innovation
- productivity
- profitability
- manager performance and development
- worker performance and attitude
- public responsibility.[17]

It is possible for objectives/goals to be in direct conflict with each other. For example, the organisation might have set a goal to reduce costs and at the same time improve product/service quality. The basic conflict in this example is that improving product quality can lead to increased costs and, similarly, reducing costs can have a negative effect on quality. In this case the organisation has to either strike a balance between the two or drop one entirely.[18]

4.4.3 Strategies

The fundamental plans that an organisation devises in order to achieve goals and objectives are termed *strategies*.[19] Strategy is the programme of activities formulated in response to objectives. In other words, it answers the question, 'How are we going to get where we want to go?' Many dictionaries quote the meaning of strategy in relation to military operations and this metaphor is accurate for business. Strategy preparation means that the organisation must examine its own strengths and weaknesses and analyse the external environment to find out how both can be harnessed to achieve objectives.

The main purpose of strategy is to build on the objectives and to communicate through a system of major objectives and policies where the organisation wants to go. Strategies, by their very nature, do not outline specifically how the organisation is to accomplish its objectives. This role is achieved by numerous other major and minor supporting plans. Strategies therefore serve as important guides for planning.

4.4.4 Policies

Policies are general guidelines for decision making throughout the organisation. They provide a direction for managers when using their judgement in achieving objectives. Policies help to establish consistency in decision making. However, they are only broad guidelines and managers can exercise discretion in their interpretation. For example, a policy might state that 'preference should be given to Irish raw materials suppliers when ordering stock'. A policy written in such terms allows a degree of managerial discretion to determine the extent and degree of preference.

Policies can be couched in two forms: express and implied. An express policy is a written or oral statement that guides managers in their decision making. For example, the human resource manual may state explicitly that the organisation is an equal opportunities employer. Implied policy is inferred from looking at the organisation's behaviour and actions, and, in this example, if an analysis of the workforce reveals that most employees are men and that there are no female managers, the expressed policy is not being adhered to but has been replaced by an implied policy of hiring and promoting men. Sometimes expressed and implied policies may conflict with or contradict each other, with the organisation pursuing an expressed policy openly yet privately applying an implied policy, as in the above example.

4.4.5 Procedures

Procedures are plans that outline methods for handling certain situations. They detail the precise manner in which activities are to be carried out. Policies and procedures are quite similar in that they both seek to influence certain decisions. However, procedures frequently involve a series of related steps that have to be taken, and differ from policies that address single issues. For example, an organisation may have a stated policy in relation to grievance and discipline; and to back this up it will have set procedures for dealing with issues of grievance and discipline, which normally follow a step-by-step approach. Other examples of procedures include purchasing equipment, hiring staff and the authorisation of travel expenses. Procedures therefore leave little room for discretion and ensure that all similar situations are handled in the same manner, which leads to consistency.

Procedures exist at all levels of the organisation but are more prevalent at the lower levels, mainly due to the need for tighter control. Procedures become more numerous at lower levels due to the economic advantages of spelling out actions in detail for employees; because managers at lower levels need less leeway; and because routine jobs can be completed most effectively when management details the best way to carry them out.[20]

Well-established procedures are commonly termed 'standard operating procedures'. These are procedures that the organisation uses in a routine manner. However, it should be remembered that procedures should be updated and reviewed to ensure that they are always appropriate for the organisation. Mistakes frequently occur when procedures become obsolete and no longer contribute to the achievement of organisational objectives.

4.4.6 Rules

Rules are statements that either prohibit or prescribe certain actions by clearly specifying what employees can and cannot do. Rules apply to situations regardless of the particular individuals involved, for example a 'no smoking' rule. Rules differ from both policies and procedures in a number of important areas. Unlike procedures discussed above, rules do not contain a specific time sequence. In fact, procedures can be viewed as a series of rules. And unlike policies, rules allow no discretion in their interpretation. So, while personal judgement can be used when applying policies, no such judgement is permitted with rules. The only element of  discretion associated with rules concerns whether the rule applies to certain situations. Organisations experience problems when they fail to clearly distinguish between rules, procedures and policies, which leads to confusion on the part of employees.

4.4.7 Programmes

Programmes are plans designed to accomplish specific goals, usually within a fixed period of time. They can be broad, such as an energy conservation programme undertaken by an organisation; or they can be narrow, focusing on particular areas within the organisation, such as a management development programme for executives. The introduction of a programme in an organisation may lead to the development of numerous supporting programmes. Taking the example of an energy conservation programme, supporting programmes might include: searching for alternative sources of energy; improving the building's insulation; making more economical use of existing energy supplies; and designing more efficient equipment. One of the key prerequisites for the successful implementation of programmes is that all the various supporting programmes are well co-ordinated and contribute to the original programme's aims.

4.4.8 Budgets

A budget is a numerical expression of a plan which deals with the future allocation and utilisation of resources over a given period of time. Budgets are normally expressed in financial terms, person hours, productivity or any other measurable unit. The budget can be seen as a tool for translating future plans into numerical terms. Examples of budgets include revenue and expense budgets, and time, space, material and product budgets.

A budget also serves as an important control mechanism (see Section 10.7). However, for it to act as a standard of control it must reflect plans. One of the major advantages of a budget is that it forces people to plan in a precise way. Since budgets are normally developed for an entire organisation, budgeting is an important device for consolidating organisation-wide plans.

The different types of plan very clearly form a hierarchy. At the top of the hierarchy is the organisation's mission or purpose, which states in the broadest sense where the organisation is going. As one moves further down the hierarchy the plans become more specific and focused until we reach budgets, which are probably the most precise and specific form of planning in which an organisation engages.

4.5 Management by objectives (MBO)

Management by objectives (MBO) is a particular approach to setting objectives and ensuring their achievement. It is a technique that can be used in conjunction with the planning process outlined above. It was developed by a group of management consultants, Urwick Orr and Partners, and was strongly advocated by theorists.[21] It came to prominence in the 1960s, when it was put into practice by a number of major organisations. The turbulent business environment of the last two decades has resulted in the usefulness of the approach being called into question, but its principles remain valid.

Instead of imposing goals or objectives on employees, MBO proposes that each subordinate be free to set goals within the framework provided by his/her superior.[22] The process originates at the top of the organisation with managers taking the decision to pursue the MBO approach. The reasons behind the decision must be communicated to the staff involved. The MBO process must also be consistent with the overall organisational goals, otherwise inconsistencies are likely to occur. The process involves the following steps:
1. The superior or manager sets performance standards that must be met by the subordinate.
2. The subordinate proposes his/her own goals depending on how s/he feels s/he can reach or exceed standards.
3. Goals are then quantified and assigned a specific time frame and finally agreed between the superior and subordinate.
4. At agreed intervals the superior reviews performance with the subordinate. The manager's role should be like that of a counsellor, helping the employee to achieve goals. The degree of goal attainment should be discussed and the causes of success or failure should be analysed.

The process assumes that individual managers are capable of assessing the goals and objectives that they can realistically expect subordinates to reach. Much depends on how MBO is communicated to those whose co-operation is required. If it is used as a 'big stick', motivation will suffer. The objective is to improve corporate performance, and this is achieved by every individual having a part in the objective-setting process. To be worthwhile an MBO programme needs complete support throughout the organisation. It also needs effort to monitor its implementation. Figure 4.6 highlights the advantages and disadvantages associated with MBO.

FIGURE 4.6. ADVANTAGES AND DISADVANTAGES OF MBO

Advantage	Disadvantage
• The employee gains a clearer understanding of the goals s/he is expected to work towards. • Planning should improve as there is greater commitment to goals. • Control should be easier as performance standards now exist. • Motivation should improve as subordinates feel they have input into the objective setting process. • Employee appraisal is simplified by reference to each individual's objectives.	• If MBO is not sold properly throughout the organisation employees may feel they are being coerced. • The focus on objectives can lead the business to strive towards incompatible goals. For example, a finance manager may have agreed to cut operating costs, while the marketing manager's objective is to promote the product more strongly. • There may be a focus on easily measurable objectives and these are not always the best ones. For example, a businessperson might want to improve the quality of his/her customer service. This is a difficult thing to measure and s/he may end up aiming for a reduction in the number of complaints, which is not necessarily the same thing. • Agreement on objectives can cause inflexibility when the environment changes. When time has been invested in hammering out objectives it is difficult to abandon them, even when circumstances change. • When goals are imposed rather than negotiated with employees, resentment and lack of commitment by employees can result.

Sources: Odiorne, G., Weihrich, H. and Mendelson, J. (eds) *Executive Skills: A Management by Objectives Approach*. Iowa: Brown & Co.; Kondrasuk, J. (1981) 'Studies in Management by Objectives Effectiveness', *Academy of Management Review* July, 419–30.

4.6 The planning process

Planning is the process of examining all aspects of the organisation in an effort to formulate strategy, incorporating strategic, tactical and operational planning, aimed at preparing the organisation for the future. Organisations typically follow certain steps in their efforts to plan: this *planning process* is illustrated in Figure 4.7.

4.6.1 Define corporate objectives

The first step in the corporate planning process is establishing corporate objectives. The previous section on objectives can be amplified in the light of corporate objective setting. Most organisations have just a few objectives, in general terms, which they hope to achieve over a long period of time. These objectives must be clarified and documented so that they can be understood by those who are trying to further the planning process.

Economists have suggested that two common types of objective are found in organisations: profit maximisers and profit satisficers. The profit-maximising organisation's aim is to make the highest possible profit, and this aim is connected to all other objectives. The profit-satisficing

FIGURE 4.7 THE PLANNING PROCESS

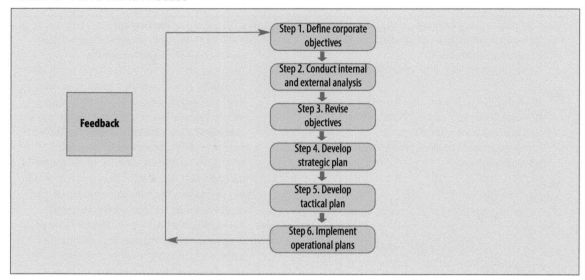

organisation, on the other hand, only seeks sufficient profits to allow it to fulfil other aims, for example to invest in new production, to enjoy a high public profile, or to allow the owner to have a good lifestyle. Many smaller businesses turn away from the chance to optimise profits in order to keep the business personal or to allow the management more free time.

Two management theories worth noting in this context are shareholder theory and stakeholder theory. **Shareholder theory** holds that all organisational objectives should be geared to maximising the return to shareholders. In a public enterprise the shareholders are a wide and diverse group including customers, employees, the government and all other interest groups whose needs have to be considered. **Stakeholder theory** holds that objectives have to be related to all those who have a stake in the organisation, which includes customers, suppliers, employees, the government and the public in general. The interests of all these groups have to be considered when setting organisational objectives. So, for example, a pharmaceutical company may be concerned with selling its products for a certain profit, providing employees with a favourable working environment, sourcing materials from local suppliers, complying with local and voluntary codes of practice and making contributions to local activities.

4.6.2 External and internal analysis

When devising corporate plans an organisation must analyse its internal strengths and weaknesses in relation to the external opportunities and threats that confront it. The assessment of an organisation's strengths, weaknesses, opportunities and threats is referred to as a SWOT analysis. Every organisation has strengths and weaknesses, which it needs to be aware of in order to capitalise on them. Unless an organisation frequently analyses its weaknesses it may find itself unprepared to respond to unanticipated threats from the environment. As noted in Chapter 3, an organisation's ability to identify and respond to opportunities in the environment is a function of its ability to effectively manage its external environment. A typical SWOT analysis involves three related steps:[23]

1. Identifying the current strategy/strategies that the organisation is following. Decision makers should identify current goals and strategies in order to determine whether the organisation is moving in the appropriate direction. This review should concentrate on the mission, strategic goals and corporate strategy.
2. Identifying the key changes in the organisation's external environment, using the techniques described in Chapter 3. The organisation should thoroughly analyse both its macro and task environment, focusing on the relative importance of each of the components for the organisation and the extent to which they are changing. This process is sometimes referred to as a PEST analysis. PEST is an acronym for political–legal, economic, socio-cultural and technological analysis of environmental influences, and this type of analysis corresponds to an analysis of the primary features of the macro environment. Due to the increasingly competitive nature of the external environment, a competitive analysis of the industry within which the organisation operates has become critically important. Chapter 3 provides details of how an organisation should undertake such a task.
3. Drawing up a resource profile of the organisation to identify its key capabilities (strengths) and key limitations (weaknesses). In order to exploit opportunities in the external environment it is necessary to know what competencies and weaknesses the organisation has.

A resource profile can be undertaken by considering resources under the following headings:
- **Human resources**. This refers to the structure and quality of the workforce. A human resource analysis might consider the age structure of employees, levels of skill, experience, staff turnover, promotion and replacement. A young, highly skilled workforce is an enormous asset, but this group also demands a lot from the organisation in high salaries, promotion and good working conditions, for example. The analysis should focus on future staffing requirements, so that areas of scarcity and surplus can be identified.
- **Financial resources**. A financial audit of resources includes the financial structure and current borrowing capacity of the organisation. Balance sheets, ratio analysis, forecast cash flow and working capital have to be examined.
- **Organisational resources**. This involves considering the strengths and weaknesses of each business unit and department. A critical examination of each area will reveal certain strengths and shortcomings. For example, a print firm might have a highly trained production staff, but this may be a drawback for the organisation in terms of its cost and the difficulty of introducing new technology.
- **Technological resources**. Every organisation has to decide whether to be leader or a follower in the area of technological capability. This will have implications for the level of production costs, which have to be traded against the capital cost of acquiring new technology.

One of the main aims of an internal organisational analysis of strengths and weaknesses is that it enables the organisation to see where it can develop a competitive advantage. In the current business environment an organisation must be able to carve out a special and distinct advantage that will endure over time.

A SWOT analysis can be performed by any organisation, and an example is shown in Figure 4.8. McDonald's is the world's leading food service retailer with more than 33,500 local restaurants serving approximately 69 million people in 119 countries every day.

McDonald's is one of the world's most famous and instantly recognisable brands and holds a leading share in the globally branded, fast service restaurant segment. The company was established in 1954 by Ray Kroc, and enjoyed huge success in the global marketplace. However, the competitive landscape has become more challenging in recent years and the company experienced difficulties in 2002/3. Since then McDonald's has turned its fortunes around, but challenges remain. A SWOT analysis for McDonald's is summarised in Figure 4.8.

FIGURE 4.8 SWOT ANALYSIS FOR MCDONALD'S CORPORATION

Strengths	Weaknesses
• Continued profitability in the face of recession • Global presence • Location of outlets at key sites • Global brand identity • Market leadership • Sponsorship of charities • Product innovation • Speed of service • Effective franchise system • Economies of scale due to size	• Staff turnover • Employee productivity • Limited product ranges in the healthy options area • Customer fatigue with the uniform nature of the product
Opportunities	**Threats**
• Continue to expand in Asia, Africa and the Middle East • Build on recent expansion in China • Expansion of range of products to appeal to changing consumer demands • Provide more information on nutritional content of food • Develop greener business practices	• Growing health-conscious consumer market which is likely to avoid traditional fast food outlets • Market saturation in some markets • Link between fast foods and obesity, particularly in children • Increased competition – from garages and convenience stores • Increased competition from other fast food chains • Economic downturn

Source: www.investmentu.com/2010/December/mcdonalds-growth-continues.html; www.mcdonalds.com.

4.6.3 Revise objectives

In the light of the foregoing external and internal analyses, the unique competitive advantage an organisation can develop should be clear. If no distinct advantage emerges, strategy formulation should centre on developing some competitive edge. Such advantages could include a unique product, market leadership, and quality of manufacturing reputation or service back-up. Developing some form of leading edge often means a complete revision of the objectives previously defined.

4.6.4 Formulate strategic plans

At this stage, the building blocks are in place, ready to be cemented together in the form of a strategic plan. Strategic plans, discussed earlier, are usually developed along two lines: first, deciding the direction of the organisation's activities (expansion, contraction, diversification or merger); second, finding the resources (human and financial) to facilitate these activities. The starting point for a strategic plan is the formulation of a strategy statement. This proposes how objectives are to be fulfilled and sets the guidelines for the development of tactical plans. Organisations typically formulate strategies on two levels: corporate and business. Corporate-level strategies relate to the conduct of business across several industries and are broad in nature. Business-level strategies relate to the conduct of business in one particular industry sector. These will be examined in more depth at the end of this chapter.

4.6.5 Formulate tactical plans

Tactical plans are formulated for every function or business unit in the organisation and normally have a medium-term orientation of perhaps one year, but this may vary from organisation to organisation. Tactical plans interpret the strategic plan to produce more medium-term plans to achieve strategic objectives. In this sense they are more precise formulations of plans. An example of a tactical plan for a specific functional area, in this case production, might include the following:
- to improve productivity in the production area
- to improve communications in the production area.

Tactical plans should be flexible enough to be altered as contingencies warrant.

4.6.6 Implement action/operational plans

When tactical plans are finally agreed it is necessary to formulate specific action plans to implement planning decisions. The link between tactical planning and implementation is the various operational or action plans that deal with the day-to-day functioning of the organisation. Action or operational plans to achieve the tactical plans outlined in the previous section could include the following:
- to increase productivity by 10 per cent by 1 June 2015
- to issue a three-page monthly newsletter by 30 June 2015.

Effective implementation means providing the necessary resources, motivating staff and holding regular (usually monthly) meetings to review how targets are being met. These meetings provide the basis for feedback to all levels of the organisation on how effective the planning process has been.

The planning process we have just outlined is a complex and highly important process for any organisation. The process is a demanding one requiring that the organisation consciously determines courses of action and bases decisions on purpose, knowledge and considered estimates.

Having completed the planning process, the organisation will have clearly identified objectives, strategies and various types of plan to achieve those goals. It is then in a position to make decisions about other managerial functions, such as organising and controlling, which will contribute to organisational efficiency.

4.7 Business-level planning and strategies

Business-level strategies refers to the operation of a single business. A single business or strategic business unit (SBU) produces a particular line of goods/services which are marketed to a clearly identifiable customer group. A number of different approaches have been taken to the classification of the various strategies available to single business organisations.

4.7.1 The Miles and Snow typology

Raymond Miles and Charles Snow[24] identified four different categories of business-level strategy:

1. A company pursuing a **prospector** strategy is typically involved in a high-growth, innovative industry and continually looks for new opportunities and market sectors. This type of organisation embraces change and rewards risk taking.
2. Companies pursuing a **defender** strategy maintain growth levels by protecting their current markets and keeping customers well served. Organisations using this style tend to be less aggressive and less entrepreneurial in style.
3. The **analyser** strategy is a combination of prospector and defender strategies. The organisation keeps its current market and customers but introduces a moderate degree of change and innovation. Organisations opt for this strategy as they do not want to miss out on certain opportunities should they arise within the business environment.
4. Finally, in a **reactor** strategy the organisation has no clear approach, merely reacting to the changes introduced by competitors rather than anticipating potential changes. Such organisations often fail to notice changes in the business environment until it is too late.

Management Focus 4.1 Miles and Snow examples in the smartphone sector

Both Samsung and Apple can be viewed as prospectors, given their high growth levels in a very innovative and competitive industry sector.

In contrast, Nokia could be viewed as a reactor with its emphasis on the handset market.

4.7.2 Porter's generic strategies

Michael Porter provides the second approach to the classification of business-level strategies. In line with his model of competitive analysis, he argues that organisations can follow one of three generic strategies: differentiation, cost leadership and focus.

1. Organisations pursuing a **differentiation** strategy try to make their products and services unique and distinctive by enhancing product quality. Customers are willing to pay more because they perceive that the product/service is more valuable. Examples of organisations pursuing such a strategy are Jack Wills and Abercrombie & Fitch (clothing) and the book publisher Dorling Kindersley.

2. Organisations can also pursue a **cost leadership** strategy, whereby the organisation offers the lowest-cost product/service by reducing manufacturing and other costs. By keeping costs low the organisation can offer its product/service at the lowest price. Both Lidl and Aldi pursue this strategy.

3. A **focus** strategy enables the organisation to concentrate on a specific regional market, product line or group of customers. The strategy could have a differentiation focus – concentrating on providing high-quality goods and services at a premium price – or a cost leadership focus – providing the lowest-cost product within a specific sector. Some of the local and regional supermarkets adopt this approach by only catering for particular regional markets.

4.8 Corporate-level planning strategies

Organisations can also develop strategies at the corporate level that may extend across many industry sectors. At the corporate level the key strategic issue for an organisation concerns the nature and degree of *diversification*. Diversification is the number of different business activities conducted by an organisation and the extent to which those activities are or are not related.[25]

It is possible to identify two main types of corporate-level strategy that can be pursued by an organisation: related diversification; and unrelated diversification.

4.8.1 Related diversification

In this case the organisation produces a range of similar products and services that are linked in some way. Organisations pursuing related diversification normally compete in the same market, have the same distributors, technology, brand name and reputation. Its main advantages are that it spreads the organisation's risk evenly, provides economies of scale and lower overhead costs, and facilitates the development of synergy. Procter & Gamble pursues a related diversification strategy.

4.8.2 Unrelated diversification

In this case the organisation produces diverse products across many different markets. Many of the business activities have no logical connection between them. Often referred to as conglomerates, many organisations pursued this strategy in the 1960s and 1970s. During this period it was widely believed that such a strategy could result in stable organisational performance because the risk was spread over many industrial sectors. In addition, there were advantages in resource allocation. However, there is evidence to suggest that unrelated diversification is associated with a decrease in organisational performance.[26] Many of the conglomerates that embraced unrelated diversification have hived off unrelated business activities. Unrelated diversification was hard to manage and control. Corporate-level managers often lacked the complete knowledge to make strategic decisions, instead relying on financial data. Unrelated diversification resulted in a lack of synergy among organisational units and there was a lack of investment in research and development (R&D).

4.8.3 Managing diversification strategies

Organisations can manage their diversification strategies by using portfolio management techniques, the most famous of which is the Boston Consulting Group (BCG) matrix. This matrix is a framework for drawing conclusions about the performance of key businesses performed by the diversified organisation. In evaluating business performance the BCG matrix considers the rate of growth in the market and the market share held by the organisation. The matrix concludes that rapidly growing sectors where the organisation already possesses a strong market share perform best. The least attractive option is where the growth rate is slow and the organisation has a small share of the market. The matrix classification is illustrated in Figure 4.9.

FIGURE 4.9 THE BCG MATRIX

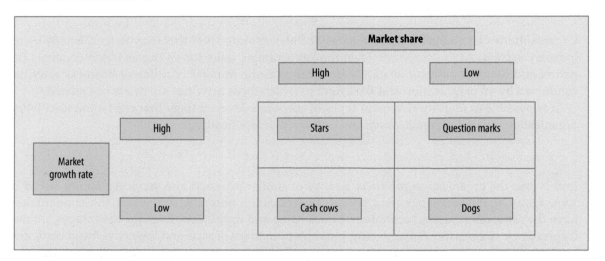

- Stars are businesses that have the largest share of the market in a rapidly growing market.
- Cash cows are businesses with a large market share which is not likely to increase in the near future. These businesses usually generate profits which can be invested in stars.
- Question marks are businesses that have a small share of a growing market. The future outlook in these sectors is often unpredictable.
- Dogs are sectors where the business has a small share of a low-growth market. The matrix advises organisations to sell dogs and invest the money in other sectors.

The BCG matrix has been used by many diversified organisations as a means of effectively managing their portfolio of business investments. However, despite its appealing nature the BCG matrix has one main disadvantage: its analysis is limited to two criteria – market growth and market share held by the organisation. It is widely recognised that other factors influence organisational performance, and these are not included in the matrix. Despite its faults, however, the BCG matrix has greatly enhanced the power of organisations to control their diversified investments.

4.10 Summary of key propositions

- Planning has been defined as a process of establishing aims and objectives and choosing a course of action to ensure that these objectives are achieved. Planning is a critically important function for all organisations; it provides the framework for all subsequent management functions.
- Planning takes place at various levels of the organisation and involves all managers to a greater or lesser degree. Strategic planning takes place at the top of the organisation, tactical at middle levels and operational at lower levels.
- In addition to the three main types of planning, organisations also engage in contingency planning. This involves generating alternative courses of action should unexpected events occur in the business environment.
- When planning, organisations can use a variety of different plans to guide future action, ranging from the most basic – the mission statement – to more precise and specific forms such as budgets, all of which form a hierarchy of plans. Typical plans used by an organisation differ across four criteria: the degree of repetitiveness; the time frame; scope; and the level at which the plan is directed.
- An example of one particular process for setting objectives is MBO. This approach has many associated advantages but also disadvantages.
- In order to ensure that planning is effective, organisations typically go through a process of planning, involving a sequence of stages, the success of which depends on the accuracy of the preceding stage. The main stages involve defining corporate objectives, internal and external analyses, revising corporate objectives and formulating strategic, tactical and operational plans.
- Business-level strategies refers to the operation of a single business which produces a particular line of goods/services marketed to a clearly identifiable customer group.
- Miles and Snow identified four different types of strategy undertaken by organisations at the business strategy level: prospector; defender; analyser; reactor. Michael Porter provided three different generic strategies undertaken by organisations: differentiation; cost leadership; focus.
- Organisations can also develop strategies at the corporate level and these may extend across many industry sectors. At the corporate level the key strategic issue for an organisation is the extent of diversification. Organisations typically pursue one of two kinds of diversification strategy. Related diversification means that the organisation produces a variety of products/services which are connected. Unrelated diversification involves the production of diverse products/services across different markets with no logical connection.
- Organisations have sought to manage their diversification strategies by using portfolio management techniques, the most famous of which is the BCG matrix.

Discussion Questions

1 Explain why planning is one of the most important managerial functions.
2 Distinguish between strategic, tactical and operational planning.
3 Identify any four types of plan and explain their importance to the planning process.
4 Explain why the planning process is necessary.
5 Conduct a SWOT analysis for an organisation with which you are familiar.
6 What are the main advantages and disadvantages associated with the MBO approach?
7 Find some recent examples of plans announced by organisations in Ireland and evaluate their nature and characteristics.
8 Explain why organisations engage in contingency planning.
9 Explain the Miles and Snow typology for business-level strategies and apply it to a market sector with which you are familiar.
10 Explain the main differences between Porter's generic strategies.
11 What are corporate-level strategies and why are they important for planning?
12 Find examples of organisations in Ireland pursuing related and unrelated diversification strategies and evaluate their success.

Concluding Case: Ryanair's competitive strategy

Ryanair operates a low-cost scheduled airline serving 178 airports with over 1,500 routes across 28 countries. It provides short-haul, point-to-point services from its 57 bases, most of which are in Europe. In 2012 Ryanair carried almost 76 million passengers, making it one of the world's largest airlines. The airline started operations in 1985, serving routes from Dublin to Luton and Gatwick, but within four years had lost €31.74 million and was on the verge of bankruptcy. In 1991  the airline was relaunched as a low-cost carrier and a new management team was appointed. Using the model of Southwest Airlines, Ryanair eliminated 14 unprofitable routes, standardised aircraft type, reduced fares by up to 70 per cent, and turned its fortunes around. By 1995 the airline had carried 2.25 million passengers and continued to expand. In 1997 Ryanair took advantages of liberalisation in the EU airline industry and developed new routes such Stansted to Stockholm, Oslo and has continued to grow ever since.

In 2012 Ryanair made a net profit of €560.4 million on operating revenues of €4,324.9 million. Table 4.3 summarises other aspects of the airline's performance during the period 2011–12.

Ryanair states that its strategy is to:

... firmly establish itself as Europe's biggest scheduled passenger airline, through continued improvements and expanded offerings of its low fares service. In the highly challenging current operating environment, Ryanair seeks to offer low fares that generate increased passenger traffic while maintaining a continuous focus on cost containment and operating efficiencies.

TABLE 4.3 ASPECTS OF RYANAIR'S PERFORMANCE 2011–12

	2012	2011	Change
Average number of employees	8,438	8,063	+5%
Passengers per average number of employees	8,983	8,942	+1%
Average yield per revenue passenger mile	0.059	0.053	
Average booked passenger fare (€)	45.36	39.42	
Ancillary revenue per booked passenger (€)	11.69	11.12	

The heart of its successful strategy is based on providing a no-frills service with low fares designed to stimulate demand, particularly from budget-conscious leisure and business travellers who might otherwise have used alternative forms of transportation or who might not have travelled at all. Ryanair's competitive strategy and airline culture centres on keeping costs to a minimum and this it achieves in a number of ways. First, Ryanair operates a 'Keep It Simple, Stupid' (KISS) philosophy in relation to its service offering. The carrier generally makes its lowest fares widely available, selling seats on a one-way basis only. The company claims that its no-frills service allows it to prioritise features important to its clientele, such as frequent departures, single-class seating, advance reservations, baggage handling and consistent on-time services. This eliminates non-essential extras that interfere with the reliable low-cost delivery of its basic flights. The eliminated free extras include advance seat assignment (this has the effect of forcing the timely boarding of passengers), in-flight meals and drinks, and checked baggage. In addition the airline does not offer air bridges to aircraft,

baggage transfer, multiclass seating, or access to frequent flyer programmes. Ryanair also phased out all reclining seats and seat back pockets in order to reduce cleaning and maintenance costs. It outsources many of its services, such as aircraft and ground handling, maintenance and repairs. In 1997, Ryanair dropped its cargo services and, without the need to load and unload cargo, the turnaround time of an aircraft has been reduced from 30 to 25 minutes.

Ryanair has, however, sought to make additional revenue from providing ancillary services, for which it charges, offered in conjunction with its core airline business. These include on-board duty-free and beverage sales, travel reservation services, gaming and bingo cards, travel insurance, baggage charges, suitcases and car rental. In 2000, Ryanair's in-flight sales of beverages and duty-free merchandise accounted for 5.3 per cent of the company's revenue, but by 2012 total revenue from ancillary services had jumped to just over 20 per cent at €846.2 million, up from €802 million the year before. Table 4.4 provides a summary of ancillary revenues per booked passenger over a four-year period.

TABLE 4.4 ANCILLARY REVENUES 2009–12

	2012	2011	2010	2009
Ancillary revenues per booked passenger (€)	11.69	11.12	9.98	10.21

Second, Ryanair uses secondary airports rather than primary airports, for example Frankfurt (Hahn) and Brussels (Charleroi). These airports have lower charges and are less congested than principal airports. There is a greater chance of obtaining a slot, a quicker turnaround, less taxi time and delays, which translates into shorter block time and maximum aircraft utilisation. Since Ryanair is able to produce high volumes for these airports it is able to negotiate favourable terms. Ryanair maintains a fleet that consists of a single aircraft type – Boeing 737s. Ryanair currently operates 305 Boeing 737-800s at an average age of four years, which leads to increased crew flexibility and cheaper maintenance.

Third, Ryanair operates short-haul, point-to-point city pair services with no connections, no interlinking and no baggage transfers, all of which avoid the costs of providing a through service for connecting passengers as well as delays caused by the late arrival of connecting flights. Finally, Ryanair operates a direct sales and distribution strategy, selling 100 per cent of its fares direct, either online or by phone – 99 per cent via its highly successful website www.ryanair.com. Further savings are achieved by issuing all tickets electronically.

Ryanair faces some challenges into the future. It has continued to be controversial in relation to employment practices and there have been several disputes. It refuses to recognise a trade union and will only do so when the majority of workers want one. Ryanair uses a performance-related pay structure so that employees are incentivised to work harder and are rewarded well for doing so. However, employees work longer hours and are paid less than their counterparts in other airlines. In the future Ryanair faces threats from high-speed rail networks and stiff competition from other airlines.

Its somewhat cavalier attitude toward its customers has not always been helpful for the airline, and some high-profile court cases have resulted in much negative publicity. EU legislation now means that all airlines must compensate passengers for lost baggage and delays. In 2012 the European Court of Justice ruled that Ryanair must pay meals, accommodation and transport, and 'means of communication with third parties' for passengers who were affected by cancellations due to volcanic ash clouds from an Icelandic volcano in 2010. Ryanair said the decision would lead to higher fares for passengers.

The company is in a strong financial position, particularly when compared to other airlines. Ryanair is one of the few airlines that have continued to make money. However, the company has predicted that market conditions in Europe will remain tough, with austerity measures, fuel costs and government charges depressing future demand for air travel. Ryanair holds a 29.8 per cent stake in Aer Lingus, which it purchased in 2006 after the partial privatisation of Aer Lingus. Its third offer for a controlling stake in Aer Lingus was rejected by the EU Commission in 2013. Ryanair has stated its intention to appeal this decision but it is difficult to see what future role it can continue to play in Aer Lingus.

The airline is also susceptible to external events that may impact on demand for air travel. Changes in fuel prices and uncertainty associated with the euro pose a risk for the airline. In addition there are risks associated with planned growth, the cost of acquiring additional aircraft and any potential changes to the Irish corporation tax rate. Ryanair's success is closely associated with its CEO and poses a question of succession management for the airline. Michael O'Leary has indicated his intention to step down from the CEO position over the next few years. The man so closely associated with building Ryanair into a low-cost carrier will be difficult to replace in the short term. Working out what type of leader would suit the airline in the future and planning a recruitment drive are key factors facing the airline. The company is targeting growth over the next 10 years, predicting it will carry up to 120 million passengers per annum within a decade. However, recession, competition and very low fare competition at new bases will constrain future profitability.

Keep up to date
www.ryanair.com

Sources: Ryanair: Q3 Results, 31 December 2012 (www.ryanair.com/doc/investor/present/ quarter3_2013.pdf); Annual Report 2012; Lynch, S. (2013) 'Ryanair Loses Ash Cloud Appeal', *Irish Times*, 31 January [online] www.irishtimes.com/business/sectors/transport-and-tourism/ryanair-loses-ash-cloud-appeal-1.1072428; Carty, E. (2013) 'Ryanair to Fight Decision to Reject its Bid for Aer Lingus', *Irish Independent,* 12 February [online] www.independent.ie/business/irish/ryanair-to-fight-eu-decision-to-reject-its-bid-for-aer-lingus-29065644.html; O'Brien, C. (2012) 'Ryanair Half-year Profits up 10%', *Irish Times*, 5 November [online] www.irishtimes.com/ newspaper/breaking/2012/1105/ breaking4.html.

Case Questions
1.   Prepare a SWOT analysis for Ryanair.
2.   What recommendations would you make for the future of the company?

Notes and References

1 Jones, H. (1974) *Preparing Company Plans: A Workbook for Effective Corporate Planning*. New York: Wiley.

2 O'Brien, C. (2012) 'New Retail Chain Plans 200 Jobs', *Irish Times* 15 November 2012 [online]. Available at http://www.irishtimes.com/business/sectors/retail-and-services/new-retail-chain-plans-200-jobs-1.748993. Accessed 17 December 2012.

3 Keogh, O. (2012) 'Jam Maker Spreads the Good News with Expansion Plans', *Irish Times* 13 November [online]. Available at http://www.irishtimes.com/business/sectors/agribusiness-and-food/jam-maker-spreads-the-good-news-with-expansion-plans-1.551166. Accessed 17 December 2012.

4 Deegan, G. (2012) 'Visitor Car Park Planned for Burren', *Irish Times* 31 October 2012 [online]. Available at http://www.irishtimes.com/news/visitor-car-park-planned-for-burren-1.559557. Accessed 17 December 2012.

5 O'Halloran, B. (2012) 'Santos to Invest €8m in Firm with Plans to Drill in Ireland, *Irish Times* 13 December 2012 [online]. Available at http://www.irishtimes.com/business/sectors/energy-and-resources/santos-to-invest-8m-in-firm-with-plans-to-drill-in-ireland-1.2686. Accessed 17 December 2012.

6 Burke-Kennedy, E. (2012) 'Bus Éireann Unveils Cost-Cutting Plan', *Irish Times* 14 December 2012 [online]. Available at http://www.irishtimes.com/news/bus-%C3%A9ireann-unveils-cost-cutting-plan-1.754806. Accessed 17 December 2012.

7 Michiels, R. (1986) 'Planning, an Effective Management Tool or a Corporate Pastime?', *Journal of Marketing Management* 1(3), 259–64.

8 Sarason, Y. and Tegarden, L. (2003) 'The Erosion of the Competetive Advantage of Strategic Planning: A Configuration Theory and Resource Based View', *Journal of Business and Management* 9(1).

9 Froot, K., Scharfstein, D. and Stein, J. (1994) 'A Framework for Risk Management', *Harvard Business Review* 63(6), 91–102.

10 Foster, J. (1993) 'Scenario Planning for Small Businesses', *Long Range Planning* 26(1), 123–9.

11 Kast, F. and Rosenweig, J. (1985) *Organisation and Management: A Systems Approach*. New York: McGraw-Hill.

12 Weihrich, H. and Koontz, H. (1993) *Management: A Global Perspective*. New York: McGraw-Hill.

13 David, F. (1989) 'How Companies Define their Missions', *Long Range Planning* 22(1), 90–7.

14 Drucker, P. (1973) *Management Tasks, Responsibilities and Practices*. New York: Harper Row.

15 Quigley, J. (1994) 'Vision: How Leaders Develop It, Share It and Sustain It', *Business Horizons* September–October, 37–41.

16 Thompson, A and Strickland, A. (1990) *Strategic Management: Concepts and Cases*. Illinois: Irwin.

17 Drucker, P. (1954) *The Practice of Management*. New York: Harper Row.

18 Vancouver, J., Millsap, R. and Peters, P. (1994) 'Multi-level Analysis of Organisational Goal Congruence', *Journal of Applied Psychology* 79(5), 666–79.

19 Shivastava, P. (1994) *Strategic Management: Concepts and Cases*. Cincinatti: South Western.

20 Weihrich, H. and Koontz, H. (1993) *Management: A Global Perspective*. New York: McGraw-Hill.

21 Drucker, P. (1954) *The Practice of Management.* New York: Harper Row; Humble, J. (1972) *Management by Objectives.* USA: Teakfield.

22 Carroll, S. and Tosi, H. (1973) *Management by Objectives.* New York: Macmillan.

23 Johnson, G. Whittington, R. and Scholes, K. (2010) *Exploring Strategy: Text and Cases.* London: Prentice Hall.

24 Miles, R. and Snow, C. (1978) *Organisational Strategy, Structure and Process.* New York: McGraw-Hill.

25 Lubatkin, M. and Chatterjee, S. (1994) 'Extending Modern Portfolio Theory into the Domain of Corporate Diversification: Does it Apply?' *Academy of Management Journal* 37(1), 109–36.

26 Hoskisson, R. and Hitt, M. (1994) *Downscoping: How to Tame The Diversified Firm.* New York: Oxford University Press.

CHAPTER 5

Decision Making

- To understand the term decision making, which means selecting a course of action from a range of alternatives. It plays an integral part in planning but is also a fundamental part of the entire management process.
- To understand the different types of decision taken by organisations and the range of conditions, from complete certainty to risk and uncertainty.
- To understand that certainty means that the available alternatives and their costs or benefits are certain: managers know with certainty that particular alternatives will lead to definite outcomes and there is no element of doubt.
- To understand that under the risk condition all the available alternatives and their potential costs and benefits are known, but the outcomes are sometimes in doubt. Therefore while the alternatives are known the outcomes are unknown.
- To understand that uncertainty is when the available alternatives, the likelihood of their occurrence and the outcomes are all unknown. Decisions made under uncertain conditions are consequently the most difficult to take due to the lack of concrete knowledge. In the current business environment more and more decisions are being made under conditions of uncertainty.
- To appreciate that organisations make hundreds of decisions each day which can be classified as programmed or non-programmed. Programmed decisions are well structured, routine, repetitive and occur on a regular basis. Non-programmed decisions are new, unstructured and have no established procedures for making them.
- To understand the barriers to effective decision making, which include decision framing, the illusion of control and time pressures.
- To understand the decision-making process, which comprises six key steps: problem identification and diagnosis; identifying alternatives; evaluating alternatives; choice of alternative; implementation; and evaluation.
- To understand the most popular approaches to decision making: the rational model; bounded rationality; escalation of commitment; and the political model.
- To understand that rationality in relation to decision making refers to a process that is perfectly logical and objective, whereby managers gather information objectively, evaluate available evidence, consider all alternatives and ultimately make choices that will lead to the best outcomes for the organisation.
- To understand the dynamics of group and individual decision making.

5.1 Introduction

Decision making can be viewed as an integral part of planning in that key decisions have to taken throughout the planning process. The following sections focus on many of the issues that arise when making organisational decisions.

Decision making can be defined as 'the selection of a course of action from among alternatives'.[1] In this sense decision making is at the heart of planning: for plans to be formulated and implemented, decisions on certain courses of action have to be taken. Some commentators have even argued that decision making can be viewed as the most fundamental managerial activity of all.[2] Decision making is discussed primarily within the context of planning; but despite the link with planning, decision making is a fundamental element of the entire management process.

Organisations make literally hundreds of decisions each day as they fulfil their operational requirements. Some of these decisions are small and minor and can be completed quickly, for example the size and colour of envelopes required by the organisation. Others are more complicated and far-reaching and require more detailed analysis, such as whether to expand into foreign markets. Decision making, which takes place at all levels of the organisation, is therefore a central part of the manager's role.

5.2 Characteristics of decisions

Making decisions in an organisational context requires good judgement and diagnostic skills. Most managers advance within an organisation as a result of their ability to make good decisions. The characteristics of decisions faced by most managers are varied in nature, depending on the type of decision in question. Given that managers make a variety of decisions during their daily lives we would expect that decisions would have different characteristics. There is no doubt that a relatively simple decision in relation to re-ordering stationery supplies will not have the same characteristics as a decision concerning establishing a new subsidiary in a foreign market. While decisions vary in nature it is possible to identify some key characteristics that define managerial decision making in the modern organisation, as shown in Figure 5.1.

FIGURE 5.1   CHARACTERISTICS OF MANAGERIAL DECISIONS

Some decisions that managers make are routine and well structured and are thus relatively easy to make. However, other decisions are poorly structured and lack full information, making them much more challenging for the manager. We can distinguish between **programmed** and **non-programmed** decisions (outlined in Figure 5.2).

Programmed decisions tend to be well structured, routine and repetitive, occurring on a regular basis. They are usually made at lower levels in the organisation, have short-term consequences and are based on readily available information. Due to the fact that the organisation is frequently presented with the decision, a decision rule can be developed that tells the organisation or decision maker which alternative to choose once the information is available. The decision rule ensures that a definite method for obtaining a solution can be found and that the decision does not have to be treated as something new each time it occurs. Frequently simple formulae can be applied to the situation. Examples of programmed decisions include ordering raw materials or office supplies and calculating holiday pay, sick pay or redundancy payments, which takes place frequently in Irish organisations.

Non-programmed decisions, in contrast, are new and unstructured and consequently a previously established decision rule cannot be applied. In other words, the organisation has no established procedures or records for dealing with the decision, which can therefore appear to be highly complex. Non-programmed decisions tend to occur at higher levels in the organisation, have long-term consequences and require a degree of judgement and creativity.[3] Examples of non-programmed decisions include the decision to try an unproven technology or to expand into a previously unknown market. Allegro, the Irish distribution company, took a major non-programmed decision in deciding to launch the American snack Pringles on the Irish market. This product is very different from traditional snack foods in that it is marketed in a distinctive tube packaging, which protects the product from breaking, and has a long shelf life of 18 months. The decision paid off, and Pringles captured a significant share of the market.

FIGURE 5.2 CHARACTERISTICS OF PROGRAMMED AND NON-PROGRAMMED DECISIONS

Programmed	Non-programmed
Well-structured	Poorly structured
Routine	New
Information available	Little information
Taken at lower levels	Taken at higher levels
Short time frame	Long time frame
Decision rules and set procedures used	Judgement and creativity used

While these two types of decision are clearly distinguishable, they represent a continuum from programmed to non-programmed, rather than being exclusive categories. Many decisions will contain elements of each category.

5.3 Decision-making conditions

In general there are three different types of condition under which managers take decisions.[4]

The first condition is **certainty**, which means that the available alternatives and their costs or benefits are certain. In other words, managers know with certainty that particular alternatives will lead to definite outcomes and there is no element of doubt. Given the current turbulent business environment it is not surprising that very few decisions can be made with certainty. Only the most minor of decisions can be taken under a condition of complete certainty.

The second condition is **risk**. Under the risk condition, all available choices and their potential costs and benefits are known, but the outcomes are sometimes in doubt. So, while the alternatives are known, the outcomes are unknown. An example of a risk condition is the throw of a die: the alternatives (one to six) are known, but the outcome is not known – there is a one-in-six chance of each number coming up. The probability of certain events can be calculated by the organisation using statistical techniques. Objective probability is the likelihood of an event occurring based on hard quantitative data, normally statistical. In contrast, subjective probability is a personal judgement of the likelihood of an event occurring. In today's business environment, risk taking has become critically important for organisations.

The final condition is **uncertainty**, under which the available alternatives, the likelihood of their occurrence and the outcomes are all unknown. Decisions made under uncertainty are the most difficult to take because of this lack of concrete knowledge. Such decisions tend to be ambiguous, intangible and highly unusual.[5] In the current business environment more and more decisions are taken under uncertainty. When making decisions under uncertain conditions, managers require intuition and judgement.

The decision-making conditions represent a continuum from certainty to uncertainty as shown in Figure 5.3.

FIGURE 5.3 DECISION-MAKING CONDITIONS

Certainty	Risk	Uncertainty
Decision is a certainty	Decision is a gamble	Decision needs courage and is a gamble

While decisions taken under conditions of certainty tend to be the easiest to make and the most successful, decision failures can occur in relation to any type of decision. Given the additional problems associated with risk and uncertainty conditions it is not surprising that there are decision failures in these conditions. Any decision can suffer from adverse conditions and bad luck, but much decision failure can be attributed to decision-making procedures, which are under the manager's control.[6]

When managers are faced with the choice of competing alternatives they frequently experience conflict, both within themselves and also from other individuals and groups in the organisation. In the first instance managers experience psychological conflict when faced with a range of alternatives, none of which they find appealing. For example, when faced with the need to reduce costs the manager can reduce the hours of work or eliminate a bonus for all staff. Neither of these alternatives is appealing and the manager may experience conflict over which choice to make. Alternatively, managers may also be faced with a range of extremely appealing alternatives but experience conflict because they have to choose only one. For example, a manager might have two very capable internal candidates going for promotion, but can only choose one.

In making decisions, managers also experience conflict with other members of the organisation. Different groups will protect the interests of their own work groups very carefully and will not want to see any reduction in status through declining resources. Unless the decision is construed to be a win–win scenario it is inevitable that some degree of conflict will emerge.

Given that most managers face lack of structure and information, and uncertainty and conflict as they make decisions, it is not surprising that managerial decision making has become all the more challenging, yet also critically important, in recent years. Decisions that managers make about strategy and direction are typically characterised by uncertainty and conflict and result in demanding decision-making scenarios.

5.4 The decision-making process

Most models of decision making include six essential steps that it is recommended managers should follow when making decisions. As shown in Figure 5.4, managers should:
1. Identify and diagnose the problem.
2. Identify alternative solutions.
3. Evaluate alternatives.
4. Choose an alternative.
5. Implement the decision.
6. Evaluate the decision.

FIGURE 5.4 STEPS IN THE DECISION-MAKING PROCESS

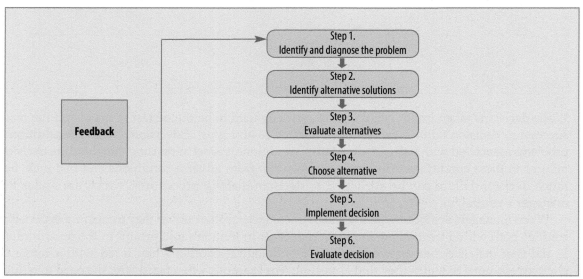

5.4.1 Step 1: Problem identification and diagnosis

The first stage of the decision-making process is recognising that a problem exists and that action has to be taken. A problem is a discrepancy between the current state of affairs and a desired state of affairs. Unless the problem is identified in precise terms, solutions are very difficult to find. In seeking to identify a problem, managers can use a variety of sources of data, including comparing organisational performance against historical performance, against the current performance of other organisations/departments or against future expected performance.

Problem identification must be followed by a willingness to do something to rectify the situation. Before taking action the problem needs accurate diagnosis. Diagnosis involves assessing the true cause of the problem by carefully selecting all relevant material and discarding information which is not relevant to the problem at hand. Sometimes decisions need to be made when a problem does not exist: for example, a company might want to grow rapidly to capitalise on market opportunities and will have to decide on what route to take.

5.4.2 Step 2: Identification of alternatives

Having identified and diagnosed the problem, the next step for an organisation is to identify a range of alternatives to solve the problem. Managers should try to identify as many alternatives as possible in order to broaden options for the organisation. In generating alternatives the organisation may look toward ready-made solutions that have been tried before, or custom-made solutions that have to be designed specifically for the problem at hand. In today's business environment more and more organisations are applying custom-made solutions to enhance competitive advantage.

Returning to the previous example of an organisation seeking growth opportunities, identifying all the alternatives is critically important when making a choice about a certain course of action. Some of the alternatives open to the company are:
- growth through acquisition
- growth through establishing an overseas facility
- using an agent to market and distribute the product abroad
- growth through diversification of the existing product line.

With such a decision the organisation has to design its own individual custom-made solution. While the organisation might be guided by previous decisions it has taken, or by what competitors have done, this decision is unique and therefore requires new solutions.

5.4.3 Step 3: Evaluation of alternatives

Having identified the available alternatives, a manager needs to evaluate each alternative in order to choose the best one. Consideration should be given to the advantages and disadvantages as well as the costs and benefits associated with each option. Most alternatives will have positive and negative aspects and the manager will have to try to balance anticipated outcomes.

Depending on the situation, evaluation of alternatives may be intuitive (based on gut feeling) or based on scientific analysis. Most organisations try to use a combination of both. When evaluating alternatives, managers may consider the potential consequences of alternatives under several different scenarios. In doing so they can develop contingency plans which can be implemented with possible future scenarios in mind. When evaluating the range of alternatives available to the organisation to handle growth, a number of different criteria can be applied. The organisation will consider the cost associated with each option as well as the time taken to complete each alternative. The chances of success of each of the options will also have to be considered, as will the impact of any decision on employees, training and culture.

5.4.4 Step 4: Choice of alternative

Having evaluated the various alternatives, the next step is to choose the most suitable one. If for some reason none of the options considered is suitable, the manager should revert back to Step 2 of the process and begin again. When there are suitable alternatives and Steps 2 and 3 have been conducted skilfully, selecting alternatives may be relatively easy. In practice, however, alternatives may not differ significantly in terms of their outcomes and therefore decisions will be a matter of judgement. In coming to a decision the manager will be confronted by many conflicting requirements that will have to be taken into account. For example, some trade-offs may involve quality versus acceptability of the decision, and political and resource constraints.

Returning to our example, using the evaluative criteria in Step 3 the organisation will make a decision about which alternative to choose for future growth. Based on an analysis of the market and the organisation's capabilities they decide to purchase a small company with a strong market presence in a geographical region presently unserved by the organisation.

5.4.5 Step 5: Implementation

Once the decision has been made it needs to be implemented. This stage of the process is critical to the success of the decision and is the key to effective decision making. The best alternative is worth nothing if it is not implemented properly. In order to successfully implement a decision, managers must ensure that those who are implementing it fully understand why the choice was made, why it is being implemented, and are fully committed to its success.

Decisions often fail at the implementation stage because managers do not ensure that people understand the rationale behind the decision and that they are fully committed to it. For this reason many organisations are attempting to push decision making further down the organisation to ensure that employees feel some sense of ownership in the decisions that are made.

To implement the decision to acquire another smaller business in a different country requires good conceptual skills and could prove challenging. In addition to legal and competitive issues the company will have to deal with assimilating aspects of the new business into their current operations.

5.4.6 Step 6: Evaluation

Once the decision is implemented, it needs to be evaluated to provide feedback. The process of evaluation should take place at all managerial levels. This step allows managers to see the results of the decision and to identify any adjustments that need to be executed. In almost all cases some form of adjustment will be made to ensure a more favourable outcome. Evaluation and feedback are not one-off activities, however, and they should form part of an ongoing process. As conditions change, decisions should be re-evaluated to ensure that they are still the most appropriate for the organisation. This also helps managers to learn about making sound decisions taking past experience into account.

Evaluation of the acquisition of a new business will be measured on the success and profitability of the venture. As the primary goal of the decision was to increase growth opportunities, the organisation should carefully monitor growth rates. The organisation, having acquired a new business, will feed back its experiences into the next decision-making process with which it is faced.

The model presented in Figure 5.4, and discussed above, is a useful framework for managers to consider when making decisions. It must be recognised, however, that the process is never as neat and sequential as the one outlined above.

5.5 Barriers to making good decisions

The decision-making process discussed in the previous section is the suggested course of action that managers should take when making decisions. Research has shown that managers make better decisions when they follow a sequential process.[7] However, as managers attempt to make good decisions they are faced with many challenges and barriers. Decisions can be framed either in terms of gains or losses, or by a reference point against which the various options can be evaluated. A manager normally applies a *decision frame* to a decision. A decision frame refers to the perception held by the manager in terms of gains or losses associated with the outcome of a decision.[8] Consequently, the same outcome could be viewed as a gain or a loss depending on the perception and reference point used. For example, if an employee received a €1,000 bonus when everyone else received a €2,000 bonus, should this be viewed as a gain or as a loss? The answer depends on the individual and whether the reference point is the employee's original salary (gain) or a comparison with others (loss).

Management Focus 5.1 Coca-Cola's negative decision frame

In the mid-1980s Coca-Cola was the biggest-selling soft drink worldwide, yet the company decided to change the formula and introduce a 'new' Coca-Cola to the market. The result was disastrous: consumers disliked the new formula and preferred the old one. As a result, after three months the company had to reintroduce the old formula, using the brand name Coca-Cola Classic. What events led to the company taking such a poor decision? The decision was the product of a negative decision frame. Coca-Cola's share of the market had been steadily declining and the company's options were to make no changes and continue to decline, or to take the risky option to change the formula. In essence, the choice was between certain loss or risk, and the company chose the latter. As it turned out, though, the decision the company made resulted in more short-term losses than anticipated.

The nature of decision framing is important because managers usually tend to avoid risky options, though when faced with a choice between losses, managers will tend to opt for a risky alternative. Choosing between losses is a choice between risky alternatives: between certain loss and possibly even greater loss. Decision framing may be responsible for many decision failures in that risky decisions that normally go wrong are the product of a choice between losses.[9] The result is a strong preference for risk rather than perceived certain loss. This motivates managers to take risks in order to avoid losses. Although such behaviour might sometimes avoid loss, the typical result is actually to increase it.

Decision making is also susceptible to psychological biases. Managers frequently allow their subjective biases to interfere with objective decision making. Individuals often allow their own personal feelings and emotions to creep into the decision-making process. Consider the example of a manager faced with a decision about where to relocate his/her office. One location is the most effective but the other alternative is in a far nicer location and is closer to where the manager lives. Which option will the manager choose? If subjective biases come into play, it will be the latter.

Managers can also be affected by the 'illusion of control'. This essentially means that managers develop a sense that they can influence outcomes even when they have no control over events. Such over-confidence can be very dangerous for decision making, particularly if an important strategic decision is in question. Managers can also pay too much attention to short-term gains at the expense of long-term sustainable success. This has tended to be a feature of national culture in Western societies. Quite often long-term strategies require short-term pain.

The final barrier to making effective managerial decisions is the issue of time. Pressures of time frequently mean that decisions are rushed. If managers are under pressure to reach a decision quickly they may not have time to thoroughly research all of the available options, and the quality of the decision could suffer accordingly. Unless the decision is a programmed one it can be very difficult to make under pressure of time.

5.6 Approaches to decision making

The four most popular approaches to the study of decision making are: the rational model; bounded rationality; the political model; and escalation to commitment. In this section each will be examined and their contribution evaluated.

5.6.1 The concept of rationality

Rationality in relation to decision making refers to a process that is perfectly logical and objective, whereby managers gather information objectively, evaluate available evidence, consider all alternatives and eventually make choices that will lead to the best outcomes for the organisation. The rational approach to decision making has its foundations in traditional economic theory, which argues that managers attempt to maximise benefits and have the capacity to make complex decisions quickly. Such a rational approach to decision making assumes that four conditions are fulfilled:

1. There is perfect knowledge of all the available alternatives.
2. There is perfect knowledge of all of the consequences of the available alternatives.
3. Managers have the capacity to objectively evaluate the consequences of the available alternatives.
4. Managers have a well-structured and definite set of procedures to allow them to make optimum decisions.

Although managers rarely have total control over all of the factors that determine how successful decisions will be, they can ensure a degree of control over the process that they use for making decisions. It is increasingly clear that few managerial decisions are taken in a completely rational manner. Indeed, some of the most effective and innovative decisions used little in the way of rational guidelines.[10]

5.6.2 Bounded rationality

As we have seen, decisions are made under varying conditions ranging from certainty and risk to uncertainty. In the current environment managers seldom make decisions under the conditions of certainty that would be needed to apply a completely rational model. For many managers today the rational approach represents an ideal approach, but one that is simply not attainable under current conditions of risk and uncertainty.

Given the fact that managers cannot always make decisions under certainty conditions, and in a rational manner, they have to apply a less than perfect form of rationality. Herbert Simon called this 'bounded rationality', and argued that decisions taken by managers are bounded by limited mental capacity and emotions, and by environmental factors over which they have no control. Due to these limitations managers rarely maximise or take ideal decisions with the best possible outcomes.

Intuition and judgement are therefore used by the manager to solve problems and make decisions. Taking a rational approach to problem solving and decision making involves clear identification of goals, objectives, alternatives, potential consequences and their outcomes. Each of these is in turn evaluated in terms of contribution to the overall aim. In judgemental decision making, the response to the need for a decision is usually rapid – too rapid to allow for an orderly sequential analysis of the situation – and the decision maker cannot usually give a veridical account of either the process by which the decision was reached or the grounds for judging it correct.[11]

As we saw in section 5.5, psychological biases can influence judgement. For example, a manager might have to make a decision about where to establish a subsidiary office of the organisation. When making the decision the manager could be influenced by personal opinions, emotions and personal bias in favour of one location over another. This might be particularly noticeable if the manager is subsequently going to work in the office, as the choice might be heavily influenced by his/her desire to live in one location. In this way, total rationality is not applied as the manager may choose a location that s/he favours and this will not necessarily be the most rational choice.

Another integral part of the bounded rationality approach is the notion that managers seek to satisfice, that is, settle for an alternative which is satisfactory, rather than continuing to search for the optimal solution. Satisficing may occur because the manager tires of the decision-making process and seeks to resolve the problem quickly with the first minimally acceptable solution rather than searching further for a better one.

Managers may also be unable to handle large amounts of complex information. Bounded rationality also recognises that managers may not have full and complete information and may experience problems processing information, which clearly affects a manager's ability to make optimal decisions.[12] Decisions made under bounded rationality may not always be the best; however, on occasion good decisions have been made on the basis of judgement and gut feeling.

Therefore the rational approach associated with traditional economic theory proposes that managers seek to maximise benefits and in this sense outlines how managers should behave. Bounded rationality, however, concentrates on how managers actually behave in practice when making decisions, and argues that limitations placed on managers mean that they will seek to satisfice rather than maximise.

5.6.3 The political model

While the previous approaches have concentrated on the role played by rationality in the decision-making process, the political model concentrates on the impact of organisational politics on decision making. Power and politics play an important role in the decision-making process.

Power is the ability to influence others. In the context of an organisation power can be viewed as the ability to exert influence over individuals, work groups or departments. There are five main types of power found in the organisational setting:

1. **Legitimate** power originates from the manager's position within the organisation's hierarchy. The power is inherent in the hierarchical position the manager occupies.
2. **Reward** power originates from the manager's ability to withhold rewards from others.
3. **Expert** power derives from the expert knowledge and information that an individual/manager has amassed.
4. **Referent** power originates from the charisma or identification that a manager has developed.
5. **Coercive** power is associated with emotional or physical threats to ensure compliance.

In the decision-making process those who possess power are clearly an important dynamic. Political decision processes are used in situations where uncertainty, disagreement and lack of information are common. Within organisations it is common to find different coalitions, all of which possess varying degrees of power depending on the situation. Coalitions can be formed by particular work groups, teams, managers, functional specialists, external stakeholders and trade unions. Each group brings with it certain ideas and values, coupled with power, in relation to the decision under discussion. It is common for each coalition to defend its own territory and to ensure that any decisions made do not negatively impact on its members (both formal and informal). The presence of coalitions therefore adds an important ingredient to the decision-making process.

Different coalitions are likely to possess different and conflicting objectives. Depending on the relative power of each coalition, negotiation and compromise will feature strongly. In some cases the compromise and outcome will be a win–lose situation, which means that one coalition's gain is another's loss. In other cases a win–win situation can be generated. The political model recognises that, apart from actually making the decision, many other factors are at work, including negotiation, compromise and power struggles. The presence of political forces can be beneficial to the decision-making process if it means that a wider range of issues is considered and greater input and commitment is achieved. On the other hand, power struggles may lead to a lack of focus on key issues and produce narrowly defined decisions largely following the self-interest of particular groups.

5.6.4 *Escalation of commitment*

While it does not explain how decisions are made, this approach concentrates on why people continue to pursue a failing course of action: that is, why commitment to a poor decision often escalates after the initial decision has been made. This approach is particularly concerned with decision makers who, even in the face of failure, continue to invest resources in a failing decision. For example, an organisation may decide to enter a particular market by introducing a certain product. After a little while it may become obvious that the product is not suited to that market. The organisation, however, continues to increase spending on advertising and marketing rather than exiting from the market.

Escalation of commitment to a failing decision is often attributed to self-justification and a feeling of personal responsibility for the decision. When individuals are personally responsible for negative consequences they may decide to increase investment of resources in a previously chosen course of action.[13] Organisations therefore have to strike a balance between persevering with a decision and recognising when a decision is failing and should be abandoned. Not all organisations fall into the escalation of commitment trap. In the previous example of Coca-Cola, the organisation realised that the decision to change the formula was incorrect and subsequently altered its course of action.

5.7 Group versus individual decision making

Task forces, teams and boards are all examples of where decision making occurs in a group setting. The basic idea behind group decision making is the notion that two heads are better than one. Generally the diversity of groups facilitates better-quality decisions.[14] However, a group can be inferior to the best individual in the group.[15] In some cases, groups will provide the best-quality decisions and in others the individual will do better.[16] In coming to a conclusion about the efficiency of groups it is necessary to consider the advantages and disadvantages of group decision making.

Group decision making: advantages and disadvantages

Advantages

- Group decision making allows a greater number of perspectives and approaches to be considered, thereby increasing the number of alternatives that can be drawn up.
- Groups generally facilitate a larger pool of information to be processed. Individuals from different areas can bring varied information to the decision-making setting.
- By increasing the number of people involved in the process it is more likely that a greater number of people will understand why the decision was made, and this facilitates implementation.
- Group decision making allows people to become involved and produces a sense of ownership of the final decision, which means that people will be more committed to the decision.
- Using a group to arrive at a decision means that less co-ordination and communication is required when implementing the decision.   ⟶

Disadvantages

- Group decisions take longer to arrive at and this can be problematic when speed of action is key.
- Groups can be indecisive and opt for satisficing rather then maximising. Indecision can arise from lack of agreement among members. Satisficing occurs when individuals grow tired of the process and want it brought to a conclusion, leading to satisficing rather than maximisation.
- Individuals who have either a strong personality or a strong position can dominate groups. The result is that a particular individual can exert more influence than others. The main problem with such a situation is that the dominating person's view of the decision need not necessarily be right; and if his/her view is the right one, convening a group for discussion is a waste of time.
- Groups inevitably have to compromise to reach a decision and this can lead to mediocre decisions. Mediocrity results when an individual's thinking is brought into line with the average quality of a group's thinking. This is called the levelling effect.
- Groups can lead to group think, which can be defined as 'a mode of thinking that people engage in when they are deeply involved in a cohesive group, when members' strivings for unanimity override their motivation to realistically appraise alternative courses of action'. Group think happens in situations where the need to achieve consensus among group members becomes so powerful that it takes over realistic evaluations of available alternatives. Criticism is suppressed and conflicting views are not aired for fear of breaking up a positive team spirit. Such groups become over confident and too willing to take risks.

Source: Irving, J. (1982) *Group Think.* Boston: Houghton Mifflin.

Having considered the advantages and disadvantages of group decision making, it is clear that group decision making is well suited to certain circumstances. We can identify factors that favour individual and group decision making.[17]

Factors favouring individual decision making include:

- Short time frame.
- Decision is relatively unimportant to the group.
- Manager has all the data needed to make the decision.
- One or two members of the group are likely to dominate.
- Conflict is likely.
- People attend too many meetings.
- The data is confidential.
- Group members are not sufficiently qualified.
- The manager is dominant.
- The decision does not directly affect the group.

Factors favouring group decision making include:

- Creativity is required.
- Data is held by the group.
- Acceptance of the solution by group members is important.
- Understanding of the solution is important.

- The problem is complex and needs a broad range of knowledge.
- The manager wants to build commitment.
- More risk taking is involved.
- Better understanding of group members is needed.
- The group is responsible for the decision.
- The manager wants feedback on ideas.

Management Focus 5.2 Baileys: the result of a brainstorming session

The concept of Baileys Irish Cream was developed from a brainstorming session. Baileys is a unique mixture of fresh, premium Irish dairy cream, spirits, Irish whiskey and a proprietary recipe of chocolate flavours.

It's now sold in 180 countries worldwide and is both the world's top selling liqueur brand and the world's top selling cream liqueur brand. Baileys accounts for over 50 per cent of all spirits exported from Ireland. Over 75% of the raw ingredients and packaging used to make and present Baileys is sourced from the island of Ireland.

Source: www.the-baileys-lounge.baileys.com/en-ie/Product-and-Company-Information.aspx.

5.8 Improving group decision making

In order to avoid the disadvantages associated with group decision making and to build on the advantages, three main ways of improving group decision making have been proposed.

Brainstorming, which became popular in the 1950s, was developed by Alexander Osborn to facilitate the development of creative solutions and alternatives. Brainstorming is solely concerned with idea generation rather than evaluation, choice or implementation. The term effectively means using the brain creatively to 'storm' a problem. It is based on the belief that when people interact in a relaxed and unrestrained setting they will generate creative ideas. The acceptance of new ideas is also more likely when the decision is made by the group involved with its implementation.[18] In brainstorming the group members are normally given a summary of the problem before the meeting. At the meeting members come up with various ideas, which are recorded in full view of all other members. None of the alternatives is evaluated or criticised at this stage. As members produce new ideas and alternatives this serves to stimulate other members in the hope that a truly good solution can be identified.

The **Delphi technique** was developed in the early 1960s as a means of avoiding the undesirable effects, while retaining the positive aspects, of group interaction.[19] Delphi was the seat of the Greek god Apollo, who was renowned for his wise decisions. The Delphi technique consists of a panel of experts formed to examine a problem. Rather than physically meeting, the various members are kept apart so that social or psychological pressures associated with group behaviour cannot influence them. In order to find out their views, they are asked to complete a questionnaire. A co-ordinator then summarises the findings and members are asked to fill out another questionnaire to re-evaluate earlier points. The technique assumes that, as repeated questionnaires are conducted, the range of responses will narrow to produce a consensus. The Delphi technique is particularly useful where experts are physically dispersed, anonymity is required and members have difficulty communicating with each other. On the negative side, however, it reduces direct interaction among group members.

Nominal grouping was developed in the 1970s. In contrast to brainstorming, it does not allow a free association of ideas, tries to restrict verbal interaction and can be used at many other stages of the decision-making process apart from idea generation.[20] In nominal grouping, members are given a problem and are asked to think of ideas individually with no discussion. They then present these ideas on a flip chart. A period of discussion follows, which builds on the ideas presented. After the discussion, members privately rank the ideas. Generation of ideas and discussion proceeds in this manner until a solution is found.[21]

The main advantage of this approach is that it overcomes differences in power and prestige between members and it can also be used at a variety of stages in the overall decision-making process. Its main disadvantages are that its structure may limit creativity and it is costly and time-consuming.

5.9 Summary of key propositions

- Decision making is the selection of a course of action from a range of alternatives. It plays an integral part in planning but is also a fundamental part of the entire management process.
- Organisations make hundreds of decisions each day, which can be classified as programmed and non-programmed. Programmed decisions are well structured, routine, repetitive, occurring on a regular basis. Non-programmed decisions are new, unstructured and have no established procedures for making them.
- Decisions are taken under different conditions ranging from complete certainty to risk and uncertainty.
- Certainty means that the available alternatives and their costs or benefits are certain: managers know with certainty that particular alternatives will lead to definite outcomes and there is no element of doubt.
- Under the risk condition, all the possible alternatives and their potential costs and benefits are known, but the outcomes are sometimes in doubt: the alternatives are known but the outcomes are unknown.
- Uncertainty is when the available alternatives, the likelihood of their occurrence and the outcomes are all unknown. Decisions made under uncertain conditions are consequently the most difficult to take due to the lack of concrete knowledge. In the current business environment more and more decisions are being made under conditions of uncertainty.
- Barriers to effective decision making include: decision framing, the illusion of control and time pressures.
- The decision making process contains six key steps: problem identification and diagnosis; identification of alternatives; evaluating alternatives; choice of alternative; implementation; and evaluation.
- The four most popular approaches to decision making are: the rational model; bounded rationality; escalation of commitment; and the political model.
- Rationality in relation to decision making refers to a process that is perfectly logical and objective, whereby managers gather information objectively, evaluate available evidence,

consider all alternatives and ultimately make choices that will lead to the best outcomes for the organisation.
- Decisions can be taken by either groups or individuals depending on the nature of the decision. The quality of group decisions can be enhanced by three main techniques: brainstorming; the Delphi technique; and nominal grouping.

Discussion Questions

1 Explain the nature and importance of decision making.
2 Explain, using your own examples, the differences between programmed and non-programmed decisions.
3 Explain the different decision-making conditions under which decisions are taken.
4 What do you understand by the term 'rationality' in relation to decision making?
5 Explain the term 'bounded rationality'.
6 What role do political forces play in organisational decision making?
7 Apply the rational model of decision making to your decision about how to spend next year's summer holiday. Evaluate its effectiveness.
8 Outline the advantages of group decision making.
9 Outline the disadvantages of group decision making.
10 Explain the terms 'group think' and the 'levelling effect'.
11 Evaluate group versus individual decision making.
12 How can group decision making be improved?

Concluding Case: Glanbia – big plans; key decisions

Glanbia plc is an international nutritional solutions and cheese group. Its headquarters are in Ireland, and it produces some of the best-known brands in Ireland. Glanbia is a major supplier of mozzarella for pizza toppings, and cheese for both McDonald's and Burger King. The company was formed from the merger of Avonmore Foods and Waterford Foods in 1997. It employs 4,300 people worldwide and has manufacturing and processing facilities in seven countries. The company is quoted on both the Dublin and London Stock Exchanges. Total group revenue for 2010 was €2.6 billion.

The company's vision is 'to be the leading global nutritional solutions and cheese group'. To this end the business strategy of Glanbia is 'to deliver attractive and growing returns to shareholders, excellent solutions and service to our customers, value adding routes to market for our milk suppliers and to provide rewarding careers to our employees'.

Operationally the group is divided into three main divisions, reflecting its history and the direction of its strategy.

1   **US Cheese and Global Nutritionals.** This division is one of the leading producers of American-style Cheddar cheese for both the US market and also for export to overseas markets. Glanbia has a large-scale cheese processing facility in Idaho, USA. The Global Nutritionals side of the business developed as a by-product associated with cheese processing, namely whey pool, which is a key raw material for nutritionals. The nutritionals business can be further divided into: Ingredient Technologies, a business-to-business nutritional ingredients solutions development sector; Performance Nutrition, consisting of health and wellness products; and Customised Premix Solutions, a business-to-business vitamins and minerals business. Examples of nutritional products include Thermax, used in ready to drink beverages, and Revive, a recovery beverage.

2.   **Dairy Ireland.** This division consists of three main sectors: Agribusiness produces and sells a wide variety of farm inputs, including animal feed, to the group's main farming suppliers; Dairy Ingredients uses 1.5 billion litres of milk to produce cheese- and dairy-based ingredients (Glanbia processes 25 per cent of the Irish milk pool and 40 per cent of the Irish whey pool) and Consumer Products uses 0.3 billion litres of milk annually to produce dairy products and liquid milk.

3.   **Joint Ventures and Associates**. Glanbia has three main international joint ventures: Southwest Cheese, based in the USA; Glanbia Cheese in the UK; and Nutricima in Nigeria.

Key strategic priorities for the group include: alignment with key customers and markets; first-class science-based innovation; effective risk and capital management and operational excellence; and strategic cost management.

TABLE 5.1 GLANBIA'S OPERATING DIVISIONS

US Cheese and Global Nutritionals	Dairy Ireland	Joint Ventures and Associates
• US Cheese • Ingredient Technologies • Performance Nutrition • Customised Premix Solutions	• Dairy Ingredients • Consumer Products • Agribusiness	• Southwest Cheese • Glanbia Cheese • Nutricima
40% group revenue	44% group revenue	16% group revenue

Glanbia's strategy centres on maximising the scale and efficiency of its businesses. To this end, the company aims to secure and enhance its strong market leadership in key sectors by continuous development in innovation, market knowledge operations and technological standards. In pursuit of this strategy and in response to events in the competitive marketplace, Glanbia has taken a number of important decisions. Some of these decisions were expansionary in nature; others were responses to strong market competition and unfavourable environmental conditions.

Following the 1997 merger, Glanbia decided to create a single group identity, which it introduced in 1999. The Glanbia group name was designed to replace the previous use of both Avonmore and Waterford. It was envisaged that this move would reduce consumer confusion, especially in the UK market, and also reduce internal divisions between the former Avonmore and Waterford staff.

After the merger and creation of Glanbia the overall focus centred on a number of sectors, the two most significant of which were nutritional products and cheese. The cheese sector involved the USA, pizza and cheese production for the EU market, and the Irish and UK retail cheese market. The USA cheese business, based in Idaho, is thriving due to its low-cost location and the scale advantages accruing to Glanbia. Glanbia benefited from strong demand and increases in the price of cheese. The competitive position of some of Glanbia's other divisions deteriorated over the same period and this presented the company with some tough decisions. Many of the problems centred on the UK market where the strength of sterling, price wars between supermarkets and strong competition among suppliers have all negatively affected Glanbia.

In 1999, the liquid milk business in the UK provided Glanbia with many problems as the company found one of its traditional markets under severe price pressure. Glanbia lost an important account with Asda WalMart and continued to face strong competition from other suppliers. In addition, the supermarkets began a process of rationalising the number of suppliers they traded with. Under such competitive pressure Glanbia decided to sell the liquid milk business in the UK to Express Dairies. The global meat market has also been faced with oversupply and falling demand. From 1998 onwards, demand from Russia and Asia declined. This was coupled with increased international competition. The extent of oversupply in the international pig meat market in the EU and USA led Glanbia to dispose of its beef operation to Dawn Meats; and it also disposed of its sheep meats division.

In 2010 Glanbia announced its intention to sell its Irish dairy business to Glanbia Co-operative Society (its 54.6 per cent shareholder) in order to focus on expansion of its international business. In 2008 the company acquired Optimum Nutrition, a US body-building supplement manufacturer. By focusing on the nutritionals side of the business Glanbia could see faster and more consistent growth. In addition, the recession had dented earnings across the food industry and global diary markets had become more volatile. However, the sale did not receive the required agreement by the Glanbia Co-operative members in May 2010 and the plan was put on hold. In November 2012 a decision was made to establish a joint venture between Glanbia Co-op and Glanbia plc (on a 60:40 basis), that would take control of the company's Irish milk processing unit. To finance the plan the co-op reduced its shareholding in Glanbia plc from 54.4 per cent to 51.4 per cent.

Keep up to date
www.glanbia.com

Sources: www.glanbia.com/glance; O'Brien, D. and Flanagan, P. (2012) 'Windfall for Irish Farmers as 82pc Vote Yes to Glanbia Share Sale', *Irish Independent* [online] www.independent.ie/irish-news/windfall-for-farmers-as-82pc-vote-yes-to-glanbia-share-sale-28941062.html.

Case Questions
1. Discuss the link between Glanbia's vision, business strategy and key strategic priorities.
2. Identify the key decisions that have been made by Glanbia.
3. What type of decisions were they? Under what conditions were they made?
4. How successful have the decisions been?

Notes and References

1 Weihrich, H. and Koontz, H. (1993) *Management*. New York: McGraw-Hill.

2 See Priem, R. (1994) 'Executive Judgement, Organisational Congruence and Firm Performance', *Organisational Science*, August, 421–32.

3 Agor, W. (1986) 'How Top Executives Use Their Intuition to Make Important Decisions', *Business Horizons* 29(2), 49–53.

4 Bass, B. (1983) *Organisational Decision Making*. Illinois: Irwin; March, J. (1994) *A Primer on Decision Making: How Decisions Happen*. New York: Free Press; Harrison, F. (1994) *The Managerial Decision Making Process*. Boston: Houghton Mifflin.

5 Boynton, A. (1993) 'Management Search Activity: The Impact of Perceived Role Uncertainty and Threat', *Journal of Management* 19(4), 725–48.

6 Whyte. G. (1991) 'Decision Failures: Why They Occur and How to Prevent Them', *Academy of Management Executive* 5(3), 23–31.

7 Dean, J. and Sharfman, M. (1996) 'Does Decision Process Matter? A Study of Strategic Decision-making Effectiveness', *Academy of Management Journal* 9, 368–96.

8 Tversky, A. and Kahneman, D. (1981) 'The Framing of Decisions and the Psychology of Choice', *Science* 59, 453–8.

9 Whyte. G. (1991) 'Decision Failures: Why They Occur and How to Prevent Them', *Academy of Management Executive* 5(3), 23–31.

10 Imparato, N. and Harari, O. (1995) *Jumping the Curve: Innovation and Strategic Choice in an Age of Transition*. San Francisco: Jossey-Bass.

11 Simon, H. (1987) 'Making Management Decisions: The Role of Intuition and Emotion', *Academy of Management Executive*, February, 57–64.

12 Saunders, C. and Jones, J. (1990) 'Temporal Sequences in Information Acquisition for Decision-Making: A Focus on Source and Medium', *Academy of Management Review* 15, 29–46.

13 Staw, B. (1976) 'Knee Deep in the Big Muddy: A Study of Escalating Commitment to a Chosen Course of Action', *Organisational Behaviour and Human Performance* 16, 27–44.

14 Shaw, M. (1981) *Group Dynamics: The Psychology of Small Group Behaviour*. New York: McGraw-Hill; Sussman, L. and Deep, S. (1984) *COMEX: The Communication Experience in Human Relations*. Cincinnati: South Western.

15 Hill, G. (1982) 'Group Versus Individual Performance: Are n + 1 Heads Better than One?', *Psychological Bulletin* 91, 517–39.

16 Locke, E., Schweiger, D. and Latham, G. (1986) 'Participation in Decision Making: Should it be Used?', *Organisation Dynamics* 14(3), 65–79.

17 Sussman and Deep, *op. cit.*

18 Summers, I. and White, D. (1976) 'Creativity Techniques: Towards Improvement of the Decision Process', *Academy of Management Review* 1(3), 99–107.

19 Dalkey, N. and Helmar, O. (1963) 'An Experimental Application of the Delphi Methods to the Use of Experts', *Managerial Science* 9, 458–67.

20 Delbecq, A. and Van de Ven, A. (1971) 'A Group Process Model for Problem Identification and Programme Planning', *Journal of Applied Behavioural Science* 7, 466–92.

21 Dowling, K. (2000) 'Asynchronous Implementation of the Nominal Group Technique: Is it Effective?' *Decision Support Systems* No. 3.

CHAPTER 6

Organisational Structure and Design

- To understand that organising, the second function of management, is the process of dividing organisational tasks between groups, individuals and departments and co-ordinating their activities to achieve organisational goals.
- To appreciate that the pattern of how activities are divided and later co-ordinated is called organisational structure. Organisational structure is the system of task, reporting and authority relationships within which the work of the organisation is done.
- To understand that organisational structure can be broken down into structural configuration and structural operation. Structural configuration is the size and shape of the structure, and it includes the division of labour, spans of control, hierarchy and departmentalisation. Structural operation, the process of the structure, includes formalisation, decision making, responsibility and authority.
- To understand the main types of departmentalisation: functional; product; geographical; and mixed. The most suitable form of departmentalisation depends on the nature of the organisation's activities.
- To understand how organisational structure has evolved and that traditional approaches to organisational design were universal in that they offered principles that were designed to work in all situations.
- To understand Mintzberg's range of structures: a simple structure; a machine bureaucracy; a professional bureaucracy; a divisionalised structure; and an adhocracy. Mintzberg concludes that there must be a fit between the structure, the structural imperatives, the organisation's strategy and components of the structure.
- To understand the four main trends in organisational design that have been developed in response to the realisation that bureaucracy can no longer cope with a changing business environment. Hierarchical levels have been reduced; the division of labour has been widened; teams have been introduced; and responsibility and decision-making authority has been pushed down the organisation.

6.1 Introduction

This chapter examines the second function of management – organising. Organising is the process of dividing the tasks to be achieved and then co-ordinating them. The framework used for organising is called organisational structure. Organisational structure has a number of components, which we shall examine in this chapter. Organisational design is concerned with how the various components of structure are drawn together to produce particular structural forms. This chapter will also look at historical approaches to structure and design, along with some more recent additions. Recent developments in structure and design have been triggered by changes in the business environment. More contemporary approaches to organisational design will be considered.

6.2 The nature and importance of organising

Organising is the process of dividing tasks between groups, individuals and departments and co-ordinating their activities to achieve organisational goals. The process usually starts with reflection on the plans and objectives devised at the planning stage, followed by the establishment of the major tasks that need to be undertaken to achieve these goals. The tasks are then divided into sub-tasks and resources are allocated to them. Finally, the outcomes of the process are evaluated and corrections made. The function of organising creates relationships between organisational areas that outline when, where and how resources are to be used.

During the organising process the organisation's activities are broken down and departmentalised. Connections and means of co-ordination are then established. The pattern of how activities are divided and later co-ordinated is called *organisational structure*, which can be defined as the system of task, reporting and authority relationships within which the work of the organisation is completed.[1] The purpose of any form of structure is to co-ordinate employees' activities in order to achieve organisational goals.

In recent years, organisational structure and design has undergone a revolution. As a result of the changes in the business environment, organisations have come to realise that in order to survive their structures must be flexible and adaptive, to enable the organisation to respond to and anticipate change.[2] Therefore, having an effective form of organisational structure has become an important source of competitive advantage. Organisations that do not adapt their structures to meet changing needs will face extinction. Those that change their structural design to reflect changed circumstances will achieve the flexibility and creativity necessary for survival. Before examining the various approaches to organisational design, including recent developments, it is necessary to understand the components of an organisation's structure.

6.3 Components of organisational structure

The main components of an organisation's structure can be divided into two main areas: structural configuration and structural operation.

6.3.1 Structural configuration

Structural configuration refers to the size and shape of the structure and includes the size of the hierarchy, spans of control, division of labour and means of co-ordination. The structural configuration of an organisation can be clearly seen from its organisational chart. In contrast, structural operation concentrates on the processes and operation of organisational structure, including decision making, formalisation, responsibility and authority. Taken together, structural configuration and operation provide a full picture of the various component parts of an organisation's structure. Each element is shown in Figure 6.1 and will be examined in turn.

FIGURE 6.1 COMPONENTS OF ORGANISATIONAL STRUCTURE

Structural Configuration	Structural Operation
• Division of labour • Span of control • Hierarchy • Departmentalisation	• Formalisation • Decision making • Responsibility • Authority

The **division of labour** in an organisation is the extent to which the work of the organisation is broken down into different tasks, to be completed by different people. It is also referred to as job specialisation, which means that one person is specialised in doing one particular task. A clear example of division of labour can be found in McDonald's, where staff are assigned to cleaning up the lobby areas, or making fries, or making burgers, or serving the public. In this case the division of labour is quite narrow – each person completes one particular task. A wider division of labour in this example could involve one person looking after customers throughout their visit, from serving them to preparing food and cleaning up after them.

It was hoped that narrow divisions of labour and job specialisation would lead to efficient use of labour, increased standardisation and the development of employee expertise through repetition of a task. However, very narrow job specialisation can lead to reduced job satisfaction and motivation, as people have to complete the same routine task over and over again.[3] It can also lead to absenteeism, high turnover and poor-quality output.

A **span of control** is the number of employees directly reporting to a supervisor. A narrow span of control means that the supervisor is in charge of a small number of employees, whereas a wide span of control means that the supervisor is in charge of a large number. Figure 6.2 shows an example of both wide and narrow spans of control. Supervisor A has only three employees directly reporting to him/her, which is a very narrow span. In contrast, supervisor B has nine employees reporting to him/her, a much wider span.

FIGURE 6.2 NARROW VERSUS WIDE SPANS OF CONTROL

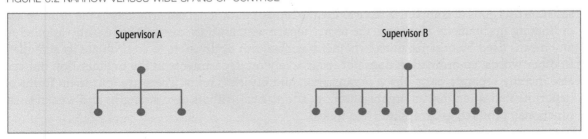

With wider spans of control, employees tend to have more freedom and discretion. In contrast, narrow spans of control usually lead to a high level of supervision, as managers can keep their eyes on the activities of all employees under their control. Effective spans of control are those where employees can be given a degree of freedom, while at the same time having some form of guidance from a supervisor should assistance be required. Many theorists have tried to identify the optimal span of control.[4] The size of the span depends on a number of factors, including the degree of specialisation, the similarity of tasks, the type of information available, the need for autonomy, direct access to supervisors and the abilities and experience of both supervisors and employees.[5] Consequently there can be no universal prescriptions in relation to the optimal span of control that hold true in all situations.

The number of levels and the extent of **hierarchy** outlines the reporting relationships within the organisation from the top to the bottom. Organisations with relatively few levels in their hierarchy are called flat structures; those with many levels are called tall structures. There is a relationship between the number of levels in the hierarchy and the spans of control, as shown in Figure 6.3.

FGURE 6.3 SPANS OF CONTROL AND LEVELS IN THE HIERARCHY

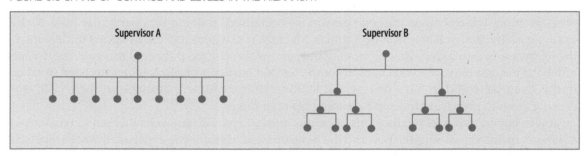

On the left-hand side of the figure it can be seen that where there are wide spans of control fewer levels in the management structure are required. In this case the span of control is nine, and only one hierarchical level is needed. However, if the spans are very narrow, as shown on the right-hand side of the figure, more supervisors and managers are needed, which increases the number of levels in the hierarchy. In this case, the span of control is two and there are three hierarchical levels in the structure. Therefore, as the span increases the hierarchy decreases and, conversely, as the span decreases the hierarchy increases.

The final element of structural configuration is concerned with co-ordinating the various activities of the organisation. This has been traditionally known as **departmentalisation** – as departments were normally set up to co-ordinate activities. In recent years business units or even separate divisions of companies have tended to replace traditional departments as the primary co-ordinating mechanism. However, the term 'departmentalisation' can still be usefully applied to any means used by organisations, whether business unit or division, to co-ordinate its activities. In other words, co-ordination does not focus solely on departments in the organisation but can also include separate parts of the organisation and business units. There are four main forms of departmentalisation that an organisation can adopt, each with its own strengths and weaknesses: functional; product; geographical; and mixed.

Functional departmentalisation

In functional departmentalisation, probably the most popular form of departmentalisation until recent years, the separate units of the organisation are organised according to the functions they perform. Functional departmentalisation is usually structured around the traditional organisational functions of manufacturing, marketing, finance, engineering and personnel. Figure 6.4 provides an example of a functional approach to structuring activities that is used by Aer Lingus. As can be seen from the chart, Aer Lingus is structured around the main functions involved in its activities, which are operations, commercial, finance, human resources (HR) and shared services (information technology, legal, regulatory affairs, procurement, security and services).

FIGURE 6.4 AER LINGUS: A FUNCTIONAL STRUCTURE

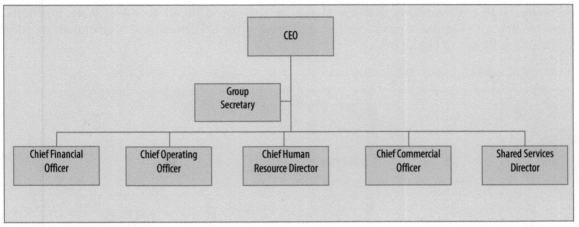

Source: Aer Lingus *Annual Report 2010* www.aerlingus.com/media/aerlinguscom/content/pdfs/corporate/AerLingus GroupplcAnnualReport2010FINAL.pdf.

The main *advantages* associated with functional structures are:
1. The functions of each individual are emphasised, allowing people to concentrate their efforts.
2. Resources are used efficiently by grouping the various functions and gaining economies of scale and reductions in overheads.
3. A clear and simple communication and decision-making system is possible.
4. It is easier to measure the output and performance of the various functional areas, so performance standards are easier to maintain.
5. The training given to specialists is simplified and employees have greater opportunities for specialised training and in-depth skill development.
6. Status is given to each of the main functional areas.
7. Control by the top of the organisation is facilitated.

However, there are also a number of *disadvantages* associated with this form of structure:
1. If departments are large it becomes difficult to co-ordinate the various departments.
2. Due to their limited outlook, employees tend to focus on departmental goals rather than wider organisational goals.

3. It can be quite costly to co-ordinate the activities of the various functions.
4. Such a structure makes it difficult to develop managers with experience in a wide variety of areas.
5. Competition and rivalry between departments can develop.
6. Such a structure can lead to lower customer satisfaction when compared to alternative means of departmentalisation.

Product departmentalisation

The second form of departmentalisation focuses on product. Instead of structuring the organisation around functional areas, it is structured on the basis of the products produced. Business units in many organisations are structured in this manner. Product departmentalisation was introduced by many large organisations that found that it was too difficult to co-ordinate functional departments. An example of product structures used by the US Cheese and Nutritionals division of Glanbia is shown in Figure 6 5.

FIGURE 6.5 GLANBIA US CHEESE AND GLOBAL NUTRITIONALS DIVISION: A PRODUCT STRUCTURE

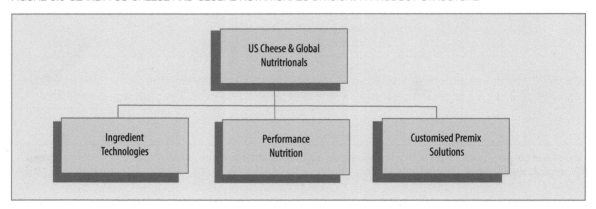

Source: www.glanbia.com/glance.

The main products of the division (Ingredient Technologies, Performance Nutrition and Customised Premix Solutions) become the focus of the structure. Each product line contains the various functional activities it requires, such as personnel and marketing. This form of departmentalisation is also commonly used by organisations operating in the service sector, including CIÉ, which structures its activities into the main services it provides. Figure 6.6 illustrates the service style of structure used by CIÉ, which focuses on its key service areas: Iarnród Éireann, Bus Éireann, Bus Átha Cliath and CIÉ Tours International.

This type of structure has a number of *advantages*:
1. Product areas or business units can be evaluated as profit centres.
2. Additions to the product line can be easily facilitated, which allows for growth. In the same way a product can be discontinued and resources reallocated to another product.
3. It allows fast co-ordination and communication between functions working on a product.
4. The structure focuses on the needs of the clients.

5.   The structure develops managers with a wide experience of various functions.
6.   Employees develop full-time commitment to a particular product line.

FIGURE 6.6 CIÉ: A SERVICE STRUCTURE

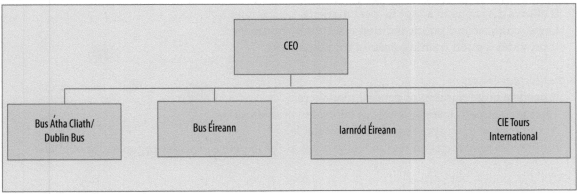

Source: www.cie.ie/about_us/annual_reports.asp.

It also has a number of *disadvantages*:
1.   Co-ordination between specialised product areas can be problematic.
2.   There is a duplication of functional services for each product.
3.   Less communication and interaction occurs between functional specialists.
4.   The emphasis tends to be on product objectives rather than wider organisational objectives.

Geographical departmentalisation

In geographical departmentalisation the organisation is structured around activities in its various geographical locations. An example of geographical structures used by the Kerry Group is shown in Figure 6.7. The Kerry Group is divided into three distinct businesses operating in geographically focused markets: America; Europe, the Middle East and Africa (EMEA); Asia/Pacific; UK; and Ireland.

FIGURE 6.7 KERRY GROUP: A GEOGRAPHIC STRUCTURE

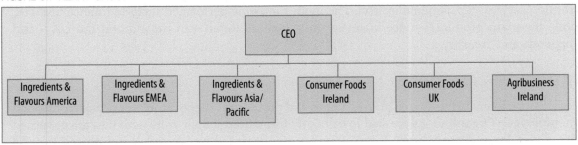

Source: www.kerrygroup.com/page.asp?pid=82.</SN>

This form of structure is particularly suitable for organisations selling in many different countries where there are significant differences in markets and customer needs. The main *advantages* of this structure are:

1 It encourages logistic efficiency.
2 It allows divisions to adapt to local markets.
3 Legal, cultural and political differences can be minimised.
4 It provides a good training ground for managers.

Its *disadvantages* are:

1 It needs a large number of general managers.
2 Top management loses a degree of control over operations.
3 A duplication of support services is inevitable.
4 Employees may focus on regional objectives at the expense of wider organisational goals.

Mixed departmentalisation

Many large organisations use a mixture of the various approaches to gain the advantages associated with the different means of departmentalisation. For example, a bank might have a geographical structure in several countries with a functional structure in each bank. An example of mixed departmentalisation can be found in the Bank of Ireland, as illustrated in Figure 6.8.

FIGURE 6.8 BANK OF IRELAND: MIXED DEPARTMENTALISATION

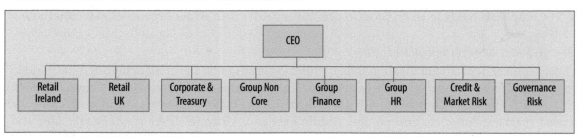

Source: www.bankofireland.com/fs/doc/wysiwyg/group-structure-chart-18-10-2012.pdf

The organisational chart clearly shows that the structure is a mixture of functional and product/service departmentalisation. The main functions performed include finance and HR, while the main product/service business units include Retail – in Ireland and the UK – and Corporate and Treasury.

6.3.2 Structural operation

Formalisation refers to the degree to which rules and procedures shape the jobs and tasks completed by employees. Organisations are said to be highly formalised if their work activities are governed by many rules and procedures. If the activities are governed by few rules and procedures the structure is said to have low formalisation. The main purpose of formalisation is to predict and control how employees behave on the job.[6]

High formalisation is designed to ensure standardisation of work and a high-quality product or service. Organisations involved in the manufacture or maintenance of transport vehicles, for example, typically display high levels of formalisation due to the requirements of stringent safety and engineering standards. On the negative side, high formalisation leads to a lack of autonomy, freedom and initiative as people come to blindly follow rules without considering whether or not they benefit the organisation.

Decision making can be either centralised or decentralised. Centralisation refers to a decision-making policy where authority resides at the top of the organisation, whereas decentralisation means that decisions are taken at all levels of the organisation. Centralisation ensures a greater uniformity of decisions as they are all taken by the same group. Those at the top of the organisation have the best knowledge and understanding of the issues facing the organisation and are therefore in a better position to take decisions. On the other hand, decentralisation ensures that lower-level problems can be solved and decisions taken on the spot. It also gives lower-level employees the opportunity to develop decision-making skills; it can increase motivation; and it spreads the work more evenly throughout the organisation.

Responsibility can be viewed as an obligation to do something with the expectation that some act or output will be achieved. In an organisational setting, managers and supervisors are responsible for achieving certain organisational goals and also for the conduct of their subordinates. Passing on responsibility is usually referred to as delegating. Most organisations delegate responsibility for certain tasks to those lower down in the organisation. Top managers cannot cope with responsibility for all tasks and consequently delegate.

Authority is power that has been legitimised within a certain social context,[7] or, in other words, the right to performance on command. In the case of organisational authority, the social context is the organisation and the authority is associated with the hierarchical position. This is referred to as position power or legitimate power. Specialists in the organisation may also possess power that arises from their expert knowledge. This is referred to as expert power. Authority and responsibility are related: for responsibility to be truly delegated the authority associated with such responsibility should also be passed on. However, managers or supervisors often pass on the responsibility for a certain task but not the authority to see it through. The end result is confusion and inefficiency.

Organisational structures, therefore, have clearly identifiable components. Structural configuration, which can be seen from an organisational chart, includes the division of labour, spans of control, hierarchy and departmentalisation. Structural operation focuses on the actual operation of the structure and includes formalisation, decision making, responsibility and authority.

6.4 Universal approaches to organisational design

Having discussed the main components of organisational structure we now move on to consider the various approaches that have been taken in relation to organisational design. Structural components are the building blocks used to configure organisational design forms in much the same way as building materials are used to produce a house. The manner in which the components are drawn together produces different types of organisational design, just as different building materials produce different types of house. Organisational design, therefore, refers to the structural components and relationships that are used to achieve organisational goals.

Universal approaches to organisational structure argued that there is always one best way of structuring an organisation's activities. In this sense, they offered prescriptions which were designed to work in all situations. These approaches concentrate almost entirely on the formal organisation and its associated structure, and ignore the role of the informal organisation.[8] Factors such as the organisation's external environment, size and technology were, therefore, largely ignored by advocates of the universal approach. Among the most popular and influential universal approaches are the classic principles advocated by Fayol[9] and Weber.[10]

As we saw in Chapter 1, Fayol is considered the father of modern management. He was the first person to identify what roughly corresponds to the modern five functions of management – planning, organising, commanding, co-ordinating and controlling. Fayol also identified 14 principles of management, which he considered vitally important for managers. Fayol's classical principles were widely applied in many organisations and therefore it is not surprising that they have had an impact on organisational structure.

Fayol's principles have served as a basis for the development of principles of organising. The application of Fayol's unity of command means that employees should only receive instructions from one person, while unity of direction means that tasks with the same objective should have the same supervisor. Fayol also advocated division of labour and a clear system of responsibility. Taken together these principles have laid the foundation for both structural configuration and structural operation.

Over time these principles have been criticised for ignoring the human element in organisations, such as motivation, job satisfaction and the informal organisation. The application of Fayol's principles leads to a rather rigid mechanical form of structure, whereby people are slotted into areas irrespective of their abilities or motivation. Fayol also neglected to outline how his principles should be put into operation to ensure success. Finally, Fayol's principles were based not on scientific analysis but on his own personal experiences, which has led many people to question their general applicability.

The second universal approach and probably the most well known and enduring is bureaucracy. Weber used the term 'bureaucracy' at the turn of the century to describe what he perceived as the preferred form of structure for business and government. Weber's bureaucratic organisation was designed to minimise the personal influence of individual employees in decision making, thereby co-ordinating the large number of decisions to be taken by the organisation. It was also designed to facilitate the allocation of scarce resources in an increasingly complex society. The bureaucratic structure advocated by Weber had six main characteristics which were discussed in Chapter 1 and are summarised here:

1. division of labour
2. managerial hierarchy
3. formal selection
4. career orientation
5. formal rules and procedures
6. impersonality.

Organisational structures based on Weber's principles of bureaucracy quickly developed. These structures emphasised a narrow division of labour, narrow spans of control, many levels of hierarchy, limited responsibility and authority, centralised decision making and high formalisation. The bureaucratic structure was particularly popular in large organisations as it allowed such organisations to perform the various routine activities needed for effective operation. This structure became the dominant form of structure used by the majority of organisations, as it appeared to offer an efficient form of structure and was technically superior to any other form.

The bureaucratic structure has a number of important *advantages*:

1   The strict division of labour advocated by Weber increased efficiency and expertise through repetition of the task.
2   The hierarchy of authority allowed a clear chain of command to develop which permitted the orderly flow of information and communication.
3   Formal selection meant that employees were hired on merit and expertise, which eliminated the nepotism associated with managerial practices in the early days of the Industrial Revolution.
4   Career orientation ensured that career professionals would give the organisation a degree of continuity.
5   Rules and procedures controlled employee performance and therefore increased productivity and efficiency.
6   The impersonality of the organisation ensured that rules were applied across the board, eliminating personal biases and ensuring efficiency.

Over time bureaucracies have produced a number of unintended negative outcomes, particularly associated with individual behaviour. The main *disadvantages* are:

1   The behaviour of employees becomes segmented and insular, with employees only focusing on their own task and having little awareness of what is going on in other areas. As a result, effective co-ordination becomes very difficult.
2   The extensive rules and procedures used by the organisation can sometimes become ends in themselves. Consequently, obeying rules at all costs becomes important irrespective of whether such action is to the organisation's advantage or not.
3   Bureaucracy also promotes rigidity and leads to a situation where the organisation is unable to react quickly or change when necessary. Bureaucratic organisations come to believe that what has worked well in the past will continue to do so.
4   Delegation of authority and the insular nature of bureaucracy can lead to a situation where employees identify more with the objectives of work groups, at the expense of the objectives of the wider organisations. This is referred to as goal displacement.
5   The extensive hierarchy makes communications particularly difficult. Middle managers frequently become overloaded with information, and bottlenecks are created.
6   Innovation rarely occurs in a bureaucratic structure because new ideas take so long to filter up the hierarchy. Each level in the hierarchy acts as a further barrier.
7   The strict division of labour can lead to routine and boring jobs where workers feel apathetic and demotivated.
8   The extensive rules and procedures provide minimum standards above which employees normally will not go. So, instead of acting as a controlling device, the rules actually reduce performance.

Despite its inherent disadvantages, the bureaucratic form of organisational structure has been very successful for large organisations operating in stable and simple external environments. Its rationality and efficiency are entirely suitable for this type of environment, which may explain why so many organisations have used a bureaucratic structure.

Taken as a whole, the universal approaches to structure, while laying the foundations for further development and analysis, were heavily flawed. Both Fayol and Weber concentrated too heavily on formal aspects of the organisation, which led to a rigid, mechanistic type of structure. Both approaches, in advocating universal principles, ignored the role of the organisation's size, technology and external environment.

6.5 The Mintzberg framework

Building on contingency theory, Mintzberg[11] (1979, 1981) identified a range of structures and the situations in which they are most commonly found. Mintzberg argued that a vitally important consideration in structuring an organisation is to achieve a match or fit between the various parts. There must be a fit between the structure, the structural imperatives (size, technology, environment and organisational life cycle), the organisation's strategy and the various components of structure (co-ordination, division of labour, formalisation and decision making). If these elements do not fit together, the structure will be ineffective. Mintzberg identified five types of structure.

6.5.1 Simple structure

The simple structure is found in small, relatively new organisations that operate in a simple and dynamic environment. Direct supervision is the main co-ordinating mechanism, which means that a supervisor or manager co-ordinates the activities of employees. The structure is quite organic with little specialisation and little formalisation. The CEO holds most of the power and decision-making authority. Due to its simple yet dynamic environment, it must react quickly to changing events. An example is a small local shop or garage.

6.5.2 Machine bureaucracy

A machine bureaucracy corresponds to a typical bureaucracy and can be found in large, mature organisations operating in a stable and simple environment. Standardisation of work processes is the main co-ordinating mechanism, which means that the methods employees use to transform inputs into outputs are standardised. There is strong division of labour, high formalisation and centralised decision making. Due to its stable and simple environment, the machine bureaucracy does not have to change or adapt quickly. An example of a machine bureaucracy is the civil service or any large mass production organisation.

6.5.3 Professional bureaucracy

Professional bureaucracies are usually professional organisations located in complex and stable environments. The primary co-ordinating mechanism is the standardisation of employee skills, which means that the skills or inputs into the various processes are systematised. The division of labour is based on professional expertise and there is little formalisation. Decision making is decentralised and occurs where the expertise is based. An example of a professional bureaucracy is a hospital or university.

6.5.4 *Divisionalised structure*

The divisionalised structure is found in old and large organisations operating in simple and stable environments with many distinct markets. It could, in fact, be a machine bureaucracy divided into the different markets that it serves. Decision making is split between headquarters (HQ) and the divisions, and standardisation of outputs is the main co-ordinating mechanism used. Due to the fact that control is required by HQ a machine bureaucracy tends to develop in each of the divisions. The most famous example of a divisionalised structure is General Motors, which pioneered the design in the 1920s.

6.5.5 *Adhocracy*

An adhocracy is found in young organisations operating in complex and dynamic environments, normally in a technical area. Co-ordination is achieved by mutual adjustment, which means that employees use informal communication to co-ordinate with each other. Decision making is spread throughout the organisation, and there is little formalisation. Specialists are placed in project teams to achieve the work of the organisation. This form of structure is designed to encourage innovation, which is very difficult to do with the other structures. Examples of organisations that use adhocracies in certain areas of their organisation are Johnson & Johnson, Procter & Gamble and Iona Technologies.

Mintzberg's framework provides guidelines for the choice of an appropriate structure depending on the age of the organisation, its external environment and the nature of its employees.

6.6 Contemporary organisation design

There have to date been two major evolutions in organisational structure. The first occurred in the early 1900s and involved a recognition of the independent roles and function of management and ownership. The second evolution took place some 20 years later and introduced the command and control organisation, more commonly called a bureaucracy, with which we are so familiar today. Now organisations are coming to terms with the third evolutionary period. The shift this time is from bureaucratic, hierarchical forms to more flexible and adaptable forms, or from modernist to post-modernist forms.[12]

The main reason for the dominance of bureaucracy as an organisational structure is that it is a rational and efficient form of structure when the environment is simple and stable. However, when the external environment becomes complex and dynamic, the rigidity of the bureaucratic structure hampers its ability to be flexible and adaptive. Recent trends in organisational structure have centred on the need to achieve competitive advantage in an increasingly complex, dynamic and competitive environment[13] (see Management Focus 6.1).

Management Focus 6.1 BP to restructure trading arm amid profit erosion

Oil major BP is restructuring its trading unit, Integrated Supply and Trading Division (IST), into a leaner and nimbler outfit in the face of eroding profits. The firm's profitability had been eroded in a trading environment where price volatility was low, inventory build-ups in landed and floating storage had limited gains on trading plays, and spare refining capacity led to thin margins. To deal with the tougher operating environment, BP has embarked on a restructuring programme that aims to shorten decision-making by cutting layers of management, including removing the position of chief operating officer of Global Oil and Global Gas. A new role, the Head of Commercial Development, to focus on major projects, strategy and regulatory developments, was also established. The review process would extend to management layers below regional trading heads, to speed decision-making and to focus accountability for trading oversight.

Source: www.businessandfinance.ie/news/bptorestructuretradingarmamidprofiterosion.

The extent of change in the business environment has meant that bureaucratic and hierarchical structures are no longer effective. Such forms of structure thrive on stability and certainty, characteristics of earlier environments but not of the environment in which most organisations now operate. The bureaucratic model, with its extended hierarchy, narrowly segmented job design, rule-bound procedures and lack of individual autonomy and responsibility, is no longer appropriate for effective organisation. The structures and systems associated with such organisational forms do not adapt readily to change and are not flexible enough to anticipate change.

Many of the developments have built on the idea that the nature of the business environment shapes the most appropriate form of structure. Due to the nature of the current business environment, organisations are now undertaking fundamental changes to their structure. To achieve competitive advantage organisations must be flexible and adaptive, to respond to and anticipate change in the business environment.[14] Many organisations have looked to organisational structure as a means of providing such flexibility and adaptability. As a result of the nature of the business environment and the ineffectiveness of traditional bureaucratic structure, organisations have experimented with four main structural trends, as shown in Figure 6.9.

FIGURE 6.9 TRENDS IN ORGANISATIONAL STRUCTURE

1. Changes in job design
2. Flatter hierarchies
3. Team mechanisms
4. Increased responsibility and decision-making authority

The first trend has been toward flatter, less hierarchical structures. Reducing the layers in a hierarchy is designed to reduce costs, free up information flows, speed up communications and allow more innovative ideas to flourish. Organisations are therefore reducing hierarchies to more manageable levels. However, hierarchy has not been eliminated totally as this would be both impractical and in contravention of all time-tested laws of management and leadership. Organisations have also widened the traditional division of labour. Previously, individuals were boxed into segmented and isolated work tasks with little knowledge or training in other areas. Due to the need to be more flexible, many organisations have now widened job categories and trained employees to be multi-skilled.

Changing attitudes in the workforce has led to the creation of new structures that allow individuals more responsibility and authority over their work and a larger role in decision making. In order to meet these demands, organisations have pushed responsibility downwards. For example, they have been allowed to inspect work where previously they were only allowed to manufacture products. The final trend has been to move away from segmented and isolated work to team-based operations. Organisations are experimenting with task forces for short-term problem-solving exercises and with cross-functional and cross-hierarchical teams to achieve longer-term objectives. Organisations are also introducing team mechanisms for completing tasks. Such team mechanisms have been called self-managed teams or autonomous work groups and they complete the work of the organisation with the guidance of a supervisor. For example, Bausch and Lomb, which manufactures sunglasses and contact lenses, introduced self-managed teams to complete tasks in teams rather than in isolation. As organisations have experimented with these four structural trends, new types of organisational structure have evolved and developed.

6.6.1 Matrix and project structures

The matrix structure, a combination of functional and product structures, was first implemented by TRW Inc. in the USA, which found that traditional functional departmentalisation was inadequate for managing complex technological developments. In a matrix structure employees are members of both a functional group and also a product group, so in effect they have two supervisors, one from their core functional area and one from the particular project area. However, when employees are involved in specific projects the project manager is the reporting supervisor. The most remarkable feature about the matrix structure is that functional and product lines of authority are overlaid to form a grid. This form of structure is usually found in organisations with diverse activities, or used for project management. Private industry has found this structure attractive, particularly for projects with a high capital investment and research and development (R&D) requirement.

An example of a matrix structure is shown in Figure 6.10.

FIGURE 6.10 AN EXAMPLE OF A MATRIX STRUCTURE

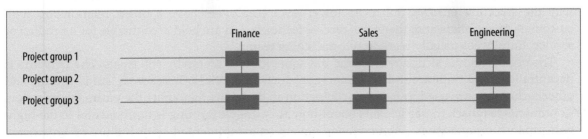

As can be seen from the diagram, employees belong to both a functional group, either engineering, sales or finance, and at the same time are also members of a particular project group.

This form of structure has a number of important *advantages*:

1 The interdisciplinary nature of the project teams contributes to a high rate of new product innovation.
2 It establishes the project manager as a focal point for all matters involving a particular project.
3 It maximises the use of a limited pool of specialists.
4 It makes specialised functional assistance available to all projects.
5 It provides a good training ground for potential managers of diversified organisations.

There are also a number of *disadvantages*:[15]

1 It leads to interpersonal and command conflict with the existence of a dual reporting relationship.
2 It creates power struggles among project managers and functional area heads.
3 It slows down decision making.
4 It can promote narrow viewpoints associated with specific projects at the expense of wider organisational objectives.
5 It can be difficult to trace accountability and authority.

The matrix structure is most appropriate in certain circumstances:[16]

- when the organisation produces short-run complex products
- when complicated product design needs innovation and timely completion
- when many kinds of sophisticated skills are needed
- when a rapidly changing marketplace requires changes even in the period between design and delivery.

Increasingly organisations are using project structures which have the added flexibility of no departments. Employees work on projects and once their objectives have been achieved they move on to a new project assignment.

6.6.2 Team-based work and new organisational forms

Instead of the traditional individual structure of tasks, newer approaches to structure concentrate on **teamwork** by introducing self-managed teams to achieve the work of the organisation. Such teams make decisions about the tasks to be completed and deal directly with the customer. In this way the structure ensures that even lower-level employees have a direct relationship with customers or suppliers and, therefore, receive feedback and are held accountable for a product or service. Employees usually work in self-managing teams.

The organisational structure is flatter, but some form of hierarchy still exists. The structure is decentralised and built around customers, products or services. Task forces, study groups and other techniques are used to foster participation in decisions that affect the entire organisation. Continuous feedback to participants about how they are performing is fundamental to the high-performance organisation. Organisations have also experimented with the use of temporary organisational forms for specific projects. Once their objectives have been achieved these teams are disbanded.[17]

The **boundaryless organisation** operates without the boundaries that more traditional organisations have, both internally and externally.[18] They are therefore much more fluid and flexible. Eliminating boundaries caused by strict specialisation and hierarchy means that relationships are established through lateral communication, decision making and goal setting. Rather than allocating responsibility and authority in line with the traditional hierarchy, the boundaryless organisation mutually shares authority, responsibility and control among people and units, which facilitates the co-operation necessary to achieve organisational goals.[19] A key element of the organisation is its ability to redesign itself to accommodate new tasks and problems and changing environmental circumstances. Organisations that have experimented with such internal networks include General Motors and Ericsson.

Moving our attention to external boundaries we can consider the emergence of a **network organisation**. This is a market mechanism that allocates people and resources to problems and projects in a decentralised manner.[20] The network organisation seeks to manage complex relationships between people and departments within the organisation and groups such as suppliers and customers outside it. The use of networks to establish relationships with external groups has become popular. Such networks frequently include suppliers, customers, trade unions and even competitors. In some cases these networks can be used to establish alliances with traditional competitors.

A dynamic network is arranged so that its major component parts can be assembled or reassembled to meet changing requirements. The traditional business functions such as manufacturing, marketing and distribution are no longer carried out by a single organisation but by independent organisations within the network. Each part of the network is therefore able to pursue its distinctive competence. Due to the fact that each business function is not necessarily part of the same organisation, a broker is used to assemble and co-ordinate the various contributions. The various networks are held together by contracts, which are market mechanisms, rather than a hierarchy.

The use of information technology, whereby networks can hook themselves together in a continually updated information system, further facilitates such developments. The illustration of an external network can be applied to the case of the manufacture of sports clothing. A sports kit could be designed in Italy for the North American market, specifically meeting its local demand, manufactured in Singapore, then sold and distributed by a transnational network. Each of the main functions, from design to manufacture, sales and distribution, is conducted by a different organisation. More and more organisations are adopting this type of structure and it is well known that brand leaders such as Nike are not involved in the actual manufacture of their products.

There are some potential problems associated with the recent move towards network structures. While developments in information technology have facilitated the development of complex business contacts and relationships, these can become difficult to co-ordinate and control, posing problems for those involved with this form of structural design. In addition, there is little hands-on control as the network operations are geographically dispersed. Continuity can also be a problem for the network organisation as it constantly redefines itself using different network partners.

6.7 Summary of key propositions

- Organising is the process of dividing organisational tasks between groups, individuals and departments and co-ordinating their activities to achieve organisational goals. The pattern of how activities are divided and later co-ordinated is called organisational structure.
- Organisational structure is the system of task, reporting and authority relationships within which the work of the organisation is done.
- Organisational structure can be broken down into structural configuration and structural operation. Structural configuration is the size and shape of the structure. It includes the division of labour, spans of control, hierarchy and departmentalisation. Structural operation is the process of the structure and includes formalisation, decision making, responsibility and authority.
- There are four main types of departmentalisation: functional; product; geographical; matrix; and mixed. The most suitable form of departmentalisation depends on the nature of the organisational activities.
- Traditional approaches to organisational design were universal in that they offered principles that were designed to work in all situations. The most popular universal approaches were Fayol's classical principles of management and Weber's bureaucracy.
- Mintzberg identifies a range of structures: a simple structure; a machine bureaucracy; a professional bureaucracy; a divisionalised structure; and an adhocracy. Mintzberg concludes that there must be a fit between the structure, the structural imperatives, the organisation's strategy and components of the structure.
- Bureaucracy has been the dominant form of structure since it became popular in the 1930s and 1940s. However, it is primarily suited to stable and simple environments. The external environment is currently complex and unstable and as a result bureaucracies have become less effective.
- Four main trends in organisational design have developed in response to the realisation that bureaucracy can no longer cope with a changing business environment. Hierarchical levels have been reduced, the division of labour has been widened, teams have been introduced and responsibility and decision-making authority has been pushed down the organisation.
- Organisations have experimented with team and project structures, and boundaryless and network forms of organisation.

Discussion Questions
1 Explain the terms 'organising' and 'organisational structure'.
2 Explain the terms 'division of labour', 'span of control' and 'hierarchy'.
3 Explain the elements of structural configuration.
4 Discuss the different types of departmentalisation an organisation can use. Which one do you think is most appropriate for a large organisation competing in many different and widespread markets?
5 Critically evaluate the universal approaches to the study of organisational design.
6 Discuss Mintzberg's contention that effective structure arises from a fit between the structural imperatives, strategy and the components of the structure.

7   Outline the most recent trends in organisational design. Find an example of a company that has introduced any of these changes.
8   Why have bureaucracies become less efficient in the current business environment?
9   Why have organisations experimented with networks?
10   Why are team-based mechanisms and project teams appealing to organisations?

Concluding Case: Tronics plc

Tronics plc is a small family-owned firm employing 100 workers manufacturing components for the electronics sector. The company is 30 years old and many of the structures and procedures have evolved over the firm's history. Work is highly specialised, with a narrow division of labour. Employees complete narrowly defined tasks on a repetitive basis. This has resulted in employees developing considerable expertise in particular areas. There are also narrow spans of control and many levels in the organisational hierarchy. Employees feel 'over-supervised' and not trusted. As a result, employee morale and job satisfaction have all fallen. Employees are considering moving to positions in other organisations with a more flexible approach to work.

Decision making is highly centralised with the owner/manager taking responsibility for all the key decisions facing the firm. Communications are slow and cumbersome and frequently only occur from the top down. The firm operates a very traditional control and command style of structure and management. The work environment is highly formalised, with many rules and procedures that have evolved over time. Adhering to these rules – whether or not they are appropriate to a particular situation – has become critically important for all employees.

In recent years, the business environment facing the firm has changed significantly. Increased competition and advances in both information technology and in the broader area of technology have all fundamentally changed the basis of competition in the electronics sector. The business environment is highly volatile and requires a structure that can respond quickly to changes. Tronics has suffered as a result of its slow and rigid organisational structure. Many people in the organisation believe that what has worked well in the past will continue to do so.

Case Questions
1   Explain why the current organisational structure is causing problems for the organisation.
2   What changes would you suggest and why?

Notes and References

1   Moorehead, G. and Griffin, R. (1989) *Organisational Behaviour*. Boston, MA: Houghton Mifflin.
2   Nadler, D. and Tushman, M. (1997) *Competing by Design: The Power of Organisational Architecture*. Oxford: Oxford University Press.
3   Sherman, J. and Smith, H. (1984) 'The Influence of Organisational Structure on Intrinsic and Extrinsic Motivation', *Academy of Management Review* 27(4), 877–85.
4   See Haimann, T. and Scott, W. (1970) *Management in the Modern Organisation*. Boston, MA: Houghton Mifflin; Koontz, H. and O'Donnell, C. (1964) *Principles of Management*. New York:

McGraw-Hill; Urwick, L. (1956) 'The Span of Control: Some Facts about the Fables', *Advanced Management* 21, 39–49; Van Fleet, D. and Bedeian, A. (1977) 'A History of the Span of Management', *Academy of Management Review*, July, 356–72.

5 Mintzberg, H. (1979) *The Structuring of Organisations: A Synthesis of Research*. New Jersey: Prentice Hall.

6 Ibid.

7 Pfeffer, J. (1981) *Power in Organisations*. Massachusetts: Pittman.

8 For a discussion on the importance of the informal organisation, see Krackhardt, D. and Hanson, J. (1993) 'Informal Networks: The Company behind the Chart', *Harvard Business Review* July–August, 104–11.

9 Fayol, H. (1916) *Administration Industrielle et Générale*. English translation (1949) *General and Industrial Management*. London: Pitman.

10 Weber, M. (1947) *The Theory of Social and Economic Organisation* (trans. Henderson and Talcott). New York: Free Press.

11 Mintzberg, *op. cit.* and (1981) 'Organisational Design: Fashion or Fit?', *Harvard Business Review* 59, 103–16.

12 Clegg, R. (1992) 'Modernist and Post Modernist Organisations' in G. Salaman (ed.) *Human Resource Strategies*. London: Sage.

13 Lei, D. and Slocum, J. (2002) 'Organisation Design to Renew Competitive Advantage', *Organisational Dynamics* 31(1), No. 1, 1–18.

14 Drucker, P. (1992) 'The Coming of the New Organisation', *Harvard Business Review* 66, 33–5.

15 Davis, S. and Lawrence, P. (1977) *Matrix*. Reading, MA.

16 Grinnel, S. and Apple, H. (1975) 'When Two Bosses are Better than One', *Machine Design* 9 January.

17 For a fuller discussion see Bakker, R.M. (2010) 'Taking Stock of Temporary Organizational Forms: A Systematic Review and Research Agenda', *International Journal of Management Reviews* 12(4), 466–86; Lundin, R.A. and Söderholm, A. (1995) 'A Theory of the Temporary Organisation', *Scandinavian Journal of Management* 11(4), 437–58; Burke, C. (2012) 'Temporary Organizing: A Review of Past Research and an Agenda for the Future', paper presented at the IFSAM Congress in Limerick, Ireland (26–29 June 2012); Cattani, G., Ferriania, S., Frederiksen, L. and Täube, F. (eds) (2011) 'Project-Based Organizing and Strategic Management', *Advances in Strategic Management* 28.

18 Dess, G.G., Rasheed, A.M.A., McLaughlin, K.J. and Priem, R. L. (1995) 'The New Corporate Architecture', *Academy of Management Executive* 9(3), 7–18.

19 Powell, W. (1990) 'Neither Market nor Hierarchy: Network Forms of Organisation' in B. Staw and L. Cummings (eds), *Research in Organisational Behavior*. Greenwich, CT: JAI Press; Chisholm, R. (1998) *Developing Network Organisations: Learning from Practice and Theory*. Reading, MA: Addison Wesley.

20 Baker, W. (1992) 'The Network Organisation: Theory and Practice', in Nohria and Eccles (eds), *Networks and Organisations: Structure, Form and Action*. Massachusetts: HBS Press.

CHAPTER 7

Managing Human Resources

CHAPTER LEARNING OBJECTIVES

- To understand the centrality of human resources (HR) to overall organisational success.
- To appreciate the historical development of the HR function in Ireland.
- To understand the core activity areas of the HR function.
- To be aware of the stages in the HR planning process.
- To be able to distinguish between recruitment and selection.
- To be able to summarise the common approaches to performance appraisal.
- To understand reward management.
- To realise the importance of training and development.
- To appreciate the context of employee relations in Ireland.

7.1 Introduction

Managing HR is one of the key elements in the co-ordination and management of any organisation. An organisation's workforce represents one of its most valuable resources and the extent to which the workforce is managed effectively may be a critical factor in improving and sustaining organisational effectiveness and efficiency. It has been argued that the successful management of the human resource may be one of those pivotal factors that distinguishes the high-performance organisation from the average performer, and that HR may represent the single most important untapped source of potential organisational competitive advantage.

Poole and Jenkins[1] note that:

> There are many ways in which companies can gain competitive edge or a lasting and sustained advantage over their competitors, among them being the development of comprehensive human resource management policies. Indeed, the adoption of sophisticated human resource management policies and practices is seen as one of the major keys to competitive advantage

in the modern world. This is not least because such practices can be formidable weapons in highly competitive environments because of the inability of competitors to formulate an effective response in the short term.

It is to this critical issue of 'people management' that we now turn. Variously referred to as personnel management or human resource management (HRM), this dichotomy presents a difficulty inherent in any discussion in this area. It is a particularly complex issue, given that neither of the two is viewed as a completely homogeneous concept. In order to avoid getting into major ideological debates or stereotypical characterisations of differences between HRM versus personnel management (which are beyond the scope of this text), here we follow Monks who, in a reflective piece on the role carried out by those who are responsible for managing the 'people' function within organisations, argues that whether the incumbents are called personnel or HR managers is not necessarily important; what is much more important is to give recognition and expression to the complexity of the task that faces those who have to take responsibility for 'people matters'.[2] Beyond this, we can suggest that the expressions 'human resource management' or 'personnel management' can be interpreted in specific or general terms. In its specific or narrow interpretation, the expression refers to the professional specialist function performed by HR or personnel managers, who are responsible for devising and executing the organisation's policies and strategies relating to the attraction, selection, rewarding, employment and welfare of people. More generally, the literature on the subject also clearly indicates that the management of the human resource may relate to any and all of those who have responsibility for people matters in their various organisational roles – a responsibility that most managers, across all functions, have to fulfil in some capacity. Accepting of course that the management of the human resource may be a function of all who have a responsibility for others, for the purpose of this chapter we shall take a narrow interpretation and concentrate on the specialist function and its activities. In Section 7.2 we provide a short historical overview of the development of the specialist HR function in Ireland. In Section 7.3 we discuss each of the main activities of the human resource function, incorporating Irish research data where available. In this section, HR planning, recruitment, selection, pay and benefits, performance appraisal, and training and development are all examined as core HR activity areas. Finally, Section 7.4 examines employee relations (traditionally the most significant area of personnel activity in Ireland) as a separate people management activity, focusing on the different actors and institutions that exist in the employee relations domain.

7.2 The historical development of the HR function

In order to help the reader fully understand the current nature of HR activity and the specialist function, it is necessary to provide a thumbnail sketch of its historical development. This overview will highlight the major transitions that personnel management has gone through and give some indications of how HRM has developed as a specialist management function.

It is difficult to pinpoint exactly when personnel management first appeared in Ireland, but Barrington, in his account of the development of the Irish administrative system, indicates that a personnel function had been established in the civil service after the First World War.[3] It has been suggested by Monks that its official recognition in the private sector is probably best dated to the setting up of the Irish branch of the Institute of Labour Management in Dublin in 1937. This body was the forerunner of the current Chartered Institute of Personnel and Development (CIPD).

For the purpose of the short historical account presented here, we distinguish between the following key phases: the early 1900s; the mid-1900s; the centralised pay bargaining period of the 1970s; and the HRM debate from the 1980s onwards.

Management Focus 7.1 The Chartered Institute of Personnel and Development

Championing better work and working lives

The CIPD is the professional body for HR and work-based learning – with over 130,000 members working across private businesses and organisations in the public and voluntary sectors. As an independent and charitable organisation, the CIPD is committed to championing better work and working lives by improving practices in people and organisation development for the benefit of individuals, businesses, economies and society.

CIPD Ireland is a branch of the CIPD which was founded in 1937. Based in Dublin, CIPD Ireland has over 5,000 members.

Source: cipd.co.uk.

7.2.1 The early 1900s

Prior to the 1930s, two key traditions can be identified. They represent the first prominent influences on managerial practice relating to HR and they laid the foundation for the development of personnel management as we now understand it.

Welfarists

The origins of personnel management lie in the Protestant work ethic and a concern, among a few enlightened employers, for the alleviation of the abhorrent working conditions witnessed after the Industrial Revolution. In Britain, the first recorded appointment of a welfare worker (in 1896) was a formal recognition of the need for specialist individuals to deal with people management issues. The early years of the twentieth century brought with them the appointment of a number of welfare workers among Irish employers. Prominent Irish examples include Jacobs and Maguire & Paterson, both in Dublin. However, the depression that followed the First World War, coupled with large-scale unemployment, led to the abandonment of much of this work.

Taylorists

As welfarism was increasingly becoming a victim of the depression, Taylorism and its associated notions of labour efficiency became an increasingly popular alternative. The quest for efficiency and profitability among employers led to the standardisation of work systems and to a more systematic approach to a wide range of managerial activities.

7.2.2 The mid-1900s

If some developments in Taylorism inspired personnel practitioners to develop a more calculative approach to managing employees, this was partially redressed by a growth in the behavioural sciences. This period was marked by a trend toward increasing organisational size and complexity and the application of personnel management practice to increasingly wide areas of management. The emerging behavioural sciences established a body of knowledge to underpin many aspects of personnel work, such as selection, training, motivation, industrial relations and payment systems. The increasing complexity during this period led to the emergence of two different traditions: bureaucrats and consensus negotiators.

Bureaucrats

As organisations became increasingly complex, the range of personnel activities widened, which in turn led to the need to formalise procedures. In this tradition, 'personnel' encompassed activities in the areas of employment, wages, joint consultation, health and safety, welfare and education/training. Personnel functions largely became custodians of the procedures that regulated the operation of these activities within the organisation.

Consensus negotiators

Following the lifting of the Emergency Powers Order in 1946, trade union density in Ireland accelerated sharply. This 'new unionism' was to have a strong impact on both the organisational environment and on the functioning of specialist personnel departments, for a number of reasons. First, trade unions enjoyed a period of legitimacy in the eyes of employers and among government, perhaps best highlighted by the establishment of the Labour Court in 1946. Second, with increasing union density came an enhanced ability to engage in industrial action in the pursuit of collective objectives. An indicator of this is the very large number of days lost in the period 1947–51 (1.742 million). The emphasis on collective bargaining required a wide range of specialist skills on the part of personnel managers. This expanding specialist skills base served to justify and enhance not only the role of the personnel specialist, but also that of the personnel function as a whole.

7.2.3 The 1970s: centralised pay bargaining

The return to centralised pay bargaining in 1970 did not result in a decline in the importance of the personnel specialist as union negotiators switched their focus to other negotiable issues at the level of the workplace, such as employment conditions and productivity. It did result in the necessity for the personnel specialist to become a legal expert. The 1970s brought with them an unprecedented wave of legislation which sought to protect employees and provide for redress in cases where rights had been infringed. In turn, this required that specialist personnel functions had a high level of expertise in all aspects of employment law. This development, in particular, added a strong impetus to the drive for greater professionalism in the field of personnel management. Clearly, interest in greater professionalism in personnel management cannot be absolutely confined to this period, although it was during this period that it received a much stronger impetus. The Donovan Commission on industrial relations (1968) highlighted the need for greater expertise in the operation of the employer/employee relationship and in 1970, the Institute of Personnel

Management (IPM – now CIPD) developed an exam-only scheme as a route to membership in an attempt to regularise and improve standards in the personnel management profession.

7.2.4 The 1980s: the emergence of HRM?

The 1980s was clearly a decade of change, and it was a period of reappraisal for personnel management. A depressed economic climate from the beginning of the decade, together with increased competitive pressures, led to a slump in business activity. These developments helped to change both the focus of personnel management and the nature of personnel activities. Internationalisation, Japanisation, excellence theories, new technology and economic pressures combined to set new priorities, forcing the personnel function to act under tighter cost controls, dismantle historical rigidities, build flexibility and accommodate a greater range of work, with little by way of extra resources. The personnel function increasingly turned to more innovative practices, embodied in the term 'human resource management', which began to replace 'personnel management' as the preferred title, and which essentially refers to the development of a strategic corporate approach to workforce management. It has its roots in US industry, which was receptive to the application of the principles of organisational psychology and behavioural science in an attempt to improve overall organisational performance. The central contention is that organisations incorporate HR considerations into strategic decision making, establish a corporate human resource philosophy and develop personnel strategies and policies to improve HR utilisation.

The overall impact of this shift from the operational to a more strategic emphasis has been debated strenuously. Some contributors, such as Keenoy,[4] argued that HRM as a development was merely a retitling exercise, while others felt it could involve a complete reorientation of the personnel function, depending on how the strategic emphasis took hold. Whatever the truth of the matter, Beardwell and Holden[5] noted that the potential for optimising competitive advantages from HR has emerged as one of the most significant debates in this new order and that it is broadly related to three key features of a firm's HR:

1. A firm's workforce must add value to the product or service being provided;
2. Levels of individual performance must matter; and
3. A firm's human capital investment cannot be easily imitated.

Management Focus 7.2 Strategic HRM

The concept of strategic HRM refers to the development of a strategic corporate approach to workforce management, whereby HR considerations become integral to strategic decision making as organisations seek to establish a corporate HR philosophy and strategy that complements their business strategy. This line of thinking is now well established and it illustrates the strategic potential and significance of HRM to all organisations.

However, several methodological problems arise when seeking to unearth the linkages between business strategy and HRM because of the differences in meaning associated with the concepts of 'business strategy' and 'HRM strategy'.

7.3 Activity areas in HRM

Thus far in this chapter, we have provided a brief historical overview of the development of personnel management and the specialist HR function in Ireland. This discussion is intended to serve as a general background for the remainder of this chapter, which focuses on the specific activities of HRM and the context for managing the employment relationship.

The range of HRM activities that may be undertaken by an organisation is extensive and, as a result, the role of the specialist HR function clearly may be different in different organisations. As Gunnigle *et al.* suggest:

> Many are basic activities common to all types of organisation, such as recruitment. Others may be appropriate in certain organisational contexts (for example, collective bargaining in unionised firms), while still others are optional in character and their use related to managerial perspectives on personnel management (such as an emphasis on personal career development).[6]

This section of the chapter will cover HR planning, recruitment, selection, pay and benefits, performance appraisal, and training and development as the major activity areas in managing HR.

7.3.1 HR planning

Before launching into more mainstream HRM activities, such as recruitment or training, an organisation must decide on an HR strategy that fits with its present and future needs. The importance of planning the material resources of an organisation has never been called into question. However, planning for people as a resource – the human resource – has rarely been accorded the same status. Because people are, arguably, the single most important resource available to an organisation, it is important that sufficient numbers of the appropriate calibre of people are available to the organisation in pursuit of its objectives. In other words, it is crucial to plan for people, much like any other resource. HR planning can be defined as an exercise that seeks to anticipate likely future business demands and to make provision for the quantity and quality of HR that will be necessary to meet those demands.

The three major objectives of HR planning are to ensure that the organisation:
1. finds and retains the quantity and quality of HR that it requires
2. makes the best possible use of its HR
3. can manage the HR implications of employee surpluses or deficits.

Thus, by definition, HR planning is not simply about numbers of people; it is also about the quality of HR and how they are deployed throughout the organisation in order to ensure optimum organisational effectiveness and efficiency. It is a process that affects every aspect of HRM (recruitment, selection, performance appraisal, training and development, industrial relations, etc.), and one that must be aligned with the organisation's corporate objectives/mission and strategic plans.

FIGURE 7.1 THE HUMAN RESOURCE PLANNING PROCESS

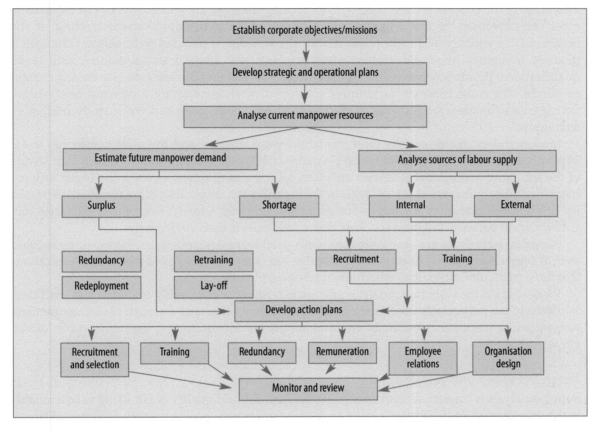

It has been suggested that sound HR planning needs to be based on the following six principles and actions, which are necessary prerequisites for any organisation.[7]

1. The plan has to be fully integrated with the other areas of the organisation's strategy and planning.
2. Senior management must give a lead in stressing its importance throughout the organisation.
3. In larger organisations a central HR planning unit responsible to senior management needs to be established, the objective of which is to co-ordinate and reconcile the demands for HR from different departments.
4. The time span to be covered by the plan needs to be defined.
5. The scope and details of the plan have to be determined.
6. The plan must be based on the most comprehensive and accurate information available.

The major stages in the process are:
• Stage 1: demand analysis.
• Stage 2: supply analysis.
• Stage 3: estimating deficits/surpluses.
• Stage 4: developing action plans.

Stage 1: Demand analysis

This stage of the process is concerned with estimating the quantity and quality of HR required to meet the objectives of the organisation. It is based on a thorough understanding of the organisation's strategy and its implications for the workforce, planned technological changes, a detailed inventory of employee characteristics (age, sex, marital status, tenure, skill level, qualifications, promotion potential and performance levels) and the attrition rate among current resources. The most common techniques employed when conducting a demand analysis are managerial estimates/judgements, statistical methods/techniques and work study methods/ techniques.

Managerial estimates are the most straightforward method and the most commonly used. Typically, individual managers draw up estimates of HR requirements based on their knowledge of the situation. Managerial estimates are often collected at different levels in the organisational hierarchy, with managers at lower levels in the organisation submitting estimates that are passed up through the hierarchy for discussion and consideration. Clearly, since these estimates rely entirely upon personal judgements, their major weakness is their subjectivity.

Statistical techniques are now more commonly used for making estimates. However, techniques such as regression analysis or econometric models are often only employed by larger organisations that have particular difficulties with human resource planning.

Work study is the systematic analysis of work in terms of people, skills, materials and machines. Work study is a particularly useful form of analysis for tasks that lend themselves to measurement; consequently, work study methods are often employed for estimating the demand for 'direct' employees.

Stage 2: Supply analysis

Supply analysis is concerned with estimating the quantity and quality of HR likely to be available to the organisation. In this instance there are two major sources to be examined: the internal labour market (existing employees); and the external labour market (the potential supply of HR available outside the organisation). With respect to supply analysis, one of the most common factors that complicates the task of HR planning is labour wastage. Both planned and unplanned losses must be accounted for. Planned losses might be those that relate to retirements, for example; unplanned losses are more difficult to deal with. The most typical source of unplanned loss is through voluntary wastage – when employees leave of their own accord. Useful indices for calculating wastage are provided in Table 7.1.

TABLE 7.1 INDICES USED IN HR PLANNING

Labour turnover index	=	$\dfrac{\text{Number of employees leaving in period}}{\text{Average number employed in period}} \times 100$
Labour stability index	=	$\dfrac{\text{Number of employees with more than one year's service}}{\text{Number employed one year ago}} \times 100$
(extent to which experienced		

Finally, there are external factors that need to be taken into account. Factors such as the nature of the competition for labour, population trends, education/training opportunities, government policies, etc. will all have an impact on the external labour market.

Stage 3: Estimating deficits/surpluses

After conducting both a demand and a supply analysis, the results can be compared in order to determine whether the supply of labour available matches the demand for labour. Equally, it is possible that the supply of labour exceeds or falls short of the estimates required. Depending on the result achieved at this stage of the process, an action plan will be prepared.

Stage 4: Preparing an action plan

This last stage is based on the information that the preceding stages have yielded. The purpose of the action plan is to ensure that the day-to-day HR needs of the organisation are satisfied. Plans emanating from the process will cover what the organisation must do, and how it will manage recruitment, selection, training and development, promotions and so on.

7.3.2 Recruitment

Information arising from the planning process will be used to make decisions about the required level of recruitment. Recruitment is concerned with attracting a group of potential candidates to apply for the vacancy or vacancies that the organisation has available. Effective recruitment procedures are a prerequisite for the development of an effective workforce. The literature has emphasised the necessity for the recruitment and selection of employees who are committed to the goals of the organisation. The terms 'recruitment' and 'selection' refer to complementary, but distinct, processes in employment. Thus, the quality of the new recruits depends upon an organisation's recruitment practices, while the relative effectiveness of the selection phase is inherently dependent on the calibre of the candidates attracted and the effectiveness of the selection processes employed.

The key choice is whether to recruit internally or externally. There are advantages and disadvantages associated with both and the choice largely depends on the position being filled. It has been suggested that the benefits of recruiting internally from current employees are that it is good HR practice, it may increase motivation, the induction time is shorter, and the costs and uncertainties of recruiting from outside are reduced. However, there is also the drawback that it limits the potential range of candidates from the wider labour market and an injection of new blood into the organisation. It may also lead to discontent among existing employees as some may feel that they have been overlooked. There has been a tendency among some Irish organisations to focus on the internal labour market, which may be linked to a preference on some occasions for so-called 'soft' HRM practices, such as career planning, counselling and employee development, in place in those organisations.

Two key stages can be identified in the recruitment process: the 'background' stage and the actual recruitment stage.

Background stage

This involves conducting what is termed a 'job analysis', which can be simply defined as 'specifying the job and defining what the job demands in terms of employee behaviour'. Typically, two important products are derived from the process of job analysis: the job description; and the person specification.

The **job description** is a statement of the main tasks and responsibilities of the job. It is clearly an important aspect of the background stage of recruitment, because the ideal individual is matched against the contents of the job description. If an inaccurate job description is prepared, the 'desirable characteristics' that the person should possess may also be inaccurate or inappropriate. Therefore, in order to achieve the best possible 'job–person fit', an accurate job description is essential. Organisations take different approaches to the preparation of the job description. Some ask current employees to keep a diary of their daily job activities and draw up a job description accordingly, while in others the task of compiling the details of the job description are reserved for managers and supervisors.

The **person specification** sets out the skills, qualifications, knowledge and experience the individual should possess in order to best match the job. The person specification often distinguishes between those characteristics considered essential and those considered desirable. It might take account of, for example:

- attainments, education/qualifications/experience
- general intelligence
- special aptitudes
- interests
- motivation
- adjustment.

TABLE 7.2 COSTS ASSOCIATED WITH DIFFERENT SOURCES OF RECRUITMENT

	DIRECT COSTS
Internal sources	
Transfer	
Promotion	
Demotion	None
External sources	
Existing workforce: recommendations from friends, relatives etc.	Minimal
Casual applications: unrequested CVs	Minimal
Advertising: local, national media, professional/technical journals etc.	Expensive (depending on media used)
Schools and colleges: contacts, careers officers, 'milk round'	Low (except for travel costs)
Government training schemes	None (can receive financial benefits for employing some categories of worker)
Employment agencies	Expensive (10–25% of starting salary)
Management consultants/executive search agencies	Very expensive (25%+ of starting salary)

In this way the person specification can be useful for focusing on the desired characteristics of potential employees that may need to be specified in the background phase. It may also be helpful in preparing for and conducting interviews in the subsequent selection phase.

Recruitment stage

Equipped with a job description and a person specification, after conducting a job analysis, the task is now to attract a pool of potential candidates. In considering possible sources of labour, it is in some ways easy to assume that these are invariably external. However, as mentioned earlier, they may be either internal or external. Internal sources may come about through transfers, promotions or, indeed, demotions. Potential external sources include schools, institutes of technology, universities and other educational establishments; government-sponsored training schemes; employment agencies; unsolicited applications previously received; advertising (local/national media, professional/technical journals); and management consultants/executive search agencies. Each of these sources should be evaluated, particularly with respect to their suitability to yield the right candidate, and the costs involved. Table 7.2 highlights the major costs associated with different sources of recruitment.

Table 7.3, drawing on data from the Cranet E Survey (2010), highlights the recruitment methods used to fill vacancies for different grades in Ireland. The data suggest that responding organisations are using a combination of recruitment methods to fill positions. Utilising the internal labour market for recruitment purposes appears to be the most common recruitment method at all levels.

TABLE 7.3 METHODS OF FILLING VACANCIES IN IRELAND (%)

	Management	Professional/Technical	Clerical	Manual
Internally	77.0	73.8	68.9	69.8
Recruitment agencies/ consultancies	68.9	69.9	42.7	32.8
Advertisement	62.1	56.3	53.4	69.2
Word of mouth	41.7	53.4	53.4	71.4
Vacancy page on company website	60.2	61.2	52.4	54.1
Vacancies on commercial job websites	49.5	50.5	58.1	34.5
Direct from educational institution	10.7	45.6	34.8	19.2
Speculative applications/walk-ins	13.6	26.2	57.7	67.7
Job centres/public recruitment agencies	9.7	17.5	41.1	45.9

Source: Cranet Ireland/UL Kemmy Business School (2010) *National Survey of HR Practices.*

Whatever method of recruitment is used to source applicants, the organisation requires details of the candidates' skills, abilities, aptitudes, etc. Typically, the choice here is between asking the applicants to submit their own curriculum vitae (CV) or to have all applicants complete a standard application form. From the point of view of getting standardised information and assessing candidates against the same parameters, application forms are preferred. An individual CV gives scope for creativity but may also include some irrelevant information and exclude some essential facts. A compromise situation lies between both of these alternatives: design an application form specific to the job, but allow some blank space for supporting information.

7.3.3 Selection

The selection process effectively begins when applications are received. Selection tools available to organisations range from the traditional methods of interviews and references to more sophisticated techniques such as biographical data, aptitude tests and psychological tests. The degree to which a selection technique is perceived as effective is determined by its reliability and validity. Reliability is generally synonymous with consistency, while validity refers to what is being measured, and the extent to which those measures are correct.

The interview is widely held to be the most commonly used selection technique. Often described as a 'conversation with a purpose', or (as McMahon[8] suggests) a contrived, interrogative conversation involving a meeting, usually between strangers, which rarely lasts for more than an hour, the interview can take a number of different forms. The three most common types are one-to-one interviews, panel interviews and group interviews/assessment.

In a one-to-one situation, there will be one interviewer and one interviewee/candidate. This type of interview tends to be less formal than a panel interview and facilitates the development of a rapport between interviewer and interviewee. It also makes less demand on management time. Perhaps its greatest weakness is the potential for subjectivity and bias.

In a panel interview, there will normally be a number of interviewers (often up to seven people) and one interviewee. The key advantage of such an interview is that it is more objective than the one-to-one and reduces the opportunity for bias. However, it may prove difficult to co-ordinate from the organisation's perspective and it clearly increases the demand on management time and resources.

Finally, a group interview/assessment, which is not an interview in the strict sense of the word, attempts to assess a group of candidates together. A relatively informal process in some respects, it attempts to observe and assess the individuals' behaviour in a group situation. It is often used as a preliminary selection tool.

Regardless of the type of interview being conducted, the interviewer(s) should have three objectives:
1. to obtain enough information about the candidate to determine how s/he will fit the job
2. to ensure that the applicant has enough information about the vacancy and the organisation
3. to leave the applicant with the genuine impression that s/he has been treated fairly.

It is important that interviewers adequately prepare for an interview and have a set plan when interviewing. The interview has a poor track record in predicting job performance. Most managers have little training in interviewing, and yet they rely on the process to find the most suitable person for the job. The effectiveness of the interview process is influenced by a host of factors, including the number of interviewers, their professionalism, and the time of day or the day of the week the interview is held! Table 7.4 highlights the interviewing errors that occur most frequently.

TABLE 7.4 COMMON INTERVIEWING ERRORS

Inadequate preparation: • little job analysis • inadequate interview preparation • poor planning and administration
Absence of interview structure
Premature judgement: • arriving at early decisions on candidate suitability and using interview to justify such decisions
Interviewer dominance: • interviewer talking too much • interviewer not listening, observing or analysing
No rapport: • atmosphere too intimidating • interviewer being overly critical and judgemental
Halo/horns effect: • allowing favourable/unfavourable characteristics or reports to influence final decision • allowing prejudices or subjective opinions to influence selection decisions
Structural rigidity: • adhering slavishly to a pre-planned structure • not adapting to the needs of individual candidates

The whole objective of the exercise is to establish a rapport with the interviewee, and to obtain all the information relevant to the post. The interviewer must be wary of allowing his/her own biases and interests to influence the decision. Clearly, since interviews are likely to retain an important role in employee selection, management should make every effort to gain the best possible results from their use.

Beyond the interview, a number of selection tests are available to assist in making selection decisions. Owing to the subjective nature of the interview, such tests are sometimes used to give a more objective rating. The most common types of tests are:

- **Intelligence tests.** These measure one's mental capacity and potential. They are particularly useful for giving an insight into a person's ability to learn. However, they are not a good indicator of subsequent job performance.
- **Aptitude tests.** These are generally used in an attempt to predict areas of special aptitude and to examine a candidate's suitability for particular types of work. However, as with intelligence tests, they cannot, in absolute terms, predict subsequent job performance.
- **Proficiency tests.** Otherwise known as ability tests of achievement, they can be a good measure of specific knowledge or skills.
- **Personality tests.** The aim of these tests is to ensure that the successful candidate has the most appropriate type of personality for the job being filled. While these tests do give a measure of an individual's suitability for certain jobs, their reliability and validity can be rather low.

Reference checking typically forms a part of most selection processes. It is the most popular selection technique after the interview. It helps to validate information already obtained and allows a picture of the individual's previous performance to be formed. References may be sought in different ways:

- writing a standard business letter, detailing the position and asking the referee to give his/her opinion of the candidate's suitability
- forwarding a standard form, asking the referee to give details of the candidate's past experience and character
- requesting information over the telephone about the candidate's past performance, etc.

Regardless of the method used, the object is the same: to seek independent corroboration of the facts as presented by the applicant.

TABLE 7.5 SELECTION METHODS MOST COMMONLY USED IN IRELAND

	Management	Professional/Technical	Clerical	Manual
Interview panel	88.4	80.6	64.1	56.1
One-to-one interviews	56.3	59.2	61.2	75.4
Application forms	43.7	47.6	53.4	68.8
Psychometric test	49.5	37.9	19.4	12.5
Assessment centre	20.4	14.6	5.8	1.9
Graphology	1.0	1.9	1.9	1.8
References	89.3	88.3	83.5	95.7
Ability tests	28.2	36.9	32.0	36.7
Technical tests	20.4	36.9	18.4	26.7

Source: Cranet Ireland/UL Kemmy Business School (2010) *National Survey of HR Practices.*

The data generated by the Cranet E Survey 2010 highlights the importance of the interview and the reference as the most common selection methods employed in Irish organisations. The interview may take the form of a one-on-one encounter between the candidate and the interviewer or a panel of interviewers meeting the candidate. Confirming earlier research in the Irish context, less use is being made of what are sometimes referred to as more 'sophisticated' selection techniques.

7.3.4 Pay and benefits

An organisation's reward system is a powerful indicator of its philosophy and approach to workforce management. The design and implementation of an effective reward system has proved a difficult task for many organisations. It has also been suggested that many employee grievances and criticisms of reward systems as they experience them may actually mask more fundamental problems. Dissatisfaction with aspects of the employment relationship, such as the supervisory style or opportunities for personal development, may manifest themselves in dissatisfaction with aspects of the reward system. Consequently, organisations experiencing problems with their reward system should examine decisions taken on other human resource issues such as selection, promotion and the work environment rather than assuming that the issue relates entirely to the remuneration system.

Employee rewards are usually classified under two broad headings: intrinsic rewards and extrinsic rewards. Intrinsic rewards spring from the job itself and include such things as autonomy, responsibility and challenge. Extrinsic rewards are more tangible and include pay, job security and working conditions. The relative importance of intrinsic over extrinsic rewards, and vice versa, is a much-debated issue, rooted in the various theories of motivation (see Chapter 9 for a fuller discussion of theories of motivation).

An organisation's reward system may attempt to incorporate the motivational principles underlying the various motivation theories in an attempt to improve or reinforce performance. Actual reward satisfaction will be one of the key determinants of performance improvements. In his analysis of rewards systems, Lawler concluded that the following five key factors influence satisfaction with a reward:[9]

1. Satisfaction with a reward depends on the amount received versus the amount the individual feels s/he should receive.
2. Comparisons with what happens to others influences people's feelings of satisfaction.
3. Employees' satisfaction with both the intrinsic and extrinsic rewards received from their jobs affects overall job satisfaction; individuals who are dissatisfied with the reward system are likely to express dissatisfaction with their jobs overall.
4. People differ widely in the rewards they desire and in what value they attach to those rewards; effective reward systems should meet employees' needs.
5. Many extrinsic rewards satisfy employees only because they lead to other rewards; for example, increased pay may only satisfy because of what it can buy.

Turning specifically to payment systems, the choice of a payment system is an important consideration for organisations. It is imperative that an organisation maintains an appropriate and equitable payment system. The particular package offered will be determined by a variety of factors, not least among them the organisation's ability to pay, labour market conditions, comparable rates/levels elsewhere and possibly the bargaining strength of the trade union. There are numerous options in the type of payment system an organisation might adopt. The more common types of payment systems utilised in Irish organisations are:

- **Flat rate only.** Flat rate schemes are by far the most popular, and involve a fixed hourly, weekly or monthly rate. Such schemes are simple, easy to administer, easily understood and provide stability of earnings for the employee. Flat rate schemes are typically used in jobs where specific performance criteria are difficult to establish.
- **Flat rate + individual, group or company-wide payment by results.** Schemes of this kind are becoming more popular. It is estimated that over one-third of manufacturing establishments in Ireland operate some type of wage incentive scheme for direct manual employees. While schemes of this kind often act as a good motivator (because the reward is immediate), they are often difficult to establish and administer and indeed may be a source of conflict due to felt inequities.
- **Merit rating.** Under merit rating schemes employees receive bonus payments based on a systematic assessment of their performance. Performance is evaluated against specified

objectives and merit payments are made on this basis. While such systems are positive because they reward good performance and do not solely involve the basis of production factors, it is clearly difficult to find an accurate measure of overall performance.

- **Profit/gainsharing.** Under schemes of this kind, employees receive a bonus related to improved company performance. That bonus/reward may take the form of money or company shares. While schemes of this nature create greater employee awareness of the organisation's overall performance and may go some way towards increasing employees' commitment to the organisation, take-up in Ireland has been low.
- **Piecework.** Employees are only paid for the work that they have completed, so payment is based solely on performance. As a payment system it may be a major source of conflict as it does not guarantee any minimum income.

Incentive schemes seem to be experiencing increased popularity in many Irish organisations (see Table 7.6 for data from the 2010 Cranet Survey in Ireland). The growth of incentive schemes in Ireland has been inexorably linked to the trend toward relating pay more closely to performance. However, the take-up of incentive schemes is correlated with organisational ownership. Thus, in the Irish context, US-owned organisations on the whole appear far more likely to utilise incentives than their counterparts, particularly Irish indigenous organisations, which demonstrate a lower take-up across the range of incentives.

TABLE 7.6 USE OF INCENTIVE SCHEMES IN IRELAND 2010 (%)

	Management	Professional/ Technical	Clerical/ Administrative	Manual
Employee share schemes	28.2	23.3	19.4	9.7
Profit sharing	23.3	13.6	8,7	3.9
Stock options	22.3	8.7	2.9	1.0
Flexible benefits	23.3	15.5	13.6	8.7
Performance-related pay	57.3	48.5	38.8	23.3
Bonus based on individual goals/performance	60.2	49.9	39.8	20.4
Bonus based on team goals/ performance	36.9	32.0	23.3	21.4

Source: Cranet Ireland/UL Kemmy Business School (2010) *National Survey of HR Practices.*

When planning pay systems, an approach that takes account of all the benefits is to be preferred. Pay should not therefore be examined without giving at least some consideration to the other benefits that may apply. The nature of voluntary fringe benefits provided to employees varies between organisations, but in general, it is estimated that fringe benefits (both statutory and voluntary) constitute an additional 25–30 per cent on top of basic weekly pay for manual grades. Employee benefits (statutory and voluntary) might include maternity leave, child care facilities, career breaks, paternity leave, holidays (above the statutory minimum), health insurance, sports/recreation facilities, parental leave, additional holiday pay, company cars, pension schemes and sick pay arrangements.

Table 7.7 presents the benefits that respondents to the 2010 Cranet Survey in Ireland indicated that they had in place.

TABLE 7.7 PERCENTAGE OF IRISH ORGANISATIONS OFFERING THE FOLLOWING BENEFITS

Workplace childcare (subsidised or not)	3.9
Childcare allowances	6.8
Career break schemes	41.7
Maternity leave	69.9
Paternity leave	42.7
Parental leave	49.3
Pension schemes	85.4
Education/training break	58.3
Private health care schemes	64.1

Source: Cranet Ireland/UL Kemmy Business School (2010) *National Survey of HR Practices.*

7.3.5 Performance appraisal

Assessing the work of employees is a key function of HRM, and, indeed, a central aspect of all managerial work. The objective is to achieve and sustain high performance standards in an attempt to ensure organisational survival and success. Designed to complement the continuous evaluation and reward of people at work, performance appraisal has been defined as a procedure and process that assists in the collection, checking, sharing and use of information collected from and about people at work for the evaluation of their performance and potential for such purposes as staff development and the improvement of that work performance.

It can therefore be seen as a periodic assessment of the performance of the individual dedicated to reviewing their past performance and future potential. Such a review and examination allows decisions to be made with respect to the training and development needs of an individual and also their reward (where salary increments, bonuses, etc. are awarded on the basis of individual performance).

Tyson and York identify six major objectives of the performance appraisal process:[10]

1. To determine how far people are meeting the requirements of their jobs and whether any changes or action are required for the future.
2. To determine developmental needs in terms of work experience and training.
3. To identify people who have potential to take on wider responsibilities.
4. To provide a basis for assessing and allocating pay increments and similar rewards.
5. To improve communication between managers and their staff.
6. To develop motivation and commitment by providing regular and scheduled opportunities for feedback on performance and discussion of work, problems, suggestions for improvement, prospects, etc.

Table 7.8 summarises the characteristics of the more common appraisal methods and highlights some of the strengths and weaknesses associated with each.

TABLE 7.8 APPRAISAL TECHNIQUES

Method	Characteristics	Strengths	Weaknesses
Ranking	Appraiser ranks workers from best to worst based on specific characteristics or overall job performance	Simple; facilitates comparisons	Little basis for decisions; degrees of difference not specified; subjective
Paired comparison	Two workers compared at a time and decisions made on which is superior resulting in a final ranking order for full group	Ease of decison-making, simple	Difficult with large numbers plus weaknesses attributed to ranking
Critical incident	Appraiser/supervisor observes incidents of good/bad performance. These are used as a basis for judging and assessing/discussing performance	Job-related; more objective	Needs good observation skills; time-consuming
Free-form/ narrative	General free-written evaluation by appraiser	Flexible	Subjective; difficulty of comparison
Self-assessment	Appraisees evaluate themselves using a particular format/structure	Participative; facilitates discussion; promotes self-analysis	Danger of lenient tendency; potential source of conflict between appraiser and appraisee
Assessment centre	Appraisees undergo a series of assessments (interviews, tests etc.) undertaken by trained assessors	Range of dimensions examined; objective	Expensive; not necessarily job specific
Performance/objectives -oriented systems	Appraiser evaluates degree to which specific job targets/standards have been achieved	Job-related; objective; participative	Needs measurable targets; danger of collusion
Rating	Appraiser specifies on a scale to what degree relevant characteristics (normally related to job-related behaviour or personality) are possessed by appraisee	Ease of comparison; range in complexity from very simple to very involved using descriptions of behaviour/performance	Subjective; personality/behavioural traits difficult to measure

Source: Gunnigle *et al.* (2011).

With respect to the take-up of performance appraisal among Irish organisations, the data from the 2010 Cranet Survey is positive and shows a growing trend towards formalising the performance management system in organisations. Across all categories of employee, the use of appraisal systems appears to have grown significantly in recent years. For example, the data show that more than four-fifths (in excess of 80 per cent) of all managerial and professional/technical employees, and over three-quarters (78.6 per cent) of clerical employees have their performance formally assessed. These figures are up significantly since 2000, when the average percentage use was closer to 61 per cent for managerial/professional grades and 55 per cent for clerical workers. Furthermore, while formal appraisal seems to be less common among manual workers, its use has also increased from reported figures in previous years – up from 33 per cent in 2000 to 48.5 per cent in 2010).

TABLE 7.9 USE OF FORMAL APPRAISAL SYSTEMS FOR DIFFERENT CATEGORIES OF EMPLOYEE (%)

Management	83.5
Professional/technical	82.5
Clerical	78.6
Manual	48.5

Source: Cranet Ireland/UL Kemmy Business School (2010) *National Survey of HR Practices.*

7.3.6 Training and development

Developing employees and enhancing their skill and competence so that they will be effective in their jobs is one of the fundamentally important HRM tasks that any work organisation has to undertake. The method of providing this help lies in training and development. Recent years have witnessed considerable efforts to improve the national system of training and development and, in line with developments in many other economies, much of this renewed effort has been instigated by heightened international competition, technological advancements leading to the emergence of skills gaps in certain areas, and renewed efforts to provide increased incentives for organisation-level training, often, in recent years and as a result of the economic downturn, supported by the state.

Management Focus 7.3 Development in Kerry Group

Kerry Group plc was established in 1972 as Kerry Co-op. It remained a co-op until 1986, when it acquired the status of a publicly owned company. This was its first major step towards becoming a multinational company. Since 1980, Kerry Group plc has become a world leader in food ingredients and flavours and it has become a leading added value chilled-food company in Ireland and the UK.

Kerry Group places a strong emphasis on training and development. It has invested in the development of its employees' competencies and skills and has built an organisational culture that is capable of delivering competitive advantage in national and international markets. It has operated a successful graduate development programme for over twenty years, employing, training and developing graduates in a range of disciplines. Because of its growth and expansion, graduates are afforded many professional development opportunities. Kerry Group established a relationship with the IMI in the mid-1990s and created an IMI/Kerry Group management development programme. The programme arose from the need to facilitate the speedy transition of graduates from the world of academia to the world of business. The programme consists of four key components:

1. graduate socialisation
2. a structured development programme
3. ongoing mentoring and coaching
4. planned work experience.

Graduates are exposed to an intensive socialisation programme that enables them to learn 'the ropes' of the organisation and to understand their role and how they fit in. The programme incorporates mentoring and coaching undertaken by Kerry Group managers and IMI faculty. Through this progress graduates are encouraged to take responsibility for their development. As part of the planned work experience component, graduates are required to undertake specific development projects. Finally, the developmental programme is systematically evaluated.

This annual rolling programme of development has proved valuable in fast-tracking young managers to positions of responsibility in the Group.

Source: Garavan, T., Hogan, C. and Cahir-O'Donnell, A. (2009). *Developing Managers and Leaders*. Dublin: Gill & Macmillan.

There is a distinction between the concept of training and the concept of development. Training is defined as a planned, systematic effort to modify or develop knowledge, skills and attitudes through learning experiences in order to achieve effective performance in an activity or range of activities. Development is typically viewed as a broader concept relating to the general enhancement and growth of an individual's skills and abilities through conscious and unconscious learning, with a view to enabling them to take up a future role in the organisation. In some quarters training and development was often seen as an optional extra – something to be indulged in when times are good but one of the first areas to suffer when cutbacks are required. However, it is generally becoming more recognised that there is a strong correlation between organisational success and investment in training and development. In recent times, the academic literature has witnessed a resurgent interest in the whole area of training and development, with much of the literature focusing on the strategic development of human resources as a means of increasing the effectiveness of organisations.

A number of factors external to the organisation are also partly responsible for the increased interest in training and development. These include the pervasive spread of new technologies, increasing global competition, especially in relation to attracting and retaining multinational investment, and the emergence of skills gaps in certain industries.

At national level, responsibility for training in Ireland lies with FÁS, which has as its primary objectives the co-ordination, promotion and the provision of training activities in Ireland. Working with individuals and enterprises in order to enhance Ireland's competitiveness, it offers a range of training courses focused on the particular needs of jobseekers. The 2013 Service Plan for Training Provision highlights that FÁS will offer some 4,000 vocational training courses to more than 70,000 unemployed persons. In addition, it will register approximately 1,500 new entrants to the apprenticeship programme and continue the ongoing training and development of some 9,000 apprentices who are at various stages of their programme. Table 7.10 provides a historical overview of training in Ireland.

The Further Education and Training Bill 2013 provides for the dissolution of FÁS and the transfer of its functions to a new body, SOLAS.

Clearly, training and development is an issue that has to be faced by every organisation. It should be thought of as a logical sequence of events:
1. establishing a policy
2. identifying training needs
3. planning and conducting the training
4. evaluating the process.

TABLE 7.10 HISTORICAL OVERVIEW OF TRAINING IN IRELAND

1098	Norman invasion	Introduction of the guild system of operation
1879	Industrial Revolution	Evolution of factory system of production
1896	Agricultural and Technical	First form of regulated apprenticeship in Ireland Instruction (Irl) Act
1930	Vocational Education Act	Established VECs to provide a nationwide system of continuing education
1931	Apprenticeship Act	Set up Apprenticeship Committees to regulate apprenticeship training
1959	Apprenticeship Act	Established An Cheard Chomhairle to co-ordinate and regulate the apprenticeship system
1967	Industrial Training Act	Set up AnCO to assume full responsibility for all industrial and commercial training, including apprenticeships. Also to promote training at all levels in industry
1987	Labour Services Act	Established FÁS – the amalgamation of AnCO, NMS and the YEA. Function to provide, co-ordinate and promote training activities in Ireland.

Source: Heraty, N. (1992) *Training and Development: A Study of Practices in Irish Based Companies*. University of Limerick.

Formulating a training policy. The objective here is that those responsible for training and development in the organisation, in conjunction with other managers, agree a definite policy with specific objectives achievable within a given time frame. The policy should clearly establish what the organisation is prepared to do with respect to the training and development of its employees. The policy should ensure that employees can find solutions to their training and development needs and that training and development is put into action through the creation of a facilitative atmosphere backed up with the necessary resources.

Identifying training needs. Accurate identification of training needs is vital for the development of effective, relevant and timely training and development interventions. It should aim to identify what is currently happening and what should actually be happening. It is, in some ways, a rather subjective area as training needs for a particular job are open to different interpretations. The most common method used to identify training needs is a survey, which will typically centre on identifying:

- Who needs to be trained? How many and which types of employee?
- What standards of performance is the training expected to achieve?
- What are the present training arrangements?
- What are the suggestions for improvements?

Planning and conducting the training. The training that is to take place needs to be planned and the most appropriate methods decided on. There is a whole range of training methods from which a suitable selection can be made, for example:

- on-the-job
- coaching
- counselling

- mentoring
- secondment
- project work
- formal lectures
- group discussions
- case study
- computer-assisted training.

When choosing a particular intervention, the guiding principle should be high learning transfer; in other words, seeking activities or interventions that focus as closely as possible on the job to be performed. The choice of training delivery method available to organisations is considerable. Therefore, when deciding on the most appropriate method to use, organisations should take account of the principles of learning, the particular needs of those to be trained and the logistics of training that affect every organisation. All training delivery methods have their own particular strengths and can be modified to suit organisational requirements. The most important criterion in determining the choice of training delivery method is the extent to which it meets the particular objectives that have been established by the training needs analysis.

Management Focus 7.4 Key learning principles that can be applied to the design and delivery of training

- Motivation to learn. The employee must want to learn and thus, in order to be committed to the process, must perceive that the learning event will result in the achievement of certain desired goals.
- Involvement of the learner. The training should be seen as an active rather than a passive process. Adults learn more effectively when they are actively involved in the learning process.
- Meaningfulness of the material. The nature of the training intervention must be seen to be relevant to the employee's work.
- Reinforcement of learning. Employees should be given an opportunity to practise what they have learned.
- Feedback. Learners need immediate and constant feedback on their performance.

Evaluating training and development activities. This ensures that control is maintained over the total process and allows a considered assessment of the outcomes, methods and overall impact of any particular training and development programme. Training evaluation can take place at a relatively informal level, for example simply asking participants how they felt about the programme and judging their reactions; or, at a more formal level, perhaps using questionnaires or tests to assess what the participant has actually learned.

7.4 The employee relations context

So far in this chapter we have argued that recent years have brought with them a concerted effort by many organisations to establish a competitive edge through improvements in quality, service and performance in an effort to survive the downturn. We have noted that one key source of competitive improvement has been an increased emphasis on the better utilisation of HR, something that can potentially be achieved through a focus on a core set of HRM activities, namely HR planning, recruitment, selection, pay and benefits, performance appraisal, and training and development. One other critical factor influencing success or failure in leveraging organisational advantage in this area is the nature of the relationship between the parties in the labour process. It is to this relationship, which encompasses the spectrum of employee, employer and state, that we now turn. The way in which this relationship is set up and managed defines the climate of employee relations in the organisation, and serves as a strong enabler for all HR activity.

At the outset it is important to clarify what is meant by industrial/employee relations as the term itself is a source of some confusion. There are, as Salaman observed, almost as many definitions of the concept as there are writers on employee relations matters.[11] The majority of classical definitions of industrial/employee relations emphasise the rules, or job regulation mechanisms, that govern the employment relationship in the workplace. For example, Dunlop defined industrial relations as 'the study of employment rules and their variation over time'.[12] This early perspective set a broad and integrated agenda for the discipline of industrial relations. Accordingly, the parties to the labour process – management, trade unions and government agencies – established a network of rules for the workplace and the work community. The central task of industrial relations is therefore to explain why these particular rules are actually established and how they are administered. The rules are divided into procedural rules and substantive rules. Procedural rules are methods for formally handling specific issues that might arise, such as trade union recognition, disciplinary issues or dispute resolution. Substantive matters are detailed outcomes of negotiations, such as percentage pay increases, extra holidays, etc.

The traditional management focus has been on the pluralist concept of industrial relations, encompassing the premise that a basic conflict of interest exists between management and labour and that this conflict can be optimally handled through collective bargaining between employers and trade unions over divisive issues, particularly pay and working conditions. Collective bargaining is the process through which agreement on negotiable issues is reached between organised employees and management representatives. The pluralist approach therefore recognises that a coalition of various interests exists, and management's role is to achieve a balance between these differing interests. Because of the existence of this coalition of interests, conflict is likely to arise and management's role is to plan how to handle this conflict and reconcile the conflicting interests.

During the 1980s it became evident that although this definition aptly described management– worker relations in many organisations, it did not encapsulate organisations where the focus was more unitarist in perspective. Unitarism as a philosophy of industrial relations is based on the existence of a mutuality of interests between the parties to the labour process. The organisation's goals are the fundamental ones and it is management's prerogative to manage. Consequently, this approach places the emphasis on dealings with individual employees using various mechanisms such as elaborate communications, career development, quality circles and merit pay.

In this chapter, 'employee relations' is seen in generic terms as incorporating all employer, employee and state interactions on employment matters. The focus is therefore on the nature of the relationship between the parties to the labour process and the term includes both pluralist and unitarist models and encapsulates both state and organisation-level arrangements. Having established the meaning of employee relations it is now pertinent to turn to the actors involved in the process, namely trade unions, management associations and state institutions, and their role in employee relations in Ireland

7.4.1 Trade unions

Essentially a trade union can be viewed as a body that aims to unite workers with common interests. It seeks to define those interests, express them and collectively advance them. Its basic strength lies in its ability to organise and unite. While employees join trade unions for a host of reasons, among the most common are a desire to influence pay claims, to have protection against arbitrary management actions and because they fundamentally believe in the function and the role of trade unions in society. By joining unions, employees provide themselves with the collective means and the strength to redress the imbalance in bargaining power that normally exists between the individual employee and the employer. Table 7.11 highlights the major objectives of trade unions in Ireland.

TABLE 7.11 TRADE UNION OBJECTIVES IN IRELAND

- Achieving satisfactory levels of pay and conditions of employment and providing members with a range of services.
- Replacing individual bargaining with collective bargaining thereby redressing the balance of bargaining power in favour of employees and reducing management prerogative in employment related matters.
- Facilitating the development of a political system where workers have a greater degree of influence on political decisions resulting in an economic and social framework which reflects employee needs rather than those of employers/management.

Irish trade unions are normally organised on an occupational basis and may be loosely grouped into three broad categories: craft unions; general unions; and white-collar unions.

Craft unions cater for workers who possess a particular skill in a trade where entry is restricted through apprenticeship or otherwise. Craft unions have traditionally been protective of their trade by ensuring that only people holding union cards carry out certain types of skilled work. This has often led to criticisms of restrictive and inefficient work practices and sometimes to demarcation disputes. Increased mechanisation and consequent de-skilling have had a detrimental impact on the membership and power of craft unions, as reflected in the reduction of their share of union members. Examples of craft unions in Ireland are the Technical, Electrical and Engineering Union (TEEU), and the Union of Construction, Allied Trades and Technicians (UCATT).

General unions cater for any workers, regardless of skill or industry. However, they have traditionally catered for semi-skilled and unskilled workers. They are typically the largest unions and account for approximately half of all trade union members. They are common in all types of organisation and in all industrial sectors. The best known is the Services, Industrial, Professional and Technical Union (SIPTU), which is by far the largest union in Ireland.

White-collar unions normally cater for professional, supervisory, clerical and managerial grades. Unions of this type have experienced significant growth in membership in recent years, as reflected in their increased share of membership from 24 per cent in 1940 to over 35 per cent in the late 1980s. The Association of Secondary School Teachers of Ireland (ASTI) is an example of a white-collar union. It represents 18,000 teachers in community schools, community colleges, comprehensive schools and voluntary secondary schools.

There are essentially three different levels in the trade union structure in Ireland (see Figure 7.2): workplace level; branch level; and national level.

FGURE 7.2 TRADE UNION STRUCTURE

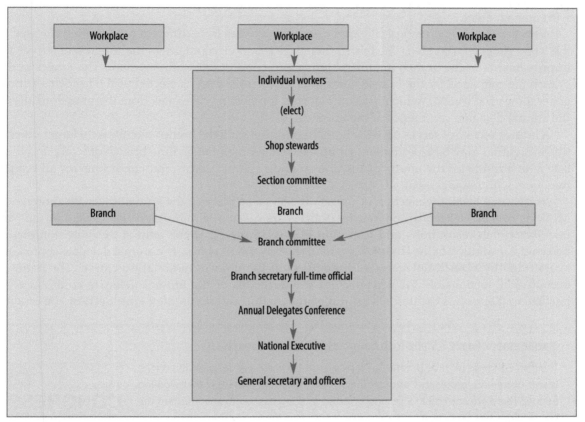

Source: Gunnigle, P., McMahon, G. and Fitzgerald, G. (1995) *Industrial Relations in Ireland: Theory and Practice*. Dublin: Gill & Macmillan.

At the workplace level, shop stewards are the main trade union representatives. The shop steward is charged with the responsibility of acting on the membership's behalf on industrial relations matters at the organisational level. Fellow trade union members elect the steward at annual elections. The steward must perform his/her job like all other employees, as well as acting as steward, and stewards are given reasonable time off from work for union business. The major functions of the shop steward are:
- to recruit new members into the union
- to collect union subscriptions from members
- to negotiate with management on behalf of the members
- to liaise with the union's central office
- to represent workers in grievance and disciplinary situations.

The section committee is a group of trade union members elected by fellow trade union members who work in a specific section of the organisation. The section committee's main activity is to help shop stewards perform their tasks effectively. On a committee of this kind, all the stewards are usually from the same trade union. If they are members of different trade unions, the committee is known as a joint shop stewards committee. Such a committee can regulate conflict between unions and support individual stewards. It also constitutes a more powerful body for negotiating with management.

A trade union branch is typically made up of employees from different organisations located in the same geographical area. The branch manages the internal affairs of the union and strives for improvements in the branch members' terms and conditions of employment. The affairs of the branch are managed by the branch committee. This committee is elected at the branch's annual general meeting (AGM), which is also the forum for electing delegates from the branch to attend the annual delegate conference of the union.

A branch secretary serves both the branch committee and the branch members. In larger unions, this individual may be a permanent employee of the union (a full-time branch official), and their role is to administer the affairs of the branch and negotiate terms and conditions for all branch members with management.

At national level, the election of union officers takes place at the annual delegate conference. Motions concerning the union and its policies are discussed and voted on. These motions are usually branch resolutions and a motion that is approved at the annual delegate conference becomes a resolution of the conference and ultimately union policy. The annual delegate conference is attended by branch delegates and members of the union's national executive. The national executive is responsible for carrying out the decisions of the annual delegate conference. In particular, it appoints the union's full-time branch officials and the staff employed by the union.

Management Focus 7.5 The Irish Congress of Trade Unions (ICTU)

The Irish Congress of Trade Unions (ICTU), the largest civil society organisation on the island of Ireland, represents and campaigns on behalf of some 832,000 working people. There are currently 55 unions affiliated to Congress, north and south of the border. Congress seeks to:

- represent and advance the economic and social interests of working people;
- negotiate national agreements with government and employers, when mandated to do so by constituent and member unions;
- promote the principles of trade unionism through campaigns and policy development;
- provide information, advice and training to unions and their members;
- assist with the resolution of disputes between unions and employers;
- regulate relations between unions and ruling on inter-union disputes.

Source: www.ictu.ie.

The union's general officers are usually full-time employees of the union and they do not have another job. In some unions they are appointed to their position by the national executive, while in others they are elected at the annual delegate conference or by a ballot of union members. The general officers are usually the general president, general secretary, general vice-president and general treasurer.

ICTU is the central co-ordinating body for the Irish trade union movement, with a majority of trade unionists in membership of unions affiliated to Congress. Individual unions maintain a large degree of autonomy, and ICTU relies on the co-operation of affiliated unions in promoting its overall goals. The annual conference of ICTU is attended by delegates from affiliated unions. The ICTU plays a critical role at national level, representing union views to government. Along with the other social partners (government, employer representatives, farmer federations), it is involved in national negotiations on pay and other aspects of social and economic policy.

7.4.2 Employer organisations

The major driving force for the development of employer organisations was the perceived need on the employers' side to organise collectively in order to counterbalance and deal effectively with emerging trade unions. Employer organisations in Ireland are of two types: employer associations and trade associations. Employer associations were established to aid in the conduct of employee relations, whereas trade associations were established with trade and commercial reasons in mind.

Employer associations have the following broad objectives:

- to effectively represent employers' views to government and to other appropriate bodies so as to preserve and develop a political, economic, social and cultural climate in which business objectives can be achieved
- to create an environment/climate that supports free enterprise and enshrines managerial prerogative in decision making
- to ensure the existence of a legislative and procedural environment that supports and co-ordinates employers' views on employee relations matters and to provide assistance to affiliated employers.

The largest employer association in Ireland is the Irish Business and Employers' Confederation (IBEC), which was formed in 1993 through an amalgamation of two previously separate institutions, the Federation of Irish Employers (FIE) and the Confederation of Irish Industry (CII). IBEC represents the alliance of a large number of companies and organisations that recognised the need for a single cohesive force capable of providing effective leadership and representation in a turbulent business environment. IBEC is dedicated to promoting a favourable climate for economic growth, investment and employee/industrial relations. IBEC has offices in Dublin, Cork, Limerick, Waterford, Galway, Donegal town and Brussels. Among its services are:

- representation in relations with government, trade unions and EU institutions on commercial, economic and industrial and employee relations issues
- membership of an appropriate sector organisation with direct links to the corresponding European association
- conferences, seminars, specialist publications, statistics, business-sector profiles and customised research
- a range of additional consultancy services on, for example, HRM, health, safety and environment, training and development issues.

Management Focus 7.6 The Irish Business and Employers' Confederation (IBEC)

IBEC was formed in 1993 as a result of a merger between the Confederation of Irish Industry (CII) and the Federation of Irish Employers (FIE).

Its vision is to be the most influential, dynamic business representative organisation in Ireland, driving our business agenda in Europe.

IBEC represents the interests of business in Ireland and provides a wide range of direct services to its 7,500 members, which range from the very small to the largest enterprises, employing over 70% of the private sector workforce in Ireland.

Source: www.ibec.ie.

At the national level, IBEC has a strong regional membership structure through which members' views on national issues are co-ordinated and representation can be made on matters of regional interest. At European level, through its Brussels office, IBEC seeks to influence EU economic and social policy, represent Irish interests in BusinessEurope (formerly the Union of Industrial and Employers' Confederations in Europe (UNICE)), and produce a range of specialist publications. IBEC also represents members' interests in many international organisations, such as the International Labour Organisation (ILO) and the International Organisation of Employers (IOE).

7.4.3 State institutions

Traditionally, the role of the state in employee relations in Ireland has been restricted to the establishment of legislative ground rules and the provision of mediation and arbitration services, leaving employers and employees relatively free to develop work rules and procedures to suit particular organisational contexts. In recent years, the role of the state in employee relations has increased, particularly through a process of reforming the system of employee relations and also through being a party to national agreements and in ongoing negotiations on public sector reform.

The state provides a number of specific institutions – the Labour Relations Commission (LRC), the Labour Court, rights commissioners, equality officers and the Employment Appeals Tribunal (EAT) – all of which are charged with various responsibilities for employee relations matters.

Labour Relations Commission (LRC)

Formally established by the then Minister for Labour in January 1991, the LRC's statutory authority and functions derive from Sections 24 and 25 of the Industrial Relations Act 1990. It is a tripartite body with employer, trade union and independent representation and has been charged with the general responsibility of promoting good industrial relations practice. The Commission provides a comprehensive range of services designed to prevent the occurrence of disputes and, where they do occur, some mechanisms for resolution. The key services provided by the LRC are:

*   an industrial relations conciliation service
*   an industrial relations advisory and training service
*   preparing, after consultation with unions and employers' organisations, codes of practice relevant to industrial relations

- guidance on codes of practice
- the appointment of equality officers and the provision of an equality service
- a rights commissioners service
- a workplace mediation service
- commissioning research into matters relevant to industrial relations
- reviewing and monitoring developments in the area of industrial relations.

The conciliation service was formerly provided by the Labour Court. The service can be seen as a proactive measure to resolve disputes before they require full Labour Court investigation. The role of the advisory service is broader than that of the conciliation service and is designed to help identify general problems which may be giving rise to employee relations difficulties. The advisory service brings with it a new dimension to the services available to Irish employers and trade unions. It has as its central brief the task of preventing industrial disputes by encouraging good industrial relations policies, practices and procedures in organisations facing management–labour difficulties. The service becomes involved in assignments either on the basis of union/management agreement or on the initiative of the LRC with the agreement of the parties concerned.

Labour Court

Established in 1946 by the Industrial Relations Act, the Labour Court is a central institution in the Irish system of employee relations. The role of the Court has changed significantly as a result of the 1990 Industrial Relations Act. Its central role is investigating and making recommendations on cases referred to it by parties in dispute. If the conciliation service provided by the LRC fails to resolve a dispute, both parties can ask the Labour Court to hear their case. The Industrial Relations Act 1990 provides that the Labour Court may normally investigate a dispute only in the following situations.

- If it receives a report from the LRC that no further efforts on its part will help resolve the dispute.
- If it is notified by the chairperson of the Commission that the Commission has waived its function of conciliation in the dispute.
- If it is hearing an appeal in relation to a recommendation of a rights commissioner or an equality officer.
- If it decides after consultation with the Commission that the exceptional circumstances of the case warrant a Labour Court investigation.
- If it is referred to under Section 20 of the Industrial Relations Act 1969.
- If it is requested by the Minister to do so.

A Labour Court hearing normally consists of an independent chairperson, a representative of an employer and a representative of a trade union. Hearings typically involve both written and oral submissions and some element of cross examination. When the Court has fully investigated the case it will issue a recommendation. The Labour Court is not a court of law. It operates as a tribunal in hearing the different sides of the argument and then sets out its opinion and the terms on which the matter should be settled.

Rights commissioners and equality officers

Rights commissioners deal with disputes concerning individual employees. Originally established under the operation of the Labour Court, the Rights Commissioner Service now operates as part of the LRC. Commissioners remain completely independent in the performance of their functions. Rights commissioners investigate disputes relating to employment legislation, including the Industrial Relations(Miscellaneous Provisions) Act 2004, the Unfair Dismissals Act 1977, the Maternity Protection Acts 1994–2004 and the Payment of Wages Act 1991. A rights commissioner will only deal with a dispute if it involves:

* a dispute that is not connected with the pay and conditions of a collective group of workers
* a dispute that has not been or is not already being investigated by the Labour Court
* a party to the dispute who does not object in writing.

Generally, a rights commissioner will investigate disputes concerning individual employees only. An objection to an investigation by a rights commissioner must be notified in writing to the commissioner within three weeks. An appeal against a recommendation from a rights commissioner must be notified in writing to the Labour Court within six weeks from the date of the recommendation.

Historically, equality officers dealt with issues relating to discrimination under legislation such as the Anti-Discrimination (Pay) Act 1974 and the Employment Equality Act 1977. They operated under the auspices of the LRC, but were independent in the performance of their duties.

The Employment Equality Acts 1998–2011 repealed the Anti-Discrimination (Pay) Act 1974 and the Employment Equality Act 1977. Under the 1998 Act, discrimination occurs where a person is treated less favourably than another person. It is forbidden on the grounds of gender, marital status, family status, sexual orientation, religious belief, age, disability, race and membership of the travelling community.

The Equality Authority, an independent body set up under the Employment Equality Act 1998, facilitates the enforcement of the Act and is charged with the responsibility of promoting equality under the Act. Equality officers now operate within the Office of the Director of Equality Investigations, and this Office is now the first place where individuals seeking redress under the Act will go.

Employment Appeals Tribunal (EAT)

The current EAT was initially established as the Redundancy Appeals Tribunal under the terms of the Redundancy Payments Act 1969, and was later renamed the Employment Appeals Tribunal under the Unfair Dismissals Act 1977. The EAT consists of a chairperson, who must be a practising barrister or solicitor, seven vice-chairpersons and a panel of ordinary members drawn equally from employer associations and ICTU. The EAT operates in divisions consisting of a chairperson or vice-chairperson and two other members, one from the employers' side and one from the trade union side. The EAT adjudicates on a number of Acts, including the Redundancy Payments Acts 1967–2007, the Minimum Notice and Terms of Employment Acts 1973–2005, the Unfair Dismissals Acts 1977–2007, and the Maternity Protection Acts 1994–2004.

Overall, state institutions play a major role in employee relations in Ireland. Operating within the framework of the Industrial Relations Act 1990 and earlier legislation, state institutions are largely concerned with conciliation and arbitration.

7.5 Summary of key propositions

- This chapter introduced the historical development of HRM in Ireland and discussed each of the major activity areas in HRM – HR planning, recruitment, selection, performance appraisal, pay and benefits, and training and development. It also outlined the context for the conduct of employee relations in Ireland, examining the roles of trade unions and employers' organisations and the machinery of the state involved in employee relations.
- Historically, HRM has gone through a number of major transitions, the most prominent being the welfarist and Taylorist phases in the early 1900s, the move towards bureaucracy and negotiators in the mid-1900s, the increased legislation in the 1970s, and the increasingly strategic role of more recent years, culminating in the emergence of HRM.
- HR planning is concerned with the quantity and quality of HR available to an organisation and how these are deployed throughout the organisation in an attempt to ensure organisational effectiveness and efficiency. The major stages in the HR planning process are: analysing demand; analysing supply; estimating deficits/surpluses; and developing action plans.
- Recruitment is concerned with attracting a group of potential candidates to apply for the position that the organisation has available. Two key stages can be identified in the recruitment process. First, the background stage is concerned with the conducting of a job analysis. Second, the actual recruitment stage is concerned with attracting a pool of potential candidates from either the internal or the external labour market.
- Selection is concerned with choosing the most suitable candidate from the pool that has been attracted during the recruitment phase. The most common methods of selection include the interview, the reference and the aptitude test.
- The choice of payment system is an important consideration for organisations as the money a person receives for carrying out work can be a source of motivation. The most common types of payment system used in Irish organisations include flat rate only, flat rate + bonus, merit rating, profit sharing and piecework.
- Performance appraisal is the process of reviewing an individual's performance and progress in a job and assessing his/her potential for future promotion. The results-oriented appraisal method is the most commonly used in Irish organisations.
- Training and development is aimed at helping employees to become more effective on the job and developing their potential. Good training practice should begin with developing a policy, followed by identifying needs, then planning and conducting the training and finally evaluating the process. On-the-job training is the most commonly used training method in Ireland.
- A trade union can be defined as a continuous association of wage earners with the objective of improving or maintaining conditions of employment. There are three major types of trade union in Ireland: craft unions, general unions and white-collar unions. Employer organisations in Ireland are of two types: employer associations and trade associations.
- The major state institutions involved in employee relations in Ireland are the Labour Relations Commission (LRC), the Labour Court, rights commissioners, equality officers and the Employment Appeals Tribunal (EAT).

Discussion Questions

1 What are the main phases in the history of HRM in Ireland?
2 Define HR planning and give reasons why it should be linked to an organisation's overall strategic plan.
3 Identify and describe the main phases in producing an HR plan.
4 What should be included in a job description and person specification?
5 What are the major sources of recruitment available to an organisation?
6 Describe the different types of selection interview that you are familiar with and highlight the advantages and disadvantages associated with each.
7 What factors will influence an employee's satisfaction with the rewards s/he receives? Describe the different types of payment system that an organisation could adopt. What factors will influence the choice of payment system?
8 Define performance appraisal and identify some of the major objectives of the performance appraisal process.
9 Describe the methods of performance appraisal that you are familiar with and the advantages and disadvantages of each.
10 Distinguish between training and development and identify the factors that are responsible for the increased interest in training and development in recent years.
11 Describe each of the main stages involved in systematic training and development.
12 Outline the main aims of trade unions and discuss the key strategies that are employed to achieve these aims.
13 Consider the Irish Business and Employers' Confederation, focusing on its role and the advantages and disadvantages of membership from an organisation's perspective.
14 Discuss the role of both the Labour Court and the Labour Relations Commission in Irish employee relations.

Concluding case: Change at Leeway and the implications for human resource management and development

Leeway, a unionised organisation with headquarters in the USA, is a leading manufacturer of computer systems and associated equipment. The company operates in highly competitive circumstances, and its external environment is both complex and dynamic. The company and its management appreciate that organisational change and adaptation is necessary in order to remain competitive and continue as a market leader.

In the past, Leeway has come to recognise the need to become a more employee-centred organisation. While it started out as what might be termed 'organic' in nature, a number of negative features have manifested themselves in the course of time: several layers of supervision; large growth in the number of technical specialists and support staff; a growth in the number of procedures and rules, leading to a deal of inflexibility; weakened general decision making with relatively little input from employees; a fall off in the level of innovation; poor communication and duplication of certain activities.

Overall the organisation was out of tune in terms of what was being demanded of it by its external environment. The negative features combined to form what the company had labelled the traditional organisation, one not conducive to high levels of performance and effectiveness.

Following a series of meetings at various levels throughout the organisation, a number of features of the new organisation scenario were identified, and can be summarised as follows: greater optimisation of technical and human resources; implementation of a philosophy whereby human assets are to be viewed as resources to be developed rather than as expendable spare parts (agents, not objects); the achievement of optimum task groupings and multiple, broad flexible skills; the promotion of ownership and responsibility lower down the organisation and the utilisation of internal controls and self-regulating sub-systems and groups; the achievement of a flatter organisation structure and a more participative management style; the encouragement of a degree of innovation and intrapreneurship; a more proactive stance in relation to the external environment.

Case Questions

1   Reflect on the characteristics of the new organisation scenario and what it represents relative to the tradition within Leeway.

2   Discuss the implications of the implementation of each aspect of the new scenario on each of the functional aspects of HRM.

Notes and References

1   Poole, M. and Jenkins, G. (1996) 'Competitiveness and Human Resource Management Policies', *Journal of General Management* 22(2), 1–14.

2   Monks, K. (1996) 'Ploughing the Furrow and Reaping the Harvest: Roles and Relationships in HRM', 1996 Examiner/University College Cork Lecture in Human Resource Management, University College Cork, September.

3   Barrington, T. (1980) *The Irish Administrative System*. Dublin: Institute of Public Administration.

4   Keenoy, T. (1990) 'Human Resource Management: A Case of the Wolf in Sheep's Clothing?', *Personnel Review* 19(2).

5   Beardwell, I. and Holden, L. (1994) *Human Resource Management: A Contemporary Perspective*. London: Pitman.

6   Gunnigle, P., Heraty, N. and Morley, M. (2011) *Human Resource Management in Ireland* (4th edn). Dublin: Gill & Macmillan.

7   Tyson, S. and York, A. (1992) *Personnel Management*. Oxford: Butterworth-Heinemann.

8   McMahon, G. (2000) 'Choosing the Right Kind of Interview for the Job', *Irish Times*, 9 October.

9   Lawler, E. (1977) 'Reward Systems' in J. Hackman and J. Suttle (eds), *Improving Life at Work: Behavioural Science Approaches to Organisational Change*. New York: Goodyear.

10   Tyson and York, *op. cit.*

11   Salaman, G. (1987) 'Towards a Sociology of Organizational Structure', *Sociological Review* 26(3), 519–54.

12   Dunlop, J. (1958) *Industrial Relations Systems*. New York: Holt.

Leadership

8.1 Introduction

Leadership as a phenomenon has throughout the course of history commanded attention from many different perspectives. From an organisational perspective, it remains a critical area of research and study, most especially in the context of the ever-increasing internationalisation of business and the challenges that that brings for all in leadership roles. But what are the characteristics of a good leader? Well, that's a good question! There is little doubt that leadership is a skill that is respected and admired, but it appears rather elusive to many people. It is also widely talked about and, at the same time, is somehow puzzling. Nicholls suggests that leadership is a seductive word that has a multitude of meanings,[1] while Leavy notes that 'few areas in management and in the wider purview of society and social organisation are more engaging and intriguing than leadership'.[2]

There are many studies and a considerable body of knowledge on leadership, the diversity of which is reflected in the breadth of the literature. Among the diverse issues investigated are: the qualities of the exceptional leader; the relationship between personality dimensions and successful leadership; the extent of the charisma possessed by the leader and its usefulness in effecting change in organisations; confidence, in particular over-confidence, among leaders; leadership perception; the effect of leadership on group behaviour and performance; trust between leaders and followers; decision making among leaders; vision creation and leadership; the role of leadership in individuals withdrawing from organisational life; the motivational consequences of different leadership approaches; the degree of emotional intelligence possessed by the leader, in particular its relationship with transformational abilities; the relationship between demonstrated leadership and organisational performance; the language patterns of leaders, which are said to have the potential to provide unique insights into their thoughts and actions; and even the physical fitness of the leader, something which some have suggested might hold the key to effective executive leadership.

The sheer diversity of the field has led Hitt to suggest that trying to 'piece together' a comprehensive theory of leadership from the numerous threads running through the extensive literature is 'like trying to find one's way out of a jungle without a map'.[3] But with or without a map, making the journey and exploring the nature of leadership is important, because studies have indicated that leadership can make a difference to organisational performance.

In making the exploratory journey the reader will discover that a good deal is now known about the leadership phenomenon. The broad sweep of the literature on the subject concerns itself with the characteristics of so-called effective leaders and the things that set them apart, the power sources of the leader, and the nature of the influence that they possess and how they wield it.

This chapter examines the nature of leadership and its significance in organisational life. We introduce the distinctions between management and leadership framed in the literature, outline the multiple roles that a leader might adopt in the organisation, and review the different schools of thought on leadership. Early trait theory, behavioural, contingency and more recent charismatic models are presented. As you will see, trait theory has its origins in the elaborate search for characteristics, dispositions and tendencies that set leaders apart from others. An assumption underpinning the thought of many of the researchers working in the trait tradition is that leaders are born, not made. The behavioural school takes as its starting point not the identification of traits but the actual behaviours exhibited by the leader. Several major contributions to this tradition point to two major dichotomous leadership behaviours, namely task-oriented behaviour or people-oriented behaviour. The contingency school concerned itself with the differing demands made on leaders, depending on the context in which they are operating. And charismatic models of leadership broadly focus on how leaders enact the achievement of highly significant accomplishments in organisations. However, before we present these different schools in greater detail, the definitional and role aspects of leadership, which abound in the literature, will be explored.

Management Focus 8.1 The many sides of leadership

One potential reason for the appearance of confusion in the literature might lie in Flanagan and Thompson's observation that 'leadership research and teaching are fast moving fields'. They note that:

> While big ideas – traits, behaviours, cognition – do not come along very frequently, intense energy goes into the 'normal science' of applying these ideas to diverse situations and changing circumstances. The results can often portray a very fragmented picture or, worse, a series of pictures whose relationship is by no means clear.

Source: Flanagan, H. and Thompson, D. (1993) 'Leadership: The Swing of the Pendulum', Leadership and Organizational Development Journal 14(1), 9–15.

8.2 Leadership defined

House and Aditya note that though the leadership phenomenon has a long pedigree, the 'systematic social scientific study of leadership did not begin until the early 1930s'.[4] Since that time there has been a sharp focus on unearthing the characteristics of the effective leader and the centrality of leadership ability to successful management. In the 1950s Selznick noted that leadership goes beyond simple efficiency or underlying arguments about efficiency and more fundamentally establishes the basic mission of the enterprise and creates and nurtures a functioning social unit capable of fulfilling that core mission.[5] In the 1960s a slightly narrower interpretation was advanced by Tannenbaum *et al.*, who suggested that leadership is an interpersonal influence that is exercised in a situation and directed specifically through the communication process towards the attainment of a specified goal.[6] More recently, Edgeman and Dahlgaard called attention to the systematics of leadership, which they view as a combination of core values and core competencies that allow the right course of action in a given situation to be chosen.[7] Systematic leadership of this nature, they suggest, is related to business excellence. This sharper focus on the bottom line and the performance impact of leadership has been especially evident in recent contributions. Dess and Picken, in their treaties on leadership in the twenty-first century, observe that the foundation of wealth creation is changing from capital-intensive manufacturing industry to information-intensive businesses and that a change of this nature and magnitude requires a new and distinct form of leadership dedicated to simultaneously fostering innovation and responsiveness. These outcomes of innovation and responsiveness are, they suggest, best attained by leadership behaviours dedicated to institutionalising employee empowerment, sharing knowledge and enabling creativity.[8] Trevelyan suggests that leadership should be a balance between a directive style, which shows the way, and a softer, devolved style, which seeks to maximise the potential of individuals.[9] The most effective leadership, she suggests, promotes motivation, creativity and performance, while also sustaining support, managerial control and expert input. In this way the leader is viewed both as enabler and constrainer.

Management Focus 8.2 Prominent writers on leadership

The notion of what constitutes effectiveness in leadership trait, behaviour or action is also highly variable in the literature. Here are some prominent thinkers' views.

- Plato: Effective leaders are philosopher kings
- Machiavelli: Effective leaders are power-wielders, individuals who employ manipulation, exploitation and deviousness to achieve their own ends.
- Weber: Effective leaders have charisma – that special spiritual power or personal quality that gives an individual influence over large numbers of people.
- Taylor: Effective leaders view management as a science.
- De Pree: Effective leaders view management as an art.
- Drucker: Effective leaders are able to carry out the functions of management – planning, organising, directing and measuring.
- McGregor: Effective leaders understand the human side of enterprise.
- Likert: Effective leaders are able to establish effective management systems.

- Blake and Mouton: Effective leaders choose a leadership style that reflects a concern for both production and people.
- Bennis and Nanus: Effective leaders have vision and are able to translate the vision into action.
- Burns: Effective leaders are able to lift followers into their better selves.

Source: Hitt, W. (1993) 'The Model Leader: A Fully Functioning Person', *Leadership and Organisation Development Journal* 11(7), 4–11.

8.3 Distinguishing leadership and management

Leadership is an essential and integral part of good management. Contrary to popular belief, leadership is not an optional extra in the manager's armoury. Managers who do not lead are often considered to be neglecting an important managerial function. It has been argued that when lacking its leadership dimensions, management is reduced to mere administration and that organisations that are managed without leadership generally perform more poorly than their counterparts where such leadership is an integral component of the management cannon. Yukl notes that while one individual might perform both managerial and leadership functions, the two activity domains involve separate and relatively distinct processes.[10] Thus, managers are oriented toward stability, while leaders are innovation-oriented. Furthermore, while managers typically get individuals to do things with ever increasing efficiency, the goal of the effective leader is to get individuals to agree about what things should actually be done and how they should be done.

Mintzberg argues that leadership behaviour can be an integral part of a manager's job;[11] in his research he identifies ten main roles grouped into three areas (see Table 8.1).

TABLE 8.1 MANAGERIAL ROLES IDENTIFIED BY MINTZBERG

Interpersonal	Figurehead Leader Liaison
Informational	Monitor Disseminator Spokesman
Decisional	Entrepreneur Disturbance handler Resource allocator Negotiator

Source: Mintzberg, H. (1973) *The Nature of Managerial Work*. New York: Harper Row.

Obviously, as Statt highlights, chief executives will spend much more of their time on the interpersonal roles than would more junior managers. However, this does not mean that they will be any more effective as leaders. He argues that the job titles and the job descriptions, and the amount of time the job demands for activity defined as leadership, simply tell us what is done. They do not tell us how it is done – and that is where leadership ability and effectiveness comes in:

But in any organisation we tend to look automatically at the apex for evidence of leadership. Indeed the greatest fallacy of leadership is that it always comes from the top down. It most certainly does not.[12]

TABLE 8.2 DISTINGUISHING BETWEEN A MANAGER AND A LEADER

Manager	Leader
Motivates people and administers resources to achieve stated organisational goals	Motivates people to develop new objectives
Short-range view	Long-range perspective
A copy	An original
Maintains	Develops
Focuses on system and structure	Focuses on people
Implements	Shapes
Relies on control	Inspires trust
Eye on the bottom line	Eye on the horizon
Narrows down horizons	Opens up horizons
Rational	Emotional
Classic good soldier	Own person
Accepts the status quo	Challenges the status quo
Does things right	Does the right thing

Source: Statt, D. (1994) *Psychology and the World of Work*. London: Macmillan.

Many believe management and leadership to be more delineated as organisational and/or societal roles. Thus, for example, Zaleznik of Harvard Business School argues forcefully that there is a difference between leadership and management and highlights a number of differences associated with their motivation, personal history and how they actually think:[13]

- Managers tend to adopt impersonal or passive attitudes toward goals. Leaders adopt a more personal and active attitude toward goals.
- In order to get people to accept solutions, the manager needs to continually co-ordinate and balance in order to compromise conflicting values. The leader creates excitement in work and develops choices that give substance to images that excite people.
- In their relationships with other people, managers maintain a low level of emotional involvement. Leaders have empathy with other people and give attention to what events and actions mean.
- Managers see themselves more as conservators and regulators of the existing order of affairs with which they identify, and from which they gain rewards. Leaders work in, but do not belong to, the organisation. Their sense of identity does not depend upon membership or work roles and they search out opportunities for change.

It has been suggested that what is becoming apparent is that organisational leadership relies on a combination of personal traits, skills, attitudes and abilities, along with situational/environmental conditions which, in combination, create the recipe for potential success. Theoretically this mix of the personal and the situational have long been debated in prominent schools of thought on leadership and it is to these schools that we now turn.

8.4 Different schools of thought on leadership

This section will introduce and discuss four major schools of thought on leadership that are prominent in the literature:

- the trait approach
- the behavioural approach
- the contingency approach
- the charismatic approach.

8.4.1 Trait theories of leadership

It is almost a truism to suggest that good leadership is essential for business performance. But what makes a good leader? Among the earliest theories of leadership were those that focused on traits.[14] The earliest trait theories, which can be traced back to the ancient Greeks, concluded that leaders are born, not made. Until around 1950, most studies sought to identify leadership traits, principally because prominent leaders seemed to possess certain 'exceptional characteristics'. In this theory, also known as the 'great man' theory, the assumption was that it is possible to identify a unifying set of characteristics that make all great leaders great; so researchers set about looking for the personality characteristics or traits that distinguished leaders from other people. If the concept of traits were to be proved valid, there would have to be specific characteristics that all leaders possess. The trait theories argued that leadership is innate, the product of our genes, given at birth. The chosen individuals are born with traits (particularly personality traits, though physical traits possibly had a role to play), which caused them to be self-selected as leaders. The findings emanating from this early work tend to disagree on what sets of traits distinguish leaders from followers. Among the characteristics identified are:

- intelligence
- initiative
- dependability
- lateral thinking ability
- self-assurance
- maturity
- visionary ability
- social well-being
- need for achievement
- need for power
- goal-directedness.

Overall, the research effort dedicated to the search for universal traits possessed by leaders resulted in little truly convincing, consistent evidence. Some have gone so far as to suggest that the hunt for such traits resulted in a lot of 'dead ends'. Certainly much of the research work identified lists of traits that tend to be overlapping or contradictory, with few significant correlations between factors. As Luthans[15] points out, only intelligence seemed to hold up with any degree of consistency, and when these findings were combined with those of studies on physical traits, the overall conclusion was that leaders were more likely to be bigger and brighter than those being led, but not too much so! Despite this, Stogdill argued that it was not entirely appropriate to abandon the study of traits, and that the best way forward was to introduce an interactional element into the equation whereby traits and their significance/universality would be considered in the context of the situational difficulties or demands facing the leader.

However, the view that leaders are 'born, not made' is much less widely held today. There has been an incremental shift away from this thinking for a number of reasons. First, the enormous range of traits potentially affecting leadership ability is problematic and it is difficult to measure them. This appears to be a critical weakness, according to House and Aditya, largely because there is little empirically substantiated personality theory to guide the search for leadership traits.[16] The lists of traits tend to be exceptionally long and there is not always agreement on how these traits should be prioritised. This resulted in an inability to produce many replicative investigations. Second, if we were to rely on birth alone to produce leaders, we would potentially not have enough leaders to go around. Third, there is a growing body of evidence on the influence of nurturing and life experiences in this area. Fourth, our leadership needs are diverse and vary enormously and are commonly dispersed throughout society, with the result that if the specific situational demands of the leader are taken into account, the replication problem once again raises its head. Overall, many remain unconvinced that there is any direct link between any specific characteristics and any form of leadership.

8.4.2 Behavioural theories of leadership

As convincing evidence failed to accumulate from trait-based research, researchers increasingly began to seek out behaviours that specific leaders exhibit. The central hypothesis in this school of thought was that critical specific behaviours differentiate leaders from non-leaders. Extensive research studies on behavioural classifications of leadership were conducted by Stogdill and Coons at Ohio State University and by Likert at the University of Michigan.[17]

Ohio State University leadership studies

These studies, which began in the 1940s, sought to identify and classify independent dimensions of leader behaviour. Questionnaires were designed containing a list of items detailing specific aspects of leadership behaviour. From a list of more than one thousand dimensions, the researchers eventually consistently identified two categories that accounted for most leadership behaviour. These two dimensions were labelled 'initiating structure style' and 'considerate style'. Initiating structure style reflects the extent to which the leader defines and structures his/her role and the roles of the followers in achieving established organisational goals. The considerate style reflects the extent to which the leader focuses on establishing trust, mutual respect and rapport between him/herself and the followers and among the group of followers.

Both styles were found to be uncorrelated, thus potentially giving rise to four possible types of leadership behaviour (see also Figure 8.1):

- low on initiating structure style/low on considerate style
- high on initiating structure style/low on considerate style
- high on initiating structure style/high on considerate style
- low on initiating structure style/high on considerate style.

FIGURE 8.1 FOUR LEADERSHIP STYLES

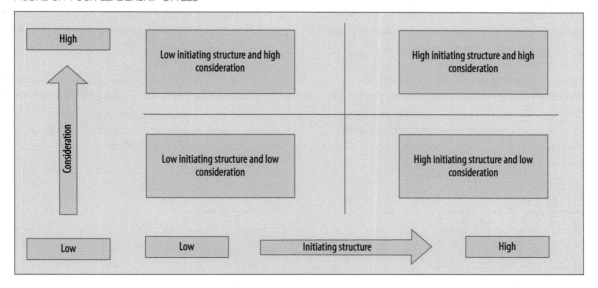

Though criticised on methodological grounds, particularly for its reliance on questionnaires, the research demonstrated that leaders high in initiating structure style and high in considerate style were generally more likely to achieve superior performance from their followers. Followers were also more likely to describe higher feelings of satisfaction when compared with their counterparts operating under the leadership of those who were low on either style, or both.

University of Michigan studies

Like the work done at Ohio, the Michigan studies, under the direction of Rensis Likert, sought to examine the nature of the relationship between the behavioural characteristics of leaders and performance effectiveness. The research resulted in a two-way classification of leadership: employee-oriented and production-oriented styles, with employee-oriented leaders emphasising interpersonal relations in the workplace, and production-oriented leaders concentrating on the technical aspects of the work. The results of the studies demonstrated that employee-oriented leaders consistently achieve higher productivity and higher job satisfaction among their work groups. Conversely, production-oriented leaders are more likely to be associated with lower group productivity and lower job satisfaction. However, it also emerged that the employee-oriented and production-oriented approaches need to be balanced. Those employee-oriented leaders taking part in the studies who achieved superior results consistently recognised that production was one of the main responsibilities of their work!

The managerial grid

The managerial grid advanced by Blake and Mouton has been particularly influential as a two-dimensional model of leadership and is generally viewed as an extension and advancement of the earlier work of the team at Ohio State University.[18] The grid has two axes – concern for people and concern for production – which can be taken to represent the initiating structure style and the considerate style of the Ohio research or, indeed, the employee-oriented and production-oriented dimensions of the Michigan work. Blake and Mouton's writings begin from the assumption that a manager's job is to foster attitudes about behaviour that promote performance, creativity and intrapreneurship and innovation in the enterprise. Such managerial competence can be taught and learned. Their managerial grid (see Figure 8.2) provides a framework for understanding and applying effective leadership.

FIGURE 8.2 THE BLAKE AND MOUTON GRID

9	Country club management – (1,9) Production is incidental to lack of conflict and 'good fellowship'.					Team management – (9,9) Production is from integration of tasks and human requirements.		
8								
7								
6								
5			Dampered pendulum – (5,5) (Middle of the road) Push for production but don't go 'all out', give some but not all. 'Be fair and firm'.					
4								
3								
2	Impoverished management – (1,1)					Task management – (9,1)		
1	Effective production is unobtainable beacuse people are lazy, apathetic and indifferent. Sound and mature realtionships are difficult to achieve because human nature being what it is, conflict is inevitable.					People are a commodity, just like machines. A manager's responsibility is to plan, direct and control the work of those subordinate to him/her.		
	1	2	3	4	5	6	7	8	9

Source: Blake, R. and Mouton, J. (1962) 'The Managerial Grid', *Advanced Management Office Executive* 1(a).

The grid results from combining two fundamental ingredients of managerial behaviour: a concern for production and a concern for people. Any manager's approach to their job will show more or less of each of these two fundamental constituents. They may show a high degree of concern for one or the other of these, or they may lie in the middle, with an equal concern for both. Different positions on the grid represent different typical patterns of behaviour. The grid indicates that different degrees of concern for production and concern for people are possible. Only five key styles are isolated here for illustration.

- **9,1:** Management focuses almost exclusively on production issues. This type is one who expects schedules to be met and wants production operations to run smoothly and methodically. Interruptions in the schedule are viewed as someone's mistakes. Disagreement is viewed as being dysfunctional and is seen as insubordination.
- **1,9:** This management style – 'country club style' – almost exclusively emphasises people concerns. People are encouraged and supported in their endeavours as long as they are doing their best. Conflict and disagreement is to be avoided and even constructive criticism is not seen as helpful because it interrupts the harmonious relationship.
- **1,1:** This style, known as impoverished management, signals little concern for either production or people. These managers avoid responsibility and task commitment. Leaders of this kind avoid contact and where possible display little commitment to problem solving.
- **5,5:** These managers display the 'middle of the road' style; they push enough to get acceptable levels of production, but in the techniques and skills that they use they also demonstrate a concern for people. They show a firm but fair attitude and have confidence in their subordinates.
- **9,9:** This manager demonstrates a high concern for production and a high concern for people issues. This is a team manager whose goal is one of integration. S/he aims for the highest possible standard and insists on the best possible result for everyone. There is usually maximum involvement and participation and the achievement of difficult goals is viewed as a fulfilling challenge. It is accepted that conflict will occur. When it happens it is handled in an open and frank manner and is not treated as a personal attack. This style, Blake and Mouton argue, is always the best style to adopt since it builds on long-term development and trust. In order to be truly effective, this style of leadership requires an appropriate cultural fit. The value set of the whole organisation must seek to support this style of leadership.

8.4.3 Contingency leadership theory

Contingency theories are based on the premise that predicting leadership success and effectiveness is more complex than simply isolating traits or behaviours: situational variables, or the context in which leadership occurs, also have strong explanatory power. Both Fiedler's investigations, in particular his concepts of the least preferred co-worker and House's path–goal theory are in the tradition of contingency theory.

Fiedler's theory

In the 1970s Fred Fiedler conducted a series of studies dedicated to the leadership of work groups. Beginning with the assumption that anyone appointed to a responsible leadership position of this kind will possess the requisite technical expertise, his research question was: What is it about leadership behaviour that leads to effective group working? ('Effective' meaning how well the group performs the primary task for which it exists.) Fiedler's research identifies two main leadership styles: relationship-motivated and task-motivated. Relationship-motivated leaders obtain satisfaction from having good relationships with others. They usually encourage participation and involvement and are always concerned about what the other team members think of them. Conversely, task-motivated leaders are strongly focused on the task. Their emphasis is on proceduralisation and task completion.

Fiedler subsequently developed an instrument to classify these two styles. The instrument asks leaders to review all people with whom they have ever worked and think of the one with whom they could work least well. They are then asked to rate this least preferred co-worker (LPC) along a number of dimensions. Fiedler found that relationship-motivated leaders will score relationship issues high in spite of their problems with the LPC. Conversely, task-motivated leaders rate the LPC low on all dimensions. Fiedler emphasises that both these leadership styles can be useful and effective in appropriate situations. He argues that it is necessary to have a contingency perspective on leadership because effective leadership will be contingent on the nature of the tasks to be completed and the context in which this is to be done.

Management Focus 8.3 Least preferred co-worker

Exhibit 8.2 Least-preferred co-worker

Think of the person with whom you work least well. S/he may be someone you work with presently, or may be someone you knew in the past. S/he does not have to be the person you like least well, but should be the person with whom you now have or have had the most difficulty in getting a job done. Describe this person as s/he appears to you by placing an 'x' at the point you believe best describes that person. Do this for each pair of adjectives.

Pleasant	__ __ __ __ __ __ __ __	Unpleasant
	8 7 6 5 4 3 2 1	
Friendly	__ __ __ __ __ __ __ __	Unfriendly
	8 7 6 5 4 3 2 1	
Rejecting	__ __ __ __ __ __ __ __	Accepting
	8 7 6 5 4 3 2 1	
Helpful	__ __ __ __ __ __ __ __	Frustrating
	8 7 6 5 4 3 2 1	
Unenthusiastic	__ __ __ __ __ __ __ __	Enthusiastic
	8 7 6 5 4 3 2 1	
Tense	__ __ __ __ __ __ __ __	Relaxed
	8 7 6 5 4 3 2 1	
Distant	__ __ __ __ __ __ __ __	Close
	8 7 6 5 4 3 2 1	
Cold	__ __ __ __ __ __ __ __	Warm
	8 7 6 5 4 3 2 1	
Co-operative	__ __ __ __ __ __ __ __	Unco-operative
	8 7 6 5 4 3 2 1	
Supportive	__ __ __ __ __ __ __ __	Hostile
	8 7 6 5 4 3 2 1	
Boring	__ __ __ __ __ __ __ __	Interesting
	8 7 6 5 4 3 2 1	

Quarrelsome	8 7 6 5 4 3 2 1	Harmonious
Self-assured	8 7 6 5 4 3 2 1	Hesitant
Efficient	8 7 6 5 4 3 2 1	Inefficient
Gloomy	8 7 6 5 4 3 2 1	Cheerful
Open	8 7 6 5 4 3 2 1	Guarded

Scoring. Your score on the LPC scale is a measure of your leadership style and indicates your primary motivation in a work setting. To determine your score, add up the points (1 through 8) for each of the 16 items. If your score is 64 or above, you are a high LPC person or relationship-oriented. If your score is 57 or below, you are a low LPC person or task-oriented. If your score falls between 58 and 63, you will need to determine for yourself in which category you belong.

Source: Fiedler, F. and Chemers, M. (1974) *Leadership and Effective Management*. New York: Scott, Foresman and Co.

House's path–goal theory

Advanced by Robert House as a contingency theory of leadership, path–goal theory extracts critical elements from expectancy theory of work motivation and the Ohio State University research on behavioural aspects of leadership.[19] Specifically, it was intended as a contribution that would reconcile the conflicting findings concerning task-oriented and person-oriented leadership. House argues that leaders are effective if they can help subordinates to identify a goal and then enable them to achieve it. The terminology 'path–goal' is used to reflect the belief that effective leadership is about clarifying the path to help others get from where they are to the achievement of their work goals and to smooth the journey along the path by reducing and/or eliminating blocks and pitfalls. House identifies four leadership styles – directive, supportive, participative and achievement-oriented – and two classes of situational variables that influence the leadership behaviour–outcome relationship – the personal characteristics of the subordinates and the environment of the subordinates. These situational variables are seen to influence the perceptions and motivations of subordinates, and consequently the leader is advised to adopt the style that in the given circumstances is most likely to result in the identification and achievement of appropriate goals. Robbins outlines a number of useful hypotheses that have emerged from path–goal theory research:[20]

- Directive leadership leads to greater satisfaction when tasks are ambiguous or stressful than when they are highly structured and well laid out.
- Supportive leadership results in high employee performance and satisfaction when subordinates are performing structured tasks.
- Directive leadership is likely to be perceived as redundant among subordinates with high perceived ability or with considerable experience.

- The more clear and bureaucratic the formal authority relationships, the more leaders should exhibit supportive behaviour and de-emphasise directive behaviour.
- Directive leadership will lead to higher employee satisfaction when there is substantive conflict within a group.
- Subordinates with an internal locus of control (those who believe they control their own destiny) will be more satisfied with a participative style.
- Subordinates with an external locus of control will be more satisfied with a directive style.
- Achievement-oriented leadership will increase subordinates' expectations that effort will lead to high performance when tasks are ambiguously structured.

Overall, in evaluating the significance of contingency theory and research in that tradition, House and Aditya note that:

> While some of the major predictions of contingency and path–goal theory were supported by meta analyses, . . . the theories did not fare well overall, and the interest of leadership scholars in these theories waned.[21]

In particular, they suggest that they were criticised for the conceptual base from which they were drawing and because of the degree of inconsistency that characterised the empirical findings that were produced. However, as they also highlight, research in this domain did eventually lead to other work that proved more influential in the field. Significantly, later work by Fiedler and Garcia[22] proved significant and House's path–goal theory eventually led to significant developments in the charismatic research tradition.

8.4.4 Charismatic leadership theories

Much like some of the early work associated with trait theory and behavioural theory, studies on charismatic leadership have been directed at identifying behaviours that differentiate charismatic leaders from their non-charismatic counterparts. House suggests that charismatic leaders are exceptionally self-confident, strongly motivated to attain and assert influence, and have strong conviction in the moral correctness of their beliefs.[23] In the tradition of trait theory, these personality traits are believed to be antecedents to charismatic leadership. Popper and Zakkai note that the growth and development of charismatic leadership in organisations is related to the presence of circumstances which deviate from organisational routine, circumstances connected with crisis situations or major changes.[24] Particularly significant here is transformational leadership (see below).

Transactional and transformational leadership

From the 1970s, research attention was paid to the hypothesis that more successful organisations (using objective performance indicators) have better top-management leadership than less successful organisations. Dedicated to identifying 'charismatic' characteristics of leaders, it was viewed as important in the context of organisations attempting to transform traditional systems, methodologies and approaches in an attempt to meet the emerging strategic imperative. Burns identified two types of political leadership: transactional and transformational (see Table 8.3).[25]

TABLE 8.3 APPROACHES OF TRANSACTIONAL VERSUS TRANSFORMATIONAL LEADERS

Transactional leader	
Contingent reward	Contracts exchange of rewards for effort, promises rewards for good performance, recognises accomplishments.
Management by exception (active)	Watches and searches for deviations from rules and standards, takes corrective action.
Management by exception (passive)	Intervenes only if standards are not met.
Laissez-faire	Abdicates responsibilities, avoids making decisions.
Transformational leader	
Charisma	Provides vision and sense of mission, instils pride, gains respect and trust.
Inspiration	Communicates high expectations, uses symbols to focus efforts, expresses important purposes in simple ways.
Intellectual stimulation	Promotes intelligence, rationality and careful problem-solving.
Individual consideration	Gives personal attention, treats each employee individually, coaches, advises.

Source: Bass, B. (1990) 'From Transactional to Transformational Leadership: Learning to Share the Vision', *Organisational Dynamics*, Winter, 22.

The more traditional transactional leadership involves an exchange relationship between leaders and followers which, as Popper and Zakkai note, 'becomes possible when there is no outstanding sense of impending threat or anxiety',[26] but transformational leadership is more about leaders adjusting the values, beliefs and needs of their followers. Bass suggests that transactional leadership is largely a prescription for mediocrity, while transformational leadership consistently leads to exceptional performance in organisations that really need it.[27] The core functions of the transformational leader are:
- to be a charismatic role model
- to be an inspirational motivator
- to provide intellectual stimulation
- to show concern and consideration for followers' needs, particularly those relating to achievement and growth.

He argues that the development and utilisation of transformational leadership through a sustained focus on the human resource (HR) policy areas of recruitment, selection, promotion, training and development will yield results in the health, well-being, and effective performance of the modern organisation. Brown suggests that transformational leaders are a very important asset when tackling technical change in organisations.[28] He notes that 'major change requires transformational leaders and one of their principle tools are social rites – elaborate, dramatic, planned sets of activities that promote change in individuals', and continues:

> The transformational leader operates by moulding the psychology and behaviour of his or her colleagues and subordinates. At the psychological or cognitive level the transformational leader is especially concerned to shape the values, beliefs and assumptions that employees have about their tasks, their colleagues and their organisation. At the behavioural level the

transformational leader strives to create social situations which dramatically and powerfully communicate significant messages to others. It is the means by which this social and psychological leadership can most effectively be accomplished in the cause of technological change management.

Transformational leadership theory has been criticised on a number of accounts. Statt describes it as the 'Loch Ness monster' of leadership theory.[29] He accepts that while a number of perfectly sober observers claim to have seen it, he has never witnessed it. Furthermore, he suggests that on close observation, transformational leadership represents a reversion back to the much-maligned 'great man' theory. Robbins agrees that it does represent a return to traits, but from a different perspective:

> Researchers are now attempting to identify the set of traits that people implicitly refer to when they characterise someone as a leader. This line of thinking proposes that leadership is as much style – projecting the appearance of being a leader – as it is substance.[30]

A more serious criticism questions the methodological foundations of the theory. Most of the research to date has relied on Bass's original questionnaire, which has been criticised, or on qualitative research that largely describes leaders through interviews.

TABLE 8.4 CONDITIONS CONDUCIVE TO TRANSACTIONAL AND TRANSFORMATIONAL LEADERSHIP

Leadership pattern	Conditions conducive to the predominance of the pattern
Transactional	Routine situations where the basic level of anxiety is not high, there is no acute sense of impending crisis or major changes.
Transformational	Situations where the basic level of anxiety is not high and attention is given to the developmental needs of the led. In general, this leadership pattern depends more on the leader's view of him/herself as transformational and less on the organisational context than does transactional leadership.

Source: Popper, M. and Zakkai, E. (1994) 'Transactional, Charismatic and Transformational Leadership: Conditions Conducive to their Predominance', *Leadership and Organisational Development Journal* 15(6), 3–7.

8.5 Leadership and leadership development in Ireland

The Global Leadership and Organizational Behavior Effectiveness research programme (GLOBE), directed by Bob House at Wharton School of Management, University of Pennsylvania, is focused on trying to establish how societal cultural variables influence organisational values, organisational practices, culturally endorsed norms, implicit theories relevant to leadership and the exercise of leadership in each of the cultures studied. As part of this global study of leadership, which aims to redress the US cultural bias of much of the extant literature, a group of researchers from the School of Business at Trinity College Dublin, employing a pluralist methodology, report data on several Irish leadership behaviours.

Using questionnaire data from a sample of 156 middle managers in the food processing and financial services industries, Keating *et al.* rank leadership behaviours in the Irish context (see Table 8.5).[31]

TABLE 8.5 IRISH LEADERSHIP ATTRIBUTES

Leadership attributes	Mean (7-point scale)
Self-centred	1.99
Face-saving	2.48
Autocratic	2.48
Bureaucratic	3.50
Status-conscious	3.62
Individualist	3.95
Humanely oriented	5.01
Possessing equanimity	5.11
Charismatic	5.11
Diplomatic	5.44
Collective	5.46
Procedural	5.60
Decisive	6.14
Having integrity	6.19
Inspirational	6.29
Visionary	6.33
Performance orientated	6.38

Source: Keating, M., Martin, G. and Donnelly-Cox, G. (1996) 'The GLOBE Project: A Case for Interdisciplinary and Intercultural Research', *Proceedings of the First Irish Academy of Management Conference*.

The scale scores reflect the validity of the leadership behaviour. The higher the score, the more favourably the behaviour is perceived.

In a qualitative phase of this study, participants were asked to define management and leadership, to identify the behavioural characteristics of an average manager, an above-average manager and an outstanding leader.

The leadership behaviours given prominence by the groups included vision, charisma, competence, inspiration, persistence and risk-taking. There was strong disagreement in the groups as to whether successful business persons on both the Irish and international stage were in fact outstanding leaders. None of the participants identified an excellent Irish business leader; reference to outstanding leaders tended in general to refer to figures outside the Irish context. The participants suggested the inability to give credit to successful business people reflected Irish culture. Contrasting with their lack of confidence in Irish leadership figures, there was a general belief among them that Irish managers are extremely adaptable and perform well abroad.

Turning to the context for leadership and management development in Ireland, Heraty and Morley assess the state of development in Ireland and identify policy, practice and structural contingencies that help to explain variations in the volume of leadership and management development activity undertaken at organisational level.[32] Basing their discussion on a much earlier debate on human capital investment and human asset accounting, they note that the ongoing development of skilled leaders and managers is now viewed as a priority for all organisations, particularly in light of research highlighting that the pattern of work of those in such positions is rather fragmented, ad hoc and challenging. Heraty and Morley focus on establishing the nature of leadership and management development in Ireland through an appraisal of the number of development days per annum and the assessment of a core set of policy, practice and structural domain characteristics that influence the volume of developmental activity undertaken.

In the survey, HR practitioners were asked to quantify the number of development days per year. The results, in relation to the volume of management and leadership development undertaken, point to a steady increase in investment with some 70 per cent of managers receiving between one and five days' development. They highlight that where a policy on development exists, the volume of developmental activity undertaken is higher. Thus, firms with an explicit written policy record a mean of 5.5 days per annum, their counterparts with no such policy displaying an average of 2.6 days. In the context of the existence of such a policy, they explored whether the level at which actual policy is determined – international headquarters (HQ), national HQ, subsidiary or establishment level – makes a difference. However, the location of where developmental policies are determined was found to have no significant influence on the number of days of management and leadership development provided. Beyond the actual number of days of development provided and the existence of a surrounding policy framework, the form and content of the development intervention matters greatly. The evidence to date suggests that the majority of Irish organisations tend to rely on formal interventions/programmes with a focus on personal skills training and management training. It has been noted that there is a strong tendency to emphasise seminars, but there is significantly less investment in coaching and mentoring programmes, self-awareness activities and personal profiling. It has also been established that more customised leadership development programmes are often the preserve of larger organisations.

Heraty and Morley tested the take-up of a range of development interventions to determine whether particular initiatives have an impact on the volume of management and leadership development undertaken. The use of formal career plans, international experience schemes and, to a slightly lesser degree, succession plans was found to have an impact on the volume of leadership and management development undertaken. The use of assessment centres or high flier schemes was not found to be significant in this respect. Assessment centres were not utilised to a high degree in the companies surveyed. The use of high flier schemes was found to be low in Ireland compared with our European counterparts.

Based on a trawl of several studies on management and leadership development conducted in Ireland, Garavan et al. summarise several trends that have a number of implications for future practice in developing a cadre of capable leaders.[33] They suggest that leadership development specialists must challenge simplistic views of development to reflect the challenges that need to be faced and that innovation and experimentation are necessary, rather than a reliance on traditional methods and approaches. Other key recommendations include:

- The need to integrate leadership development initiatives with business strategy and the need to take proactive steps to demonstrate how they contribute to business performance.
- Organisations should benchmark their leadership developmental effort against organisations of a similar size.
- Organisations should evaluate the internal and external factors that facilitate or inhibit leadership development
- Those charged with leadership development roles should combine qualitative and quantitative approaches to evaluate leadership development activities and their impact on practice.

8.6 Summary of key propositions

- Leadership may be interpreted in simple terms, such as 'getting others to follow', or more specifically as, for example, 'the use of authority in decision making'. It may be exercised as an attribute of position, or because of personal knowledge or wisdom.
- Leadership behaviour can be an integral part of a manager's job.
- Leadership activities can be classified into five key areas: task functions; cultural functions; symbolic functions; political functions; and relational functions.
- Leadership trait theory argues that leaders are born, not made. Also known as the 'great man' theory, this assumption is that it is possible to identify a unifying set of characteristics that make all great leaders great.
- Behavioural theories argue that specific behaviours differentiate leaders from non-leaders. Critical studies include the Ohio and Michigan studies and the managerial grid.
- Contingency theories are based on the premise that predicting leadership success and effectiveness is more complex than the simple isolation of traits or behaviours. Situational variables, or the context in which leadership is occurring, are also viewed as having strong explanatory power.

  END OF ASSIGNMENT
- Charismatic leadership has been directed at identifying behaviours that differentiate charismatic leaders from their non-charismatic counterparts. Transformational leadership has been influential here.

Discussion Questions

1. Distinguish between leadership and management.
2. Outline and describe 10 key roles that a leader should perform in an organisation.
3. In what way would you say effective leadership can impact on an organisation?
4. Name two business leaders you consider to be particularly effective. Compare and contrast their leadership styles, setting down those particular traits and behaviours that you deem to be important to their leadership abilities.
5. 'Leaders are born, not made.' Discuss.
6. What are the main problems with the trait theory of leadership?
7. What is the managerial grid?
8. What do you understand by the contingency theory of leadership?
9. From your reading of the chapter, outline three areas for future research in the leadership area that you think could prove fruitful to further building knowledge in this area.

Concluding Case: Leadership at Leadmore Ice Cream[34]

Back in the 1940s, operating from his farm at Leadmore, Kilrush, George Glynn was looking to the future. He was selling his farm's produce from a downtown outlet. Innovative by nature, he believed that anything he did he should do properly. The farm had two acres of land under glass for vegetable production and a separate unit for mushrooms and tomatoes. The glasshouse was heated by an engine he had constructed himself.

George also supplied milk to the townspeople. Even at a time of little emphasis on quality control, he carried out a regular bacteria count. Leadmore Farm provided west Clare with its first taste of homogenised bottled milk. During a glass shortage, he travelled door to door providing a service whereby customers could take milk from the churn with their own containers. George saw how this could potentially lead to health problems, so he imported cartons from Sweden, becoming one of Ireland's first distributors of cartons for pasteurised milk .

By 1946, the company, now called Leadmore Dairies, faced a surplus of milk, but George viewed this as an opportunity to realise a lifelong ambition to produce ice cream commercially. He had already done much research on the idea but now, with the possibility of realising the ambition, he began to tour ice cream plants in Ireland and the UK. Once he was fully satisfied that he had the know-how, he began making ice cream at the farm, and brought it to his downtown shop. He laid emphasis on experimentation and quality control. On numerous occasions throughout the 1950s, 1960s and 1970s, Leadmore Dairies won awards for excellence in competitions held by the Ice Cream Alliance. By the 1960s, Leadmore ice cream was distributed throughout the Clare–Limerick region. George had a marketing-oriented approach to his business and developed the market for his ice cream in this area. A logo of two Eskimos was developed, much point-of-sale material was distributed, including posters, stickers, badges and flags, and a significant marketing effort was carried out until the 1980s.

In 1969 demand for Leadmore had far outgrown supply, so George oversaw the construction of a new modern plant with sufficient production and storage capacity to facilitate nationwide distribution. George had this operational by 1971. Furthermore, during the 1970s, George sought to acquire several depots throughout the Republic and Northern Ireland.

The 1980s began on a high note. With Peter Glynn in full control of his father's company, a new brand image and some significant interests in the UK, the company was gaining much penetration in stores. In-store refrigeration was constantly updated, with state-of-the-art freezers coming from Gramp Corporation of Denmark. A succession of two poor seasons, due to bad weather conditions, lay at the heart of the decision to rely more on agents to decrease distribution costs. During the busier seasons, however, the smaller the distribution network they had to control themselves, the less costly it was for the firm. Agents seemed to be performing to a capacity which production could barely meet. For the peak months the factory was manufacturing over six days a week, 24 hours a day, to meet demand. In 1989, a heatwave in early August was a godsend for the company.

After this successful season, Peter Glynn oversaw a major investment in refrigeration in order to maintain the quality of the ice cream. The decision was taken to reconstruct the enormous cold storage facility in order to maximise wind-chill factors and minimise temperatures. New freezer compressors were purchased and new delivery trucks invested in.

Disaster struck with a run of five bad seasons, due primarily to poor weather. In response, some emergency management decisions were made, such as changing the company name, this time from Leadmore Ice to Leadmore Farm, and more investment in quality, in particular the introduction of foil wrapping, creamier recipes and changing the one-pint brick wrap to the same colour as a competitor's product.

In 1993, due to the increasingly poor health of his mother, Peter took the decision to step back from the day-to-day running of the company and he engaged marketing consultants to do an overall review of the company's strategy. The study was carried out by James Hoblyn and Peter O'Hara of Grant Thornton Consulting. James Hoblyn proposed himself as the person who could implement a turnaround strategy, and in October 1993 he took up the position of managing director of the company. In addition to appointing this new MD, fresh equity of approximately £75,000 was put into the company by family members. The board faced 1994 with confidence in the new management and the potential for an upturn in company fortunes.

Midway through the summer of 1994 it became apparent that targets were not being reached and that a serious cash flow problem had developed. The company was left with two key options: either secure outside investment or sell the company in its entirety. Creditors were demanding payment. Little progress was made and on 9 December 1994, protective notice was served to employees. The company was liquidated in 1995.

Case Question

Compare and contrast the leadership styles of George and Peter.

Notes and References

1 Nicholls, J. (1993) 'The Paradox of Managerial Leadership', *Journal of General Management* 18(4), 1–14.

2 Leavy, B. (1995) 'Strategic Vision and Inspirational Leadership' in B. Leavy and J. Walsh (eds), *Strategy and General Management: An Irish Reader*. Dublin: Oak Tree Press.

3 Hitt, W. (1993) 'The Model Leader: A Fully Functioning Person', *Leadership and Organisation Development Journal* 11(7), 4–11.

4 House, R. and Aditya, R. (1997) 'The Social Scientific Study of Leadership: Quo Vadis?', *Journal of Management* 23(3), 409–73.

5 Selznick, P. (1957) *Leadership in Administration*. New York: Harper Row.

6 Tannenbaum, R., Weschler, I. and Masserik, F. (1961) *Leadership and Organization*. New York: McGraw-Hill.

7 Edgeman, R. and Dahlgaard, J. (1998) 'A Paradigm for Leadership Excellence', *Total Quality Management* 9(4/5), 75–80.

8 Dess, G. and Picken, J. (2000) 'Changing Roles: Leadership in the 21st Century', *Organisational Dynamics* 28(3), 18–35.

9 Trevelyan, R. (1998) 'The Boundary of Leadership: Getting it Right and Having it All', *Business Strategy Review* 9(1), 37–44.

10 Yukl, G. (1994) *Leadership in Organizations*. Englewood Cliffs, NJ: Prentice Hall.

11 Mintzberg, H. (1973) *The Nature of Managerial Work*. New York: Harper Row.

12 Statt, D. (1994) *Psychology and the World of Work*. London: Macmillan, p. 337.

13 Zaleznik, A. (1977) 'Managers and Leaders: Are they Different?', *Harvard Business Review* May–June, 67–78.

14 Gibb, C. (1947) 'The Principles and Traits of Leadership', *Journal of Abnormal and Social Psychology* 42, 267–84; Stogdill, R. (1948) 'Personal Factors Associated with Leadership: A Survey of the Literature', *Journal of Psychology* 25, 35–71.

15 Luthans, F. (1992) *Organizational Behaviour*. New York: McGraw-Hill.

16 House, R. and Aditya, R. (1997) 'The Social Scientific Study of Leadership: Quo Vadis?', *Journal of Management* 23(3), 409–73.

17 Stogdill, R. and Coons, A. (1957) *Leader Behaviour: Its Description and Measurement*. Columbus, OH: Ohio State University Press of Bureau for Business Research; Likert, R. (1961) *New Patterns of Management*. New York: McGraw-Hill.

18 Blake, R. and Mouton, J. (1962) 'The Managerial Grid', *Advanced Management Office Executive* 1(9).

19 House, R. (1971) 'A Path–Goal Theory of Leader Effectiveness', *Administrative Science Quarterly* 16, September, 321–38.

20 Robbins, S. (1991) *Organizational Behavior: Concepts, Controversies, and Applications*. Englewood Cliffs, NJ: Prentice Hall.

21 House and Aditya, *op. cit.*

22 Fiedler, F. and Garcia, J. (1987) *New Approaches to Effective Leadership: Cognitive Resources and Organizational Performance*. New York: John Wiley and Sons.

23 House, R. (1977) 'A 1976 Theory of Charismatic Leadership' in J. Hunt and L. Larson (eds), *Leadership: The Cutting Edge*. Carbondale, IL: Southern Illinois University Press.

24 Popper, M. and Zakkai, E. (1994) 'Transactional, Charismatic and Transformational Leadership: Conditions Conducive to their Predominance', *Leadership and Organisational Development Journal* 15(6), 3–7.

25 Burns, J. (1978) *Leadership*. New York: Harper Row.

26 Popper and Zakkai, *op. cit.*, p. 6.

27 Bass, B. (1990) 'From Transactional to Transformational Leadership: Learning to Share the Vision', *Organizational Dynamics*, Winter, 22.

28 Brown, A. (1994) 'Transformational Leadership in Tackling Technical Change', *Journal of General Management* 19(4), 1–10.

29 Statt, D. (1994) *Psychology and the World of Work*. London: Macmillan.

30 Robbins, S. (1991) *Organizational Behavior: Concepts, Controversies, and Applications*. Englewood Cliffs, NJ: Prentice Hall, p. 354.

31 Keating, M., Martin, G. and Donnelly-Cox, G. (1996) 'The GLOBE Project: A Case for Interdisciplinary and Intercultural Research', *Proceedings of the First Irish Academy of Management Conference*.

32 Heraty, N. and Morley, M. (2003) 'Management Development in Ireland: The New Organizational Wealth?', *Journal of Management Development* 22(1), 60– 82.

33 Garavan, T., Hogan, C. and Cahir-O'Donnell, A. (2009), *Developing Managers and Leaders: Perspectives, Debates and Practices in Ireland*. Dublin: Gill & Macmillan.

34 This case is adapted from Garavan, T. and Garavan, M. (1997) 'Leadmore Ice Cream', in Garavan *et al.* (eds), *Entrepreneurship and Business Start-Ups in Ireland*, Vol. 2: *Cases*. Dublin: Oak Tree Press.

Motivation

9.1 Introduction

Motivation is typically viewed as a set of processes that activate, direct and sustain human behaviour focused on goal accomplishment. The study of motivation at work has been based on analysing employee behaviour at work and thus motivation theory is essentially concerned with explaining why people behave as they do, or why people choose different forms of behaviour in order to achieve different ends. However, there is no simple answer to the crucial question: How do you motivate people? Among the long list of things considered to be important motivational drivers are the human needs for interesting and stimulating work, achievement, self-development, variety, social contact, appropriate rewards, traction, structure and routine. Conversely, among the major causes of demotivation identified in the research literature are repetitive work, low pay, long hours, poor communication, poor training and a failure to be offered responsibility.

Achieving and maintaining high levels of motivation is vital. It is an important concept and has much relevance to the practising manager. How to be better at motivating people and getting the best from them continues to be an important theme in the management, leadership and organisational literature. However, as Nelson suggests, although the term 'motivation' is widely used, many managers do not understand how to motivate their employees.[1] Nelson's research highlights several incongruities and inconsistencies between what is commonly practised and what actually works. This trail of dichotomous evidence leads him to emphasise the importance of recognition, suggesting that recognition for a job well done is the top motivator of employee performance. Nelson further suggests that managers should strive to ensure that employees feel appreciated because attempting to regenerate flagging morale is a much more demanding task than doing relatively straightforward things regularly to maintain it at an acceptable level.

In exploring the area of motivation, this chapter highlights definitional aspects of motivation and outlines the key theoretical perspectives that have been adopted in relation to this concept. The long pedigree of the concept in management thinking is established through the examination of both content and process theories of motivation. Hierarchy of needs theory, existence–relatedness–growth theory, achievement motivation theory, two factor theory, expectancy theory, equity theory and goal theory are all discussed. These can be considered established contributions on motivation and, though criticised in some quarters, they remain highly significant in the literature. As Ambrose and Kulik conclude in their review of empirical work on motivation published during the 1990s, while some new motivational theories have been introduced, the traditional ones appear firmly entrenched and continue to receive considerable empirical support.[2] The importance to motivation in the workplace of pay and the structuring and design of work are also considered as motivation theory locates its analysis of employee performance around whether work and its rewards satisfy individual employee needs.

9.2 The ongoing centrality of motivation in organisational life

Motivation at work has been the object of sustained attention since the emergence of the industrial society. Steers and Porter advance a number of factors that account for the prominence of motivation as a focal point of interest.[3] First, they suggest that managers and organisational researchers cannot avoid a concern for the behavioural requirements of the organisation. The necessity of attracting the right calibre of employee and engaging him/her in such a way as to ensure high performance remains a central concern of the productive process. Second, they argue that the pervasive nature of the concept itself has resulted in it remaining a central area of inquiry. As a complex phenomenon it has an impact on a multitude of factors and any worthwhile understanding of organisations requires a good deal of attention to be focused on this array of factors and how they interact with one another to create certain outcomes. Third, international competitive trends in business, coupled with increased business regulation, have forced organisations to seek out any mechanisms that might improve organisational effectiveness and efficiency. The ability to direct employees' efforts toward these twin goals of effectiveness and efficiency are seen as crucial. A fourth reason for the sustained interest in motivation concerns the issue of technological advancement. An organisation must continually ensure that its workforce is capable of and willing to use advanced technologies to achieve organisational goals. A final reason, according to Steers and Porter, centres on the issue of planning horizons. Taking a longer-term perspective of the human resource in an attempt to build up a reservoir of well-skilled, enthusiastic employees brings the concept of motivation to the fore.

9.3 Motivation defined

The word 'motivation' is derived from the Latin word *movere*, which means 'to move'. Modern interpretation of motivation is somewhat broader, expressing various understandings of how we view people and organisations. Thus, while Vroom conceptualises motivation as a process governing choices made by persons or lower organisms among alternative forms of voluntary activity,[4] DuBrin suggests that motivation centres on the expenditure of effort toward achieving an objective the organisation wants accomplished.[5] Arnold *et al.*, using a mechanical analogy, suggest that the motive force gets a machine started and keeps it going; they argue that motivation concerns the factors that push or pull us to behave in certain ways.[6] Bennet suggests that an employee's motivation to work consists of all the drives, forces and influences – conscious and unconscious – that cause the employee to want to achieve certain aims,[7] while Forrest considers that motivation can be simply defined as 'consistently putting effort, energy and commitment into desired results'.[8] Most of the early work on motivation was centred on getting more out of the employee, although many theorists were also concerned with finding an answer to the problem that was consistent with the essential dignity and independence of the individual. Motivation theory bases its analysis of employee performance on how work and its rewards satisfy individual employee needs.

Numerous theories have been developed over the years to aid management in identifying employee motives and needs, the most influential of which will be discussed here.

9.4 Content theories of motivation

Content theories of motivation focus on the question: What initiates or stimulates behaviour? Content theorists implicitly assume that needs are the most important determinant of individual levels of motivation.

9.4.1 Maslow's hierarchy of needs

Most managers will be familiar with the hierarchical classification of human needs first proposed by Maslow in his 'Theory of Human Motivation'.[9] Maslow, a clinical psychologist, suggested that human motivation is dependent on the desire to satisfy various levels of needs. Maslow's hierarchy of needs is perhaps the most publicised theory of motivation. Based on the idea of a series of needs that range from basis instinctive needs for sustenance and security to higher-order needs, such as self-esteem and the need for self-actualisation, it seeks to explain different types and levels of motivation that are important to individuals at particular times in their lives.

Maslow suggests that there are in all five levels of needs ranked in the order shown in Figure 9.1 – this is the order in which the individual will seek to satisfy them.

Hierarchy of needs theory states that a need that is unsatisfied activates seeking/searching behaviour. Thus, the individual who is hungry will search for food; s/he who is unloved will seek to be loved. Once this seeking behaviour is fulfilled or satisfied, it no longer acts as a primary motivator. Needs that are satisfied no longer motivate. This clearly illustrates the rationale for arranging these needs in a hierarchy. The sequential ascending order implies that it is the next unachieved level that acts as the prime motivator. Need propensity means that higher-order needs cannot become an active motivating force until the preceding lower-order need is satisfied. However, individuals will seek growth when it is feasible to do so and have an innate desire to ascend the hierarchy. Such higher-order needs will act as a motivator when lower-order needs have been satisfied. Self-actualisation is the climax of personal growth. Maslow describes it as the desire for self-fulfilment; the desire to become everything that one is capable of becoming.

FIGURE 9.1 MASLOW'S HIERARCHY OF NEEDS

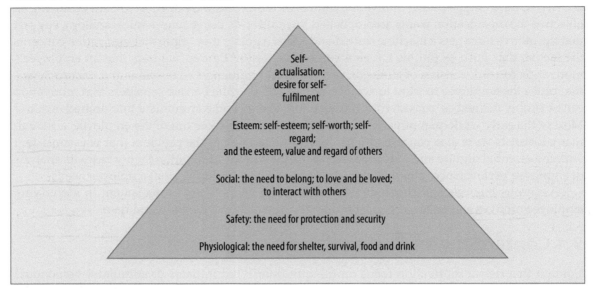

Maslow's hierarchy of needs theory recognises that needs motivate people in different ways. Furthermore, it identifies important categories of individual needs and encourages us to consider the variety of needs that stimulate or initiate behaviour at different times.

However, Maslow's theory has been the subject of much commentary and criticism over the years and it is generally agreed that the theory has a number of deficiencies. First, Maslow's work was based on general studies of human behaviour and motivation and as such was not directly associated with matters central to the workplace. Arising from this the theory is extremely difficult to apply because of the elusive nature of the needs identified, particularly in the context of the workplace. Researchers have also found little support for the concept of exclusive pre-potency. There is plenty of evidence to suggest that needs are not organised in the hierarchical structure suggested in Maslow's framework. People regularly sacrifice lower-order needs in order to satisfy those at a higher level on the hierarchy, for example people who risk their lives to save other people (ignoring their own needs for safety in favour of, say, attachment or esteem needs); people who go on hunger strike (depriving themselves of their basic survival needs in order to satisfy a higher-order need); or even someone who stays up all night to study for an exam (bypassing the need for sleep in order to fulfil their individual potential). All these provide clear evidence that the need order is not as straightforward or as linear as the hierarchy suggests.

A more realistic scenario is that individuals have several active needs at the same time, which implies that lower-order needs are not always satisfied before one concentrates on higher-order needs. An implicit assumption of Maslow's hierarchy is that need deprivation is what motivates people's behaviour. The theory is based on a 'fulfilment progression' dynamic that indicates that when a need has been sufficiently satisfied, it no longer acts as a motivator. There is a connotation inherent in this assertion that suggests that in any attempts to motivate people, needs should be deprived in order to sustain motivated behaviour. Both intuitively and empirically, this implication points to a flaw in the theory. Need deprivation may motivate for a certain length of time, after which its effects may yield quite the opposite reaction. If people are continually denied an opportunity to satisfy needs they are experiencing, this eventually leads to demotivated, apathetic and disheartened behaviour. Finally, it has also been suggested that the theory attempts to demonstrate an imputed rationality in human actions that may not necessarily exist. The conceptualisation of our needs in such a logical sequential fashion, while useful as a frame of reference to which we can all compare ourselves, has not resulted in convincing evidence in the research community.

The strongest implication emerging from the hierarchy is that unless people's basic deficiency needs are satisfied, they will not be motivated to pursue goals that relate to higher-order needs. Therefore, activities that demand the organisationally popular dimensions of teamwork, 'empowerment', creativity, innovation or knowledge enhancement will not be relevant or important to people who don't earn enough money to survive, or who are not sufficiently protected from danger in their workplace. According to Maslow's theory, people in low-paid work or who face hazardous or dangerous environments in the workplace will be less interested in developing social networks, achieving high status in their jobs or realising their potential in other ways.

9.4.2 Existence–relatedness–growth theory

Existence–relatedness–growth (ERG) theory, developed by Alderfer (1969), reduces Maslow's hierarchy of needs into a three-fold taxonomy (see Figure 9.2).[10]

FIGURE 9.2 EXISTENCE–RELATEDNESS–GROWTH THEORY

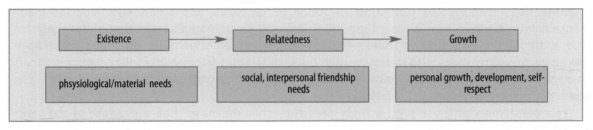

Building on Maslow's work, ERG theory avoids some of the issues that have led to criticism of Maslow's work. Here there is no emphasis on a hierarchical structuring of needs. Instead, needs are arranged along a continuum, giving them all equal status in terms of their ability to serve as a goad to action at a particular point in time. Alderfer suggests that motivated behaviour can be activated either via 'need fulfilment progression' or by another dynamic referred to as 'need frustration regression'. Fulfilment progression refers to a situation where once a need is satisfied in someone, s/he ceases to be motivated by that need category and moves on to another, higher-order, category of need, while frustration regression refers to the situation where, if a need is consistently frustrated, an individual 'regresses' to being motivated by lower-order needs that are already being fulfilled to a sufficient degree. Therefore, another important difference from Maslow's theory is the proposition that an already satisfied need may be reactivated as a motivator when a higher-order need cannot be satisfied. Furthermore, more than one needs category may be important and influential at any one time and thus the notion of pre-potency is rejected here.

9.4.3 McClelland's achievement theory

McClelland concentrated on developing and identifying motivational differences between individuals as a means of establishing which patterns of motivation lead to effective performance and success at work.[11] The needs identified by McClelland can be useful in helping managers to recognise the diversity of behaviours that people display at work. According to this theory, needs that people experience can be directly related to people's work preferences. McClelland's theory of achievement motivation argues that the main factor in willingness to perform is the intensity of an individual's actual need for achievement. He proposes that the organisation offers an opportunity to satisfy three sets of needs:

1. The need for achievement (nAch), which is a desire for challenging tasks and a good deal of responsibility.
2. The need for affiliation (nAff), which refers to the need for developed social and personal relations.
3. The need for power (nPow) which refers to the need for dominance.

These are need categories that are learned through life experiences, and a person will tend to be driven more or less by any one of the three needs identified. McClelland's research has shown that people who are mainly driven by a need for achievement will have distinctly different work preferences than those driven by a need for power or by a need for affiliation. Individuals with a high need for achievement tend to view organisational membership as a means of solving problems and providing a platform from which they can excel. Individuals with a high nAch tend to take personal responsibility for providing solutions to problems and desire feedback on their performance. Persons who have a high nAff desire to participate in tasks that allow them to frequently interact with others. Those who demonstrate a high nPow view the organisation as a means of providing them with status through the position they occupy. McClelland suggests that these needs are acquired throughout one's life and thus may be triggered and developed through the appropriate environmental conditions.

The motivation of those with a high need for achievement is thus a product of the task responsibilities, how attainable the task goals are and the nature and regularity of the feedback that they receive. It has been argued that people are often motivated by tasks that give them a feeling of competence, something which is especially true of people who have a high nAch. Such individuals tend to work at tasks that lead to difficult but achievable goals. Achieving difficult goals causes them to feel competent, while goals that are too easy to achieve or that are unattainable do not. Finally McClelland maintains that individuals can actually learn to increase their nAch. This may be achieved through exposing them to human resource development programmes that place an emphasis on achievement and that are didactic with respect to the methods that can be put in place for achieving.

9.4.4 The two-factor theory

Herzberg's 1960s research involved questioning people about those factors that led to either extreme satisfaction or extreme dissatisfaction with their jobs, the environment and the workplace.[12] His original study was based on intensive interviews with a sample of 200 engineers and accountants. The factors that resulted in satisfaction Herzberg labelled 'motivators', while those that resulted in dissatisfaction he labelled 'hygiene factors' (see Figure 9.3).

FIGURE 9.3 THE TWO FACTOR THEORY

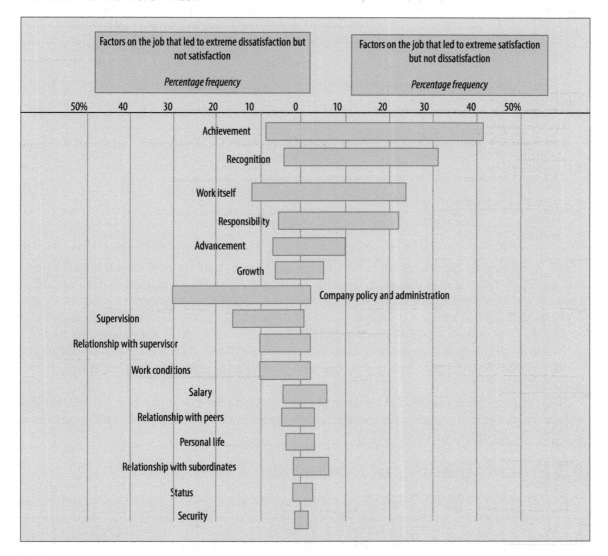

Herzberg was concerned with the impact of the job and the environment on an individual's motivation. His objective was to identify the factors at work that led to the greatest levels of satisfaction and dissatisfaction in an attempt to design work that provided job satisfaction and promoted high levels of performance.

The motivators Herzberg identified were:

- achievement
- recognition
- the work itself
- responsibility
- advancement
- growth.

The implication is that management can stimulate employee motivation by structuring work to incorporate these dimensions.

The hygiene factors he identified were:

- company policy
- supervision
- salary
- peer and subordinate relationships
- status
- security.

These, according to Herzberg, are factors that, where good, will not of themselves make people feel satisfied. Thus, if they are good, dissatisfaction is removed but satisfaction does not accrue. However, if these aspects of work are poor, extreme dissatisfaction is experienced. Herzberg's findings indicate that satisfaction and dissatisfaction are not at opposite ends of the same spectrum: rather, they are on two separate spectra. The opposite of satisfaction is not dissatisfaction but no satisfaction; similarly, the opposite of dissatisfaction is no dissatisfaction. Thus, pleasant or good working conditions do not actually produce motivation – as hygiene factors, they simply prevent dissatisfaction.

The major criticisms levelled at Herzberg's work centre on the extent to which his original study was methodologically sound; for example, the extent to which accountants and engineers are actually like all other workers.

9.5 Process theories of motivation

The work of the process theorists proposes that people are more complex, more pragmatic and more contemplative than the need theorists suggest, or at least imply, and that motivation at work is subject to more than an individual's needs. In researching what motivates people at work, process theories seek to establish not only what people want from their work situations, but how they believe they can actually achieve it and what influences the process.

9.5.1 Theory X, theory Y

Advanced by Douglas McGregor in his seminal work, *The Human Side of Enterprise*, this is an attempt to focus on managerial assumptions about employees and the implications of such assumptions for subsequent managerial behaviour, particularly with respect to how managers seek

FIGURE 9.4 THEORY X, THEORY Y

Theory X	Theory Y
Employees are inherently lazy, dislike work and will do as little as possible.	Employees like work and want to undertake challenging tasks.
Consequently, workers need to be corrected, controlled and directed to exert adequate effort.	If the work itself and the organisational environment are appropriate, employees will work willingly without need for coercion or control.
Most employees dislike responsibility and prefer direction.	People are motivated by needs for respect, esteem, recognition and self-fulfilment.
Employees want only security and material rewards.	People at work want responsibility. The majority of workers are imaginative and creative and can exercise ingenuity at work.

to motivate their subordinates.[13] McGregor outlined two sets of assumptions concerning human nature that a manager might adopt and labelled them theory X and theory Y. Autocratic managers, McGregor suggested, are likely to subscribe to the assumptions of theory X, while those who are less bureaucratic are likely to work with the assumptions of theory Y (see Figure 9.4).

This dichotomous framework is particularly useful for allowing us to classify different managerial styles. McGregor himself maintained that in the majority of circumstances theory Y assumptions are the most accurate reflection of employee attitudes toward work because work is natural to the human species and those who perform work will normally devote their attention to the completion of a task. Consequently, to the extent that these theory Y assumptions are valid, they should be reflected in organisational structures, systems and practices.

9.5.2 Expectancy theory

Associated with Vroom, this theory focuses on outcomes rather than needs.[14] The theory identifies important expectations that individuals bring to the workplace and focuses on the relationship between the effort put into the completion of particular activities by the individual and the expectations concerning the actual reward that will accrue as a result of expending the effort. Expectancy theory attempts to combine individual and organisational factors that impact on this causal effort–reward relationship. Broadly, this theory argues that individuals base decisions about their behaviour on the expectation that one behaviour or another is more likely to lead to needed or desired outcomes. The relationship between one's behaviour and particular desired outcomes is affected by individual factors such as personality, perception, motives, skills, abilities, etc., and by organisational factors such as culture, structure, managerial style (the context in which one is operating). Thus, expectancy theory avoids attempts to isolate a definitive set of employee motives, but seeks to explain individual differences in terms of goals, motives and behaviours. It postulates that employee motivation is dependent on how the employer perceives the relationship between effort, performance and outcomes.

FIGURE 9.5 EXPECTANCY THEORY

Motivation = Expectancy × Instrumentality × Valence

- **Expectancy** is the probability assigned by the individual that work effort will be followed by a given level of achieved task performance (value = 0 to 1).
- **Instrumentality** is the probability assigned by the individual that a given level of achieved task performance will lead to various work outcomes (rewards) (value = 0 to 1).
- **Valence** is the value attached by the individual to various work outcomes (rewards) (value = -1 to +1).

Therefore the motivational appeal of a given work path is drastically reduced whenever any one or more of the factors approaches the value of zero. The model suggests that an individual's level of effort (motivation) is not simply a function of rewards. The individual must feel that s/he has the ability to perform the task (expectancy), that this performance will impact on the reward and that this reward is actually valued. Only if all conditions are satisfied will employees be motivated to exert greater effort. It is thus critical that individuals can see a connection between effort and reward and that the reward offered by the organisation will satisfy employees' needs. However, there is no simple formula because individuals possess different preferences for outcomes and have different understandings of the relationship between effort and reward. They may well be motivated in very different ways. Among the criticisms levelled at the theory are the difficulty associated with testing the theory empirically, and the fact that it assumes a type of rationality, which may not actually exist, with respect to how the individual thinks and behaves.

Porter and Lawler extended the original work of Vroom and advanced a revised 'expectancy framework' (see Figure 9.6).[15] They examined the role that abilities and role perceptions play in producing various outcomes and, drawing upon earlier motivation theory, highlighted the differences between intrinsic and extrinsic rewards, the former being rewards that are generated by the individuals themselves (for example, a sense of achievement, personal satisfaction, a feeling of pride in work, and so on) and the latter being rewards that are provided from external sources (pay, promotion, praise, recognition, etc.).

FIGURE 9.6 PORTER AND LAWLER'S EXPECTANCY FRAMEWORK

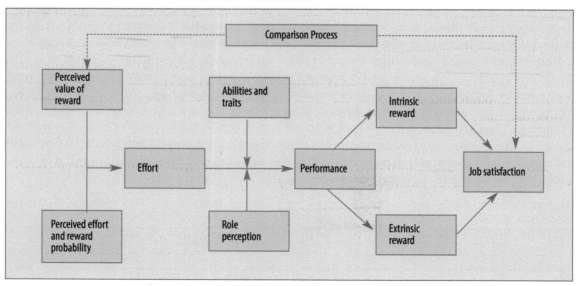

As in the original expectancy theory, Porter and Lawler also highlight that before people make a decision to exert effort, they need to value the rewards that are available and to feel that, if they do exert effort, the rewards will be available to them.

In relation to the implications of expectancy theory for management, Vroom suggests that managers must seek to understand individual employee goals and motives, ensure these are clearly and positively linked to desired performance levels which in turn are achievable from the employee's perspective. Nadler and Lawler go a little further and highlight specific areas for management action:[16]

- Establish what the valued outcomes are.
- Specify desired and achievable performance levels.
- Ensure that there is a clear link between effort, performance and desired outcomes.
- Ensure adequate variation of outcomes available.
- Ensure equity and fairness for the individual employee.

Expectancy theory does not attempt to identify a universal set of motivational factors. Rather, it highlights the importance of a range of potential motivational factors. These may be either intrinsic or extrinsic. Intrinsic outcomes are those originating from doing the job (sense of achievement, satisfaction), while extrinsic outcomes are those provided by other people, particularly management, and include pay, promotion, etc.

9.5.3 Equity theory of motivation

The concept of a fair day's work for a fair day's pay is often used to express how the parties in the labour process perceive the employment relationship. Equity theory, sometimes referred to as justice theory, resembles expectancy theory in that it sets down the individual's cognitive process that determines whether or not s/he will engage in the effort–reward bargain struck with his/her employer.

Developed by Adams, equity theory of motivation is based on the comparison between two variables: inputs and outcomes. 'Inputs' refer to that which the individual brings to his/her employment and include things such as effort, experience and skills.[17] 'Outcomes' describes the range of factors the employee receives in return for his/her inputs – pay, recognition, fringe benefits, status symbols. Adams suggests that individual expectations about equity correlations between inputs and outcomes are learned during the process of socialisation in the home or at work and through comparison with the inputs and outcomes of others. Adams suggests that individuals can:

- change inputs – reduce effort if underpaid
- try to change their outcomes – ask for a pay rise or promotion
- psychologically distort their own ratios by rationalising differences in inputs and outcomes
- change the reference group to which they compare themselves in order to restore equity.

Huseman et al. enumerate the core propositions of equity theory as follows:[18]
1. Individuals evaluate their relationships with others by assessing the ratio of their outcomes from, and inputs to, the relationship against the outcome–input ratio of another comparable individual.

2. If the outcome–input ratios of the individual and the comparable other are deemed to be unequal, inequity exists.
3. The greater the inequity the individual perceives (in the form of either over-reward or under-reward), the more distress the individual experiences. In this respect, there are two types of perceived inequity that people can experience:
   a) negative inequity – when people feel that the unfair treatment affects them in negative ways such as less pay, or fewer positive work outcomes than other people in the same or similar work situations
   b) positive inequity – when individuals feel that the unfair treatment affects them in positive ways, such as when they receive more positive work outcomes than their colleagues, including pay.
4. The greater the distress an individual experiences, the harder s/he will work to restore equity. Among the possible equity restoration techniques the individual might use are: distorting inputs or outcomes; disregarding the comparable other and referring to a new one; or terminating the relationship.

Thus, employees will formulate a ratio between their inputs and outcomes and compare it with the perceived ratios of inputs and outcomes of other people in the same or a similar situation. If these two ratios are not equal the individual will take action in an attempt to restore a sense of equity.

An amount of research interest has been generated in testing the relationships advanced by Adams, particularly those relationships that focus on employee reactions to pay. Overall, the research highlights support for Adams's theory about employee reactions to wage inequities.

9.6 Motivation and pay

The utility of using pay to motivate and promote performance has been a subject of debate for many years, with some support for both sides of the argument. Most managers instinctively believe that money is a motivator, even though empirical evidence to support this is far from conclusive. Perhaps the key point that can be drawn from the available evidence is that pay is a complex, multifaceted issue that serves as both a tangible and intangible motivator, offering intrinsic and extrinsic rewards. Thus, the applicability of pay-related incentive schemes across a wide range of organisational contexts is difficult to generalise on and is largely dependent on organisational circumstances, employee profile and prevailing conditions.

Kohn suggests that punishment and rewards are two sides of the same coin.[19] Rewards have a punitive effect because, like outright punishment, they are manipulative. 'Do this and you'll get that' is not very different from 'Do that and here's what will happen to you.' In the case of incentives, the reward itself may be highly desired but, by making that bonus contingent on certain behaviours, managers manipulate their subordinates, and the experience of being controlled is likely to assume a punitive quality over time. Similarly, others have argued that just because too little money can irritate and demotivate does not mean that more money will bring about increased satisfaction, much less increased motivation. Doubtless, pay is important to employees. It provides the means to live, eat, and achieve other personal or family goals. It is a central reason why people hold down and move between jobs. However, a key question is not the importance of financial incentives as such, but whether they motivate employees to perform well in their jobs.

Once an individual has been attracted to the organisation and the job, the role of money as a motivator is debatable. Clearly money, or the lack of it, can be a source of dissatisfaction, grievance, etc. However, if an employee is reasonably happy with his/her income, does that income induce him/her to perform at higher levels? Many of the theoretical prescriptions suggest that money is important in satisfying essential lower-order needs, such as basic physiological and security needs.

This line of argument suggests that once such lower-order needs are satisfied, it is factors intrinsic to the job that are the prime motivators, especially at the self-actualisation level. Others suggest that money is important at all levels and may be a prime motivator where it is a valued outcome and where there is an obvious or tangible link between effort, performance and the achievement of greater financial reward.

It has been argued that during the 1960s and 1970s many organisation behaviour theorists emphasised the importance of job enrichment and organisation development, with less of an emphasis on the importance of money as a motivator. The more contemporary emphasis on performance, productivity and cost reduction has tended to focus on primary job values such as employment security, benefits and, more particularly, the pay package. Most managers will agree that remuneration – especially the money element – has an important role in motivating employees. However, it is only one factor in the entire motivation process. Clearly many people are not primarily motivated by money but by other factors such as promotion prospects, recognition or the job challenge itself. All employees do not have a generalised set of motives. Rather, an organisation's workforce will be made up of people with varying sets of priorities relating to different situations and work contexts resulting in differing employee motives and goals. These motives and goals will vary from one employee to another and also in the experience of individual employees over time. For example, a young single person may prioritise basic income and free time and the job itself may not hold any great interest. Later, that person, now married and with a mortgage, may be more concerned with job security and fringe benefits such as health insurance and a pension plan.

Arguably, there are four key issues that should be considered when exploring the extent to which employees are motivated by pay:

1. It is clear that employees must value financial rewards. If people are paid at a very high level, or simply not concerned with financial rewards, higher pay would have little incentive value for employees. Other factors related to the job and work environment must have the potential to motivate employees.
2. If money is a valued reward, employees must believe that good performance will allow them to realise that reward. This suggests that pay should be linked to performance and differences in pay should be large enough to adequately reward high levels of performance. This approach obviously rejects remuneration systems that reward good, average and poor performance equally, such as regular pay increments based on seniority.
3. Equity is an important consideration. Employees must be fairly treated in their work situation, especially in terms of the perceived equity of pay levels and comparisons with fellow employees. They will be keen that rewards (pay, incentives and benefits) adequately reflect their input (effort, skills, etc.). Should employees feel they are not being treated fairly on these criteria, performance levels may fall.

4.   Employees must believe that the performance levels necessary to achieve desired financial rewards are achievable. The required performance criteria and levels should be clearly outlined and communicated to employees. Organisations must also ensure that employees have the necessary ability, training, resources and opportunity to achieve such performance levels. Otherwise, employees will either not be able, or else will not try, to expend the necessary effort.

Thus, from the motivational perspective, effective payment systems should:
* Be objectively established.
* Clarify performance levels required and rewards available.
* Reward the achievement of required performance levels adequately and quickly.
* Ensure that employees have the ability, training resources and opportunity to achieve the required performance level(s).
* Recognise that financial incentives are only one source of motivation and that jobs should be designed in such a way as to ensure that employees can satisfy other needs through their work (for example achievement, challenge).
* Take regular steps to identify employee needs and ensure that these can be satisfied within the organisational environment.

Even where these factors are present, success is not guaranteed. For example, an incentive scheme based on output figures may be established to encourage employees to achieve high performance levels. However, unofficial norms established by the work group may dictate 'acceptable' performance levels and ensure these are not exceeded through various social pressures. Equally, such an approach may signal to employees that management are clearly in charge and may either lessen employee feelings of control and competence or encourage conflict over the standards set. It should always be appreciated that while pay is an important source of employee motivation, it is not the only one.

9.7 Motivation and the design of work

Fox *et al.* suggest that the provision of meaningful work is a way of tapping into people's self-motivation and desire for achievement at work.[20] The nature of work organisation and design will significantly influence the degree to which work is intrinsically satisfying for employees and promotes high levels of motivation. Organisations should therefore carefully consider their approach to work design in order to promote and maintain acceptable levels of motivation in the workplace.

Broadly speaking, the design of work is the way the various tasks in the organisation are structured and carried out. It reflects the interaction of management style, the technical system, HR and the organisation's products or services. Davis defines the process of job design as that which is concerned with the 'specification of the contents, methods, and relationships of jobs in order to satisfy technological and organisational requirements, as well as the social and personal requirements of the job holder'.[21] The design of individual jobs is seen to impact particularly strongly on employees since it influences job content, employee discretion, the degree of task fragmentation and the role of supervision. Decisions on the organisation of work are primarily a management responsibility and the particular approach chosen will be a good indicator of corporate beliefs about how employees should be managed, how jobs are structured, and the role of supervision. It will also reflect the organisation's approach to many aspects of human resource management (HRM) as manifested in attitudes to recruitment, employee development, motivation, rewards and management/employee relations.

Over the years the field of job design has been characterised by shifts from one theoretical perspective to another. The primary shifts have been from task specialisation to job enlargement, job enrichment, socio-technical systems theory and the quality of working life (QWL) movement, and high-performance work design.

9.7.1 Task specialisation

Variously referred to as task specialisation, scientific management or Taylorism, the traditional approach to the organisation of work was dominated by a desire to maximise the productive efficiency of the organisation's technical resources. Choices on the organisation of work and the design of jobs were seen as determined by the technical system. Management's role was to ensure that other organisational resources, including employees, were organised in such a way as to facilitate the optimal utilisation of the technical system. This efficiency approach is based on scientific management principles and has been a characteristic of employer approaches to job design since the beginning of the twentieth century. Jobs were broken down into simple, repetitive, measurable tasks, the skills for which could be easily acquired through systematic job training. The rationale for this approach to work and job design was based on technological determinism: the organisation's technical resources were seen as a given constraint and the other inputs, including employees, had to accommodate the technical system. It also reflected managerial assumptions about people at work. Close supervision, work measurement and other types of control indicate a belief about employees akin to McGregor's theory X discussed above, which suggests that employees need to be coerced to work productively and that this is best achieved by routine, standardised tasks.

This traditional model of job design has undoubtedly had benefits for many organisations. It helped improve efficiency and promoted a systematic approach to selection, training, work measurement and payment systems. However, it has also led to numerous problems, such as high levels of labour turnover and absenteeism, and, most significantly in the context of our debate here, low motivation. Thus short-term efficiency benefits were often superseded by long-term reductions in organisational effectiveness. Many behavioural scientists argued that organisational effectiveness could be increased by recognising employee ability and giving employees challenging, meaningful jobs in a co-operative working environment.

More recently, the increased emphases on improving quality, service and overall competitiveness have led to the emergence of other schools of thought aimed at restructuring work systems to increase employee motivation and performance. Much of the focus of the work of the successors to task specialisation has been on the restructuring of jobs to incorporate greater scope for intrinsic motivation. Subsequent schools questioned traditional management assumptions about why employees work. The traditional approach saw employees as essentially instrumental in their attitudes to work. Jobs were seen as a means to an end and it was these extrinsic rewards that motivated employees. Consequently, employers created work systems that closely circumscribed jobs, supervised work and rewarded quantifiable performance.

9.7.2 Job enlargement and job enrichment

The job enlargement and job enrichment schools differ in their emphasis: the former makes a job 'bigger'; the latter adds some element to the job that is dedicated to increasing the employee's psychological growth. Job enlargement grew from the arguments of humanitarians in the 1950s that production methods prevalent at the time created poor working conditions, which led to high levels of job dissatisfaction. The proposed solution was job enlargement, which, when introduced, would lead to more variety and less routine work. This assumption was drawn upon by Walker and Guest in their study of automobile assembly lines.[22] They studied 180 workers and identified six main characteristics of mass production technology:

1. repetitiveness
2. low skill requirement
3. mechanically paced work
4. little alteration of tools or methods
5. low requirement for mental attention
6. minute subdivision of product.

It was concluded that the solution to eliminating the ills of mass production technology lay in job enlargement.

Job enrichment, which was largely attributed to Herzberg, was developed for the advancement of the two-factor theory of work motivation discussed earlier in this chapter (see section 9.4.4). The job enrichment approach suggested that employees gain most satisfaction from the work itself and it is intrinsic outcomes arising from work that motivates employees to perform well in their jobs. Herzberg establishes the concept of vertical loading as a means of moving away from the addition of 'one meaningless task to the existing (meaningless) one'. Vertical loading, dedicated to the addition of more challenging dimensions to the job, remains the mainstay of job enrichment (see Figure 9.7).

FIGURE 9.7 PRINCIPLES OF VERTICAL JOB LOADING

Principle		Motivators involved
A.	Removing some controls while retaining accountability	Responsibility and personal achievement
B.	Increasing the accountability of people for their own work	Responsibility and recognition
C.	Giving a person a complete natural unit of work (module, division, area, etc.)	Responsibility, achievement and recognition
D.	Granting additional authority to an employee in their activity; job freedom	Responsibility, achievement and recognition
E.	Making periodic reports directly available to the worker rather than to the supervisor	Internal recognition
F.	Introducing new and more difficult tasks not previously handled	Growth and learning
G.	Assigning people specific or specialised tasks, enabling them to become experts	Responsibility, growth and advancement

Source: Herzberg, F. (1966) *Work and the Nature of Man*. New York: Staples.

In a similar treatise on intrinsic outcomes and job satisfaction, Hackman and Oldham enumerate three basic conditions necessary for promoting job satisfaction and employee motivation:[23]

1. Work should be meaningful for the 'doer'.
2. 'Doers' should have responsibility for the results.
3. 'Doers' should get feedback on the results.

This approach suggests that it is the design of the work, not the characteristics of the employee, that have the greatest impact on employee motivation. Hackman and Oldham identified five 'core job characteristics' that need to be incorporated into job design to increase meaningfulness, responsibility and feedback:

1. **Skill variety** – the extent to which jobs draw on a range of different skills and abilities.
2. **Task identity** – the extent to which a job requires completion of a whole, identifiable piece of work.
3. **Task significance** – the extent to which a job substantially impacts on the work or lives of others, either within or outside the organisation.
4. **Autonomy** – freedom, independence and discretion afforded to the job holder.
5. **Feedback** – the degree to which the job holder receives information on his/her level of performance, effectiveness, etc.

Having identified the factors necessary to promote satisfaction and intrinsic motivation, the next stage is to incorporate these characteristics into jobs through various job redesign strategies. Hackman and Oldham suggest five implementation strategies to increase task variety, significance and identity, and to create opportunities for greater autonomy and feedback:

1. **Form natural work groups.** Arrange tasks together to form an identifiable, meaningful cycle of work for employees, for example responsibility for a single product rather than small components.
2. **Combine tasks.** Group tasks together to form complete jobs.
3. **Establish client relationships.** Establish personal contact between employees and the end user/client.
4. **Vertically load jobs.** Many traditional approaches to job design separate planning and controlling (management functions) from executing (employee's function). Vertically loading a job means integrating the planning, controlling and executing functions and giving responsibility to employees (for example, for materials, quality, deadlines and budgetary control).
5. **Open feedback channels.** Ensure maximum communication of job results (for example service standards, faults, wastage, market performance, costs).

These changes would have positive long-term benefits for both the organisation and the individual employee. Not all employees are expected to respond favourably to such redesign initiatives. Only those with a strong desire for achievement, responsibility and autonomy will be motivated by increased intrinsic satisfaction and hence motivated to perform better. For others, such change may create a source of anxiety and lead to resentment and opposition to changes in the work system.

FIGURE 9.8 JOB CHARACTERISTICS MODEL

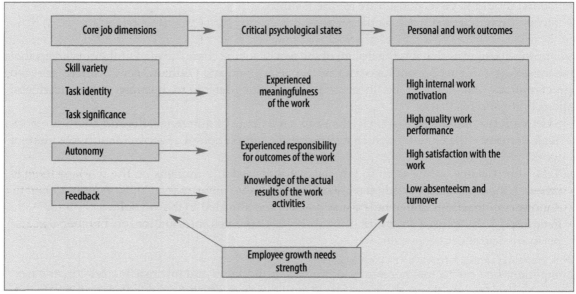

Source: Hackman, J. and Oldham, G. (1980) *Work Redesign*. New York: Addison Wesley.

9.7.3 *The quality of working life movement*

Concern with the nature of work organisation and its potentially adverse effects on employee motivation has encouraged many organisations to take steps to ensure that job design incorporates the intrinsic needs of employees. This has been manifested in the emergence of the quality of working life (QWL) movement, which aims to eliminate many of the problems associated with traditional work systems, making work more meaningful for employees and ensuring more positive benefits for employers.

Apart from the job enrichment initiatives mentioned above, the QWL movement has also been characterised by steps to increase employee influence and involvement in work organisation and job design. Again, this challenges some traditional management assumptions about employees. It involves recognising that employees can and want to make a positive input into organisational decision making. It assumes that such involvement is valued by employees and results in greater commitment, responsibility and performance.

Increased employee influence in work system design also addresses the issue of employee supervision as an aspect of the management role. If employees are to be involved in making decisions about the organisation of work and responsible for the subsequent execution of such decisions, much of the 'control' aspect is removed from the supervisory role. It necessitates a change in attitude to workforce management. Supervisors become less concerned with monitoring and controlling employee performance and more involved in advising and facilitating employees in carrying out their jobs.

This approach requires high levels of commitment and trust from both management and employees. Management must feel confident that employees have the required competence and will use their greater levels of influence positively and to the benefit of the organisation. Employees must be happy that their increased commitment and sense of responsibility will not be abused or exploited by employers.

There are various mechanisms available to encourage increased levels of employee participation in the design and operation of work systems. Possibly the best-known approach is quality circles. These are small groups of employees and managers who meet together regularly to consider means of improving quality, productivity or other aspects of work organisation. They are seen as having played an important role in the success of Japanese organisations and have been successfully applied in Western economies, including Ireland.

There are numerous other participative and consultative mechanisms that can work effectively in the appropriate organisational environment. Creating such an environment has become an important concern for organisations. Past experience in applying various techniques to improve employee motivation and involvement have demonstrated that these operate best where there is a change in the overall corporate approach. The issue for senior management is how to create a corporate culture whose values, beliefs and practices establish an organisational environment within which employees are highly committed to and work towards the achievement of business goals.

9.7.4 High-performance work design

The high-performance concept, which advocates an integrated approach to structuring work and managing the human factor, has its roots in the individualistic and group approaches to job restructuring of previous decades. There is a shift in language and emphasis away from job enlargement, job enrichment and quality circles towards a more all-inclusive approach that links individual contributions, group performance and competitive advantage, which, according to Buchanan and McCalman, brings a new acceptability to these traditional strategies.[24] Thus, they argue, the 'high performance' label reflects a strategic shift in our approach to the management of human assets, and may serve to encourage a wider understanding of the applications of traditional job restructuring techniques, variations of which have enjoyed a renaissance in recent times in light of the strategic imperative of the 1990s.

The concept of high-performance work systems is very much associated with the new high-tech companies of the 1980s, and especially those that located at greenfield sites in an attempt to establish a fundamentally different type of organisation and organisation culture. The essence of high-performance systems appears to lie in the adoption of a culture of continuous improvement and innovation at all levels in the organisation; and the implementation of a range of work organisation and HR systems to sustain and develop this culture, particularly teamworking, quality consciousness, employee autonomy, and flexibility. They are also felt to reflect an increased management emphasis on developing broadly defined, challenging jobs within more organic, flexible organisation structures. The high-performance work organisation has a distinctive structure which is designed to provide employees with skills, incentives, information and decision-making responsibilities that will lead to improved organisational performance and facilitate innovation. High-performance work systems are thus seen as being much more than a change in the nature of jobs. Rather, they appear to embrace fundamentally different assumptions about organisational structure and orientation, so that all aspects of organisational management are altered to embrace a 'new' culture designed to improve performance and responsiveness through developing a more committed, flexible and skilled workforce.

It is clear from our preceding discussion that a critical focus of high-performance work systems entails the development of new (or different) approaches to the management of employees as well as the structure of jobs and systems. Almost all contributors highlight the need to empower employees in an attempt to make the organisation more effective. While commentators may differ on detail, there is overwhelming support for the use of group- or team-based work systems as a means of developing a highly skilled, flexible and motivated workforce within a leaner, flatter, more responsive organisation structure.

In Ireland, the first prominent examples of organisations that sought to develop high-performance work systems along the lines described above were firms that had experimented with such systems elsewhere. These were mostly US 'high-tech' companies such as Digital and Apple. More recently we have seen greater diversity in the range of companies undertaking such initiatives. One of the mostly widely quoted Irish examples is Bord na Móna, which undertook a number of radical initiatives during the 1990s. First, a new multidisciplinary and team-based management structure was established. The initial challenge was to reduce costs, and this was addressed by a major redundancy programme that saw 2,500 workers (out of approximately 5,000) leave the company. After this, management initiated a more fundamental overhaul, including the introduction of autonomous work groups (AWGs), which meant that instead of working in isolation, the workers became team members. Leaders were selected for these AWGs, which then assumed responsibility and authority for the completion of tasks. In addition to the establishment of AWGs, Bord na Móna also reduced the number of levels in the management hierarchy, fundamentally restructuring the organisation. Today, under its vision 'A New Contract with Nature', Bord na Móna is successfully diversifying from peat extraction to wind power, waste management and resource recovery.

9.8 Summary of key propositions

- This chapter explored the concepts of motivation at work and argued that motivation as a concept continues to be central to organisational life. Taking a longer-term perspective of the human resource in an attempt to build up a reservoir of well-skilled, enthusiastic employees has brought the concept of motivation to the fore.
- Motivation is typically viewed as a set of processes that activate, direct and sustain human behaviour dedicated to goal accomplishment. It is essentially concerned with explaining why people behave as they do, or why people choose different forms of behaviour in order to achieve different ends.
- The content theories of motivation focus on the needs that people experience and how these needs might drive or initiate behaviour. Maslow's hierarchy of needs, Alderfer's ERG theory, McClelland's achievement motivation theory and Herzberg's two-factor theory all attempt to explain, from a variety of perspectives, the role that needs play in motivating people's behaviour.
- Process theories are based on the assumption that individuals and groups think consciously about the effort they expend at work and its relative utility in reaching valued goals. Expectancy theories and equity theories focus on how people consider or weigh up various factors that contribute to their decisions to engage in effort at work.

- The utility of using pay to motivate and promote performance has been a subject of debate for many years, with some support for both sides of the argument. Importantly, while most managers instinctively believe that money is a motivator, empirical evidence to support this is far from conclusive.
- The nature of work organisation and design will significantly influence the degree to which work is intrinsically satisfying for employees and promotes high levels of motivation. Organisations should therefore carefully consider their approach to work organisation in order to promote and maintain acceptable levels of motivation in the workplace. Among the key approaches examined here were scientific management, job enlargement, job enrichment, the QWL movement and high-performance work design approaches, all of which involve different ideas on how to design work in order to keep the individual motivated in the workplace.

Discussion Questions

1 What lessons does motivation theory have for practising managers?
2 Debate to what extent Maslow's hierarchy of needs has practical relevance to effective people management.
3 A manager's perceptions of the workforce will profoundly influence his/her attitudes in dealing with people. Discuss.
4 Compare three different need theories of motivation. In what ways are they similar and how do they differ in their approaches to motivation at work?
5 Is pay a motivator?
6 Distinguish between the different approaches to job design and highlight the aspects of each approach, if any, that were seen to be motivating.

Concluding Case: Motivation case study

Kathy Murphy checks the time, logs off her computer and heads out of the office. She is late already and is supposed to be meeting her friend Paula Byrne in the nearby sandwich bar for lunch and a chat. Along the corridor she bumps into Mark O'Driscoll, the training manager. 'Surely it's not lunchtime already, Kathy?' he queries. 'I have some memos here I want sent out before three this afternoon – I was hoping you could get them started before lunch. Also, can you drop these off to Áine on B Shift? She's scheduling safety training for her group this afternoon.' Kathy takes the notes, assures Mark that she will attend to them as soon as she gets back and detours to Áine's desk with the safety schedules.

By the time she sits down for lunch with Paula, half her lunch break is already over and she is feeling seriously put out. 'You're cutting it fine,' says Paula. 'Don't get me started,' replies Kathy, 'you wouldn't believe the morning I've had. Honestly, some people are just too much . . .' and she launches into a tirade about the running around she has had to do all day culminating in Mark's last-minute request (although she wouldn't exactly call it a request). 'I was supposed to be sitting in with Ciara for a couple of operator interviews this afternoon but I'm not going to be able to do that now as I have to type Mark's bloody memos. Oh hell, Paula, I'm so sick of it all sometimes.'

'So why don't you leave then, Kathy?' Paula retorts. 'You've been complaining for months that you're fed up with the way work's going for you and that you want to get more experience in personnel work. Why don't you do up your CV and see what's out there?'

'I know you're right, Paula, and some days I feel I just can't take it any more. But I've almost finished my Diploma course and the company is sponsoring me to do it – I don't want to leave until I have that finished. Plus, most of the time I like working for Diamond Computing and there are lots of opportunities, if only people would give me a chance.'

'What exactly do you mean?' asks Paula.

'Well, take this afternoon, for example,' replies Kathy. 'Ciara Brennan is our recruitment manager and she knows I am doing the CIPD Diploma in Personnel Management in the evenings at the university. We were talking about it last week and I was telling her that while I love the course it's often difficult to apply the theory as my job involves the administration side of HR work and not the people side of things. Anyway, when I told her that we did a practical module on interviewing skills she asked whether I'd like to sit in with her on some interviews. I jumped at the chance but had to run it by the HR manager first – he was fine with it, and thought it was a great idea provided I still did my regular work.'

'But I don't understand,' says Paula. 'What's the problem, so?'

'Mark O'Driscoll – he's the problem,' replies Kathy. 'He's constantly calling in to me at the last minute with work that has to be done asap. Plus, he sometimes has me doing stuff that technically is not part of my job at all. Take last week. He was supposed to be designing an induction training programme for new graduates but, Paula, he hadn't a clue. He'd organised a focus group with some of our graduates who have been here a while, but he just didn't know what he wanted to ask them. I was involved just to take notes but I ended up feeding some ideas to him in order to get the discussion going. And then you should have seen what he put together afterwards. It was woeful. I was putting the document together and I restructured and virtually rewrote the whole thing for him. Honestly, I know more about his job than he does.'

'I hope he was suitably grateful for you getting him out of a bind,' says Paula.

'Him? Grateful? You must be joking!' retorts Kathy. 'He never mentioned it again save "Thanks for typing this for me, Kathy" and "By all accounts the HR manager really likes the final version and it's going to be introduced within the next couple of months."'

'What? He never let on that you were involved in designing it?' asks Paula disbelievingly. 'How can you bear to work for him?'

'Well, that's the thing, you see,' replies Kathy. 'I don't work for Mark per se. Both Marjorie and myself provide general administrative assistance to the HR function, although I seem to be doing a lot more of Mark's work lately. I wouldn't mind so much except I don't really want to specialise in training. I much prefer the generalist HR side of things – you know, recruitment, rewards and the like.'

'So what are you going to do then?' asks Paula. 'Wait until you finish your course, get your HR qualification and then leave?'

Kathy puts on her coat and heads back to work. 'I don't know', she replies. 'What else can I do?'

Case Questions

1   How would you describe Kathy's work needs and values?
2   At what motivation level is she working now?
3   What would you advise Kathy to do?
4   What practical action can the company take to improve Kathy's intrinsic motivation?

Notes and References

1   Nelson, B. (1999) 'The Ironies of Motivation', *Strategy and Leadership* 27(1), 26–33.
2   Ambrose. M. and Kulik, C. (1999) 'Old Friends, New Faces: Motivation Research in the 1990s', *Journal of Management* 25(3), 231–92.
3   Steers, R. and Porter, L. (1987) *Motivation and Work Behaviour*. New York: McGraw-Hill.
4   Vroom, V. (1964) *Work and Motivation*. New York: John Wiley and Sons.
5   DuBrin, A. (1978) *Human Relations: A Job Oriented Approach*. Reston, VA: Reston.
6   Arnold, J., Cooper, C. and Robertson, G. (1995) *Work Psychology*. London: Pitman.
7   Bennet, R. (1991) *Management*. London: Pitman.
8   Forrest, C. (2000) 'Motivation for the Millennium', *Training Journal* January, 10–15.
9   Maslow, A. (1943) 'A Theory of Human Motivation', *Psychological Review* 50(4).
10   Alderfer, C. (1969) 'An Empirical Test of a New Theory of Human Needs', *Organizational Performance and Human Behaviour* 4.
11   McClelland, D. (1960) *The Achieving Society*. New York: Von Nostrand-Reinhold.
12   Herzberg, F. (1966) *Work and the Nature of Man*. New York: Staples.
13   McGregor, D. (1960) *The Human Side of Enterprise*. New York: McGraw-Hill.
14   Vroom, *op. cit.*
15   Porter, L.W. and Lawler, E.E. (1968). *Managerial Attitudes and Performance*. Homewood, IL: Dorsey Press.
16   Nadler, D.A. and Lawler III, E.E (1977). 'Motivation: A Diagnostic Approach' in B.M. Staw (ed.), *Psychological Dimensions of Organizational Behavior* (3rd edn). Upper Saddle River, NJ: Pearson Education, pp. 25–36.
17   Adams, J. (1965) 'Inequity in Social Exchange' in Berkowitz, L. (ed.), *Advances in Experimental Psychology*. New York: Academic Press.
18   Huseman, R., Hatfield, J. and Miles, E. (1987) 'A New Perspective on Equity Theory: The Equity Sensitivity Construct', *Academy of Management Review* 12.
19   Kohn, A. (1993) 'Why Incentive Plans Cannot Work', *Harvard Business Review* September–October.
20   Fox, D., Byrne, V. and Rouault, F. (1999) 'Performance Improvement: What to Keep in Mind', *Training and Development* 52(8), 38–41.
21   Davis, L. (1966) 'The Design of Jobs', *Industrial Relations* 6(1).
22   Walker, C. and Guest, R. (1952) *The Man on the Assembly Line*. Boston: Harvard Business School Press.
23   Hackman, J. and Oldham, G. (1980) *Work Redesign*. New York: Addison Wesley.
24   Buchanan, D. and McCalman, J. (1989) *High Performance Work Systems: The Digital Experience*. London: Routledge.

CHAPTER 10

Control

CHAPTER LEARNING OBJECTIVES

- To understand the centrality of control to organisational survival and success.
- To know the different stages in the control process.
- To appreciate the characteristics of effective controls.
- To distinguish feedforward, concurrent and feedback controls.
- To identify and illustrate common financial and non-financial controls.

10.1 Introduction

Control is critical to organisational success and sustainability and it is a core managerial function. At the outset, it is important to note that controlling is recognised as one of the major activities of managers, and that it is generally viewed as an integral link that binds together other essential managerial functions such as planning, organising and leading.[1] While this is as true for small firms as it is for large ones, for public organisations as well as private ones, and for those operating in the not-for-profit sector, it is being increasingly recognised that management control procedures and systems do vary between organisations, sectors and societies. Whitley highlights that four particular characteristics of control systems differ considerably in different contexts.[2] These are:

1. the extent to which control is exercised overwhelmingly through formal rules and procedures
2. the degree of control exercised over how unit activities are carried out
3. the influence and involvement of unit members in exercising control
4. the scope of the information used by the control system in evaluating performance and deciding rewards and sanctions.

Similarly, Bhimani notes that cross-national studies of management control systems and internal accounting practices suggest that there are distinct national differences.[3] Beyond country-level national differences, organisational characteristics have also been found to be important in explaining differences in the approach to exercising control. For example, Kald *et al.* identify variations in management controls depending on the nature of the particular strategy being pursued by the organisation,[4] while Modell discusses the linkage between the management controls in place and the nature of the human resource management system being followed by the organisation.[5]

Regardless of the institutional context or variations in organisational characteristics, control seeks to ensure the achievement of organisational objectives and goals by measuring actual performance and taking corrective action where needed. In this way it can be viewed as that aspect of managerial work that tries to ensure that there is a conformance between what is planned for and what unfolds.

This chapter examines the control process and the various types of control that can be used in organisations. Following a consideration of the characteristics of effective controls, the two main methods of control – classified as financial and non-financial controls – are examined. Financial controls examined include budgets, break-even analysis and ration analysis. Non-financial controls looked at here include project controls, management audits and inventory, production and quality control.

10.2 The nature and importance of control

The control function of modern management is the process dedicated to ensuring the effective and efficient achievement of organisational objectives. Sridhar and Balachandran argue that any task assignment decision must be accompanied by an appropriately designed managerial control system, as each affects the other.[6] The control process typically involves measuring progress toward planned performance and, where necessary, applying corrective measures so that performance can be improved. Therefore, control is concerned with making sure that objectives are attained. It is strongly related to planning in that for control to occur, plans have to be available against which to measure performance. Similarly, it is unlikely that planning can operate effectively if there are no control mechanisms to correct deviations from the plans themselves. In this way, the relationship between planning and control has been likened to that of the two blades of a pair of scissors – the scissors cannot work unless there are two blades.[7]

Control, however, has been the most neglected and, it has been argued, the least understood function of management. Kirsch notes that while much discussed, managerial control is an inadequately studied phenomenon in organisational research.[8] Baker and Jennings, among others, consider this surprising, given that it has been demonstrated that poor control mechanisms often have a have a negative effect on organisations.[9] The core managerial role of control has frequently been equated purely with financial control. In this sense, control has been regarded as an activity associated with accountants and financial departments rather than as a broader, more all-encompassing management function. The very word itself has been a source of some confusion. It can have the status of a portmanteau term, sometimes considered to be largely about directing people, sometimes about evaluating outcomes and, on other occasions, about taking corrective action.

In the modern organisation, control is the function of every manager. Top-level managers are concerned about controlling sales and profits. Middle managers are concerned about controlling direct labour hours and production outputs. Front-line supervisors are concerned about controlling quality and scrap. So while the scope of control varies depending on the managerial level, all managers have responsibility for implementing plans and consequently are responsible for their control.

In recent years the control function has changed. Traditionally, the majority of organisations were involved in labour-intensive industries. However, today more and more organisations are involved in the service sector, where it is more difficult to measure performance. In this context the control function becomes more complex and at the same time more important.

Information technology (IT) has revolutionised control systems but has also added complexity to the control process. Naveh and Halevy note that low-cost data control and communications systems are now being applied to the control function and such advancements have made possible organisation-wide information systems with which process improvements across the entire organisation can be achieved.[10] The result is a more flexible and speedy system. IT allows organisations to speed up changes in strategies by revising financial plans and testing changes ahead of time by quickly running and comparing various 'what if' scenarios.

Management Focus 10.1 IT and control

An often-quoted example of the application of IT to a control system can be found in the scanning machines used in supermarkets and retail outlets. These electronic devices allow the organisation to:

- Instantly identify and calculate the type, quantity and price of each individual item purchased. The control of inventory is therefore much easier: the organisation no longer has to undertake a physical stock-take as the scanners produce inventory records instantly. This system also identifies slow-moving products that may need to be reduced in price to sell or perhaps should not be reordered. The system also tracks consumer tastes and patterns, which facilitates reordering of stock.
- Calculate employee productivity by assessing how many customers and items are dealt with per minute. If, for example, the checkout person is very slow, this could lead to customer frustration. To prevent this, the checkout person can be sent for retraining.
- Calculate precisely how much money or revenue is generated hourly, daily and weekly from each till, store or regional area. This makes financial control far simpler and more accurate. It is also possible to pinpoint how the organisation is deviating from overall budgets.

As a result of these changes, store managers have been able to lower inventory levels, boost turnover and match product mixes to consumers' changing tastes. These developments have all meant that the control function has assumed far greater importance.

10.3 Stages in the control process

Various frameworks for management control systems are suggested in the literature, but the underlying core objective of all of them is the effective management of overall organisational performance. For the purposes of this chapter, control can be considered an ongoing process involving three interconnected activities as shown in Figure 10.1. Control is designed to ensure that different organisational stakeholders such as individual employees, teams and business units meet agree objectives and to minimise any deviations from such objectives.

FIGURE 10.1 THE CONTROL PROCESS

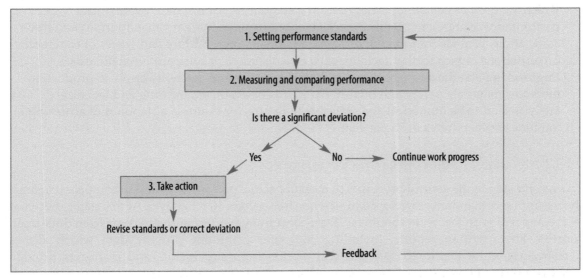

10.3.1 Setting performance standards

The first step in the control process is the establishment of agreed performance standards. All organisations have goals, and a standard related to a particular goal can be thought of as the level of expected performance for the achievement of that goal. Weihrich and Koontz view standards as selected points in an overall planning programme that measure performance, so that managers can observe how things are going without watching every step in the process.[11] In this way, standards are yardsticks for performance. Unless standards are established and enforced, performance across the various parts of the organisation is likely to vary widely. Standards of performance can be set for almost any organisational activity, as the following examples illustrate:

- **Market share:** Increase market share by 20 per cent.
- **Quality:** Product deviations should not be higher than 2.5 defects per million.
- **Costs:** Costs should be reduced by 15 per cent.
- **Innovation:** 25 per cent of turnover should be generated by products less than three years old.
- **Employees:** Turnover should not exceed 4 per cent per month.
- **Customers:** All customer complaints should be answered within 24 hours.

Establishing standards of performance is a complex task, given the wide variety of standards that have to be established, but they are particularly important in the context of avoiding or rectifying poor performance. In general, standards can be generated from three different sources: historical, comparative or engineering-based.

- **Historical standards** are based on the organisation's past experience. Previous production, sales, profits and costs can be used as a basis from which to establish performance standards. However, standards based on historical data assume that the future will be the same as the past: abrupt changes render historical standards useless.

- **Comparative standards** are based on the experience of other organisations and competitors, which are used as benchmarks in generating standards. For instance, the financial performance of another organisation can be used to judge market value. Journals and trade associations provide information on sales, advertising expenditure and wages of competitor organisations, which further facilitates the establishment of comparative standards.
- **Engineering standards** are based on technical analyses and generally apply to production methods, materials, safety and quality. Standards based on engineering and technical analysis tend to be numerical and objective in nature, for example a standard of achieving 'on time' delivery rates of 95 per cent.

10.3.2 Measuring and comparing performance

The second step in the control process is to measure actual performance and to compare it against the performance standards developed in step one (see section 10.3.1 above). At this stage, the 'what is' is compared with the 'what should be'. Data concerning performance can come from three main sources. First, written reports, including computer printouts, provide data which allows performance to be measured. Second, oral reports from supervisors and managers provide information about levels of performance on a day-to-day basis. Third, personal observation, which involves touring the various areas and observing activities, can provide important information about performance. However, personal observation is by its very nature subjective and does not often generate sufficient quantitative data. Too much personal observation can be construed by employees as management showing a lack of trust. Despite these disadvantages, many managers still believe that personal observation provides important insights that quantitative data is simply unable to do.

Actual performance can meet, surpass or fall below the established performance standards. If performance meets the standards, no control problem exists and the work can continue. Where standards have not been reached due to exceptional circumstances such as a strike, no further action is usually taken in the control process. If performance fails to meet or exceeds expectations, further examination is required. If standards have been exceeded it is possible that the standards were inappropriately set or that superior talent and effort was put in to the process. When performance fails to meet standards this could be caused by inappropriate standards but, more worryingly, could arise from poor talent, lack of effort or failure to use resources efficiently.

In cases where actual performance falls below or exceeds standards the critical issue facing managers is how much of a deviation is acceptable before corrective action should be taken. In reality, actual performance rarely matches established performance standards and consequently deviations are the norm. Managers, however, have to know when deviations are significantly different and require corrective action. Because managers cannot react to every deviation, performance ranges that state both upper and lower control limits are used. Managers apply the principle of exception by concentrating on significant deviations or exceptions from expected results. Therefore, as only exceptional cases need to be corrected, managers can save time and money by effectively applying the principle of exception.

10.3.3 *Taking action*

The final step in the control process is to take action based on the comparisons made in the previous step. At this stage of the control process, control can be clearly seen as part of the management system and can be related to the other management functions of planning, organising and leading. Where a significant deviation has occurred management should take vigorous corrective action. Effective control demands that prompt action is taken to rectify the situation. An organisation can either correct the deviation or revise the standards applied. When correcting deviations, both positive and negative deviations should be examined as a basis for learning.

Corrective action can be taken by the top of the organisation, by a specialist or by the operators themselves. Managers or supervisors, for example, can change procedures, introduce new technology or training, or even take disciplinary action. An organisation can also alter or revise standards if it is felt that they are unacceptable or unrealistic. Standards based on historical data may no longer be appropriate due to changed environmental circumstances.

Having either taken corrective action or revised standards the organisation will feed back lessons learned from the process into the first step, establishing standards, and the process continues in this cyclical manner.

10.4 Types of control

As we have seen, control is necessary to identify problems, adjust plans and take action. Therefore, control is designed to regulate aspects of the organisation. While performance can be continuously monitored, there are what can be considered to be three critical control points: before the activity, during the activity and after the activity has been completed. Control that occurs before the activity has been completed is referred to as **feedforward control**. Control exerted while the activity is actually being completed is referred to as **concurrent control**. Control that occurs after the activity has been completed is referred to as **feedback control**. The various types of control points are shown in Figure 10.2.

FIGURE 10.2 TYPES OF CONTROL

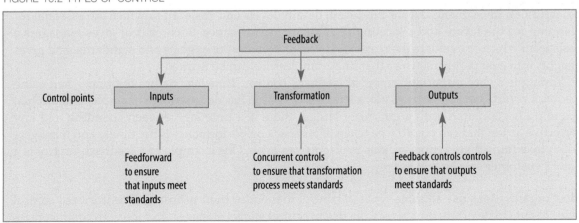

Adapted from Bedeian, A. (1993) *Management* (3rd edn). New York: Dryden Press..

10.4.1 Feedforward control

Feedforward control is future-directed and aims to prevent problems before they occur. Because managers need to react quickly to correct mistakes, they find control that might prevent mistakes occurring in the first instance appealing. Feedforward control carefully examines the various inputs to make sure that they meet the standards needed for successful transformation into outputs. Feedforward controls regulate the quantity and quality of financial, physical and human resources before they are transformed. For example, in order to prevent bad debts or loan defaults, banks ask for documentation about salary, other loans and credit history before granting loan approval. In this way they are seeking to control the activity of giving a loan before it actually happens. Similarly, in the manufacture of food products, Marks & Spencer uses extremely effective feedforward controls in relation to the quality of the supplies used, ensuring that all ingredients meet exacting quality standards. Feedforward control, therefore, strongly emphasises the anticipation of problems and preventive action at an early stage in the production process.

10.4.2 Concurrent control

Concurrent control occurs while inputs are being transformed into outputs. It monitors the transformation process to make sure that the outputs meet standards by producing the right amount of the right products at a specified time. Concurrent controls ensure that materials and staff are available when needed, and that breakdowns are repaired speedily.

Because concurrent controls occur at the same time as the transformation process, they can cope with contingencies that were not anticipated. Concurrent controls allow adjustments to be made while the work is being done. For example, if a machine has a minor fault the manager has to decide whether to follow an alternative course or to stop and correct the situation.

10.4.3 Feedback control

Feedback control monitors outputs to ensure that they meet standards. This form of control takes place after the product/service has been completed. As a result, feedback control focuses on end results as opposed to inputs or transformation activities. Feedback control provides information on the return on investment, output produced, quality levels and costs, all of which are essential for planning for the future and allocating rewards for performance. Such control gives managers a basis from which to evaluate the reasonableness of organisational goals and standards, and gives insights into past performance so that important lessons can be learned.

Timing is a very important aspect of feedback control. Time lags naturally occur when using feedback control because it takes place after the deviation has occurred. For example, when actual spending is compared with a quarterly budget there is a time lag between spending and any corrective action that can possibly be taken. If feedback on performance is not timely and managers fail to take immediate action, serious problems can arise. One example of a feedback control is a hotel's customer satisfaction survey.

Most organisations use all three types of control to monitor their processes. Feedforward control helps to anticipate future problems. Concurrent control allows managers to cope with contingencies that cannot be anticipated. Feedback control tries to ensure that the organisation does not make the same mistakes again and captures any defects.

10.5 Characteristics of effective control

Irrespective of the type of control being used, the literature highlights that effective controls share a number of important characteristics, as shown in Figure 10.3.

FIGURE 10.3 CHARACTERISTICS OF EFFECTIVE CONTROLS

1. Appropriate
2. Cost-effective
3. Acceptable
4. Emphasise exceptions at critical points
5. Flexible
6. Reliable and valid
7. Based on valid performance standards
8. Based on adequate information

10.5.1 Appropriateness

Controls must be suitable and appropriate for an organisation's goals and plans. In other words, controls should be tailored to the plans and various units/locations within the organisation. Controls should provide clear and concise information that lets managers know how well plans are progressing. Effective controls should not generate information that is irrelevant in fulfilling organisational plans.

Controls should also reflect the position in which they are used. A control used by a top-level manager is very different from one used by a front-line supervisor. Different areas in an organisation require different types of control. For example, controls used in a finance department are very different from those used in marketing. Similarly, small and large organisations use different types of control. Controls should be tailored to the individual manager, who must clearly understand them; and they should also reflect the organisational structure, which shows responsibility for the execution of plans and any deviations from them.

While certain techniques for controlling finance and human resource planning have general application, none of them is completely applicable to any one situation. Consequently, it is important to ensure that controls are tailored to the individual needs of the organisation.

10.5.2 Cost-effectiveness

The benefits achieved by control processes must offset the cost of using them. To be cost-effective, the controls used must be tailored to the job and to the size of the organisation. Larger organisations can gain economies of scale and can often afford expensive and elaborate control systems. Control techniques are economical when they show up potential or actual deviations from the minimum cost. For example, the cost of inserting electronic strips in library books which then bleep when they go through an alarm system more than offsets the cost of books lost through theft. However, employing a full-time library detective in addition to this system would probably not be cost-effective, as the cost of stolen books would not cover both forms of control.

10.5.3 Acceptability

Controls must be accepted as fair and adequate by those to whom they apply. Controls that are arbitrary or unnecessary will have little impact. Controls that are harmful to an individual's social or psychological well-being are also ineffective. For example, some organisations search their employees as they go home or come off shifts to make sure that they have not stolen goods. This form of control is frequently considered unnecessary and illustrates a lack of trust in the employees. The end result is normally frustration, apathy and distrust of management and their motives. It is therefore important that controls are accepted by people as fair and necessary if they are to be effective.

10.5.4 The relative emphasis on exceptions at control points

Controls should be designed to make sure that they show up significant deviations. Controls that do so allow managers to benefit from management by exception and detect those areas that require further action. However, it is not sufficient just to identify deviations. Some small deviations in certain areas may be more important than larger deviations in other areas. For example, a 10 per cent increase in labour costs is far more worrying than a 25 per cent increase in the cost of postage stamps. As a result, exceptions must be looked for at critical points, which then facilitates corrective action.

10.5.5 Flexibility

Effective controls must be flexible enough to withstand changing circumstances or unforeseen developments. In the current business environment, the need for flexible controls has become much more important. For example, budgets that specify how much money is to be spent on certain resources are normally based on a predicted level of sales or profits. If for some reason sales fall below the expected target the budget becomes obsolete. Unless the budget is flexible, its efficiency as a control device is questionable. Over the years it has been argued that budgets are extremely inflexible and therefore are not an effective means of control. This point will be examined in greater detail later in the chapter (see section 10.7.1).

10.5.6 Reliability and validity

For controls to be effective they should be dependable (reliable) and must measure what they claim to measure (valid). Validity and reliability are important characteristics of effective control systems. A control that is unreliable and invalid can cause lack of trust in the control process and lead to serious problems. For example, unreliable sales figures can lead to problems with inventory and future forecasts. Similarly, controls should be based on objective criteria rather than personal opinion. For example, a manager in charge of ordering materials who bases the order on how s/he thinks things are going is not as effective as the one who bases the order on computerised numbers of units produced and sold.

10.5.7 Controls based on valid performance standards

Effective controls are always based on accurate standards of performance. Such controls incorporate all aspects of performance. However, managers should be careful not to have too many measures in place as this can lead to over-control and potential resistance from employees. In order to avoid over-control, managers can set specific standards for a number of important areas and set satisfactory standards of performance for other areas. Managers can also prioritise certain targets or standards, such as quality, costs and inventory.

10.5.8 Controls based on accurate information

Managers must effectively communicate to employees the rationale and importance of control and also provide feedback on their performance. Such feedback allows employees themselves to take corrective action and motivates them. Naturally, however, in this context information about controls should be accessible and accurate.

10.6 Methods of control

Organisations use a variety of methods of control. These can be classified as either financial or non-financial. Most organisations use a variety of both types to ensure effective control of relevant areas. Figure 10.4 provides a summary of commonly used forms of financial and non-financial control, each of which is discussed in this chapter.

FIGURE 10.4 THE MAIN METHODS OF CONTROL

Financial Controls	Non-Financial Controls
1. Budgetary control	1. Project controls
2. Break-even analysis	2. Management audits
3. Ratio analysis	3. Inventory control
4. Production control	
5. Quality control	

10.7 Financial controls

Three common types of financial control typically used by organisations are budgetary control, break-even analysis and ratio analysis.

10.7.1 Budgetary control

Budgetary control is one of the most widely recognised and commonly used methods of managerial control. It ties together all three types of control – feedforward, concurrent and feedback – depending on the point at which it is applied. Budgeting involves formulating plans for a given period in numerical terms. Budgetary control is the process of ascertaining what has been achieved and comparing this with the projections contained in the budget. Most budgets use financial data, but some contain non-financial terms such as sales volume or production output. However, a budget is predominantly a financial control device. Budgets are important because they force people to plan in a precise manner, which produces a degree of order in the organisation. Budgets must reflect organisational goals and be well co-ordinated throughout the organisation if they are to serve as an effective control instrument.

Types of budget include:

- **Revenue and expense budget:** develops projections of revenue and expenses. The most common example of a revenue and expense budget is a sales budget, illustrated in Figure 10.5. Actual revenues, expenses and sales can be compared to the expected budgetary levels.
- **Time, space, material and production budget:** develops projections for machine hours, space allocated, materials required and production output. Actual and expected levels can then be compared.
- **Capital expenditure budget:** develops projections for expenditure on items such as plant and machinery. Actual expenditure can then be compared to the projected level.
- **Cash budget:** develops projections about cash receipts and disbursements, against which actual levels can be compared.

FIGURE 10.5 EXAMPLE OF A SALES BUDGET

	January		February	
	Expected	*Actual*	*Expected*	*Actual*
Sales	1,500,000		2,000,000	
Expenses				
General	510,000		775,000	
Selling	292,000		323,000	
Production	377,000		425,000	
R & D	118,000		120,000	
Office	70,000		75,000	
Advertising	52,000		59,000	
Estimated gross profit	**80,100**		**232,000**	

All budgetary control should focus on performance in what are termed 'key result areas'. These are areas that are crucial to the organisation's business, such as sales of the main product, manufacturing costs, stock levels and cash position. There are also areas where problems or failures will have repercussions elsewhere, such as supplier failures, increases in material costs and strikes or stoppages. Identifying these key result areas allows performance to be reviewed in precise terms, while allowing for some leeway elsewhere.

Stewart notes that over time, budgetary control, in certain instances, has become inflexible and cumbersome.[12] Over-budgeting has occurred, whereby managers are constrained by budgets to such an extent that they cannot use freedom and initiative in managing their areas. Frequently, abiding by budgetary forecasts becomes the overriding objective of managers at the expense of wider organisational goals. Budgets also hide inefficiencies by establishing strong precedents, especially for capital expenditure. The fact that a capital expenditure was made in the past becomes an important justification for its inclusion in future budgets, regardless of whether or not it is needed. Finally, budgets can lead to inflexibility if they are formulated for long periods of time. As environmental conditions can change quickly, budgets become obsolete, causing inflexibility.

New approaches to budgeting have been developed in order to overcome the inflexibility associated with traditional budgets. Variable budgets, which have been introduced by many organisations, analyse expense items to work out how individual costs will vary with the volume of output. Variable budgets distinguish between fixed and variable costs. Fixed costs do not vary with the volume of output and include depreciation, maintenance of plant and equipment and insurance. Costs that rise and fall depending on the volume of output are called variable costs and include materials and labour. Variable budgets attempt to calculate the extent to which variable costs change with given levels of output. An example of a variable budget chart is provided in Figure 10.6.

FIGURE 10.6 EXAMPLE OF A VARIABLE BUDGET CHART

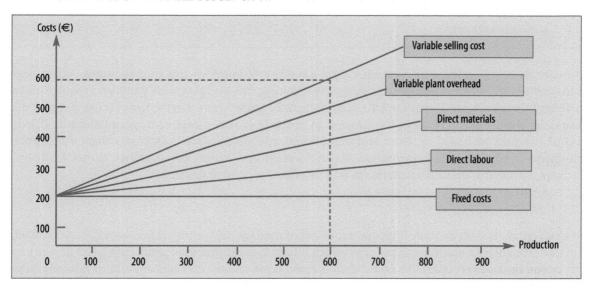

This variable budget shows the level of costs that will be incurred for different levels of output. For example, a planned production of 300 units will cost around €450. However, if actual volume increases to 600 units, costs will increase to €600, according to the budget guideline. Variable budgets therefore give the organisation a good guide as to how costs will increase with increased volume. Variable budgets work well when sales or output can be reasonably well forecast in advance. Fixed budgets can work well with good plans and sales forecasts. However, the variable budget forces the organisation to examine factors that increase as production increases.

Another development in budgeting is *zero-based budgeting*. This approach means that managers start from zero in creating a budget each year. It is an attempt to eliminate the inefficiencies that creep in as elements are carried over from one year to the next without being questioned. Zero-based budgeting is best applied to ancillary or support areas of an organisation, such as research and development (R&D) or marketing, rather than core areas like production, where certain expenses have to be carried forward every year. The main advantage of zero-based budgeting is that it forces managers to plan each year afresh. During the process reference is not made to the expenditure of the previous year. Its core advantage is that it focuses on the efficient allocation of resources at a point in time, rather than relying on the historical way of doing things.

Effective budgets

All budgets must be tailored to the specific task and used by all managers, not just controllers, if they are to be effective. It has been argued that effective budgetary control is characterised by four key elements, as shown in Figure 10.7.[13]

FIGURE 10.7 CHARACTERISTICS OF EFFECTIVE BUDGETS

1.	Top management support
2.	Participation
3.	Based on reliable standards
4.	Accurate information available

In order to be effective, budgets must first have the support of top management. When top management support the budgeting process by ensuring that budgets meet plans and require units to defend their budgets, the organisation as a whole becomes more alert to the process. Second, all managers should participate in the process in order to ensure effective implementation. Third, budgets should be based on clear and valid standards. Finally, for budgets to work effectively managers need available information about forecast and actual performance under budgets. Budgets displaying these characteristics will be effective control devices.

10.7.2 Break-even analysis

Break-even analysis is another important method of managerial control. It involves the use of fixed and variable costs to analyse the point at which it becomes profitable to produce a good or service, that is, the break-even point. As noted above, fixed costs remain constant no matter how much is produced, whereas variable costs change. Fixed costs and variable costs, when added together, are referred to as total costs.

By analysing the level of both fixed and variable costs it is possible to identify the volume needed to break even: that is, the point at which income generated from a given volume of output breaks even with total costs. Break-even analysis has many applications in control and managerial decision making and is especially useful for decisions concerning dropping or adding product ranges and the choice of distribution channels. Figure 10.8 provides an example of break-even analysis in graphic form.

In this case, the break-even point at which revenues cover total expenses or costs is a volume of 1,000 units, which cost €5,000 to produce. Producing fewer than 1,000 units would mean that a loss is being incurred and anything higher than 1,000 units means a profit can be made.

FIGURE 10.8 BREAK-EVEN ANALYSIS

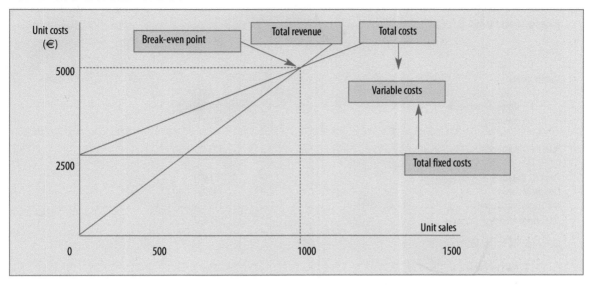

Showing the break-even point in chart form highlights the relationship between costs and profit. The fixed costs have to be covered before anything is produced. It is assumed in Figure 10.8 that total costs increase in direct proportion to the units produced. Only when total costs are equal to the revenue earned can the organisation break even. In reality, the relationship between costs and output would probably not be linear. If an organisation upgrades a machine that produces 10,000 units to one that produces 25,000, we would expect to see a large bump in the cost curve. Similarly, the relationship between revenue and sales could be uneven because of bulk discounts or price cutting. On the whole, though, break-even analysis provides a graphic illustration of how much needs to be produced before profits can be made. However, due to its simplistic approach, break-even analysis is better used with other control tools rather than in isolation.

10.7.3 Ratio analysis

Several types of control have been developed for understanding and assessing an organisation's financial performance. Such guidelines for financial performance serve as control mechanisms in that they provide benchmarks for evaluation. These guidelines are commonly termed *financial ratios* and express relationships between individual or group items on an organisation's balance sheet and profit and loss account. Because the guidelines involve ratios, this process has been called ratio analysis. Ratio analysis provides important mechanisms for interpreting organisational performance and allows an organisation to track its performance over time and to compare it with that of competitors. There are four basic types of financial ratio – liquidity, activity, profitability and leverage – each of which will be discussed and calculated using the balance sheet and profit and loss statement of the fictitious organisation ABC, as shown in Figure 10.9.

FIGURE 10.9 ABC ACCOUNTS

Balance Sheet for ABC	
Assets	€
Current assets	
Cash	9,521
Accounts receivable	88,329
Inventory	401,273
Total current assets	499,123
Property and plant	161,000
Less depreciation	44,251
Net property and plant	116,749
Total assets	615,872
Liabilities and stockholder equity	
Notes payable	22,679
Accrued expenses	51,736
Accounts payable	9,321
Corporation tax payable	23,251
Total current liabilities	106,987
Stockholder equity	
Capital stock	358,885
Preferred stock	50,000
Retained earnings	100,000
Total stockholders equity	508,885
Total liabilities and stockholder equity	615,872

Liquidity ratios

An organisation's liquidity is its ability to pay for its short-term liabilities. A commonly used indicator of an organisation's liquidity is its *current ratio*. The current ratio is a comparison of an organisation's current assets and current liabilities. To obtain the current ratio the current assets are divided by the current liabilities. In ABC's case the figures are as follows:

$$\text{Current ratio} = \frac{\text{Current assets } 499{,}123}{\text{Current liabilities } 106{,}987} = 4.6{:}1$$

A ratio of 4.6:1 means that for every €1 in current liabilities there is €4.60 in current assets to cover it. Most financial analysts believe that a ratio of 2:1 is desirable. While current ratios vary from industry to industry, a large current ratio, as seen in the case of ABC, is not necessarily a good thing as it could mean that it is not using its assets efficiently.

Another method of assessing liquidity is the *quick asset ratio*. This is preferred by some financial analysts, who fear that slow-moving inventory can lead to a misleadingly high level of current assets under the current ratio method. Quick assets are those that are available to cover emergencies and therefore exclude inventory which has yet to be sold. An organisation's quick asset ratio is calculated by subtracting the value of inventory yet to be sold from the current assets and dividing that figure by the current liabilities. The larger the ratio, the greater the liquidity. In the case of ABC the figures are as follows:

$$\text{Quick asset ratio} \quad = \quad \frac{\text{Current assets} \quad 499{,}123}{\text{Less: Inventory} \quad 401{,}273} \quad =$$

$$\frac{\text{Quick assets} \quad 97{,}850}{\text{Current liabilities} \quad 106{,}987} \quad = \quad 0.91{:}1$$

In this case, for every €1 in current liabilities only €0.91 is available to cover liabilities.

When the ratio is 1:1 the organisation is deemed liquid. So in this case ABC appears to be overstretched.

Activity ratios

These aim to show how efficiently an organisation is using its resources. There are three main activity ratios: inventory turnover ratio; asset turnover ratio; and accounts receivable turnover ratio.

Inventory turnover ratio measures the number of times that an organisation's inventory has been sold during the year. It is therefore the ratio between an organisation's cost of goods sold and the current inventory. The ratio for ABC is:

$$\text{Inventory turnover ratio} \quad = \quad \frac{\text{Cost of goods sold} \quad 567{,}215}{\text{Current inventory} \quad 401{,}273} \quad = 1.4{:}1$$

ABC's inventory has therefore been sold 1.4 times during the last year.

The *asset turnover ratio* assesses how well the organisation is using its assets. It is calculated as the ratio between an organisation's sales and the total assets. The figures for ABC are as follows:

$$\text{Asset turnover ratio} \quad = \quad \frac{\text{Sales} \quad 899{,}000}{\text{Total assets} \quad 615{,}872} \quad = 1.45{:}1$$

Therefore for each €1 invested in assets, sales have generated €1.45.

The *accounts receivable turnover ratio* measures an organisation's collection period on credit sales. It is calculated by dividing the sales by accounts receivable. The figures for ABC are:

$$\text{Accounts receivable turnover ratio} \quad = \quad \frac{\text{Sales } 899,000}{\text{Accounts receivable } 88,329} \quad = \quad 10.1{:}1$$

If we divide the 360 (days) by 10.1 it is possible to calculate the average collection period for accounts. For ABC the figure is 35.6 days. Greater than 40 days usually indicates slow accounts receivable. However, much depends on the credit policy of the organisation.

Profitability ratios

These determine how profitable an organisation's performance has been and involves the use of two ratios – net profit ratio and the rate of return on assets.

The *net profit ratio*, which is a good indicator of short-term profit, is the ratio between net profit and sales. The net profit ratio for ABC is:

$$\text{Net profit ratio} \quad = \quad \frac{\text{Net profit } 41,785}{\text{Sales } 899,000} \quad = 0.04$$

This means that for every €1 in sales, four cents is made in profit. In the region of 4–5 per cent is the average for successful organisations, although this obviously varies from industry to industry.

The *ratio of the return on assets* is the ratio between an organisation's net profit and total assets and is designed to measure an organisation's efficiency in generating profit. It is calculated by dividing total assets into net profit. The figures for ABC are:

$$\text{Return on assets ratio} = \quad \frac{\text{Net profit } 41,785}{\text{Total assets } 615,872} \quad = 0.06$$

This means that for every €1 invested in total assets, six cents in profits is eventually made. Organisation ABC has an average ratio as the industry norm is around 0.07 or 7 per cent.

Leverage ratios

Leverage ratios attempt to identify the source of an organisation's capital. Leverage is the increased rate of return on stockholder equity when an investment earns a return larger than the interest paid for debt financing. The most popular measure is the debt equity ratio, which is total liabilities divided by the total equity (that is, liabilities plus stockholder equity). The ratio for ABC is:

$$\text{Debt equity ratio} \quad = \quad \frac{\text{Total liabilities } 106,987}{\text{Total equity } 615,872} \quad = 0.17$$

This means that for every €1 in equity, 17 cents is borrowed capital. Total liabilities should not exceed total equities.

10.8 Non-financial controls

In addition to financial controls, organisations employ a range of non-financial controls. The most common forms of non-financial control are project controls, which include Gantt charts and programme evaluation review technique (PERT) analysis; management audits; inventory; production control; and quality control. Each of these key controls will be examined in this section.

10.8.1 Project controls

Project controls are designed to control the operation of certain projects undertaken by an organisation. Keil and Montealegre note that such controls can prevent a project going awry or can assist in extricating the organisation from a failing project.[14] The two most popular devices are Gantt charts and PERT analysis.

Gantt charts

Gantt charts were developed by Henry Gantt, who was an advocate of scientific management (see Chapter 1). A Gantt chart is a simple bar chart that portrays the time relationship between events and their outcome. The chart therefore depicts the sequence of activities required to complete a task and allocates a time frame for each activity. Figure 10.10 shows an example of a Gantt chart.

FIGURE 10.10 EXAMPLE OF A GANTT CHART

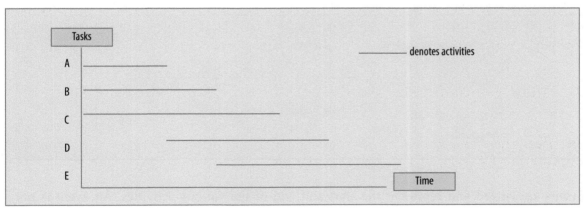

All activities represented by overlapping bars can be completed at the same time. In this example, tasks A, B and C can all be completed concurrently. Activities represented by non-overlapping bars must be undertaken in the sequence illustrated. For example, task D cannot be started until task A is finished. The Gantt chart therefore represents the steps of a project over time and can be used to track whether a project is ahead, behind or on schedule. An example of a Gantt chart for the development of a particular product is illustrated in Figure 10.11.

FIGURE 10.11 GANTT CHART FOR THE DEVELOPMENT OF A PRODUCT

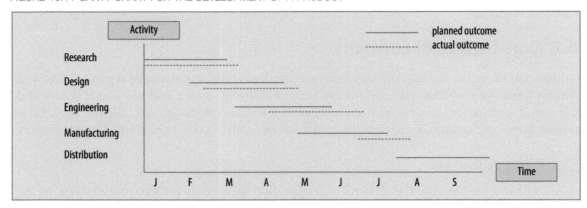

As the chart shows, progress on the development of the new product is behind schedule at the end of the year because the product has not yet been distributed due to the fact that each stage took longer than originally planned. Gantt charts help to co-ordinate activities and schedule labour. They are most useful for activities that are unrelated and are less effective when dealing with many interrelated activities.

PERT analysis

PERT involves the development of a network which shows the most likely time needed to complete each task required to finish the product or project. Figure 10.12 is an example of a PERT network.

FIGURE 10.12 EXAMPLE OF A PERT NETWORK

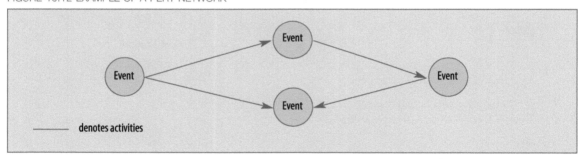

Events are circled and represent the start and end of the various activities. An event is not completed until all activities leading to it have been finished. Activities are depicted with arrows and mark the work that has to be done. An activity cannot begin until all preceding activities to which it is connected have been completed. In developing a PERT chart the following steps should be taken:

1. Identify each event that must be completed and assign a time frame to it.
2. Based on Step 1, draw a network including the various activities that need to be done and keep them in chronological order.
3. Estimate the time needed to complete each activity (usually in weeks).

4. Estimate the total time for each activity in a sequence or path of activities. The path with the longest time is the critical path. The critical path is therefore the earliest date when a project can be finished.

FIGURE 10.13 A PERT NETWORK FOR THE MANUFACTURE OF A CAR

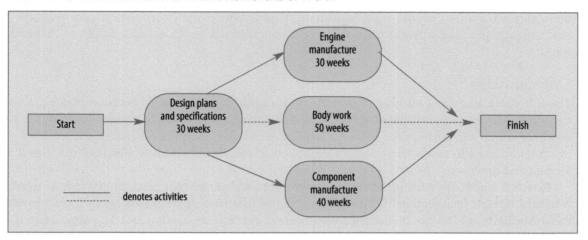

Figure 10.13 illustrates a PERT network for the manufacture of a car. In this example, the critical path is 80 weeks. Having identified the critical path, a project manager can focus on either reducing the time of the various activities or, at the very least, watch for any delays. PERT is widely used as an important control for undertaking projects. Figure 10.14 outlines the main advantages and disadvantages associated with its use.

FIGURE 10.14 ADVANTAGES AND DISADVANTAGES OF PERT ANALYSIS

Advantages
1. It emphasises areas where delays are most likely to occur.
2. It is a detailed means of controlling a given project.
3. It frequently stimulates alternative plans and schedules.

Disadvantages
1. Event times must be accurately calculated.
2. It can be costly.
3. It is difficult to apply stringently when outside suppliers are involved.
4. It is unsuitable for repetitive sequences of events since all events fall along a single critical path.

Whatever project control techniques are used by an organisation, Hutchinson notes that the objective is to help managers deliver projects that ensure business benefits on time and within budget.[15] Consequently, what must be emphasised is the need for traceability to be built into the project so that the accuracy and speed of impact assessment is improved.

10.8.2 Management audits

Management audits have developed as a means of evaluating and controlling the various elements of an organisation. They can be either external or internal. With external audits, managers conduct investigations of other competitor organisations. Internal audits investigate the operations of the organisation itself. The same control techniques can be used for both. Both internal and external management audits provide vital information from which the organisation can evaluate its performance and take corrective action. In addition, internal audits act as a deterrent to internal fraud.

External audits

These involve analysing another organisation, normally to aid strategic decision making. Other organisations can be investigated for possible mergers or acquisitions, to assess the strengths and weaknesses of competitors, or even to look at a possible supplier of materials. Most of the information used to assess these factors is publicly available information which simply has to be located and analysed.

External audits are a useful source of control for an organisation. Such audits can be used in feedback control (see section 10.4.3) to discover irregularities or problems on an industry-wide basis. Similarly, audits can be used for feedforward control (see section 10.4.1), particularly if an organisation is planning an acquisition. In this way, an external audit will highlight any potential problems that could arise from an acquisition. Finally, audits can be used to learn lessons from the mistakes of other organisations. Learning where other organisations have gone wrong can lead to suggestions for updated or enhanced concurrent controls.

The use of external audits as a control technique has increased rapidly in recent years. The nature of the current business environment, with its emphasis on cut-throat competition, has further augmented this trend.

Internal audits

Internal audits concentrate on the activities of the organisation itself. Organisations frequently undertake reviews of their planning, organising and leading functions. Control is the essential ingredient in any internal audit. When conducting an internal audit a manager should concentrate on financial stability, production, sales, HR, and ethical and social responsibility. Problems often uncovered by an internal audit include duplication of resources, poor utilisation of resources and the uneconomical use of plant and machinery.

10.8.3 Inventory control

Inventory control involves control of stock levels to ensure that the organisation has stock when needed yet at the same time does not have too much money tied up in stock that is not immediately required. Up to one-third of an organisation's total costs can be tied up in storing and handling inventory. Therefore, a control system is needed to keep these costs to a minimum. A good inventory control system tries to answer three questions:
1. How much of the required inventory items should be bought at a time?
2. At what point should inventory items be reordered?
3. What are the most economic order quantities of each item?

In the first instance, production experience and knowledge of the sources of supply will dictate how much inventory should be bought. Some items may be seasonal or scarce, so it may make sense to buy these in large lots. The timing of the reorder depends on two factors. First, the lead time involved – the time between the placement of the order and its delivery. Second, the problem of knowing what safety stock to keep so that production will not be disrupted because of supplier transport problems. The third question is resolved by reference to the economic order quantity (EOQ) model. The formula for EOQ is as follows:

$$\text{EOQ} = \frac{2 \times \text{order costs} \times \text{annual consumption}}{\text{Annual holding costs}}$$

and is portrayed graphically in Figure 10.15.

FIGURE 10.15 RELATIONSHIP BETWEEN COSTS AND ORDER QUANTITY

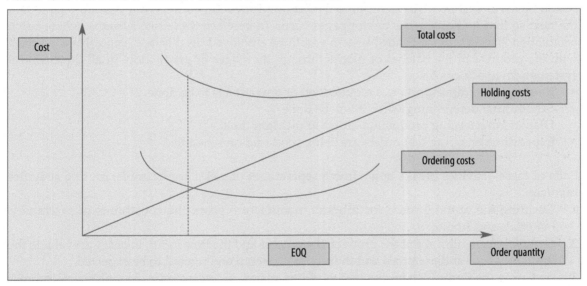

Holding costs include storage space, handling and security. Ordering costs include administration and shipping. The most economic order quantity is where the cost of ordering the goods is not greater than the cost of holding, and the total cost curve is at its lowest point. Models like the EOQ model are removed from the real world in that they cannot take account of factors like strikes, transport problems or supplier discounts. On the other hand, they give guidelines as to how inventory costs can be reduced.

Developments in IT have facilitated the control of inventory. New inventory tracking systems enable organisations to trace an order, update account balances, monitor inventory and alert suppliers of upcoming requirements. Some systems have linked their ordering function to suppliers to benefit from low inventory without shortages, for example in the automobile industry.

Automated order entry and inventory tracking can help organisations vary sales and pricing strategies between regions and customer types.

10.8.4 Production control

In the production area, planning and control systems are intertwined because the outputs of the planning system are the inputs of the control system, and vice versa. The aim of a production control system is to ensure that goods are produced on time at the right cost and conform to quality standards. A good production control system should reflect the organisation's production methods and product characteristics. The type of control required in a 'job shop' situation, where there is an element of craft work, will be different from that needed in an assembly line where mass production takes place, but whichever process is employed, an effective production control process is required. The type of product will influence the control system. An organisation that makes one-off products according to buyer specifications would have a job shop where an order control system is used. The emphasis would be on controlling each order as it passes from design through manufacture to shipment. In assembly operations, on the other hand, the flow control system would be used. This involves controlling the rate of production between one assembly point and the next so that no bottlenecks or stoppages occur. In between these two systems, where batch production is used a block control system would be employed. In this case, control is concerned with the progress of the batches or blocks through the stages of production. In all three control systems activities focus on:

- **Routing:** determining where a required job or operation is to be done.
- **Scheduling:** determining when it will be done.
- **Dispatching:** issuing production orders at the right time.
- **Expediting:** ensuring that orders are being produced on schedule.

Each of these activities breaks down into a separate set of tasks. For example, routing activities involve:

1. Deciding the optimal route for product manufacture given the constraints of machinery, materials and labour.
2. Getting information about the product, the process and the time input, in order to evaluate the input of labour and materials and the amount of scrap and rework to be expected.
3. preparing the forms for a production reporting system including order routing sheets, process information details and timesheets.

Once again, advances in IT have had an enormous impact on the production control process. Monitoring systems can track errors per hour, highlight down time, and measure machine speeds and worker productivity. All of these advances allow managers to remedy production problems at an early stage. Previously, systems relied on a controller to spot variations. Early detection allows for early correction and improves the economics of manufacturing.

10.8.5 Quality control

Quality control and production control are intertwined in that quality control is a check on the efficiency of production. A good quality control system can offer significant cost savings due to the savings on rejected products as well as warranty and servicing costs, but, according to Davies and Kochhar, its implementation and operationalisation is best guided by a number of key stages:[16]
* identifying the need to improve operational performance
* identifying best practices for the areas of performance to be improved
* prioritising practices based on the impact of specified measures of performance
* assessing predecessor practices of the practice to be implemented
* implementing the desired practices
* evaluating the improvement in operational performance.

When Japan first entered the world market its products were cheap and of inferior quality. In a drive to increase the volume and the value of its exports Japan decided in the early 1950s to institute a set of laws demanding that products meet certain quality standards before they were exported. This was backed by a campaign to make employees more aware of the need for quality. That led to the establishment of quality circles, which became a standard feature of many Japanese organisations. The circle or committee, staffed by shop-floor employees and supervisors, is concerned with maintaining high quality and screening supplies. Another interesting facet of the Japanese system is that each employee is responsible for the quality of his/her output, which reduces the need for quality control inspectors.

Quality means fitness for the intended purpose and is therefore a relative term. Quality standards are designed to be met at a reasonable cost by the producer, while at the same time presenting an acceptable face to the consumer. The relationship between quality levels and cost is shown in Figure 10.16.

FIGURE 10.16 THE COST–QUALITY RELATIONSHIP

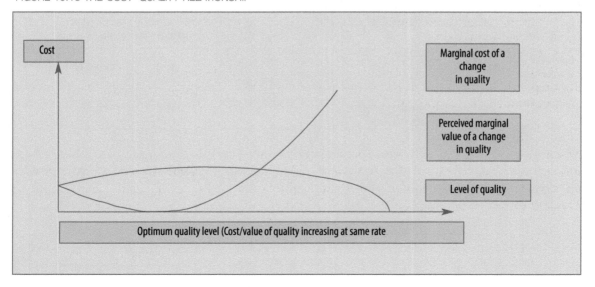

As quality is improved, the cost of producing that quality goes up and the return for higher quality declines. All products have a 'most economic' quality level. So while a modern car may have lower-quality components, it is cheaper and therefore has a mass market. Quality control offers the benefits of reduced costs and fewer customer complaints. It also enhances the corporate image, as high-quality producers are usually looked upon as leaders in the market. It must be emphasised that quality control is a continual and ongoing effort, not a sporadic effort to meet standards.

The ever-increasing emphasis on quality has led many organisations to adopt an integrated total quality management (TQM) approach (see Figure 10.17). A successful TQM system requires the continuous commitment of the top-management team. This commitment must be translated into action and embedded in attitudes and behaviour. The approach must also apply company-wide. Quality must be the responsibility of everyone and the underlying philosophy must be one of prevention.

FIGURE 10.17 LEVELS IN THE EVOLUTION OF TQM

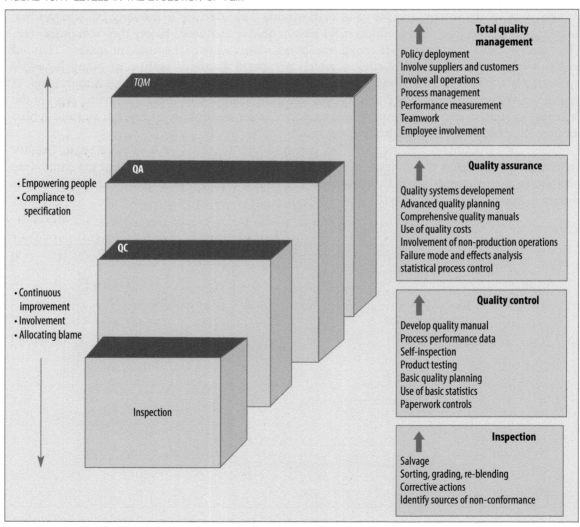

Source: Dale, B. and Plunkett, J. (1990) *Managing Quality*. Phillip Allen.

This approach integrates detection and control into the process and directs attention toward the process rather than the outputs of the process per se. Rothschild and Ollilainen note that TQM represents an elaborate and evolving managerial control mechanism in organisations.[17]

Management Focus 10.2 TQM at Analog Devices

Analog Devices is a multinational company manufacturing computer peripherals in Ireland. The principles of TQM have been integrated into the company ethos. The TQM programme at Analog is centred on the following principles:

- **Management leadership:** Management leads the commitment and the organisation's total effort to ensure that goals are achieved. Management leadership means focusing on the vital few goals, aligning of activities, maintaining constancy of purpose, and creating an environment where employees are not fearful of exposing weaknesses.
- **Respect for people:** One of the major principles of TQM is to have and demonstrate respect for other people. Respect for people, which applies to everyone in the company, has several important aspects. We listen to each other and trust the members of the team to do their jobs.
- **Teamwork:** Both daily work and improvement work often require several people within a work group, or among work groups, to work in teams. The most important quality problems, such as performance, cost, and delivery of products and services, inevitably require teamwork across organisational boundaries.
- **Satisfying customer needs:** Several 'voice of the customer' techniques have been developed for learning from our customers. Analog Devices' methods include benchmarking, customer visits, user surveys, company-wide metrics, focus group meetings, on-site time at the customer's location and product beta tests. All of these sources of data are used for improvement and for developing customer requirements.
- **Celebrating quality:** Annual Quality Festivals are held to recognise and reward the teams for their efforts. These are day-long events at which stories are presented and staff come together to share success stories.
- **Societal learning:** An important characteristic of the TQM programme is societal learning. Societal learning can be viewed as the network of learning within and between companies, customers, suppliers and others who are trying to improve their quality practices. It is too limiting for each company to work on developing TQM by itself.
- **Commitment:** Analog Devices continues to be committed to the long-term adoption of TQM into our overall organisational culture. We believe that TQM is a major means to achieving our business objectives. The involvement of all Analog employees has been critical to meeting our goals and will continue to be essential in the twenty-first century.

Source: www.analog.com/en/qnd.

10.9 Summary of key propositions

- Control is the final management function. It is the process of ensuring the efficient and effective achievement of organisational goals and objectives.
- The control process involves three steps: first, establishing performance standards; second, measuring and comparing actual performance; and third, taking corrective action where necessary.
- An organisation does not have automatic controls and therefore some form of control is needed to regulate its activities. There are three types of control: feedforward control; concurrent control; and feedback control. Feedforward control monitors inputs. Concurrent control monitors the transformation process. Feedback control monitors the outputs.
- Effective controls have a number of important characteristics. They should be appropriate, cost-effective, acceptable, should emphasise exceptions at critical points, be flexible, reliable and valid, and based on valid performance standards and accurate information.
- Methods of control typically used by organisations are either financial or non-financial. Financial controls include budgetary control, break-even analysis and ratio analysis.
- Budgetary control is the process of ascertaining what has been achieved and comparing this with projections contained in the budget. Common examples of budgets are: revenue and expense; time; space; material and production; capital expenditure; and cash. Newer approaches to budgets include variable budgets and zero-based budgets.
- Break-even analysis uses both fixed and variable costs to identify the point at which it becomes profitable to produce a certain product.
- Ratio analysis involves the use of financial ratios to assess the financial performance of the organisation. Ratios are used to assess liquidity, profitability, activity and leverage.
- Non-financial controls include project controls, management audits and inventory, production and quality controls. The project controls most commonly used are Gantt charts and PERT analysis.
- Management audits, whether internal or external, are designed to provide information about competitor organisations to aid strategic decision making and to highlight internal problems.
- Inventory, production and quality control are designed to ensure that levels of inventory are appropriate, the production process is efficient and that quality standards are high. The advances made in information technology have greatly improved these controls.

Discussion Questions
1 Define 'control' and explain its importance.
2 Explain the three steps in the control process.
3 Define and explain the various types of control an organisation can use.
4 What are the characteristics of effective control?
5 Explain the concepts of variable and zero-based budgeting.
6 What is break-even analysis? How can it be used as a control device?
7 Use the accounts from XYZ Company below to calculate these ratios: current ratio; quick asset ratio; asset turnover ratio; net profit ratio; return on assets ratio; debt equity ratio.

BALANCE SHEET FOR XYZ COMPANY

Assets	€
Current assets:	
Cash	10,000
Accounts receivable	75,323
Inventory	327,421
Total current assets:	412,744
Property and plant	356,357
Less: Depreciation	89,462
Net property and plant	266,895
Total assets	679,639
Liabilities and stockholder equity	
Current liabilities:	
Notes payable	53,424
Accrued expenses	87,932
Accounts payable	27,624
Corporation tax payable	56,528
Total current liabilities	255,508
Stockholder equity:	
Capital stock	224,131
Preferred stock	100,000
Retained earnings	100,000
Total stockholder equity	424,131
Total liabilities and stockholder equity	679,639

PROFIT AND LOSS STATEMENT FOR XYZ COMPANY

Revenues:	
Sales	1,000,000
Other income	25,000
Total	1,025,000
Costs and expenses:	
Cost of goods sold	775,000
Total expenses	200,000
Total costs and expenses	975,000
Profit	50,000

8   Explain what Gantt charts and PERT analysis try to achieve. What is the difference between the two approaches?

9   Critically evaluate management audits as a control technique in the current business environment.

10   What three questions should a good inventory control system try to answer? How can it achieve this?
11   How have advances in IT shaped the control function?
12   In the current business environment, what controls should an organisation focus on?

Concluding Case: Roads authority pays £2.8 million after mistake [18]

The National Roads Authority will have to pay £2.8 million as part of a £3.15 million settlement to SIAC, a Dublin-based construction company, after a mistake made in a tender for the building of a new Limerick–Adare national primary route was spotted by Limerick County Council staff.

The mistake in the tender put forward by the company which eventually won the £33 million contract, Pat Mulcair Contractors, was initially not noticed by county council staff, or the National Roads Authority, the secretary of the council, Mr Jim Feane, said yesterday. Mr Feane said that during a legal dispute with SIAC over the form of the tender documents used, the error was discovered.

'The county council, in the process of preparing a defence against that particular action, was re-examining the tenders. In the exercise of re-examining the tenders, the error was detected by our staff,' he said. The dispute over the format of documentation used, which is similar to that used by all local authorities, has not yet been resolved.

Originally eight tenders were assessed for the contract to build a 10-kilometre stretch of road which will run adjacent to the rail link between Limerick and Adare. County council roads division staff in Mungret, Co. Limerick, in conjunction with the National Roads Authority, carried out the assessments.

'We accepted the contract subject to the approval of the National Roads Authority,' Mr Feane said.

Separately, computing errors were made by the council and new tender totals were reached for both SIAC and Pat Mulcair Contractors, with the latter winning the contract.

'SIAC would have been aware that the tender total as submitted by them would have been lower than the tender total as submitted by Pat Mulcair Contractors,' Mr Michael Tobin, Chief Executive of the National Roads Authority, said. Errors in tenders were frequent because they had to be submitted 'in ink' after being drawn up electronically, he added. He hoped a new pilot electronic tendering process would be operational within two months.

Following a process of arbitration, with a consulting engineer as arbitrator, the settlement of £3.15 million compensation for SIAC was reached. Mr Feane said that the council was insured for £250,000 of the amount and would pay a further £100,000. The balance of £2.8 million will be paid by the NRA.

Case Questions
1   Drawing on the theory of control, analyse the nature of the control breakdowns in this case.
2   Outline what controls you would put in place to avoid such errors being made in the future.

Notes and References

1   Baker, H. and Jennings, K. (1999) 'Dysfunctional Organisational Control Mechanisms: An Example', *Journal of Applied Management Studies* 8(2), 231–9.

2   Whitley, R. (1999) 'Firms, Institutions and Management Control: The Comparative Analysis of Coordination and Control Systems', *Accounting Organizations and Society* 24(5/6), 507–24.

3   Bhimani, A. (1999) 'Mapping Methodological Frontiers in Cross-national Management Control Research', *Accounting Organizations and Society* 24(5/6), 413–40.

4   Kald, M., Nilsson, F. and Rapp, B. (2000) 'On Strategy and Management Control: The Importance of Classifying the Strategy of the Business', *British Journal of Management* 11(3), 197–212.

5   Modell, S. (2000) 'Integrating Management Control and Human Resource Management in Public Health Care: Swedish Case Study Evidence', *Financial Accountability and Management* 16(1), 33–54.

6   Sridhar, S. and Balachandran, B. (1997) 'Incomplete Information, Task Assignment and Managerial Control Systems', *Management Science* 43(6), 764–78.

7   Weihrich, H. and Koontz. W. (1993) *Management: A Global Perspective*. New York: McGraw-Hill.

8   Kirsch, L. (1996) 'The Management of Complex Tasks in Organizations: Controlling the Systems Development Process', *Organization Science* 7(1), 1–21.

9   Baker and Jennings *op.cit.*

10   Naveh, E. and Halevy, A. (2000) 'A Hierarchical Framework for a Quality Information System', *Total Quality Management* 11(1), 87–112.

11   Weihrich and Koontz, *op. cit.*

12   Stewart, T. (1990) 'Why Budgets are Bad for Business', *Fortune*, 4 June, 115–19.

13   Weihrich and Koontz, *op. cit.*

14   Keil, M. and Montealegre, R. (2000) 'Cutting Your Losses: Extricating Your Organisations When a Big Project Goes Awry', *Sloan Management Review* 41(3), 55–69.

15   Hutchinson, R. (2000) 'Project Change Control', *Project Manager Today* 12(5), 18–21.

16   Davies, A. and Kochhar, A. (2000) 'A Framework for the Selection of Best Practices', *International Journal of Operations and Production Management* 20(10), 1203–18.

17   Rothschild, J. and Ollilainen, M. (1999) 'Obscuring but not Reducing Managerial Control: Does TQM Measure up to Democracy Standards?', *Economic and Industrial Democracy* 20(4), 583–623.

18   This case originally appeared as an article by Eibhir Mulqueen in the *Irish Times*, 20 July 2000.

Index

Abercrombie & Fitch 134
ABN AMRO 66, 67
Accenture 73
accounts receivable turnover 275, 276
achievement theory 242
acquisitions 120, 280
activity ratios 275–6
Adams, J. 247–8
adhocracy 175
administrative management 18–20, 32
advertising 45, 98, 104, 105, 121, 192, 193
Aer Lingus 17, 41, 112, 113–15, 140
airline case study 111–16
    departmentalisation 167
Africa 34, 61, 85, 88, 90, 91
agribusiness 39, 72, 73, 160
Agricultural Credit Corporation (ACC) 39
agriculture 13, 39, 40, 42, 47
AIB (Allied Irish Banks) 45, 56, 57, 58, 98
AIG 66
Air Berlin 111
Air France 112, 113
airline industry 92, 105
    case studies 111–16, 138–41
    strategic alliances 109
    see also Aer Lingus; Ryanair
AirTricity 74, 76, 93
Alderfer, C. 241
Aldi 103, 104, 135
Allegro 146
alliances 83, 86, 109, 179, 209
Allianz Ireland 3
Allied Irish Bank see AIB
    alternatives
    choosing 150
    evaluation of 149–60
    identification of 149
    implementation 150
Amazon 74

Ambrose, M. and Kulik, C. 238
Analog Devices 76
    TQM programme 285
analyser strategy 134
analysis of strengths and weaknesses 130–2
Anglo Irish Bank 56, 57, 58
Anglo-Irish Free Trade Area Agreement (AIFTAA)
    43, 44
Anti-Discrimination (Pay) Act 1974 212
Apple 48, 72, 95, 104, 105, 134, 256
application forms 193–4, 196
appraisal of performance 184, 188, 199–201, 205
    techniques 200
apprenticeships 202, 203, 206
aptitude tests 194, 195
Ardnacrusha power plant 39
Argentina 86, 87
Argos 97
Arnold, J. et al. 239
Arvato 73
Asahi 48
Asda Walmart 161
ASEAN (Association of Southeast Asian Nations)
    83, 85, 87–8
ASEAN–China Free Trade Area (ACFTA) 87
ASEAN–Japan Comprehensive Economic
    Partnership (AJCEP) 87–8
ASEAN–Korea Free Trade Area (AKFTA) 88
asset turnover ratio 275
assets 274–6
ASTI (Association of Secondary Teachers of Ireland)
    206
AT&T Technologies 20
audits 280
authoritarianism vs democracy 93
authority 171, 173
    centralisation 11
    scalar principle 11
automobile industry 83, 86, 252, 279, 281

online purchasing 107
see also Ford Motor Company
autonomous work groups (AWGs) 177, 256
autonomy 166, 171, 176, 197, 253, 254
Avonmore Foods 159, 161

Bailey's Irish Cream 157
Baker, H. and Jennings, K. 261
balance of payments 48, 49
balance sheets 131, 273
    examples 274, 287
Bank of America 54
Bank of England 54
Bank of Ireland 45, 56, 57, 58
departmentalisation 170
Bank Wiring Observation Room Experiments 22
banking sector
    bailout 56–7
    bank debt 63
    financial crisis 55–6
    government guarantee 56
    see also EU/IMF; financial services sector
Barnard, Chester 19, 20, 31
Barnes & Noble 124, 125
Barrington, T. 184
Bass, B. 229
batch production 282
Bausch & Lomb 48, 177
BCG matrix 136
Bear Stearns 54
Beardwell, I. and Holden, L. 187
Bedeian, A. 265
behavioural theories of leadership 222–5
benchmarking 232, 264, 273, 285
benefits, employee 198–9
Bennet, R. 239
Bennis, W. and Nanus, B. 219
Bethlehem Steel Works Company 14–15
Bhimani, A. 260
biases in decision-making 152, 153
Bio-Energy & Forestry Ireland 62
biotechnology sector 49, 79
Black & Decker 50
Blake, R. and Mouton, J. 219, 224–5
block control system 282
BNP Paribas 66
bond markets 63–4

Bord Gáis 62, 93
Bord na Móna 41, 256
Bose 74
Boston Consulting Group (BCG) matrix 136
Boston Scientific 72, 78
boundaryless organisation 179
bounded rationality 153–4
brainstorming 157
brand loyalty 105, 107, 115
brands, global 73, 82, 132
Brazil 61, 83, 86–7, 101
break-even analysis 272–3
brewing industry 38, 96
    see also Guinness
BRICs 61, 89–91, 101, 109
British Airways (BA) 112–13
British Petroleum (BP) 82, 176
Broadband 21 62
Brown, A. 229–30
Buchanan, D. and McCalman, J. 255
budgets 127–8
budgetary control 127–8, 269–72
    effective budgets 272
    flexibility and 268
    sales budget example 270
    types of 270
    variable budget example 271
Bulgaria 84
bureaucracy 16–18, 172–3
    advantages/disadvantages 173–4
    organisational structure 171–6
    Tronics plc case study 181
Burger King 159
Burns, J.M. 219, 228
Burns, T. and Stalker, G. 30, 31
Burren National Park 119
Bus Átha Cliath 168, 169
Bus Éireann 119, 168
business activities (Fayol) 18, 19
business environment 80–116
    case studies 111–16, 138–41, 181
    competitive environment 102–8
    diversity and uncertainty 29, 109
    globalisation 81–3
    international markets 108–10
    macro environment 91–102
    regional trading alliances 83–8

Business and Finance 3, 98
business sector, development of 38–68
    Celtic Tiger 51–4
    key business sectors 73–9
    macroeconomic environment 61
    semi-state companies 41, 62, 63
    top companies in Ireland 72–3
business services 73
business-level strategies 134–6
BusinessEurope 210
butter manufacturers 105
buyers, bargaining power of 103, 107

Cadbury 20, 45
Cameron 75
Canada 34, 60, 86, 89
Cancun conference 92
capital gains tax (CGT) 52, 55
Capital Investment Advisory Committee 43
CARICOM 83
cash cows 136
Cathay Pacific 114
Catholic Church 11, 42
Celtic Tiger 51–4
Census of Population 1821 38
Central African Republic 88
Central Bank 67
Central Statistics Office (CSO) 55, 58
centralisation in decision making 171, 181
centralised pay bargaining 185, 186–7
certainty vs uncertainty 147, 153
chain of command 17, 173
charismatic leadership theories 228–30
Charter of Fundamental Rights 85
Chartered Institute of Personnel and Development
    (CIPD) 185
Chavez, Hugo 86
Cheard Chomhairle, An 203
chemical industry 44, 46, 48
Chile 86
China 60–1, 82, 83, 84, 87, 88, 89–90, 101
CIÉ 41, 168, 169
CIÉ Tours international 168, 169
Citi 78
Cityjet 112, 113
civil law 94
civil service 17, 39, 44, 174, 184

classical approaches to management 10, 13–25, 32
clean technologies 74
closed systems 27
cloud computing 77
CMC 72
coaching 201–2, 203, 232
coalitions 154
Coca-Cola 83, 151, 155
coercive power 154
collaboration 29
collective bargaining 205
Comhlucht Siúcra Éireann 41
Commission for Energy Regulation (CER) 93
commitment, escalation of 155
Committee on Industrial Organisation (CIO) 45
Common Agricultural Policy (CAP) 47
common external tariff (CET) 84
common law system 94
Common Market for Eastern and Southern Africa
    (COMESA) 88
comparative standards 264
competitive advantage 31, 47, 102–3, 201–2, 255
*Competitive Advantage: Creating and Sustaining
    Superior Performance* (Porter) 103
competitive economies 60
competitive environment 102–8
    bargaining power of buyers 103, 107
    bargaining power of suppliers 103, 106–7
    case studies 111–16, 138–41, 181, 201–2
    competitive advantage 31, 47, 102–3, 201–2, 255
    favourable/unfavourable 107–8
    rivalry among existing firms 103, 104
    threat of new entrants 103, 105–6
    threat of substitutes 103, 105
competitive niches 95
*Competitive Strategy: Techniques for Analysing
    Industries and Competitors* (Porter) 103
competitiveness of Ireland 42, 45, 51, 53, 55, 60–1,
    64
computer-aided design (CAD) 96
computer-aided manufacturing (CAM) 96
computers 48, 77, 95, 96, 214–15, 285
    see also e-business; software industry
conceptual skills 7, 8
concurrent control 265, 266, 269
Confederation of Irish Industry (CII) 209, 210
conflict, in decision making 147–8

consensus negotiators 186
construction industry 54, 59
consumer products sector 65, 74
consumers
    demands 151
    environmental awareness 99–100
    globalisation and 82–3
    products and service providers 74, 75
    social changes and 99
    see also customers
contemporary approaches to management 25–35,
    33
contingency leadership theory 225–8
contingency planning 122
contingency theory 28–30, 33
continuous improvement 255, 284
control 4, 260–88
    budgets as control mechanism 127–8, 269–72
    effective control characteristics 267–9
    financial controls 261, 262, 269–77
    information technology and 262
    methods 269
    nature of 261–2
    non-financial controls 277–85
    roads authority case study 288
    span of control 165–6
    stages in control process 262–5
    types of 265–6
Control of Manufacturers Act 1932 40, 44
Cooper Industries 72
Cooper and Whelan Report (1973) 47
co-operatives 49, 161
co-ordination 19, 29, 164, 165, 166
core competencies 218
corporate-level strategies 135–6
    see also planning
corporation tax 45, 48, 49, 51, 52, 61, 62, 64, 67
cost advantage 105
cost leadership 103, 135
cost-effectiveness, and control 267
costs
    fixed and variable 112, 113, 271, 272–3
    holding and ordering 281
    inventory control 280–2
    start-up costs 105, 115
    switching costs 106, 115
Cotonou Agreement 85

Courtaulds 48
craft unions 206
Cranet E Survey 193, 196, 198, 199, 200, 201
Creans 41
CRH (Cement Roadstone Holdings) Group 72–3
critical path 279
Culliton Report 51
cultural environment 100–2
current assets and liabilities 274–5, 287
current ratio 274–5
customers
    bargaining power of 103, 107, 108
    complaints 263
    loyalty 105, 114, 115
    satisfaction 168, 266, 285
    support services 74, 75
    see also consumers
CVs 193–194
Cyprus 84
Czech Republic 84

Dairy Ireland 160
Dale, B. and Plunkett, J. 284
Daly, Simon 112
Davies, A. and Kochhar, A. 283
Davis, L. 250
Dawn Meats 161
DCC 72
de Valera, Éamon 40
Debenhams 97
debt equity ratio 276
debt/GNP ratio 49
decentralisation in decision making 171, 175–6
decision frame 151–2
decision making 145–61
    approaches and models 152–5
    barriers to making good decisions 151–2
    biases 152, 153
    centralisation 171, 181
    characteristics of decisions 145–6
    conditions 146–8
    conflict in 147–8
    decentralisation 171, 175–6
    definition 145
    evaluation and feedback 150–1
    Glanbia case study 159–61
    group decision making 155–8

decision making, *continued*
  process 148–51
  programmed/non-programmed decisions 146
decisional roles 8, 9
defender strategy 134
delegation 9, 17, 171, 173
Dell 59, 61, 72, 77
Delphi technique 157–8
demand analysis (human resources) 190
Democratic Republic of the Congo (DRC) 88
demographics 99–100
departmentalisation 166–70, 177
depreciation 271, 274, 287
De Pree, Max 218
deregulation 92–3, 105, 115
Desmond, Dermot 67
Dess, G. and Picken, J. 218
development 202
  see also training and development
deviations, and control 268
Dickson, W. 20
differentiation 29, 30, 103, 114, 134
Digital 256
discrimination 212
diversification 74, 133, 135, 149
  related/unrelated 135
  strategies 136
division of labour 12, 17, 19, 35
  organisational structure 165, 172–5, 177, 181
divisionalised structure 175
Doha Development Agenda 92
Donoghue, Kieran 68
Donovan Commission 186
Dorling Kindersley 134
Dresdner Bank 67
Drucker, Peter 2, 218
Dublin Airport Authority (DAA) 112
Dublin Bus 169
Dublin Lockout 1913 38
DuBrin, A. 239
Dukes, Alan 50
Dunlop, J. 205
Dunnes Stores 72, 73, 104
Dynamic Administration (Follett) 20
dynamic economies 90
dynamic environment 174, 175, 214

E-bookers 116
e-business 96–7, 106, 107, 116
East African Community (EAC) 88
Eastern Europe 84
easyJet (EU) 112
eBay 75
ECCO 44
Economic Development (Whitaker) 43, 64
economic growth 53–4
economic integration 82, 84
economic order quantity (EOQ) model 281
economic partnership agreements (EPAs) 85
Economic War 41
economies of scale 12–13, 45, 82, 115, 135, 167, 267
Edgeman, R. and Dahlgaard, J. 218
EDS 51
education 45–6, 62
Educational Building Society (EBS) 56, 57
effective managers 2, 9, 10
effectiveness of organisation 27–8
Egypt 11, 90, 94
EI 44
Electric Ireland 93
electricity market 93
Electricity Supply Board (ESB) 39
Elements of Administration (Urwick) 20
emigration 41, 42, 43, 49, 58–9
Emirates 103
employee relations 204–12
  see also human resource management
employer organisations 209–10
employment 42, 46–7, 49, 51–3
  by sector 38, 39, 41, 59, 66, 140
equality 212
  financial crisis and 58
  government policies 63
  trends 2005–12 59
  unemployment 49, 58
  see also human resource management
Employment Appeals Tribunal (EAT) 212
Employment Equality Act 1977 212
Employment Equality Acts 1998–2011 212
empowerment 218, 241, 256, 284
EMRO 66
engineering industry 75
engineering standards 264
entertainment and media sector 75

entrepreneurial roles 8
entrepreneurs 12, 34
environment (of business) *see* business environment
environmental issues 94, 99–100
environmental uncertainty 29, 109
equality 212
Equality Authority 212
Equality Officers 210, 211, 212
equity 249
equity theory 247–8
ERG theory 241
Ericsson 179
ESB (Electricity Supply Board) 39, 72, 93
escalation of commitment 155
Estonia 84
EU–South Korea free trade agreement 85
EU/IMF
   bailout 56, 59, 63, 64
   financial assistance programme 56–7, 58, 65
euro 52, 84
European Atomic Energy Community
   (EAEC/Euratom) 47
European Central Bank 59
European Coal and Steel Community (ECSC) 47
European Commission 85
European Court of Justice 140
European Economic Community (EEC) 43, 47–8
   see also European Union (EU)
European Investment Bank 63
European Monetary System (EMS) 48
European Monetary Union (EMU) 51
European Stability Mechanism (ESM) 63
European Union (EU) 52, 59, 84–5
   Charter of Fundamental Rights 85
   Economic Partnership Agreement 85
   enlargement 84–5
   free trade agreements 85
   Ireland's membership 47–8, 64
   legislation 140
   Social Fund 48
   Structural and Cohesion Funds 48, 52
   tariffs 84
   trade 84–5
evaluation
   of decisions 150–1
   of performance 199–201, 263–5
exceptions 268

principle of exception 264
exchange rates 95
existence-relatedness-growth theory (ERG) 241
expectancy theory 245–7
Expedia 116
expert power 154
Export Profits Relief Act 1956 42, 48
exporting 109
exports 42, 46, 52
expropriation risk 94
external audits 280

Faber-Castell 44
Facebook 61
factors of production 26
family businesses 181, 234–5
Fannie Mae 54
Fanta 83
FÁS 202
Fayol, Henri 18–20, 32, 172, 174
Feane, Jim 288
Federation of Irish Employers (FIE) 209, 210
feedback
   decision-making 150–1
   work performance 253, 254, 269
feedback control 265, 266, 269
feedforward control 265, 266, 269
ferries 105, 114–15
Fianna Fáil 40
Fiedler, Fred 225–7
   and Chemers, M. 227
   and Garcia, J. 228
FIFA World Cup (2014) 90–1
financial bailout 56, 63–4
financial controls 261, 262, 269–77
financial crisis (2008) 54–9, 64, 82
financial information systems (FIS) 96
financial ratios 273–7
Financial Regulator 56, 67
financial resource analysis 131
financial services sector 66–8, 77–8
   see also banking
Fine Gael–Labour coalitions 49, 59
Finland 38, 60, 84
First Programme for Economic Expansion 43, 64
Fitzpatrick, M. 40, 42, 45
fixed costs 271, 272, 273

Flanagan, H. and Thompson, D. 217
flat rate schemes 197
flexibility, and control 268
Flora 105
flow control system 282
focus strategy 135
Folláin 119
Follett, Mary Parker 19, 20
food and drinks sector 45, 151, 157, 266
  case studies 34–5, 159–61, 234–5
  organic foods 99–100
  see also Kerry Group; McDonald's
Foras Tionscal, An 42, 44
Ford Motor Company 15, 41, 124, 125
foreign direct investment (FDI) 43–4, 46, 48, 49, 51, 61–2
  future prospects 59–60, 62, 64
  via a subsidiary 110
formalisation 170–1
Forrest, C. 239
Fox, D. *et al.* 250
franchises 34–5, 105, 109
Freddie Mac 54
Free State 38–9, 64
free trade 42, 43–7
free trade agreements (FTAs) 85–7
Free Trade Area of the Americas (FTAA) 86, 87
Friedman, Thomas 81–2
fringe benefits 198–9
front-line managers 5, 6, 7, 122, 261
Fruit of the Loom 50, 53
Fujitsu 48, 96
functional departmentalisation 167–8
Functions of the Executive, The (Barnard) 20
functions of management 4–5, 18, 172
Further Education and Training Bill (2013) 202

G7 economies 89, 90, 110
gainsharing 198
Game 59
Gantt charts 277–8
Gantt, Henry 15, 277
Garavan, T. *et al.* 202, 232
GasLink 62
General Agreement on Tariffs and Trade (GATT) 44, 92
General Electric 44

General and Industrial Management (Fayol) 18
General Motors 175, 179
generic strategies 134–135
Genzyme 79
geographical departmentalisation 169–170
Germany 39, 40, 60, 63, 89, 96, 101
Gibbons, Niall 3
Gilbreth, Frank and Lillian 15–16
Gillette-Braun 48
Glanbia 27, 72, 73
  key decisions case study 159–61
  product departmentalisation 168
Glanbia Co-operative Society 161
GlaxoSmithKline (GSK) 79
global brands 73, 82, 132
Global Competitiveness Report (2012–2013) (WEF) 59–61
Global Europe Strategy (2006) 85
global financial crisis 54, 55, 58
Global Leadership and Organizational Behavior Effectiveness (GLOBE) 230
globalisation 81–3
global brands 73, 82, 132
Glynn, George and Peter 234–5
GOA 75
goal displacement 173
goals *see* objectives
Goldman Sachs 89, 90
Good Friday Agreement 3
Google 61, 72, 75, 77, 98
government debt 57
governments 92–4
Grant Thornton Consulting 235
graphology 196
Gray, Danuta 3
Great Depression 41, 57
Greece 57, 84, 101
Griffith, Arthur 40
grocery sector *see* supermarkets
Gross Domestic Product (GDP) 48, 57, 58
Gross National Product (GNP) 46, 48, 49, 51, 58
group decision making 155–8
group think 156
Guinness 20, 38, 41, 96
Gulf Wars 111
Gunnigle, P. *et al.* 188, 200, 207

Hackman, J. and Oldham, G. 252–3, 254
Harland and Wolff 38
Harvard Business School 29, 103, 220
Hawthorne Effect 21, 22
Hawthorne Studies 20–2, 24, 33
HBOS 54
health and safety 186, 209
Heraty, N. 203
  and Morley, M. 231–2
Herzberg, Frederick 24, 25, 242–3, 252
Hewlett-Packard 76, 77
hierarchy 17, 29, 32, 102, 119
  of authority 173
  flatter hierarchies 178–9
  and spans of control 166
hierarchy of needs (Maslow) 22–4, 239–41
hierarchy of plans 123–4, 128
high-performance work design 255–6
Higher Education Authority (HEA) 46
historical standards 263
history of management 10–35
Hitt, W. 217, 219
Hoblyn, James 235
Hofstede, Geert 100–2
Hogan, John 67
Holland and Barrett 100
hotel chains 82
House, R. 228
  and Aditya, R. 218, 222, 228
  and GLOBE programme 230
  path-goal theory 227–8
human relations movement 20–4, 25, 33
human resource analysis 131
human resource management (HRM) 6, 15, 183–215
  employee relations 204–12
  historical development 184–7
  Leeway case study 214–15
  pay and benefits 196–9
  personnel management and 184
  planning 188–91
  recruitment and selection 191–6
Human Side of Enterprise, The (McGregor) 244–5
Hungary 84
Huseman, R. et al. 247
Hutchinson, R. 279
hygiene factors 243–4

hyperglobalisation 82

Iarnród Éireann 17, 124, 168, 169
IBEC (Irish Business and Employers'
    Confederation) 209–10
IBM 50, 100
IBRC (Irish Bank Resolution Corporation) 57, 58
ICT sector 76–7, 95
ICTU (Irish Congress of Trade Unions) 208–9
IDA (Industrial Development Authority) 41–2, 46,
    47, 48, 52, 64
  advertising campaign 49–50
  and financial services sector 67
  foreign direct investment 43–4, 46, 47, 48, 51, 53,
    61–2
  industrial products and services 75–6
  new policy 1990s 53
  Strategic Plan (1982–92) 49–50
Illumination Experiments 21
illusion of control 152
IMED 48
immigration 52, 99
imports 41, 52
incentive schemes 198, 248
incentives 248, 249, 250
  see also motivation and pay
India 61, 82, 83, 84, 89, 91
indigenous companies 44, 47, 48–9, 50–1, 64, 74, 198
Indonesia 87, 90
Industrial Credit Corporation (ICC) 41
Industrial Development Act 1969 44, 64
Industrial Development Act 1981 50
industrial estates 46
Industrial Policy Review Group 51
industrial product businesses 75–6
industrial relations 186, 205–12
  see also human resource management
Industrial Relations Act 1990 210, 211, 212
Industrial Revolution 12–13, 32, 38
industrial services sector 75–6
industry see business sector, development of
inflation 39, 51, 52, 65, 94–5
information and communications technology 76–7,
    95, 262, 281, 282
informational roles 8, 9
Infrastructure and Capital Investment Framework
    63, 64

Ingersoll Rand 76
innovation 125, 132, 263
    technological 95–6, 105
        inputs 26–7, 106, 265, 266, 282
Institute of Labour Management 184–5
Institute of Personnel Management (now CIPD)
        186–7
instrumentality 246
integration 29–30, 224, 225
    economic 82, 84
Intel 51, 62, 76
intelligence tests 195
interest rates 54, 56, 94–5
internal audits 280
International Air Transport Association (IATA) 111,
        112
International Court of Justice (ICJ) 86
International Financial Services Centre 66–8
International Labour Organisation (ILO) 210
International Monetary Fund (IMF) 43, 56, 59
International Organisation of Employers (IOE) 210
International Services Programme 50, 64
International Telecommunication Union 97
Internet 97–8
    see also e-business
interpersonal skills 6–7, 8, 9
interviews 194–5, 196
intrapreneurship 215, 224
inventory control 280–282
Investment in Education (OECD) 46
Iona Technologies 175
iPod 95, 105
Iraq 92, 94
Ireland 1912–1985: Politics and Society (Lee) 50
Irish Autism Action 124
Irish Congress of Trade Unions (ICTU) 208–9
Irish Ferries 105, 114
Irish Life and Permanent 56, 57, 58
Irish Management Institute (IMI) 45, 201
Irish Nationwide Building Society 56, 57
Irish Shipping 41
Irish Times 61, 98
Irish Transport and General Workers' Union
        (ITGWU) 38
Irish Water 62
Irving, J. 156
Italy 38, 57, 89, 96, 101, 179

J. Milroy & Sons 45
Jack Wills 134
Jacobs 185
Japan 83, 84, 87–8
    quality circles 10, 255, 283
Jefferson Smurfit 42
JetBlue 112, 114
job characteristics model 253, 254
job description 192
job design 250–1, 253, 254
    defined 250
job enlargement 252–3
job enrichment 252–3
job specialisation 165
    see also division of labour
Johnson & Johnson 78, 175
joint ventures 109, 160, 161
JPMorgan Chase 66
justice theory 247–8

Kald, M. et al. 260–1
Katz, D. and Kahn, R. 31
KCI 78
Keating, M. et al. 230, 231
Keenoy, T. 187
Keil, M. and Montealegre, R. 277
Kellogg's 74
Kemmy Business School 193, 196, 198, 199, 201
Kennedy, K. 43
Kennedy, Patrick 3
Kerry Group 3, 72, 73, 169, 201–2
Kerrygold 105
key result areas 270
Kingston 72
Kirsch, L. 261
KISS (Keep It Simple Stupid) philosophy 139
Kohn, A. 248
Kondrasuk, J. 129
Koontz, H. 25
Korea, South 60, 87, 88, 90
    EU–South Korea free trade agreement 85
Kostal 48
Kroc, Ray 132
Krups 44

Labour Court 186, 211
Labour Market Statistics 58

labour movement 38
Labour Relations Commission (LRC) 210–11
labour wastage 190
Labour–Fianna Fáil coalition 51
laissez-faire 229
land annuities 40
Larkin, Jim 38
Latvia 84
Lawler, E. 197
Lawrence, P. and Lorsch, J. 29–31
lead time 95, 281
leadership 4, 8, 10, 216–35
    active leaders 10
    behavioural theories 222–5
    charismatic leadership theories 228–30
    contingency leadership theory 225–8
    defined 218–19
    distinguished from management 10, 219–21
    Irish research 230–2
    Leadmore case study 234–5
    trait theories 221–2
    transactional/transformational 228–30
Leadmore Ice Cream 234–5
least preferred co-worker (LPC) theory 226–7
Leavy, B. 216
Lee, Joseph 46, 50
Leeway 214–15
legal systems 94
legitimate power 154
Lehman Brothers 54
Lemon's 45
levelling effect 156
levels of management 5–7
leverage ratios 276–7
Levitt, T. 82
liaison 8, 219
liberalisation 92, 93, 115, 138
Libya 92, 111
licensing 109
Lidl 103, 104, 135
Liebherr 44, 76
life cycle of organisation 174
life sciences sector 78, 79
Likert, Rensis 31, 218, 223
Limerick Post 98
LinkedIn 61, 98
liquidity ratios 274–6

Lisbon Treaty (2009) 85
List, Friedrich 40
Lithuania 84
Lloyds TSB 54
Lotus Ireland 50
Luthans, F. 222

Maastricht Treaty 51, 65
McCarthy, Stan 3
McClelland, H. 242
McDonald's 82, 159
    case study 34–5
    division of labour 35, 165
    Plan to Win strategy 34–5
    SWOT analysis 131–2
McGregor, Douglas 24, 25, 31, 218, 244–5, 251
Machiavelli, Niccoló 11, 218
machine bureaucracy 174
McLoughlin, Thomas 39
McMahon, G. 194
macro environment 61, 91–102
    economic context 94–5
    political-legal context 92–4
    socio-cultural context 99–102
    technological context 95–9
Maguire & Paterson 185
Malta 84
management 2–35
    classical approaches 10, 13–25, 32
    contemporary approaches 25–35
    definition 2
    distinguished from leadership 10, 219–1
    early management thought 10–12, 13
    effective managers 2, 9, 10
    Fayol's principles 18, 19
    functions of 4–5, 32
    Irish managers' backgrounds 3
    levels and skills 5–7
    myths 9
    roles 7–9
    theories and evolution 10–35
management audits 280
management by exception 15
management by objectives (MBO) 128–9
management development programme 127, 201
management information systems (MIS) 9, 96
management process 5

management theory jungle 25
Management and the Worker (Roethlisberger and Dickson) 20
managerial estimates 190
managerial grid 224–5
managerial roles 32
manufacturing process 82, 106
markets
    globalisation of 82–3
    international 108–10
Marks & Spencer 97, 103, 266
Marshall Aid 44
Maslow, Abraham 22, 239–41
mass production 12, 82, 174, 252
Maternity Protection Acts 1994–2004 212
matrix structure 177–8
Mayo, Elton 20, 21, 33
mechanistic structures 30, 174
media business sector 75
medical technologies sector 53, 65, 78
mentoring 201–2, 204, 232
Merck Sharp & Dohme 48, 79
Mercosur 83, 86
mergers 56, 73, 120, 133, 159–61, 210, 280
merit rating 197–8
Merrill Lynch 54
Meteor 104, 107
Mexico 76, 86, 90, 101
Michigan University studies 223, 224
Microsoft 50, 72, 77
middle managers 5, 6, 7, 122, 261
MIKT (Mexico, Indonesia, South Korea, Turkey) 90
Miles, Raymond 134
Miles and Snow typology 134
Minimum Notice and Terms of Employment Acts 1973–2005 212
Mintzberg, Henry
    leadership 219
    managerial roles 7–9, 219
    Mintzberg framework 174–5
mission statements 124–5
Mitchelstown 105
mixed departmentalisation 170
mobile phone industry 104, 107, 134
Modell, S. 261
Monks, K. 184
Moriarty Task Force Report 51

mortgages, sub-prime 54, 82
Mostek 48
motivation 237–58
    case study 257–8
    centrality of 238
    definition 238–9
    pay and 248–50
    theories of 239–48
    work design 250–6
motivators 197, 237, 239, 243–4, 248–9, 252
Motorola 51
multinational corporations (MNCs) 47, 64, 82–3, 94
    see also foreign direct investment
Murphy, Brendan 3
Murphy, William Martin 38
Musgrave Group 72, 73

Nadler, D.A. and Lawler, E.E. 247
National Asset Management Agency (NAMA) 56, 57, 58
National Economic and Social Council (NESC) 50
National Income and Expenditure Accounts 55
National Lottery licence 62
National Pension Reserve Fund (NPRF) 56, 58, 63
National Recovery Bond 63
National Recovery Wholesale Bank 62
National Roads Authority (NRA) 288
Naveh, E. and Halevy, A. 262
NCB Stockbrokers 67
needs
    hierarchy of human needs 22–4, 239–41
    hierarchy of organisational needs 23
negotiator role 8
Nelson, B. 237–8
network organisation 179
NewERA programme 59, 62–3, 64
'Next 11' 90
niches 95, 124
Nicholls, J. 216
Nike 124, 125, 179
9/11 terrorist attacks 53, 111, 112
Nintendo 105
Nissan 83
Nokia 104, 134
nominal grouping 158
non-programmed decisions 146
Noonan, Michael 57

North American Free Trade Agreement (NAFTA) 83, 86
Northern Ireland 62
Northern Rock 54
NTMA (National Treasury Management Agency) 57
NuaSoft 97
Nutricima 160

objective probability 147
objectives 125
   defining corporate objectives 129–30
   management by objectives 128–9
   revising 132
O'Brien, D. and Flanagan, P. 161
Ocean Energy 74
O'Cofaigh, Tomas 67
Odiorne, G. et al. 129
Office of the Director of Equality Investigations 212
O'Hara, Peter 235
Ohio State University leadership studies 222–3, 227
oil crises 48
O'Leary, Michael 141
Olympics (2016) 91
O'Malley, Donagh 46
O'Neil, Jim 89
Oneworld 109
online advertising 98
online banking 98
online media market 98
online shopping 96–7
online ticket sales 115
Only 119
open systems 27
operational managers 6
operational planning 121, 123, 133
operations managers 6
operator control 265
Oracle 72
order control system 282
organic structures 30
organisation, objectives 4
Organisation for Economic Co-operation and Development (OECD) 45–6
organisational behaviour (OB) 25–6
organisational chart 165, 170, 171
organisational control see control

organisational culture 201, 245, 255, 285
organisational effectiveness 27–8
organisational life cycle 174
organisational needs 23
organisational resource analysis 131
organisational structure 164–81
   approaches 171–4
   contemporary design 175–9
   definition 164
   Mintzberg framework 174–5
   structural configuration 164–70
   structural operation 170–1
   trends and new forms 176–9
   Tronics plc case study 181
organising 4, 5, 164
   see also organisational structure
Osborn, Alexander 157
outputs 26–7, 106, 265, 266, 282
outsourcing 73, 82, 109, 139

Pacioli, Luca 11
Paddy Power 3
Páircéir, Seamus 67
Paraguay 86, 87
paralysis by analysis 120
parental leave 99, 198, 199
Partnership 2000 52
partnerships, social 50–2, 53, 65
Pat Mulcair Contractors 288
patents 62, 94, 109
path-goal theory 227–8
pay bargaining 186
pay and benefits 196–9
   motivation and 248–50
Payment of Wages Act 1991 212
PayPal 61, 75
Peninsula Petroleum 72
Penney's 72, 73
pensions 23, 198, 199, 249
performance appraisal 199–201
   standards 263–5, 269
   techniques 200
Perot Systems 73
person specification 192
personality tests 195
personnel management 184–5, 186–7, 188
   see also human resource management

PERT analysis 278–9
PEST analysis 92, 108, 131
Pfizer Corporation 44, 79, 124
Pfizer Global Supply 72
pharmaceutical industry 79
piece-rate system 14–15, 16, 198
planning 119–41
    business-level strategies 134–5
    contingency planning 122
    corporate-level strategies 135–6
    definition of 119, 137
    management by objectives 128–9
    management function 4
    process of 129–34
    Ryanair case study 138–41
    types of planning 120–2
    types of plans 122–8
plant managers 6
Plato 218
Poland 39, 59, 84, 96
policies 126
political model of decision making 154
Poole, M. and Jenkins, G. 183
Popper, M. and Zakkai, E. 228, 229, 230
Porter, L.W. and Lawler, E.E. 246–7
Porter, Michael 103, 108, 111
    expectancy framework 246
    generic strategies 134–5
    and Lawler E. 246
portfolio management 136
Portugal 38, 57, 84
power 154
    empowerment 218, 241, 256, 284
    types of 154, 171
Pramerica 78
price competition 104, 113–15
Prince, The (Machiavelli) 11
principle of exception 264
Principles of Scientific Management (Taylor) 14, 16
Pringles 146
probability 147, 246
problem identification 149
procedures 126–7
Procter & Gamble 135, 175
product
    departmentalisation 168–9
    differentiation 112–16

innovation 95–6, 105, 132, 134, 160, 263
production
    control 277, 282
    globalisation of 82
    mass production 12, 82, 174, 252
    techniques 96
production managers 9
professional bureaucracy 175–6
proficiency tests 195
profit and loss statement 287
profit maximisers and satisficers 129–30
profit/gainsharing 198
profitability ratios 276
Programme for Competitiveness and Work (PCW) 51–2, 65
Programme for Economic and Social Progress (PESP) 51, 65
Programme for National Recovery (PNR) 50–1
Programme for Prosperity and Fairness (PPF) 53
programmed decisions 146
programmes 127
project controls 277–9
project structures 177–8
property bubble 55
prospector strategy 134
protectionism 40–2, 64
psychometric tests 196
public-private partnership (PPP) 63
Putin, Vladimir 91

Qantas 114
quality circles 10, 255, 283
quality management 284–5
    contingency theory and 28–9
    control 263, 283–5
    total quality management 284–5
quality of working life (QWL) movement 254–5
quick asset ratio 275

Rabobank 67
rate of return 276
Rathbornes 41
ratio analysis 273–4
rationality 152–3
    bounded rationality 153–4
reactor strategy 134
recession 54–9, 65, 82

and recovery 49–51
recruitment and selection 191–6
Redundancy Payments Acts 1967–2007 212
reference checking 196
referent power 154
Regional Development Fund 48
regional policy 46–7, 49, 53
regional trading alliances 83–8
regulatory framework 93
Relay Assembly Test Room Experiments 21–2
reliability and control 258
resource profile 131
reward power 154
reward system 196–9, 248
   see also motivation and pay
Rights Commissioners 212
risk 147
   bounded rationality 153–4
rivalry 103, 104, 113
Roadmap to Deregulation (CER) 93
Robbins, S. 227, 230
Roethlisberger, Fritz 20
roles of managers 7–9, 219
Roman Empire 11
Romania 84
Rothschild, J. and Ollilainen, M. 285
routing 282
Rowntree 20
Rowntree Mackintosh 45
rules 127, 205, 210, 229
   bureaucracy and 17
   procedural and substantive 205
   procedures and 170–1, 172, 173, 181, 214
Russia 61, 83, 89, 91, 101
Ryanair 72, 103
   airline case study 111–16
   case study 138–41

safety 94, 171, 186, 209
Salaman, G. 205
sales managers 9
Samsung 104, 134
sanctions 92
Sandisk 72
Sandoz 51
Santos 119
SAP 76

satisficing 153, 154, 156
Saudi Arabia 60, 94
scanners 262
scientific management 14–16, 32
scope 122, 123, 124, 189
Second World War 41, 44
segmentation 29
selection of staff 17, 194–6
self-managed teams 177, 178
self-regulating systems 215
self-sufficiency 40–2
Selznick, P. 218
semi-state companies 17, 41, 62, 63
service providers 65, 66, 74, 98, 104
Shannon Scheme 39
shareholder theory 130
Shell 82
Shop Management (Taylor) 14
shop stewards 207
shopping, online 96–7
SIAC 288
'Sicks' 89, 91
Siemens 75, 76
Simon, Herbert 153
Singapore 60, 85, 87, 179
single-use plans 123
Sinnott, Eamonn 62
SIPTU (Services, Industrial, Professional and
   Technical Union) 206
skill variety and job design 253, 254
skills, of managers 5–7, 11
Skyteam 109
Slovakia 84
Slovenia 84
Smart Grid 62
Smith, Adam 12
Smurfit Kappa 72
Snia Viscosa 48
Snow, Charles 134
social changes 99–100
social partnerships 50–2, 53, 65
social responsibility 20, 280
Socrates 11
soft information 9
software industry 50, 73, 74, 75, 76, 77
software solutions centre 61
SOLAS 202

South Africa 61, 88, 90, 91, 92
South America 83, 86–87
South Korea 60, 90
    free trade agreements 85, 87, 88
Southern African Development Community
    (SADC) 88
Southwest Cheese 160
sovereign debt 56, 58, 63
Spain 40, 57, 84, 96
span of control 165–6
specialisation 11, 12, 35, 165–6, 251
Spirit 112
spokesperson role 8
sports clothing 179
Sridhar, S. and Balachandran, B. 261
staff managers 9
stakeholder theory 130
stamp duty 55
standard plans 123
standards of performance 263–5
Star Alliance 109
Statt, D. 219–20, 230
Steers, R. and Porter, L. 238
Stena Line 105, 114
Stewart, T. 270
stock *see* inventory control
Stogdill, R. 222
and Coons, A. 222
strategic alliances 109
strategic business unit (SBU) 134
strategic managers 5
strategic planning 120, 121, 123, 133, 137
strategies 28, 125–6, 133, 134–6
Strategy and Development 1986–1990 (NESC) 50
strategy statement 133
Stratus 51
structural configuration 164–70
structural imperatives 174
structural operation 170–1
structure *see* organisational structure
sub-prime mortgage market 54, 82
sub-systems 27–8
subjective probability 147
substitute products 103, 105
Sumitomo Bank 66
Sunday Independent 40, 42
superintendents 6

supermarkets 104, 106, 107
    cost leadership strategy 135
    customer demands 99
    focus strategy 135
    Irish supermarket sector 104
    IT and control systems 262
scanners 262
strategic, tactical, operational plans 121
suppliers 161
Superquinn 107
SuperValu 104
supervisors 6, 122, 261
suppliers, bargaining power of 103, 106–7, 108, 161
supply analysis (human resources) 190–1
supply chain management 74, 82, 106
Sweden 56, 60, 84, 99, 101
sweet manufacturers 45
Switzerland 60, 61, 96
SWOT analysis 130–2
synergy 28, 135
Syntex 48
systematic leadership 218
systems theory 26–28, 31, 81, 106, 251

tactical managers 6
tactical planning 120–1, 133
Taiwan 60, 101
Tamboran Resources 119
Tannenbaum, R. *et al.* 218
tariffs 40–1, 43–4, 64, 84
task significance 253, 254
task specialisation 251
tax
    capital gains tax 52, 55
    concessions 52
    corporation tax 45, 48, 49, 51, 52, 61, 62, 64, 67
    income tax reduction 51
    remission on export sales 42
    rosary beads 40
    stamp duty 55
tax credit system 52
Taylor, Frederick 14, 16, 218
Taylorism 185–6, 251
teamwork 241, 255, 284, 285
    self-managed teams 177, 178
Technical, Electrical and Engineering Union (TEEU)
    206

technical skills 6, 7
technological determinism 251
technological innovation 95–6, 105
technological resource analysis 131
technology, development 95–9
Telectron 50
Telefonica 02 Ireland 3
Telesis Report (1982) 50, 64
Teradata 51
terrorist attacks 9/11 53, 111, 112
Tesco 72, 73, 104
textile industry 38, 53
theocratic law 94
theory X, theory Y 25, 244–5, 251
'Theory of Human Motivation' (Maslow) 239
'therbligs' 15
3 (service provider) 104, 107
time and motion studies 14
Tobin, Michael 288
top companies in Ireland 72–3
top managers 5–6, 7, 121–2, 171, 261
Topaz 72
total costs 272, 273, 280, 281
Total Produce 72, 73
total quality management (TQM) 284–5
Tourism Ireland 3
trade agreements 85–6
trade sanctions 92
trade unions 16, 186, 206–11
   development of 186
trading blocs 83–8
training and development 201–4
   historical overview 203
   training policy 203
trait theories of leadership 221–2
transactional/transformational leadership 228–30
travel agents 115–16
Travelocity 116
Treaty of Rome 47–8
Trevelyan, R. 218
Trinity College Dublin research 230
Troika 59, 63
Tronics plc 181
TRW Inc. 177
Turkey 84, 90
turnaround times 139, 140
Twitter 98

two factor theory 25, 242–4
Tyson, S. and York, A. 199

uncertainty 147–8
   avoidance 100–2
   bounded rationality 153–4
   environmental 29–30
Underdeveloped Areas Act 1952 41
unemployment 49, 58
Unfair Dismissals Acts 1977–2007 212
Unilever 45
Union of Construction, Allied Trades and
      Technicians (UCATT) 206
Union of Industrial Employers' Confederations in
      Europe (UNICE) 210
unitarism 205
United Arab Emirates 60
United Kingdom 13, 101, 112, 115, 161, 169, 170
United Nations (UN) 92
United Parcel Service (UPS) 73
United States 60, 84, 101
unity of command 11, 19, 172
universal principles of management 18, 20, 24, 174
Urneys 45
Uruguay 86, 87, 92
Urwick, Lyndall 19, 20
Urwick Orr and Partners 128
US Cheese & Global Nutritionals 160, 168
US Cheese 160, 168
US National Research Council 21
U-Scan 96

valence 246
Valeo 76
variable budgets 271
VECs 203
Verbatim 48
vertical loading 252, 253
video games 105
Virgin Money 54
Vita Cortex 59
Vocational Education Act 1930 45
Vodafone 104, 107
Vroom, V. 238–9, 245–6

Walker, C. and Guest, R. 252
Wall Street Crash 40

Wang Laboratories 48
Warner-Lambert 48
waste management 256
Waterford Foods 159, 161
Waterford Glass 45, 59
Wavebob 74
Wealth of Nations, The (Smith) 12
Weber, Max 16–18, 32, 172–3, 174, 218
websites 98
    see also e-business
Weihrich, H. and Koontz, W. 263
welfarism 185
Western Electric 20
Wharton School of Management 230
Whelan, Noel 47
Whitaker, T.K. 43, 64
Whitley, R. 260
Wikipedia 98

Windows Live 98
work design 250–6
work study 190
World Bank 43, 88
World Economic Forum (WEF) 59–61
World Trade Organisation (WTO) 92
World War II 41, 44

Yamanouchi 50
Yelp 61
Youghal Carpets 45
YouTube 98
Yukl, G. 219

Zaleznik, A. 220
zero-based budgeting 271–2
Zurich 78